Pre-publication REVIEWS, COMMENTARIES, EVALUATIONS . . .

"Once again Ron Nykiel has demonstrated his ability to provide a highly useful book for the hospitality industry. This book should be on the desk of every hospitality marketing executive. Chapter 8, 'The Design and Components of a Feasibility Study,' offers information not found in most hospitality books."

—James C. Makens, PhD
Consultant to the Hospitality
and Tourism Industry

"This book represents the only aggregated resource of all elements of marketing research that hospitality, travel, and tourism marketers and executives need to know. It is bound to serve as a timeless reference for the development of marketing strategies that will position organizations for success."

—Robert A. Gilbert, CHME, CHA
President and CEO,
Hospitality Sales & Marketing
Association International

"Dr. Nykiel's handbook can best be described using the retail mantra of 'convenient one-stop shopping.' It represents an excellent broad-brush overview of the many research methodologies that can and should be used to better develop and conduct marketing studies in hospitality and tourism. While academic in nature, it is written so concisely and clearly that it will also be valuable to marketers and management.

Each of the 18 chapters is well organized, beginning with objectives and ending with discussion questions and case discussion questions. Thus, readers can better understand how the information presented can be practically used in business. And the graphics used to illustrate various points are supportive and easily understood.

This handbook should be on the library shelf of all hospitality students, professors, and practitioners alike."

—Bonnie J. Knutson, PhD
Professor, The School
of Hospitality Business,
Broad College of Business,
Michigan State University;
Editor, *Journal of Hospitality
& Leisure Marketing*

Handbook of Marketing Research Methodologies for Hospitality and Tourism

Handbook of Marketing Research Methodologies for Hospitality and Tourism

Ronald A. Nykiel, PhD

THHTP

The Haworth Hospitality & Tourism Press™
An Imprint of The Haworth Press, Inc.
New York

For more information on this book or to order, visit
http://www.haworthpress.com/store/product.asp?sku=5927

or call 1-800-HAWORTH (800-429-6784) in the United States and Canada
or (607) 722-5857 outside the United States and Canada

or contact orders@HaworthPress.com

Published by

The Haworth Hospitality & Tourism Press™, an imprint of The Haworth Press, Inc., 10 Alice Street, Binghamton, NY 13904-1580.

PUBLISHER'S NOTE
The development, preparation, and publication of this work has been undertaken with great care. However, the Publisher, employees, editors, and agents of The Haworth Press are not responsible for any errors contained herein or for consequences that may ensue from use of materials or information contained in this work. The Haworth Press is committed to the dissemination of ideas and information according to the highest standards of intellectual freedom and the free exchange of ideas. Statements made and opinions expressed in this publication do not necessarily reflect the views of the Publisher, Directors, management, or staff of The Haworth Press, Inc., or an endorsement by them.

Cover design by Jennifer M. Gaska.

Library of Congress Cataloging-in-Publication Data

Nykiel, Ronald A.
    Handbook of marketing research methodologies for hospitality and tourism / Ronald A. Nykiel.
        p. cm.
    ISBN: 978-0-7890-3426-7 (soft : alk. paper)
    1. Hospitality industry—Marketing—Handbooks, manuals, etc. 2. Tourism—Marketing—Handbooks, manuals, etc. I. Title.
TX911.3.M3N93 2007
910.68'8—dc22
                                                                                        2006034083

CONTENTS

PART IV: PLANNING AND COMMUNICATIONS

APPENDIXES

Acknowledgments

First I would like to acknowledge Dr. John Ellison and the President's Commission on Executive Interchange for providing me the opportunity to both learn and put into practice qualitative and quantitative research methodologies early on in my career. Thank you, Dr. Robert Haigh, former president of Xerox Education Group, and Bill Marriott, Chairman and CEO Marriott International, for the chance to demonstrate how competitive and environmental research and analysis could be applied in the corporate development and strategic planning areas. A special thank you goes to the late Kemmons Wilson, founder of Holiday Inns, and Mike Rose, currently Chairman of Gaylord Entertainment, for their faith in me to serve as their strategic planning officer and for the great opportunity to experience the strategic planning process in full gear. Thank you, Jim Biggar Sr., former Chairman and CEO of Nestlé North America, for your faith in my research and strategic brand and marketing decisions. Thank you, Dr. Jim Myers, for sharing your knowledge on benefit and needs segmentation and for your encouragement over the years. Also, I would like to acknowledge the leadership at the University of Houston, which has provided me the opportunity to continue my research endeavors and to participate in various planning activities. Finally, a special thank you goes to my late father who encouraged me to research and plan both in my career and present endeavors.

Handbook of Marketing Research Methodologies for Hospitality and Tourism
© 2007 by The Haworth Press, Inc. All rights reserved.
doi:10.1300/5927_a

ABOUT THE AUTHOR

Dr. Ronald A. Nykiel, PhD, CHA, CHE, is currently the Conrad N. Hilton Distinguished Chair and Professor of Hotel and Restaurant Management at the Conrad N. Hilton College at the University of Houston and the Chairman of the Hospitality Industry Hall of Honor. He has addressed many corporate and association groups and lectured at the Harvard Graduate School of business and other prestigious universities on corporate strategy, marketing, consumer behavior, brand management, service excellence, and executive development topics. He is recognized as an international authority in the field of hospitality, travel, and tourism marketing, and is author of a leading hospitality industry marketing text. He serves on the Board of Directors of the Travel Industry Association of America. Dr. Nykiel authored a number of books on business strategy, marketing, consumer behavior, and service excellence. He has also appeared on national television and radio, and has contributed to a variety of journals, magazines, and other publications. He is the publisher of the *Hospitality Business Review.*

Introduction

Knowledge of the trends in the marketplace, consumer perspectives, and competition are essential to increase the odds of success with marketing programs, developmental endeavors, and customer solicitation and retention. There are a plethora of data and information resources and services to utilize in marketing research and analysis today. This text provides a guide both to qualitative and quantitative research methodologies as well as to identifying key sources for information acquisition. It focuses on how to apply research and analysis with sample outlines for various types of research commonly utilized in the business world today. Specific industry-related techniques, such as site selection studies, project feasibility studies, and the application of marketing analysis to the strategic planning process, are discussed in depth.

The text is organized into four parts. Part I provides a guide to research and methodologies. Part II focuses on market analysis and assessment, industry locational analysis, site selection, feasibility studies, and development research techniques. Part III provides techniques and applications of marketing research in support of various strategies. Research approaches and findings are discussed within the context of strategy selection related to marketing, brands, pricing, customer service, and quality initiatives. Part IV focuses on planning and communications and marketing research and market analysis. A research-based business review process and a comprehensive strategic marketing planning process are presented. This part concludes with suggested methods of presenting and communicating research findings.

The reader will obtain knowledge of how to utilize and apply different research and analytical techniques. There are ample examples within each chapter of how to effectively communicate and present research and analytical findings to groups, management, and others. The text provides detailed formats, outlines, and lists of sources for data collection. Also, there are numerous diagrams and graphic presentations to help clarify processes and procedures.

Each chapter begins with a list of learning objectives and includes examples, applications, discussion questions, key words/definitions, and a summation of major points covered. Case examples are included at the end of the chapters. These case examples demonstrate successful application of research findings and analysis in the service sector.

Also, included in the appendixes are comprehensive lists for intelligence and informational sources. Finally, a detailed glossary covering many of the key terms is provided along with a bibliography.

Handbook of Marketing Research Methodologies for Hospitality and Tourism
© 2007 by The Haworth Press, Inc. All rights reserved.
doi:10.1300/5927_01

PART I:
RESEARCH AND METHODOLOGIES

In Part I of the text, we begin in Chapter 1 with the definitions of market and research, marketing research, market segmentation, targeting, and positioning. All of these are key concepts and the terms are supported by research. In Chapter 2, we point out the differences between primary research and secondary research as well as discuss the concept of sampling. In Chapters 3 and 4, we look at the roles and related research techniques associated with qualitative and quantitative research. In Chapter 5, we examine integrative research, its advantages and disadvantages, and the concept of triangulation. Overall, this part should provide an understanding of where research plays a significant role in marketing strategy and market analysis. Further, a synopsis of the major qualitative and quantitative research methodologies and related techniques is provided.

Chapter 1

Defining Marketing Research, Market Analysis, and Applications

CHAPTER OBJECTIVES

- To provide an overview of the purpose of marketing research in the decision process.
- To define marketing research, market research, and types of research studies.
- To relate the types of research studies applicable to the various stages of product development and the product life cycle.
- To delineate the marketing research process, formulation, and approach.
- To present various marketing research techniques and applications.

PURPOSE

Marketing research is the active process of identifying and gathering information pertinent to assisting in the decision-making process. The type of information gathered for analysis is dependent upon the purpose of the research. In addition there are a variety of research methodologies and information-gathering processes utilized by market researchers. One definition of marketing research is that it is the "function that links the consumer, customer, and public to the marketer through marketing information."[1]* However, this is but one of many different definitions. Frequently, businesses want to know what the market for a specific product is or service before it can be sold to the consumer. And, frequently the term market research is used to describe the process of identifying and gathering information related to the specific product or service. In this latter case the focus is on consumer demand, product and/or service supply, the present and future scenarios, and many other factors that can impact the decision process. Again, the type of information gathered for analysis is dependent upon the purpose of the research.

The purpose of the research can be focused on analyzing customer needs, product/service attributes, competitors' strengths and weaknesses, and even external events likely to impact the product or service offering. The research might focus on the product/service offering in terms of supply and demand, both current and future. The research may focus on actual markets, countries, and cities, seeking to identify opportunities for or threats to an existing product/service offering. Research may focus on new product/service development by identifying market segments or product/service offerings currently not being served.

Market research must be timely, accurate, and reliable to be of value in assisting decision making.

*Quotations appearing in this book from W. Dillon et al., *Marketing Research in a Marketing Environment* (Burr Ridge, IL: Irwin, 1994) are reproduced with permission of The McGraw-Hill Companies.

Handbook of Marketing Research Methodologies for Hospitality and Tourism
© 2007 by The Haworth Press, Inc. All rights reserved.
doi:10.1300/5927_02

5

Research can be designed to measure and evaluate the performance of actual marketing programs, the quality of service delivery, the faults in a production process, the mix of products being offered, price points, sales approaches, and more. Research, be it qualitative or quantitative, should be designed so that the result of the information-gathering process is applicable to reducing uncertainty in managerial decisions. Decisions on pricing, product/service positioning, distribution, promotion, and any changes to product/service offerings should be based on carefully structured and conducted marketing research.

Finally, marketing research must be timely to support the decision process. And, equally important, marketing research must be ongoing to truly contribute to purposeful managerial decisions. Virtually all products and services find their environment to be very dynamic in today's marketplace. Change not only is constant but also occurs at a more rapid pace due to technology. Research can focus on the dynamics of change by identifying the needs for everything from a minor change in pricing to a major change in product/service design or offering.

Marketing research may be conducted and/or coordinated internally within the corporation and/or by an external commercial marketing research firm or service. It is also common practice to utilize both internal functions and external research firms to conduct research. Marketing and product managers, corporate managers, marketing information systems and marketing decision support system managers, R&D managers, and advertising and promotion agencies may individually, cooperatively, or collectively all be involved in the research process or subcomponents of the process. Sometimes it is more efficient and effective to utilize what is referred to as "syndicated" research. Syndicated research is based on common pools of data such as diary and scanner-panel based studies, standardized research services, and customized research services.

To succeed as a marketing manager, it is beneficial to have an understanding of the research process and to have a working knowledge of how to use marketing research and how to interpret and apply findings. Mastering this base of knowledge combined with understanding the position and life cycle stage of your product/service offerings can give you the support you need along with the knowledge to make informed and successful strategic marketing decisions. The other obvious benefit is that the facts and research-based knowledge will assist in selling senior management to support recommendations needed for the ultimate success of the marketing program.

Research should be an ongoing process as the marketplace is ever changing.

Marketing research needs tend to be dynamic or ever changing over time. These needs and even approaches to research may vary considerably during the life cycle of the product or service offering. Predevelopment research activities may involve site selection and feasibility studies. Prelaunch of new products/services might require concept testing, product attribute research and packaging, and name testing. In the introductory and growth stages of the product life cycle, research may be more focused on sales trends, pricing sensitivity, consumer attitudes and preferences, competitive responses, and other patterns that emerge. In the maturity phase, marketing research may focus on alternative portfolio scenarios, new product development, acquisitions, segmentation, and rejuvenation/rebirth strategic research. In the decline cycle, research might focus on sales strategies, dispositions, and asset redevelopment. Figure 1.1 profiles types of research and product life cycle stages.

PROCESS

Almost all companies have some informal or formal process for finding and using marketing research data. The level of sophistication varies widely and often the process is evolutionary.

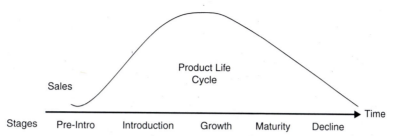

➲ Pre-Intro
- Attribute identification
- Brand testing
- Concept tests
- Copy testing
- Feasibility studies
- Focus groups
- Market studies
- Package evaluation
- Pre-test markets
- Pricing studies
- Test markets

   ➲ Introduction
   - Awareness measurements
   - Attitude studies
   - Initial demand patterns
   - New advertising measurements
   - Product refinement tests
   - Site selection
   - Tracking studies
   - Usage studies

      ➲ Growth
      - Awareness studies
      - Attitude studies
      - Market share studies
      - Tracking study
      - Positioning
      - Pricing
      - Promotion test
      - Segmentation study

         ➲ Maturity
         - Acquisition studies
         - Alternative portfolio studies
         - Decision trees/linear strategy
         - Lifestyle research
         - Market structure studies
         - Refurbishment studies
         - Repositioning studies
         - Portfolio analysis studies
         - Segmentation studies
         - Strategy grid

            ➲ Decline
            - Alternative use studies
            - Cost reduction studies
            - Disposition studies
            - Price elasticity studies
            - Sell alternatives

PRELAUNCH ⟶ ROLL OUT ⟶ ESTABLISHED MARKETS

FIGURE 1.1. Types, Studies, and Stages. *Source:* Adapted from W. R. Dillon, T. J. Madden, and N. H. Firtle, *Marketing Research in a Marketing Environment* (Burr Ridge, IL: Irwin, 1994), p. 20.

Some organizations have a highly structured and formal process for marketing research while others utilize an informal approach. As in any research methodology undertaking, in marketing research also there is a multiple-step process.

At the outset, an organization must recognize the need for research. This is where the process begins. Once there is a need to assess performance, to view competition, or do a forecast, the first step of recognizing a need has occurred. In Figure 1.2, the following eight-step research process is graphically presented.

1. *Recognizing the need.* Sometimes the need might be difficult to recognize, especially if the need is related to an external event unassociated with the existing product or service. Simple changes in tax laws in the late 1980s had dramatic effects on the lodging industry, real estate industry, and savings and loan industry. Often new products that had resulted from external technological advances can have substantial impact on traditional products and services, even render them obsolete, that is, 8-track audio, 45 and 78 rpm records, wiring, etc. Many other unexpected events can dramatically alter the marketplace. Recognizing the need to continually assess trends, the environment, and competition may prove to be extremely significant to a product or service in its struggle for market share or even survival.

2. *Defining the problem.* At this stage, marketing managers and researchers need to jointly define the purpose for which marketing research will be conducted, including the types of questions that the research must answer, the types of information already available, additional information wanted, and the use to which research results will be put. Exploratory research at this stage helps clarify what the problem really is and generates ideas on alternate research approaches.

3. *Designing the research.* This entails setting the research budget and identifying data sources. The researcher must identify how much is already known about the research question, including the data, models, and analytic techniques available. Further, the need to identify whether the research is *descriptive* (i.e., attempting to describe a marketing phenomenon, such as how consumers shop) or *causal* (i.e., attempting to predict cause-effect relationships, such as sales changes when a product package change is introduced). The type of data required and the manner in which they are collected are driven by the research design. For example, qualitative data may be sufficient for descriptive research, but experiments or quasi-experiments may be necessary for causal research. When identifying data sources, the researcher must answer questions such as which is the target population, whether a sample is required, and, if so, what sampling frame will be used, what type of sample will be drawn, how it will be drawn, and how large it will be.

4. *Collecting data.* Decisions at this stage include who will collect the data, the timeframe for data collection, required supervision, and the methods that will be used to ensure data quality and comparability across samples and studies. Data can be collected in a variety of ways. At the initial exploratory stage of the research process, including problem definition and hypotheses generation, managers may collect information informally through discussions with colleagues, field marketing personnel, distributors, customers, and noncustomers; all can provide valuable information. Additional data may be collected from secondary sources (published sources, syndicated studies) and through primary research, which includes a variety of research methods, such as interviews, surveys, focus groups, observation, and experiments. Figure 1.3 lists the types of data and data collection methods and provides brief descriptions of key uses of each.

5. *Assessing the data.* Often researchers tend to skip this very important step in the process. Once the data have been collected, it is a good practice to review all information and develop a list of what is not there or has not been collected and assess its significance to helping answer or provide solutions to the problem. Frequently, this exercise and the subsequent round of data collection result in the most significant of findings to influence the decision process.

6. *Analyzing the data.* Marketing researchers rely on both qualitative and quantitative research analyses to analyze their data. The analytic procedures to be used are generally selected prior to data collection, so that the data-collection procedures used are appropriate. Decisions at this stage relate to data coding, tabulations, and analytic techniques.

7. *Interpreting the results.* Interpretation of the results should be viewed within the context of the defined problem. Other significant findings outside the realm of the defined program can be noted or placed in an appendix. Naturally, objectivity in interpreting findings is most important. One recommended approach in more complex analyses is to categorize the interpreted results as near-term significant and long-term significant or urgent, somewhat urgent, important, and so on.

8. *Communicating the results.* It has been stated that analytical types of individuals are left-brain driven and marketing types of individuals are right-brain driven—herein may lie a potential problem in communication of research results. Researchers who are presenting results need to always focus on who the target audience is for their written or oral presentation. Yes, all related statistics, backup data, methodology, and so on, are important, but may be so complex or time-consuming to delineate that the target audience does not have the time or interest in hearing that detail. Researchers should present the findings that first answer the critical questions or problems that were assessed in an orderly manner. Depending upon the audience, this can be a logical flow of findings to the conclusion and recommendations or just the key conclusion and recommendations. Know your audience and you will be an effective communicator.

TECHNIQUES

Selecting the appropriate marketing research techniques is dependent upon the nature of the questions to be answered, time and budget constraints, and the complexity of the issues. Since marketing research aims to provide data/facts that assist in decision making, it must be not only

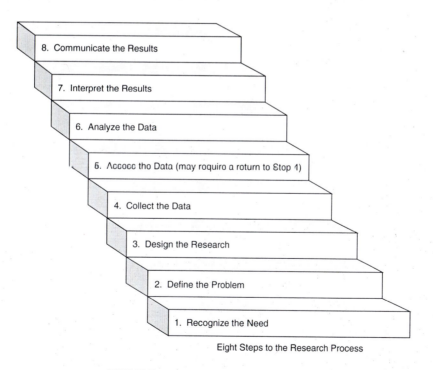

Eight Steps to the Research Process

FIGURE 1.2. The Research Process

Type of Data/Data Collection Method	Description	Use
Secondary data	Already exist as a result of routine company record keeping and previous research, or external sources of published data (e.g., sales and shipment reports, MIS data, supermarket scanner data).	Good starting point for most research because data are readily available and relatively low cost (e.g., analysis of sale and shipment data may be used to forecast demand, identify usage segments, plan logistics, and develop channels).
Primary data	Collected specifically as part of the research process; may be demographic, socioeconomic, psychological, or relate to attitudes, opinions, knowledge, purchase intentions, or behavior.	Key use where secondary data are unavailable or unreliable (e.g., address a large number of research questions such as what consumer attitudes and preferences are, how they shop, and how they consume).
Observational data	Collected via observation of natural or contrived market settings; variety of techniques include personal and mechanical observation.	Useful to gain understanding of actual consumer behavior, particularly when the researcher believes that the consumers are unable or unwilling to articulate their motivations and preferences.
Focus group data	Collected from observation of small groups of people brought together to discuss a subject of interest; discussion moderated to ensure that all individuals participate.	Useful for generating hypotheses for further testing; collecting information to help structure interview and survey questionnaires; obtaining overall consumer reaction to new concepts.
Interview data	Collected from personal or telephone interviews with one or more participants on subjects of interest.	Useful to gain in-depth knowledge of the areas of interest, especially where focus groups may interfere with candid responses (e.g., doing research on competitors, sensitive and personal topics for which privacy is essential).
Survey data	Collected from mail, telephone, fax, and electronic mail interviews of a sample of respondents from the population of interest. Questionnaires may be self-administered or interviewer administered, and include a number of different types of response formats, including fixed alternative, open-ended, and projective questions.	Useful where a larger sample is required, so impersonal survey methods offer benefits; also useful where the purpose of the research is descriptive and the researcher needs a lot of information on the population of interest (e.g., segmentation studies).
Experimental data	Collected in carefully controlled conditions where the researcher can manipulate variables of interest and examine their effects on other variables.	Useful for causal research where hypotheses generated at other stages of the research process are tested (e.g., test marketing).

FIGURE 1.3. Data—Types, Collection Methods, and Key Uses

timely but also, and most important of all, accurate and reliable. In essence, marketing research must be scientific and well documented. Figure 1.4 delineates the scientific method for marketing research.

Great invention often has its origins in great research.

Frequently, it may be advisable to use multiple methods to collect and analyze data and test several models related to the context of the data. These steps will help in building credibility and in convincing communications of the findings. There are numerous marketing research tools and models. We will discuss key marketing research techniques within the context of the questions that these techniques help answer. Further, we will present a few statistical techniques or processes that researchers utilize for marketing analysis. For example, in the analysis of variance, we concentrate on describing the processes and applications in market segmentation, in positioning products/services and related interactions.

In nonequivalent, quasi-experimental, research designs, the analysis of variance is an important tool to understand the statistical difference between the averages or the "means" of two different populations; however, they are distinguished by research design. When the statistical significance of the differences of means can be assessed, then a more accurate comparison can be made between groups. Statistical differences are assessed through an ANOVA analysis (Table 1.1). In an ANOVA analysis, the relationship between measurements of the mean and the variance or "random error" of each group provides the information needed to determine whether the difference between the two is significant. First of all, an ANOVA analysis assumes that there is a cause-effect relationship. The statistical analysis upon which the ANOVA is used describes the relationship between cause and effect through statistics:

$$Y = B0 + B1x1 + e$$

where:

Y = the effect;
$B0$ = the intercept;
$B1$ = the coefficient of the variable;
$x1$ = the variable;
e = random error.

The aforementioned formula describes a "mean" or an average effect based on either a sample from a population or an entire population. If the statistical regression is representative, it has what is called a nor-

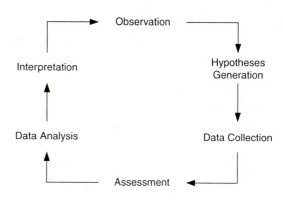

FIGURE 1.4. The Scientific Method

TABLE 1.1. Analysis of Variance

Process	Description	Applications	Probe Examples
ANOVA (analysis of variance)	Statistical procedure for analyzing the effects of one or more categorical independent variables, which are typically manipulated in a controlled experiment, on the means of a dependent variable measured at lease intervally	To determine main and interaction effects of independent variables on a dependent variable (ANOVA) or on multiple dependent variables (multivariate ANOVA)	Changes in consumer attitudes, preference, and intention to purchase as a function of exposure to rational, emotional, and other advertising messages
		To determine the effects of independent variables on a dependent variable, while controlling for the effects of one or more intervallic scaled variables (analysis of covariance)	The extent to which consumption may vary as a function of different market segments
			Sales variations as a consequence of low versus moderate price changes

mal distribution. That is, not every piece of data can be measured at the mean. Rather, the data for the population are contained within three standard errors from the mean either to the positive or negative side. An ANOVA calculation is derived from a statistical calculation for significance based on a t-statistic calculated from the regression formula based on the least squares fit. A relatively higher mean (Y) compared to the errors (e) indicates a more "precise" system or group from which the data were derived. From the relative calculations of averages and errors for each group, a more precise determination on the significance of the difference between the two groups can be assessed.[2]

Cluster analysis is an exploratory data analysis tool for solving classification problems (Table 1.2). Its object is to sort cases (people, things, events, etc.) into groups, or clusters, so that the degree of association is strong between members of the same cluster and weak between members of different clusters. Each cluster thus describes, in terms of the data collected, the class to which its members belong, and this description may be abstracted through use from the particular to the general class or type.

"Cluster analysis is thus a tool of discovery. It may reveal associations and structure in data which, though not previously evident, nevertheless are sensible and useful once found. The results of cluster analysis may contribute to the definition of a formal classification scheme,"[3] such as a taxonomy for related animals, insects, or plants; or suggest statistical models with which to describe populations; or indicate rules for assigning new cases to classes for identification and diagnostic purposes; or provide measures of definition, size, and change in what previously were only broad concepts; or find exemplars to represent classes. In most businesses, the chances are that sooner or later you will run into a classification problem. Cluster analysis might provide the methodology to help you solve the problem.

"The objective of conjoint analysis is to determine what combination of a limited number of attributes is most preferred by respondents. It is used frequently in testing customer acceptance of new product designs and assessing the appeal of advertisements. It also has been used in product positioning"[4] (Table 1.3).

TABLE 1.2. Cluster Analysis

Process	Description	Applications	Probe Examples
Cluster analysis	Method for classifying things into relatively homogenous groups (i.e., clusters)	To group customers on the basis of common characteristics	Seeks to identify groups of customers in a market as defined by the unique benefits they seek in a product
		To categorize products on the basis of like competitive attributes	Seeks to ascertain which brands in a market share like attributes and constitute competitive groups with rivalry primarily within clusters
		To cluster markets on the basis of common properties	
			Determine if homogenous markets be defined on the basis of geography or other factors

TABLE 1.3. Conjoint Analysis

Process	Description	Applications	Probe Examples
Conjoint analysis	Method for measuring consumer utilities for levels of product attributes	To ascertain the relative importance of product attributes	Identifies which attributes of a brand are most salient for consumers
		To aid in the decision of the optimum level of product attributes	Determines how much of each attribute and which features a brand should incorporate to maximize consumer satisfaction while minimizing costs
		To estimate market share for a new product	Ascertains what level of sales and market share will be achieved for alternative attribute levels

The basic steps of conjoint analysis are as follows:

- Select features to be tested.
- Show product feature combinations.
- Respondents rank the combinations.
- Input the data from a representative sample of potential customers into a statistical software program and choose the conjoint analysis procedure. The software will produce utility functions for each of the features.
- Incorporate the most preferred features into the new product or advertisement.

Respondents are shown a set of products, prototypes, mock-ups, or pictures. Each example is similar enough that consumers will see them as close substitutes, but dissimilar enough that respondents can clearly determine the preference. Each example is composed of a unique combination of product features. Rank-order preferences are obtained. The responses are codified and input into a statistical program like SPSS or SAS.

The computer then uses monotonic analysis of variance or linear programming techniques to create utility functions for each feature. These utility functions indicate the perceived value of the feature and how sensitive consumer perceptions and preferences are to changes in product features.

Correlation is a bivariate measure of association (strength) of the relationship between two variables (Table 1.4). It varies from 0 (random relationship) to 1 (perfect linear relationship) or −1 (perfect negative linear relationship). It is usually reported in terms of its square (r^2), interpreted as percent of variance explained. For instance, if r^2 is 0.25, then the independent variable is said to explain 25 percent of the variance in the dependent variable.

There are several common pitfalls in using correlation. Correlation is symmetrical, not providing evidence of which way causation flows. If other variables also cause the dependent variable, then any covariance they share with the given independent variable in a correlation will be falsely attributed to that independent. Also, to the extent that there is a nonlinear relationship between the two variables being correlated, correlation will understate the relationship. Correlation will also be attenuated to the extent there is measurement error, including use of subinterval data or artificial truncation of the range of the data. Correlation can also be a misleading average

TABLE 1.4. Correlation Analysis (Bivariate Contingency Table Analysis)

Process	Description	Applications	Probe Examples
Correlation or bivariate contingency table analysis	Statistical procedure for ascertaining the strength of association between two variables	To determine the correlates of a focal variable with other variables To discover patterns of association among a set of variables	Seeks to identify if market share correlates with profitability Determines the association between advertising expenditures and sales Determines if attitudes toward a brand are positively correlated with intentions to try it

if the relationship varies depending on the value of the independent variable (lack of homoscedasticity).[5]

Besides Pearsonian correlation (r), the most common type, there are other special types of correlation to handle the special characteristics of such types of variables as dichotomies, and there are other measures of association for nominal and ordinal variables. There is also "multiple correlation," which is the correlation of multiple independent variables with a single dependent. Also, there is partial correlation, which is the correlation of one variable with another, controlling for a third or additional variables.

Discriminant analysis attempts to find the combination of independent variables that best discriminates between two or more predefined clusters or groups (Table 1.5). It is the appropriate statistical technique used when the dependent variable is categorical (e.g., cluster membership) and the predictor variables are metric.[6]

Factor analysis is a statistical technique used to reduce a set of variables to a smaller number of variables or factors (Table 1.6). Factor analysis examines the pattern of intercorrelations between the variables, and determines whether there are subsets of variables (or factors) that correlate highly with each other but that show low correlations with other subsets (or factors).[7]

Multidimensional scaling (MDS) can be considered to be an alternative to factor analysis (Table 1.7). In general, the goal of the analysis is to detect meaningful underlying dimensions that allow the researcher to explain observed similarities or dissimilarities (distances) between the investigated objects. In factor analysis, the similarities between objects (e.g., variables) are expressed in the correlation matrix. With MDS, one may analyze any kind of similarity or dissimilarity matrix, in addition to correlation matrices. In general, MDS attempts to arrange "objects" in a space with a particular number of dimensions. As in factor analysis, the actual orientation of axes in the final solution is arbitrary. The final orientation of axes in the plane or space is mostly the result of a subjective decision by the researcher, who will choose an orientation that can be most easily explained.

MDS is not so much an exact procedure as rather a way to rearrange objects in an efficient manner, so as to arrive at a configuration that best approximates the observed distances. It actually moves objects around in the space defined by the requested number of dimensions, and checks how well the distances between objects can be reproduced by the new configuration. In

TABLE 1.5. Discriminant Analysis

Process	Description	Applications	Probe Examples
Discriminant analysis	Statistical technique where membership in a group is related to a set of independent variables (where the latter are typically measured at the interval level)	To determine on what bases two groups differ To predict the classification of an object (e.g., person) to one of two groups on the basis of a set of predictors	Seeks to determine if two market segments differ in terms of the attitudes, opinions, and lifestyles of consumers based on personal characteristics and past behavior Ascertains the likelihood that a given customer applying for a loan will be a credit risk Identifies how users and nonusers of a brand differ in terms of their judgments of product attributes

TABLE 1.6. Factor Analysis

Process	Description	Applications	Probe Examples
Factor analysis	Statistical procedure for reducing a set of measures to a smaller number of underlying variables termed factors	To build scales from items and test for unidimensionality in questionnaire development To identify valid measures for variables to be used, in turn, as independent and dependent variables in other hypothesis testing or predictive contexts To construct perceptual maps based on consumer reactions to product attributes	Identifies the underlying attribute dimensions governing consumer perceptions of a brand Looks at how different brands score on the key attributes of a product class Determines if the measures of a scale validly indicate the underlying construct they are purported to measure

more technical terms, it uses a function minimization algorithm that evaluates different configurations with the goal of maximizing the goodness-of-fit (or minimizing "lack of fit").

MDS helps researchers draw pictures of data so that they can visualize and communicate the relationships in complicated data that may be obscure when viewing just the numbers. Researchers recognize two important issues. First, consumers may use perceptual dimensions to

TABLE 1.7. Multidimensional Scaling (MDS)

Process	Description	Applications	Probe Examples
Multidimensional scaling (MDS)	Procedure for representing perceptions spatially, typically in two or three dimensions	To reveal the dimensions underlying consumer perceptions of brand attributes	Identifies the underlying attribute dimensions governing consumer perceptions of a brand
		To locate one's own and competitors' brands on the dimensional space of attributes	Ascertains how consumer preferences correspond to existing perceptions of brands in the attribute space
		To identify opportunities for positioning a new brand or repositioning an old one	Determines attributes a new brand emphasizes
			Views how an existing brand should change its attributes or consumer perceptions of its attributes

evaluate the product, which may not overlap with or share anything in common with the objective attributes of the product. Second, consumers' perceptions, even when they are the same as the objective dimensions the marketer uses, may not always be consistent.

These procedures are complicated by the reality that each consumer is different. Consumers may not all use the same dimensions in their evaluations. Even when they do, they may not all attach the same level of importance to the dimensions. And they may change both the dimensions and the importance of each over time, and as they are exposed to marketing stimuli.

Once the data are collected and sorted, they may be analyzed using one of a number of MDS approaches to arrive at a map. "As with cluster analysis, in addition to some objective statistics, researcher judgment is required to decide on the appropriate number of dimensions. The dimensions may actually be labeled by asking respondents or experts to interpret the maps subjectively. Or they may be identified in terms of objective attributes."[8]

Multiple regression is the simplest of all the multivariate statistical techniques (Table 1.8). Mathematically, multiple regression is a straightforward generalization of simple regression, the process of fitting the best straight line through the dots on an *x-y* plot or scattergram.

Regression (simple and multiple) techniques are closely related to the analysis of variance (ANOVA). Both are special cases of the general linear model or GLIM. You can combine the two when what you have is an analysis of covariance (ANCOVA).

Multiple regression is distinguished from other techniques in a number of ways. First, in multiple regression, we work with one dependent variable and many independent variables. In simple regression, there is only one independent variable; in factor analysis, cluster analysis, and most other latent variable multivariate techniques, there are many dependent variables. Second, in multiple regression, the independent variables may be correlated. In analysis of variance, we arrange for all the independent variables to vary completely independently of each other. And, third, in multiple regression, the independent variables can be continuous. For analysis of variance, they have to be categorical, and if they are naturally continuous, we have to force them into categories, for example, by a median split.

TABLE 1.8. Multiple Regression

Process	Description	Applications	Probe Examples
Multiple regression	Statistical technique for determining the degree of dependence that a dependent variable has on two or more independent variables	To identify valid causes of a dependent variable of interest and compare their relative effect	Identifies which perceived attributes of a brand contribute to consumer intentions to purchase it
		To predict the values of a dependent variable as a function of independent variables	Ascertains the relative contribution of pricing and promotion, advertising, and distribution expenditures on sales of a product
			For a given level of couponing, free sampling, advertising, and other marketing expenditures planned, projects what the level of sales will likely be

This means that multiple regression is useful in the following general class of situations. We observe one dependent variable, whose variation we want to explain in terms of a number of other independent variables, which we can also observe. These other variables are not under experimental control—we just have to accept the variations in them that happen to occur in the sample of people or situations we can observe. We want to know which, if any, of these independent variables is significantly correlated with the dependent variable, taking into account the various correlations that may exist between the independent variables. "So typically we use multiple regression to analyze data that come from natural rather than experimental situations. Like many statistical procedures, multiple regression has two functions: to summarize some data, and to examine it for (statistically) significant trends."[9]

Path analysis is an extension of the regression model, used to test the fit of the correlation matrix against two or more causal models that are being compared by the researcher (Table 1.9). The model is usually depicted in a circle-and-arrow figure in which single arrows indicate causation. A regression is done for each variable in the model as a dependent on others, which the model indicates are causes. The regression weights predicted by the model are compared with the observed correlation matrix for the variables, and a goodness-of-fit statistic is calculated. The best-fitting of two or more models is selected by the researcher as the best model for advancement of theory.

Path analysis requires the usual assumptions of regression. It is particularly sensitive to model specification because failure to include relevant causal variables or inclusion of extraneous variables often substantially affects the path coefficients, which are used to assess the relative importance of various direct and indirect causal paths to the independent variable. Such interpretations should be undertaken in the context of comparing alternative models, after assessing their goodness-of-fit, discussed in the section on structural equation modeling (SEM packages are commonly used today for path analysis in lieu of stand-alone analysis programs). When the variables in the model are latent variables measured by multiple observed indicators, path analysis is termed structural equation modeling (Table 1.9), treated separately.[10]

TABLE 1.9. Path Analysis and Structural Equation Modeling

Process	Description	Applications	Probe Examples
Path analysis and structural equation modeling	Technique for relating independent and dependent variables in complex chains and patterns	To discover if one or more variables mediate the effects of a set of independent variables on a set of dependent variables To model complex sequences of effects, feedback, and recipro-cal causation	Seeks to identify how intentions translate preferences and normative pressure into action Ascertain if attitudes influence choices or if choices determine attitudes Determines how attitudes toward a brand, attitudes toward an ad, brand loyalty, and background factors affect decisions and actual purchase behaviors

SEGMENTATION, TARGETING, AND POSITIONING (STP)

Many of the research processes and applications previously delineated result in helping to identify and clarify market segments, primary and secondary targets, and brand-positioning strategy. The goal of segmentation, targeting, and positioning is to sharpen the applications of the various marketing weapons (advertising, database marketing, electronic marketing, pricing, promotions, etc.) and to ultimately improve marketing results.

Segmentation is the process of describing the market in terms of the number of distinct groups of similar consumers that exist and their characteristics. Before segmenting their markets, managers must define their markets on the basis of product functions and technology, type of customer, geography, or stage in the production-distribution system. The segmentation process involves selecting variables that best differentiate between consumers, and using those variables in a segmentation procedure to group consumers. Consumers and organizational marketers use demographic, geographic, psychographic, and behavioral variables as segmentation bases. In the services sector, there are a number of self-segmentation processes, such as heavy user segmentation, prestige/ego seekers, and value segments. These are discussed later in the book (Chapters 10 and 11).

With the exceptional amount of data from government sources, such as the census and commercial research service organizations, extensive computer-based geographic and demographic segmentation data are readily available. Thus, geographic and demographic segmentations are relatively easy to perform for most products or services. However, neither geographic nor demographic segmentation provides information on consumer attitudes, issues, opinions, motivations, preferences, and behavior.

Psychographic segmentation attempts to address this issue by collecting lifestyle data from large samples of consumers and using these as segmentation variables. However, this method attempts to make predictions about consumer purchases based on their attitudes. Behavioral segmentation uses actual past behavior in the product category and consumer benefits sought for segmentation. Thus, it has been one of the most successful of the segmentation approaches.[11]

Targeting refers to evaluating identified segments and selecting segments to be served. In identifying the best segment opportunities, marketers evaluate segment attractiveness—size, growth potential, profitability, competitor profiles—and fit it with organizational objectives and resources. When selecting segments, marketers also decide between concentrating their efforts on one segment and serving many segments. When concentrating on one segment, they may offer the single segment an undifferentiated offering (a single-segment focus) or a differentiated offering (a market focus). When multiple segments are selected, the firm may choose a product focus—offering a single product to all segments—or may differentiate its offering in an attempt to provide each segment with a customized product—a market-dominance approach.

Positioning strategy refers to the approach that a firm uses to achieve a desired and distinct position in the customer's mind. In addition to real product differences, distinctive positioning stems from good communication. Managers must decide how to position—attributes, benefits, usage occasions, user categories, and competitors—as well as how many aspects to include when positioning. A unique selling proposition with one clear basis for positioning is easy to communicate. Perceptual mapping is a useful and widely used analytic technique that aids positioning decisions and has a number of other important marketing uses. Chapters 10, 11, and 12 provide a more in-depth look at positioning and perceptual mapping.[12]

To select the right marketing weapons you need to understand your target and your position.

CHAPTER REVIEW

Informed decisions are one of the products of reliable research. Individual needs and cultural nuances create a complex marketplace where mass marketing approaches of the past no longer are efficient or effective. Further, the marketplace is dynamic and change is the only constant. This marketplace scenario strongly supports the need for reliable, accurate, and timely marketing research. The ultimate goals of marketing research are to assist in decision making and to improve marketing performance.

In order to attain these goals, marketing research should adhere to both structured methodology and the scientific process. This structure and process includes observation and problem identification, data collection and assessment, data analysis, processing and interpretation, and effective communication/presentation.

Research requirements, structure, and techniques may vary based on the environment, competitive situation, external factors, and the stage in the product/service life cycle. Selecting the appropriate research process and related techniques enhances and expedites research findings.

KEY CONCEPTS/TERMS

Analysis of variance
Benefit segmentation
Cluster analysis
Conjoint analysis
Correlation
Discriminant analysis

Factor analysis
Market research
Marketing research
Multiple regression
Multidimensional scaling
Path analysis
Perceptual mapping
Positioning
Targeting

DISCUSSION QUESTIONS

1. Why is it important to assess the information collected before moving on to analysis and interpretation?
2. How is segmentation different from targeting?
3. How would you determine which aspects of a travel-related (airline, hotel, etc.) frequency/rewards program customers most appreciate?
4. How might a club or restaurant apply the concepts of segmentation, targeting, and positioning to improve its profitability?
5. What steps/processes would you employ to improve your response rates in a direct mail program?
6. Why is clear positioning important for product/service success?
7. Which marketing research tools/processes would you utilize to assist in the decision process related to new products?
8. Which research process and marketing research tools would be beneficial to help identify customer satisfaction levels and methods to improve in this area?
9. Make a list of three product/service offerings and see whether you can identify their positioning target market and market segments.

CASE 1.1. HYATT CORPORATION—A VARIATION OF THE SINGLENESS STRATEGY THROUGH PRODUCT TYPE/ IDENTIFICATION AND MARKET SEGMENT POSITIONING

In its own way, Hyatt Corporation had a dramatic impact on shaping the "look" of the hotel and resort product in today's hospitality industry. Working with renowned architect John Portman, Hyatt placed its Regency brand on the first major modern "atrium" hotel with the opening of the Hyatt Regency in Atlanta. With its spectacular atrium design and revolving rooftop restaurant and lounge, this hotel would not only start the atrium hotel and resort design trend but also establish a new image for Hyatt.

Hyatt Corporation opened its first hotel on September 27, 1957. Today, the company operates over 200 hotels throughout the world. At the time of this writing, Hyatt has two subordinate companies: Hyatt Hotels and Resorts and Hyatt International. Hyatt International operates over 60 hotels and 20 resorts in 37 countries, while Hyatt Hotels and Resorts operates over 120 hotels and resorts in the United States, Canada, and the Caribbean. Hyatt specializes in luxury hotels, with facilities for meetings and special services catering to the business traveler. There are three brand names under the Hyatt operation: Hyatt Regency, Grand Hyatt, and Park Hyatt. Each maintains the general level of quality and service associated with the Hyatt brand with slight variations.

Hyatt Regency hotels are Hyatt's core brand of hotels, with a contemporary image recognized by the brand's distinguished atrium architectural design. Hyatt Regency hotels are located in metropolitan areas, targeting the business traveler. Most Hyatt Regency hotels are typical business transit hotels. Major competitors are Hilton and Marriott.

Hyatt Regency hotels are positioned to serve the individual upscale business traveler market segment with full services, lodging, and amenities. Most Hyatt Regency hotels have medium-sized meeting facilities.

Grand Hyatt hotels serve major business destinations that attract major conventions and meetings as well as business and leisure travelers. Major competitors are Hilton, Marriott, and Westin. The hotels include features such as state-of-the-art technology, business centers, leisure amenities, and banquet and conference facilities. Grand Hyatt hotels are positioned to serve meetings and conventions as a primary target market and business and leisure individual travelers as a secondary target market.

Park Hyatt hotels are smaller, luxury hotels designed to cater to the discriminating individual traveler seeking the privacy, personalized service, and amenities of a small boutique hotel. Park Hyatt hotels, with other deluxe hotels, such as Ritz Carlton and Four Seasons, are located in major cities and popular upscale resort destinations.

Hyatt's hotel brands as represented in Exhibit 1.1 are positioned with slight differences in price, levels of service, and targeted market segments. The image and perception of each type of Hyatt hotel brand is upscale and consistent. Hyatt's Gold Passport Program (frequency program) is honored by all three Hyatt brands and contributes to their success by building repeat business. Hyatt believes that this multiple positioning/branding strengthens their appeal and the link to their frequency program helps capture the individual and the group segments. Hyatt's quality and service levels, as well as pricing strategies, support the concept of a varied singleness strategy for the overall brand.

In summary, beginning with the Hyatt Regency Atlanta three decades ago, Hyatt's growth strategy has focused on the upscale market with "product" as a key differentiator. Prior to this development, Hyatt had a mixed product line ranging from West Coast motels to some less-spectacular, full-service hotels. By selecting the "singleness" strategy, deleting the lower-end product, and concentrating on design leadership in the upper-level segment, Hyatt Corporation built a very strong and consistent brand in the hospitality industry.[13]

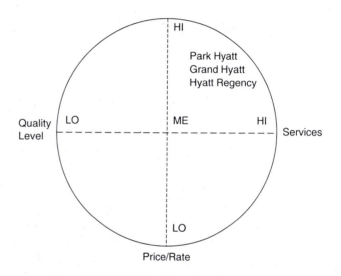

EXHIBIT 1.1. Hyatt Positioning

Case Discussion Questions

1. What are the advantages of a "singleness" strategy such as Hyatt's?
2. How does the physical product external and internal perception influence a brand's positioning?

CASE 1.2. TOYOTA MOTOR CORPORATION— POSITIONING TO PERFECTION

Launching a new brand requires an in-depth understanding of competition and the consumer. A key ingredient for success is selecting the correct positioning. This involves researching the market and analyzing both the product/service offerings and competitive strengths and weaknesses. It further involves a thorough understanding and analysis of the consumer needs and wants. When the Toyota Motor Corporation introduced the Lexus, they did so in an extraordinary manner. They knew that they had a problem. They recognized that in the U.S. market, and others, they did not have a reputation for building larger cars, luxury cars, or cars in a high price range. But they knew they had one thing going for them: the Toyota car brand was widely associated with value and quality. Clearly, they had to take that reputation and convince customers they could deliver on a whole new type of product.

To begin with, Toyota spent countless hours on consumer market research. The results allowed them to conclude which specific steps they would need to take to break into this new market of upscale automobile owners and lessees.

Research indicated what people disliked most was the auto service establishment (the dealership) and related servicing. Research also indicated that people don't strongly associate the name Lexus with Toyota. So Toyota made the extraordinary investment in building all new state-of-the-art dealerships and service shops just for the Lexus. It built these facilities with the customer's desires in mind. But the facilities would be perceived to be only as good as the service personnel and service experience itself. So Toyota provided training for all employees from the receptionist to the sales executive, from service manager to mechanic. The common denominator in this extensive training was the customer experience. The motto was as follows: Make it pleasant and, if possible, eliminate all frictional points of encounter.

Lexus keeps all their showrooms and the repair facilities clean enough to eat off the floor. They offer pick-up and delivery for even routine maintenance as another common practice. There are new (or like new) loaner cars for those who desire a car while theirs is in repair. Lexus goes one step further with follow-up phone calls, sporadic calls to see "how you like the car," and an 800 number for 24-hour road service just in case it is ever needed.

For years, customers had learned to accept less from car dealers. Research showed that Lexus not only ought to be able to achieve a 100 percent satisfaction level but also could exceed it without going overboard. Their definition of a perfect car experience was actually higher than the consumers'. So, Lexus aimed to deliver 110 percent while the consumer expected 85 percent. The result is extraordinary customer satisfaction. Of course, it helps when your product is a state-of-the-art, very low-maintenance, extraordinary, high-quality automobile. And this high quality allowed extraordinary promises to be made through advertising, promotion, and publicity when the car was first introduced.

Here's another example of Lexus's 110 percent effort. A dealer phoned a customer shortly after the purchase to ask whether anything was wrong. The customer was greatly pleased; the only thing wrong was "the wind noise from the phone antenna," he responded. When the customer went to get his car after the next maintenance visit (which was brought to the curb next to the door), he said, "That's not my car!" The service manager looked puzzled. "It's the same color and model, but the phone antenna is different and my car was coated with mud." The service manager smiled and said, "We contacted our technicians about that wind noise you referred to and they designed a new windless antenna. It's on us and we really appreciate your calling it to our attention. Also, it is our standard procedure to clean and vacuum your car before returning it to you." There are many more such stories from many other very satisfied customers.

Did this passion for customer service excellence pay off? You bet. Lexus was rated number one for customer satisfaction the very first year it was measured, scoring the highest in the index of any car in history. Lexus sales soared in a down market, which was experiencing a particularly severe downtrend in the luxury car category. Lexus sales increased nearly 30 percent in its second year while its two primary established competitors experienced declines of as much as 34 percent and 27 percent. This is taking into account the market share. Granted, some of the gain was due to value (quality at a fair, and in this instance, lesser price), but a lot of it was due to customer satisfaction.

Lexus knew the keys to winning new customers and is building a loyal base for repeat business with a highly fickle consumer group, and in a highly competitive industry. Lexus is succeeding with sales and marketing savvy closely integrated with a never before offered level of customer service. Expect Lexus to remain rated the very best for a long time.

Case Discussion Questions

1. Why is it important to understand positioning when conducting research for new products/services?
2. How can market research help improve service levels and design?

NOTES

1. W. Dillon, T. Madden, & N. Firtle, *Marketing Research in a Marketing Environment* (Burr Ridge, IL: Irwin, 1994), p. 1.
2. N. Johns & D. Lee-Ross, *Research Methods in Service Industry Management* (London: Cassell, 1998), p. 116.

3. J. Myers, *Segmentation and Positioning in Marketing Decisions* (New York: American Marketing Association, 1996), p. 68.

4. Ibid., p. 55.

5. http://www.edu.rced.ak.uk/statistics/Definitions%20in%20statistics.htm.

6. Johns & Lee Ross, *Research Methods,* p. 119.

7. Ibid., p. 117.

8. Myers, *Segmentation and Positioning,* pp. 201-202.

9. R. Daft, *Management* (Chicago: Dryden Press, 1988), p. 200.

10. http://www2.chass.ncsu.edu/garson/pa765/path.htm and www.NorthCarolinaStateUniversity.com.

11. R. Nykiel, *Marketing in the Hospitality Industry* (4th ed.) (Lansing, MI: Educational Institute, 2003), pp. 15-16.

12. Ibid., p. 38.

13. http://www.hyatt.com.

Chapter 2

Primary and Secondary Research Data

CHAPTER OBJECTIVES

- To delineate the difference between primary and secondary data.
- To discuss primary data collection methodologies.
- To identify types of secondary data.
- To discuss the usage of internal and external databases.
- To provide potential sources for locating data.

Research data may be classified as primary or secondary. Primary research is when the researcher actually interfaces with the consumer and seeks answers to specific questions, solicits opinions, or actually observes behavior. Secondary research is data obtained from third party sources such as government agencies, syndicated services, and research publications.[1] Both primary and secondary research are discussed in this chapter along with their advantages and shortfalls. Further, sources for secondary research and methods to identify and locate secondary data are provided.

PRIMARY RESEARCH DATA

It is usually wise to begin with a search of secondary research data before embarking on, designing, and/or contracting for primary research. It may well be a thorough search of secondary data that provides the researcher the information he or she is seeking. This same thorough research may also help shape the parameters of the primary research. Primary research data can be generated through a number of techniques (Figure 2.1).

Surveys and Questionnaires

Surveys and questionnaires are tools often used when researchers need to identify primary data. These interchangeable words reflect obtaining data by personal interviews, telephone interviews, computer-based interviews, or direct mail questionnaires. Selecting the best approach or approaches can be influenced by time or money requirements. There are advantages and disadvantages to each of the various approaches (Figure 2.2).

Irrespective of which technique is used, a questionnaire of some type will need to be developed. The

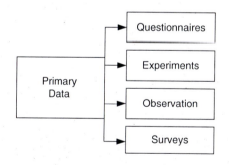

FIGURE 2.1. Primary Research Techniques

Handbook of Marketing Research Methodologies for Hospitality and Tourism
© 2007 by The Haworth Press, Inc. All rights reserved.
doi:10.1300/5927_03

Techniques	Advantages	Disadvantages
Telephone surveys	▪ Speed ▪ Low cost ▪ Reasonable response rate ▪ Flexible questioning	▪ Short/brief ▪ Sample representative ▪ Legislation ▪ Local restrictions
Personal interviews	▪ Great flexibility ▪ Higher response rate ▪ Group interaction	▪ Expensive ▪ Interviewer influence ▪ Group dominators
Direct mail surveys	▪ Good distribution ▪ No interviewer bias ▪ Convenient for respondents ▪ Focused mailing lists	▪ Time-consuming ▪ Low response rate ▪ Nonresponsive bias ▪ Structural simplicity
Computer surveys	▪ Speed ▪ Accuracy ▪ No interview bias ▪ Relative anonymity	▪ Limited access ▪ Excludes open-ended probes ▪ Varying level of respondents' technical knowledge

FIGURE 2.2. Advantages and Disadvantages of Selected Research Techniques

process of developing a good questionnaire is multifold. First, a determination of what specific information/data are being sought or are needed must be arrived at prior to beginning the solicitation process. Second, which data collection technique or approach is required is to be decided. Third is the structure of the questionnaire format, that is, open-ended questions, multiple choice, and so on. Fourth is phrasing the questions carefully or choosing how each question should be worded. Fifth is determining the order or sequence of the questions. Initial questions should be concise and easy to answer. And, questions on the same topic should be located together. Sixth is maximizing the questionnaire appeal and utility. Is the questionnaire laid out in a specific manner? Seventh is pretesting the questionnaire. The pretest will reveal which, if any, questions are not clear. And, finally, eighth is the actual distribution of the questionnaire in final form. Figure 2.3 recaps the eight-step questionnaire development process.[2]

Experiments

Experiments differ from surveys and observations in that changes (treatments) are introduced into an environment and the effects of these changes on dependent variables are measured. In most survey and observation situations, the information is gathered under normal, or near normal, conditions, and the researcher intervenes only to gather data, not to manipulate the environment. Of the three procedures, experiments provide the most conclusive evidence and are considered the backbone of "scientific research."

Experiments can be conducted either under laboratory conditions or in the field. The problem with field (real-world) experiments is that their results can be greatly affected by any number of

Experiments provide the most conclusive evidence and are considered the backbone of scientific research.

N. Johns and D. Lee-Ross
Research Methods in Service Industry Management (1998)

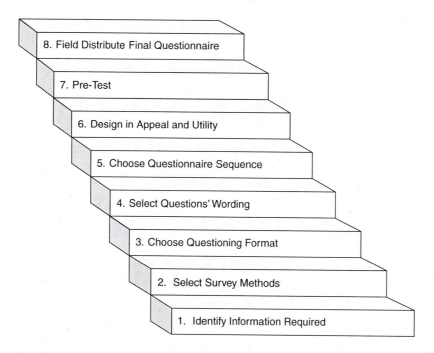

FIGURE 2.3. Questionnaire Development Process

outside factors (weather, competitors' actions, economic conditions, etc.). If an appropriate statistical design is used, the influence of some of these outside factors can be measured. The advantage of conducting experiments in a tightly controlled environment (laboratory) is that these outside factors can be eliminated, or their impact on the treatment can be measured fairly precisely.

Two key requirements for any experiment are that its results be valid and reliable. Validity refers to how well the experiment measures what it claims to measure.[3] Was the treatment totally responsible for the outcome, or did some other factor also have a major impact? Was the decline in sales due solely to the price increase, or were there other outside influences, such as competitors' actions, that led to the decline in sales?

Reliability refers to the stability or consistency of the experiment's outcome.[4] If the same treatment was repeated a number of times, would the results be fairly similar? Testing the experiment's reliability requires that the experiment be repeated a number of times, an action often ignored because it is both costly and time-consuming.

The most elaborate type of field experiment is a test market. Some component(s) of the marketing mix (price, product, place, or promotion) is tested in the field, providing the researcher with information about the reaction of the marketplace to the tests. This is an expensive and time-consuming process, however, and should be used only when a wrong decision involves a fairly significant amount of money.

Observation

This technique is used when a high degree of accuracy is required. Observation involves the personal and/or electronic recording of selected behavior as it occurs. One major benefit of observation is that it identifies what is actually occurring, whereas the survey technique relies on either the respondents' recall of what took place or their prediction of future actions (which are often subject to change).

The advantages of the observation method are (1) increased accuracy can be obtained if it is well planned and executed, (2) data can usually be gathered under normal conditions, and (3) it does not depend on the subject's communication abilities, a condition crucial to the success of many surveys.

Some possible shortcomings of using the observation method are (1) much time can be wasted waiting for the particular activity to be observed to take place, (2) people, knowing they are being observed, may act in an abnormal manner, (3) certain activities can't be observed because of their intimate or private nature, and (4) since only the final action is observed, this provides little insight into the factors influencing such a decision. Thus, it may be necessary to supplement observations with some type of survey.

The observation method can be a valuable tool to researchers, but it is a mistake to look on it as an "easy" way to obtain information. Proper planning prior to its use accompanied by careful, consistent, and critical gathering of data are necessary if useful and accurate data are to be obtained.[5]

SAMPLING

Sampling is defined as obtaining information from a percentage of the group being studied (i.e., 10 percent). In sampling, if each member of a group has a known chance of being included, it is a probability sample. If the selection is subjective, then it is a nonprobability sample. The major advantage of using probability samples is that they enable a sampling error to be estimated. Sampling error is the difference between the population's real value (which is unknown) and the value obtained from the sample. Sampling errors will always occur because the sample is never a perfect replica of the population from which it is drawn.

Types

There are many types of both probability and nonprobability samples. These are categorized based on the method used to select individual sample members. Figure 2.4 presents the categories of probability samples and their criteria.

Nonprobability samples are samples that are chosen in a subjective way. Since nonprobability samples are not randomly selected, you cannot estimate the sampling error. Figure 2.5 presents the categories of nonprobability samples and their criteria.

Category	Criteria
Simple random samples	Each member has a known and equal chance of being selected.
Systematic sample	A selection process is followed that ensures each member of the population has a known chance of being selected (e.g., every tenth name on the list).
Stratified sample	Population is divided into segments on the basis of some key characteristic, such as income or education, and sample members representing each stratum are chosen in an objective manner.
Area sample	Population is grouped into clusters (usually a geographic boundary such as a zip code or a census tract), and the sample members are selected in such a way that each cluster has a known chance of being chosen.

FIGURE 2.4. Categories and Criteria of Probability Samples

Category	Criteria
Judgment sample	Someone makes a subjective judgment about which group in the population can provide the information needed.
Convenience sample	Sample members are chosen primarily on the basis of how easy they are to contact.
Quota sample	Similar to stratified sample since the population is divided into segments, but sample members are then chosen in a subjective manner.

FIGURE 2.5. Categories and Criteria of Nonprobability Samples

Sampling Considerations

Decisions with respect to choosing a sample category and design criteria usually take into consideration a number of factors. Among these factors are time requirements, budget allocations, and how representative of the total population the sample is to be. Also, the researcher needs to consider whether the sampling error needs to be estimated and whether the user will be satisfied basing decisions on the sample data.

Generally, nonprobability samples are less expensive and take less time to develop and the findings can be as accurate as those obtained from a probability sample (assumes if properly conducted). It should also be taken into consideration that as a result of the procedures used to select the individual sample members in a nonprobability sample, sampling error cannot be estimated.

SECONDARY RESEARCH DATA

Information that is developed or gathered by someone other than the researcher and/or for other purposes than the research project under development is classified as secondary data. The benefits of using secondary research data are that it is usually quick to obtain information and usually much less costly than structuring and fielding a piece of primary research. The trade-off is that you do not control how the research was designed, collected, manipulated, interpreted, and documented.

In the use of secondary data you do not have control of how the data was designed, the sample, collection, interpretation, and documentation.

N. Johns and D. Lee-Ross
Research Methods in Service Industry Management (1998)

As a result of the Internet and technology related to data storage and manipulation, we are truly in an age of information overflow. This plethora of data can create a major problem for researchers in that it requires the ability to select the best data and sorting through many potential sources for the data. Let's briefly look where data may originate and be located.

Internal and External Data

Internal secondary data may be collected by an organization from its normal activities. Sales data, payroll data, inventory records, and production data are some examples of the types of data generated within most firms on a regular basis.

External secondary data come from a variety of sources outside the organizations. These sources include most government agencies, industrial organizations, and academic institutions, along with commercial firms, such as Dataquest or the Nielsen Company, that specialize in data gathering. Most of the internal data and much of the useful external data should be available through the organizations information system, its agencies, associations, and suppliers. Figure 2.6 provides an outline of the major external sources where secondary data can be located.

FIGURE 2.6. External Sources for Secondary Data

SOURCES OF DATA

Marketing intelligence information sources can provide substantial data. It is important for researchers to develop a working knowledge of the major secondary research information sources. As previously indicated it is a good idea to search the Internet and also contact the U.S. Government Web site. There are numerous government publications issued by virtually every branch of the government on a regular basis. The Department of Commerce has numerous field offices, as does the Small Business Administration. Also, check the Government Printing Office Publications Center in Washington, DC. You can order publications directly from this source. Specific types of marketing and consumer-related information are also abundant from the U.S. Census, Bureau of the Census. Also, media representatives and trade and consumer publications (i.e., *American Demographics*) are excellent sources of data. There are a number of non-government-related sources that provide a variety of marketing information services. Here is a sample of marketing-related resources:[6]

Source	Provides
A. C. Neilsen Company 299 Park Ave. New York, NY 10171 212-707-7500	Demographics, retail sales, and media information for each DMA (designated market area) in the United States (i.e., television audience data, retail purchases, etc.).
The Arbitron Company 142 West 57th St. New York, NY 10019 212-887-1300	Local market demographic/product usage profiles and media usage reports with target audience profiles, etc.
The Circulation Book P.O. Box 994 22619 Pacific Coast Highway Malibu, CA 90265	Circulation and penetration for all daily newspapers, Sunday papers, newspaper supplements, and magazines by metro area and TV viewers.
Claritas, Inc. 1525 Wilson Blvd., Suite 1000 Arlington, VA 22209-2411 1-800-234-5973	Offers PRIZM, a market segmentation system that divides the United States in numerous lifestyle clusters and social groups.
ClusterPlus 2000 Strategic Mapping, Inc. Corporate Headquarters 3135 Kifer Rd. Santa Clara, CA 95051-0827 1-800-472-6277	Demographic, media habits, and purchasing data on 50 plus classifications of American consumers in geographic targets down to the block level.
Dun's Marketing Services Offices nationwide 1-800-526-0651	Direct mail lists and 500 (standard industrial classifications) category and geographical information on business.
Equifax National Decision Systems 1979 Lakeside Parkway Tucker, GA 30084-5847 770-496-7171	Is where to find Micro Vision, a service that classifies consumers into 50 plus segments down to the zip + 4 level.
Fairchild Fact Files Fairchild Books 7 West 34th Street New York, NY 10001 212-630-3880	Files on market trends, buying habits, advertising expenditures, sales and demographic profiles by product category.
Gale Research Company 835 Penobscot Building Detroit, MI 48226-4094 1-800-877-4523	The encyclopedia of associations (U.S. and international), consultant directories, and the Trade Show and Professional Exhibits Directory; also, management information guides and a variety of topical reports.
Leading National Advertisers (LNA) 11 West 42nd Street, 11th Floor New York, NY 10036 212-789-1400	Competitive spending information by medium, summary of national advertising expenditures bt brand and industry category, etc.

Radio TV Reports, Inc.
317 Madison Ave.
New York, NY 10017
212-309-1400

Source for copies of all competitive radio and television ads.

Rome Report
11 West 42nd Street, 11th Floor
New York, NY 10036
212-789-1400

Contains business-to-business and trade advertising expenditures.

SRI International
333 Ravenswood Ave.
Menlo Park, CA 94025-3493
415-859-3032

Source of the VALS (values and lifestyles) program, which segments U.S. consumers into a number of distinct lifestyle groups for predicting consumer behavior.

Simmons Market Research Bureau, Inc. (SMRB)
420 Lexington Ave.
New York, NY 10170
212-916-8900

Products/services include MRI and SMRB, which provide information on demographics, size, and media habits of the user/purchaser groups for various products/brands, etc.

Standard Rate and Data Service (SRDS)
1700 West Higgins Road
Des Plaines, IL 60018
708-375-5000

Newspaper rates and data service provides population, expenditures for individual states, counties, etc., with household information; also, provides numerous "source books" for mailing lists, media rate information, etc.

Viking and Penguin Books
Viking Penguin, Inc.
375 Hudson Street
New York, NY 10014
212-366-2000

Information U.S.A., a reference guide for direct access to government experts, commerce data sources, census data sources, etc.

Yesawich, Pepperdine & Brown
1900 Summitt Tower Blvd., Ste. 600
Orlando, FL 32810
407-875-1111

MONITOR, an annual research tool that provides insight into social, behavioral, and travel-related trends among American consumers.

There are numerous additional resources for marketing data. These include but are not limited to Internet search engines. Netscape's NetSearch provides a list of search engines and directories; American Demographics, the Lifestyle Market Analysts (SRDS); Dunn's Market Identifiers (DMI), the Gallup Poll; Mediamark Research; Market Facts, Inc. (consumer mail panel); Nielsen Television Index; Nielsen Scantrack (market definitions); Nielsen Retail Index, Roper Reports, Simmons Market Research Bureau; SRI Vals-2 Program; Starch Readership Survey, and the Yankelovich Monitor.

In addition to these resources, there are numerous market research companies; focus group specialists' directories of market research reports, studies, and surveys; and many directories of mailing lists. Most major trade publications publish an annual issue in directory format, listing these various resources.

Online Databases

First, a distinction is made between online database producers and database vendors. Database producers are organizations that collect and/or create data largely focused on an industry or combination of similar industries (i.e., airline industry and travel industry). Three of the better known producers are the U.S. Department of Commerce (BLS-Service contains data on consumer price index, employment, earnings, etc.); Predicasts, which creates and assembles data on high-tech industries; and FIND/SVP, which generates its own studies and also acquires industry assessments and market research reports.

Database vendors subscribe to a number of databases, combine them, and make them available to subscribers. The primary advantage in using these vendors rather than going directly to the database producer is that a single vendor can provide access to a number of major databases.

There are hundreds of database vendors, two of the better known being DIALOG (offers access to databases, most of which deal with business-related topics) and ORBIT (Systems Development Corporation, online systems that contain databases on such varied topics as energy, agriculture, law, etc.). The typical procedure for using an online database is to pay an annual subscription fee plus a charge for each subject search.

Finally, there are some databases that provide actual sales or production data for an industry or locale over a number of time periods. This type of database is of most interest to forecasters using time series or causal models. Locating secondary data can be challenging with or without the help of a computer. With respect to non-computer-based data resources, there are indices, directories, and other aids to help in the research process. In Figure 2.7, a list of these resources is provided.

Other resources include the *Dissertation Abstracts International* (Microfilm Library Service) and the *Index of University Publications of Bureaus of Business and Economic Research*. Finally, directories can help identify firms, organizations, associations, and other entities and individuals that might have data related to your research. Major directories include *Standard and Poor's Register of Corporations, Directors, and Executives,* which classifies firms by products/services and geographically; the *Million Dollar Directory* published by Dun and Bradstreet, and *Moody's Manuals*. The latter two also contain data on American business firms. Another publication is the *Encyclopedia of Associations* published by Gale Research, which provides both statistical data and lists the publications of associations.

Data Source	Indices and Other Helpful Aids
Books	Card Catalogs, Publishers Weekly, Book Review Index (Gale Research), Economic Abstracts
Periodicals	Business Periodicals Index, Readers Guide to Periodical Literature, Applied Science and Technology Index, Predicasts F&S Index of Corporations and Industries, Ulrich's Periodical Dictionary, and the Public Affairs Information Services Bulletin
Newspapers and Business News	Wall Street Journal Index, New York Times Index, and the National Newspaper Index
Government Information	Government Publications Index, Monthly Catalog of U.S. Government Publications, and the Monthly Checklist of State Publications

FIGURE 2.7. Indices and Other Aids for Finding Printed Data

Statistical Publications

Many times marketing researchers are more interested in statistical data for purposes of trend identification, forecasts, and model development. The publications in Figure 2.8 actually contain statistical data or identify where such data can be obtained.

Publication	Source/Publisher	Content
American Statistical Index	Congressional Information Service	A comprehensive guide and index to statistical publications of the U.S. Government
Statistical Abstract of the United States	Government Printing Office	Statistics on wide variety of industrial, political, and social subjects
Survey of Current Business	Department of Commerce	Comprehensive statistical series covering business indicators, income and employment by industry, and real-estate activity
Statistics Sources	Gale Research	Identifies statistical data from government, business, and international sources
The Country and City Data Book	Government Printing Office	Statistics for cities, standard metropolitan areas, and countries
A Graphic Guide to Consumer Markets	The Conference Board	Statistics on population, income, expenditures, market prices, advertising, and production
Economic Indicators	Council of Economic Advisors? Government Printing Office	Key data on the gross national product, personal consumption, expenditures, and so on
Federal Reserve Bulletin	Federal Reserve System Board of Governors	Data on banking, savings, interest rates, industrial production, and some data on international trade
Monthly Labor Review	Bureau of Labor Statistics	Presents current data on employment, earnings, wholesale and retail prices
Business Conditions Digest	Bureau of Economic Analysis	Provides indicators of current business activity; useful for forecasting
Consumer Buying Indicators	Bureau of the Census, Department of Commerce	Purchase estimates for autos, homes, furniture, carpets, appliances, and home improvements
County Business Patterns	Government Printing Office	Individual state reports on employment and payroll figures using SIC and SMA categories
Predicasts Forecasts	Predicasts, Inc.	Short and longer range projections on economic indicators, products, and industries
Sales and Marketing Management Survey of Buying Power	Sales and Marketing Management	Statistics on population, retail sales (categories), and household incomes by state, county, SMSA, etc.

FIGURE 2.8. Publications Containing Statistics

Standard Industrial Classification

Researchers seeking information about firms or entire industries need to be familiar with the SIC. In its simplest definition, SIC codes are a sequence of numeric digits that identify major groups (types of products and services), specialized segments within each group, and firms engaged in providing goods in these segments. Further, groups of products and services are also identified. Most government and industry publications use the SIC code to present their data and describe a firm's activity. The *Standard Industrial Classification Manual,* which lists all industries and their SIC codes, is readily available in almost all libraries. A major weakness of the SIC system is that it was developed initially to classify manufacturing activities and does not really cover the service industry in an adequate manner. Whereas over 70 percent of the jobs in the U.S. economy currently are service related, only one-third of SIC codes pertain to service industries.

CHAPTER REVIEW

In this chapter, the discussion noted that primary data are data that the researcher obtains as a result of actually asking the customer, target market, or nonusers. Surveys and questionnaires as well as observational techniques may be used to obtain primary research data. Secondary data are data that already exist and can be obtained from external sources. The U.S. government is one of the largest sources of secondary data. Also discussed was the value of internal and external databases.

To acquire external data, the researcher must know how to use various indexes, directories, guides, and abstracts to identify data. While secondary data may be readily available and less expensive, there are some drawbacks, such as the age and accuracy of the data itself. Primary data are developed from the application of surveys, questionnaires, observations, and experiments. The strength of observations is that activities are studied as they take place.

When experiments are used, the researcher manipulates certain conditions in an environment and then measures the impact of those manipulations. Experiments can be conducted under laboratory conditions or out in the field. The problem with field experiments is that outside factors often influence the experiment's results. If a statistical research design is used in the experiment, the influence of some of these extraneous factors can be measured.

In most situations where primary data are generated, some type of sampling will be involved. The researcher will have to decide between a probability or nonprobability sample. Probability samples enable sampling errors to be estimated and, thus, provide a more precise estimate of the population's values.

KEY CONCEPTS/TERMS

Abstracts
Databases
Directories
Experiments
Observation
Primary data
Questionnaires
Reliability
Sampling
Secondary data

Standard Industrial Classification (SIC)
Surveys
Validity

DISCUSSION QUESTIONS

1. What are three advantages of conducting a telephone survey?
2. What are the potential disadvantages of secondary data?
3. How can the SIC code be of help to a marketing researcher?
4. Can you identify three of the better known database suppliers?
5. What is the first step a researcher should take in developing questionnaires?
6. What are the advantages and disadvantages of the observation method?
7. What is the difference between validity and reliability?

CASE 2.1. LOOKING WITHIN—OBSERVATION

Perhaps one of the least discussed research techniques is observation. In reality, applying the observation technique has often resulted in major breakthroughs in virtually every area of the service industry. Observation has led to scientific and medical discoveries as well as to new processes and products. This case example provides one simple example of using observation to develop a new product.

At the North American headquarters of a major global food corporation, there was a formal process of ongoing research on everything from new formulas to new packaging. The market research committee would meet at a different company facility across the country on a regular basis to exchange ideas, findings, etc. There was an extensive, formalized research budget. Competitive moves were monitored and monthly competitive/environmental reports, along with periodic "flash" reports, were issued. A great deal of "looking around" and "looking ahead" research was going on at all times. However, not many were "looking within" to see whether there were any key focal points of interest.

One of the organization's marketing managers (the one with the smallest research budget) decided to look within utilizing an inexpensive technique called observation. The marketer observed that the employees were provided complimentary coffee, soft drinks, and certain snack and candy products, which were made by the company. Focusing on the employees' habits, the marketer observed that most employees would drink regular coffee with their first fill-up in the morning. However, the second and third fill-ups were different. Employees (eight out of ten) would pour one-half cup of regular coffee and one-half cup of decaffeinated coffee most of the time. This observation was followed up with a simple questionnaire seeking the reasons for this mixing. The results/answers were twofold. One group stated that they wanted to cut down on caffeine. The other group stated that they just didn't like the taste of the decaffeinated coffee and rather than switch they would improve its taste with a little regular coffee.

The marketer soon discovered that the mix/blend process was pretty much a standard procedure at many coffee stations around the company. This observational research led to a formal recommendation to the new products group to develop a reduced caffeine product with the taste of regular coffee. It seemed that half regular and half decaffeinated would do the job from observation. After formal lab work and field testing, it turned out that the formula was pretty close and the "market" would respond. The new 50 percent less caffeine product with the taste of regular coffee was launched. First-year sales surpassed $100 million dollars!

Case Discussion Questions

1. Utilizing the process of observation in your daily environment, seek to identify how you or others could change existing products to meet your specific needs.
2. How do your needs and the benefits you seek in products or services change over time? During the day, week, month, season, or year?

CASE 2.2. THE POWER OF THE SURVEY AND AWARD

Survey results can be of tremendous help in positioning a product or service as well as in providing the catalyst for a major strategic marketing campaign. Survey results, even conducted by others, can prove very beneficial or very destructive. Applying survey findings can also demonstrate how these basic research tools can be very powerful.

There are two ways to use the power of the survey or award. One is to be fortunate enough to be ranked number one in an external objective consumer survey of products or services in your category. The other is to conduct and report on your own survey. This latter practice is frequently used by politicians and political parties to create perceptions that their policies are on target, or to create momentum for a candidate. The former is an extraordinarily valuable marketing weapon if used to the fullest extent and if it lives up to service delivery and/or product quality.

Continental Airlines won the J. D. Power and Associates number one ranking in customer service in 1997. It went on to win this ranking in 1998 and 1999, three consecutive years. Granted, this is a highly visible award/survey; however, once it is released, it could be yesterday's news unless it's reinforced in a methodical manner. Continental Airlines did a masterful job of doing just that, reinforcing its accomplishment with all constituencies. This included employee-based internal public relations programs and incentives, external advertising campaigns, and constant reminders in its promotional literature, timetables, frequent traveler programs, etc. In fact, Continental CEO, Gordon Bethune, even wrote a book, *From Worst to Best,* that further publicized the achievement. In a business where service is the business and a major competitive advantage, Continental has the edge as a result of reinforcing its achievement through an aggressive internal and external public relations program that is also interlinked to its other marketing weapons.

Case Discussion Questions

1. Identify a hospitality industry service organization that has been positively recognized in a consumer survey and determine how these results were incorporated into their overall organizational strategy.
2. Select another firm or brand that bases its overall marketing strategy on its performance in a third-party survey and state how the firm executes the strategy.

NOTES

1. W. R. Dillon, T. J. Madden, & N. H. Firtle, *Marketing Research in a Marketing Environment* (2nd ed.) (Homewood, IL: Irwin, 1987), p. 117.

2. R. Nykiel, *Marketing Strategies* (New York: CORMAR Business Press, 1997), p. 117.

3. N. Johns & D. Lee-Ross, *Research Methods in Service Industry Management* (London, UK: Cassell, 1998), p. 60.

4. Ibid.

5. Ibid., pp. 128-129.

6. Adapted from R. Hiebing Jr. & S. Cooper, *The Successful Marketing Plan* (2nd ed.) (New York: McGraw-Hill, 1998), pp. 20-27.

Chapter 3

Qualitative Research

CHAPTER OBJECTIVES

- To define qualitative research and its role.
- To identify the parameters of qualitative research.
- To review the basic types and techniques of qualitative research.
- To discuss the analysis of qualitative research data.

Qualitative research can be extremely valuable in marketing analysis and applications. More than one major new product concept has come directly from qualitative research. Examples include the Ford Mustang, Diet Coke, caffeine-reduced and caffeine-free coffee, a variety of soft drinks, and scores more. This chapter looks at the definition and scope of qualitative research, related advantages and disadvantages, and applications. Various types and techniques of qualitative research are also examined. Finally, the analysis techniques associated with qualitative research are reviewed and discussed.

DEFINITION AND ROLE

There are a number of definitions applicable to qualitative research. One of the basic definitions is that qualitative research is a set of research techniques, which is used in marketing (also in the social sciences), in which data are obtained from a relatively small group of respondents and not analyzed with statistical techniques. This differentiates from quantitative research in which a large group of respondents provides data that are statistically analyzed.

A more marketing-oriented definition is that qualitative research provides definitive market information regarding the opinions and behaviors of the subjects in the market research study. Qualitative research helps identify attitudes, opportunities, and problems from a given target market or market segment.

Finally, a third definition of qualitative research is described as "using 'unstructured' forms of data collection, both interviewing and observation, and employing verbal descriptions and explanations rather than quantitative measurement and statistical analysis."[1]

These definitions contrast qualitative research with quantitative research by indicating that qualitative research is nonstatistical in nature. In reality, qualitative research can provide excellent data that can feed into structuring quantitative research and can lead to statistical analysis and refined interpretation.

Handbook of Marketing Research Methodologies for Hospitality and Tourism
© 2007 by The Haworth Press, Inc. All rights reserved.
doi:10.1300/5927_04

The Role of Qualitative Research

As inferred in the aforementioned definitions, qualitative research methods may be used primarily as a prelude to quantitative research. Qualitative research methods are used to define a problem, generate hypotheses, identify determinants, and develop quantitative research designs. Qualitative research methods may be inexpensive and fast because of the low number of respondents utilized. Qualitative research often cannot be generalized to the whole population. However, qualitative research findings are very valuable for exploring an issue (especially in the services sector) and are used by most market researchers. Qualitative research can also be viewed as being better than quantitative research as a method to probe below the surface for effective drives and subconscious motivations. Also, qualitative research methods assist in uncovering complex issues, although this usually requires a greater amount of time.

Qualitative research can be extremely valuable. . . . More than a few major new products, services, and concepts have originated from qualitative methodologies.

It should be pointed out that due to the role of qualitative research, two different approaches may be undertaken. Most qualitative methods use a direct approach by clearly disclosing the purpose of the study and the organization that is conducting it and/or commissioned it. Questions are direct and to the point. Many other qualitative techniques use an indirect approach. In this case, the true intent of the research is disguised, either by claiming a false purpose or by omitting any reference to the study's purpose. Some researchers believe that this latter approach provides more honest and accurate responses.

ADVANTAGES, DISADVANTAGES, AND PERSPECTIVES

Researchers often express their own opinions and attitudes related to a preferred research methodology. There are strong proponents and opponents of each research methodology. While qualitative research mostly gathers information using interviews and observations that seem less structured than quantitative techniques, this does not mean it is less effective. In fact, a great deal of planning is often involved in qualitative research. Also, a variety of skills are needed to perform effective qualitative research. It is necessary to step back and critically analyze situations, to recognize and avoid bias, to obtain valid and reliable data, and to think abstractly.[2]

Thus, qualitative researchers have to be able to maintain distance between themselves and the phenomena under investigation, and to draw upon practical and theoretical knowledge to interpret what they see. However, in the interests of methodological rigor, this interpretation needs to conform to some agreed-upon criteria. The following criteria for research are to be generally accepted:

- *Credibility:* Researchers' interpretations must be acceptable to others (other researchers, managers of service organizations, etc.).
- *Transferability:* Results must be relevant to other organizations and situations.
- *Dependability:* Findings must permit forecasting or extrapolation (e.g., to support related theories).
- *Conformability:* Similar groups in similar organizations should also be able to duplicate the research findings.

Opponents of qualitative research believe that qualitative findings lack factual data-based validity. They assert that qualitative research should be conducted systematically enough to render it valid in the sense that quantitative research is valid. This view ignores the flexibility of qualitative research and its ability to cope with the needs and exigencies of organizations. Research projects in service organizations often need to be dynamic because organizational and environmental conditions change continually.[3]

Service organizations are not scientific laboratories with controlled conditions, nor are individuals always willing to take part in research projects. Research programs conducted within them are always subject to practical constraints, and researchers must have contingency plans. Most service organizations are labor intensive, with personnel interacting with customers much of the time. (Indeed, this "service encounter" is a crucial element of service "products.") It is, therefore, generally important to assess the attitudes of employees, customers, and managers. This usually involves tailoring research flexibly to organizational needs. Qualitative research provides an effective way to do this, and it is important that both researchers and managers understand the basic techniques available.

TYPES AND TECHNIQUES

The main types of qualitative research include in-depth interviews, focus groups, mail and electronic surveys, observation, documents, and projective techniques. This section briefly discusses each of these looking at the research type itself and its advantages and disadvantages. Figure 3.1 summarizes the qualitative research types and techniques.

In-Depth Interviews

An "in-depth interview" is conducted one-on-one and usually lasts between thirty minutes to an hour. The in-depth interview is considered one of the best methods for in-depth probing of personal opinions, beliefs, and values. Normally, a very rich depth of information can be collected and this technique offers great flexibility. Probing is very useful at uncovering hidden issues. In-depth interviews may be structured (loosely) but are usually unstructured. This unstructured approach differentiates them from survey interviews in which the same questions are asked of all respondents. Naturally, unstructured in-depth interviews are time-consuming and often responses can be difficult to interpret. Further, interviewers should be skilled in order to reduce interviewer bias. Skilled interviewers can run up the cost of the research using the in-depth approach. In in-depth interviews there are no social pressures on respondents to conform and no group dynamics. The technique usually begins with general questions and rapport-establishing questions, and then proceeds to more purposeful questions.

In-depth interviewing techniques include laddering, hidden issue questioning, and symbolic analysis.

- *Laddering* is a technique used by in-depth interviewers that starts with questions about external objects and external social phenomena and then proceeds to internal attitudes and feelings.
- *Hidden issue questioning* is a technique used by in-depth interviewers in which they concentrate on deeply felt personal concerns and pet peeves.

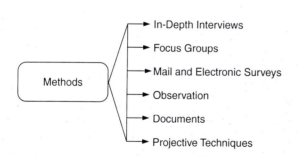

FIGURE 3.1. Types and Techniques of Qualitative Research

• *Symbolic analysis* is a technique used by in-depth interviewers in which deeper symbolic meanings are probed by asking questions about their opposites.

Focus Groups

Focus groups are interactive group discussions led by a trained moderator. While usually appearing to be unstructured or loosely structured discussions, a well-thought-out question guide is predeveloped. In a focus group, the moderator encourages the free flow of ideas from all group members. Groups can vary in size but are usually made up of eight to twelve individuals. Focus groups usually last from one to two hours; some conducted over a meal can go up to three hours. The classic perspective of a focus group is usually portrayed by a group sitting around a table in a room with a large one-way glass window or hidden cameras. Participants can't see out and/or know there is a closed circuit broadcast of the conversations to skilled researchers behind the glass or viewing monitors. Focus groups are fairly quick to set up and usually not that expensive to conduct. More and more focus groups are being conducted by using computers and Internet technology online. In a focus group, respondents may feel a great deal of peer or group pressure to respond and even conform. The group dynamics are useful in developing new streams of thought and covering an issue in a thorough manner.

Surveys

As previously delineated, a survey is usually structured and the same questions are provided to all respondents. Surveys can be conducted in a number of ways including in person, over the phone, online, and through the mail. Surveys allow for structure and are usually limited to ten to fifteen minutes without an incentive and can run as long as thirty to forty minutes with an incentive. Surveys allow for quantification, sample sizes, and can easily be adapted. Dependent upon the execution method selected, the scope of the analysis, and size of the sample, surveys can vary widely in cost and response time.

Figure 3.2 provides a synopsis of some of the advantages and disadvantages in the different delivery approaches for surveys.

Observation

Observation techniques are when the researcher observes social or market phenomena in their natural setting. Observations can occur cross sectionally (observations made at one time) or longitudinally (observations occur over several time periods). Observation is what it implies, watching the behavior of individuals or groups of people. The scope of observation is very wide because observation may take place on a comparatively broad and general scale. Choice and type of observational technique are usually influenced by the actual setting in which the observation will take place. Figure 3.3 identifies the different observational roles.

Observation is an everyday reality in many service industry settings, particularly in large service organizations. For example, a mystery guest in a hotel or a mystery shopper in a retail outlet is a type I "complete participant," usually with directions to act covertly. In contrast, a "time and motion" researcher of operational efficiency is a type IV "complete observer," observing openly, and clearly differentiated from the workers themselves. A trainee is often a type II "participant as observer," doing part of the job while observing. An outsider engaged in job shadowing is a type III "observer as nonparticipant."

Observation is an everyday reality in most service industry settings.

Technique	Advantages	Disadvantages
Personal surveys	• Interviewer can observe reactions, probe, and clarify answers • Technique usually nets a high percentage of completed surveys • Flexibility with location and time for gathering information • Interviewer can use visual displays • Allows for good sampling control	• Costly • Time-consuming • May contain interviewer biases
Telephone surveys	• Fast • Lower cost than personal surveys • Small response bias • Wide geographic reach compared to personal surveys	• Survey length is limited • Difficult to reach busy people • Difficult to discuss certain topics • Can be expensive compared to mail surveys
Mail surveys	• Wide distribution and low cost • Interviewer bias is eliminated • Anonymity of respondents • Respondent can answer at leisure	• Accurate lists are not always available • Response is not necessarily representative of the target population • Limited to length of survey • Not timely • Clarifying and probing of answers is not possible • Question order bias • Unable to guarantee a specific total sample

FIGURE 3.2. Advantages and Disadvantages of Survey Techniques

Type I: Complete participant	Type II: Participant as observer	Type III: Observer as non-participant	Type IV: Complete observer
Participant, similar age, interests, activities, covert	Participant, overt or covert	Overt, non-participation but present among subject groups	Observation at a distance, non-participation

FIGURE 3.3. Synopsis of Observational Roles

Covert observation in research situations is effective because the researcher is unknown to the subjects. The observer can pose as a work colleague of equal status, so that those being observed are more likely to behave "normally." However, covert observation raises ethical issues and researchers should consider whether it is morally acceptable to occupy a covert or type I position. This is particularly the case if the findings may be used to manipulate or exploit the subjects. In addition, if covert observers are "discovered" by observers, results may be compromised and violent situations may even develop.[4]

Observational researchers should remain objective at all times. Their own opinions, motivations, and attitudes must be set aside during the observational research process and during analysis. Observations may be recorded in note form; however, video is usually much more effective.

One other technique of the observation method is referred to as ethnography. "Ethnography is an anthropological approach which uses a rigorous style of participant observation. It allows the researcher to use participants' socially acquired and shared knowledge to account for observed patterns of their behavior."[5] Ethnography focuses on the ways in which people interact with one another in their everyday situations. Ethnographers attempt to learn about the culture of their subjects and interpret it in ways compatible with the way the members of the group see it. This research approach considers that social interactions cannot be studied under artificial conditions of experiment or interview, but only in their natural situation in "the field." Tourism research has found this approach very fruitful.

Documents

Qualitative research also generates documents, for example, the notes and transcripts of observations and interviews. However, in addition to these considerations, documents are qualitative research sources in their own right.

For example, public archives can provide information about events in the past, where the original subjects are dead or cannot be reached. They may contain useful visual materials such as photographs, sketches, or maps, which can enhance and illuminate data that have already been collected from live sources. Archives can also give clues to behavior, either directly, by describing it, or indirectly. For example, advertisements, instructions, notices and codes, and practices may provide evidence of how people once lived and behaved.

Another useful source of data may be provided by administrative documents. These include minutes of meetings, letters, memos, and financial records. Administrative documents have a similar status to archives but are usually privately (often informally) held, and for this reason may be incomplete, with access to them having to be negotiated.

Projective Techniques

Projective techniques are unstructured prompts or stimuli that encourage the respondents to project their underlying motivations, beliefs, attitudes, or feelings onto an ambiguous situation. Projective techniques are all the indirect techniques that attempt to disguise the purpose of the research. Examples of projective techniques include the following:

- *Word association:* Respondents are asked to say the first word that comes to mind after hearing a word (only some of the words in the list are test words that the researcher is interested in; the rest are fillers); this is useful in testing brand names; variants include chain word association and controlled word association.
- *Sentence completion:* Respondents are given incomplete sentences and asked to complete them.

- *Story completion:* Respondents are given part of a story and are asked to complete it.
- *Cartoon tests:* Pictures of cartoon characters are shown in a specific situation and with dialogue balloons; one of the dialogue balloons is empty and the respondent is asked to fill it in.
- *Thematic apperception tests:* Respondents are shown a picture (or a series of pictures) and are asked to make up a story about the picture(s).
- *Role-playing:* Respondents are asked to play the role of someone else; researchers assume that subjects will project their own feelings or behaviors into the role.
- *Third-person technique:* A verbal or visual representation of an individual and his or her situation is presented to the respondent. The respondent is asked to relate the attitudes or feelings of the person. Researchers assume that talking in the third person will minimize the social pressure to give standard or politically correct responses.

Ethics plays a significant role in qualitative research—it is usually a good practice to ask for interviewees' permission and to give subjects access to transcripts and recorded data.

QUALITATIVE DATA ANALYSIS

Qualitative data include notes, documents, text, and videotaped behavior. Select qualitative analysis methods are summarized in Figure 3.4.

Qualitative data are generally complex and highly dependent upon the timing and circumstances under which they are gathered. It is best practice to record data instantly or as soon as possible after observation. It is also important to record contextual information and subtle nuances of speech and behavior if the full value is to be mined from the situation. Respondents frequently reveal information that seems irrelevant at the time but later gains significance. Some recorded situation may also result in something that the researcher has not considered, and that data could very well change the whole basis of the analysis.

Data analysis tends to be an ongoing and iterative (nonlinear) process in qualitative research. The term used to describe this process is interim analysis (i.e., the cyclical process of collecting and analyzing data during a single research study). Interim analysis continues until the process or topic that the researcher is interested in is understood. Throughout the entire process of qualitative data analysis it is a good idea to engage in memoing (i.e., recording reflective notes about what is learned from the data). The idea is for the researchers to write memos to themselves when ideas and insights arise and to include those memos as additional data to be analyzed. Qualitative researchers usually transcribe their data; that is, they type the text (from interviews, observational notes, memos, etc.) into word processing documents. It is these transcriptions that are later analyzed, typically using one of the qualitative data analysis computer programs.

Coding and Category Systems

Coding and category systems are the next major step in qualitative data analysis. It is here that researchers carefully read transcribed data, line by line, and divide the data into meaningful analytical units (i.e., segmenting the data). When meaningful segments are located they are coded.

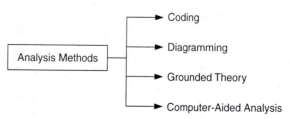

FIGURE 3.4. Select Qualitative Analytical Methods

Coding is defined as marking the segments of data with symbols, descriptive words, or category names.

N. Johns and D. Lee-Ross
Research Methods in Service Industry Management (1998)

Again, whenever a meaningful segment of text is inserted in a transcript, it is assigned a code or category name to signify that particular segment. The process is continued until all text is segmented and all data have undergone the initial coding. During coding, it is a good practice to keep a master list (i.e., a list of all the codes that are developed and used in the research study). Then, the codes are reapplied to new segments of data each time an appropriate segment is encountered. Consistency in coding is important when it comes to data analysis. Inter-coder reliability refers to consistency among different coders. Intra-coder reliability refers to consistency within a single coder. There are many different types of codes that are commonly used in qualitative data analysis. A researcher may decide to use a set of already existing codes in their data. These are called a priori codes. A priori codes are codes that are developed before examining the current data. Many qualitative researchers like to develop the codes as they code the data. These codes are called inductive codes. Inductive codes are codes that are developed by the researcher by directly examining the data. Researchers sometimes discover that the same segment of data gets coded with more than one code. These sets of codes are called co-occurring codes. Co-occurring codes are codes that partially or completely overlap. In other words, the same lines or segments of text may have more than one code attached to them.

Oftentimes researchers may have an interest in the characteristics of the individuals they are studying. Therefore, they may use codes that apply to the overall protocol or transcript being coded. These codes that apply to the entire document or case are called facesheet codes.

After the researchers finish the initial coding of their data, they will attempt to summarize and organize the data. They will also continue to refine and revise their codes. This next major step of summarizing results includes such processes as enumeration and searching for relationships in the data.

Enumeration is the process of quantifying data, and, yes, it is often done in "qualitative" research. When reading "numbers" in qualitative research, always check the basis of the numbers. For example, if one word occurs many times and the basis is the total number of words in all the text documents, then the reason could be that many people used the word or it could be that only one person used the word many times.

Sometimes codes or categories can be organized into different levels or hierarchies. This is called creating hierarchical category systems. The idea is that some ideas or themes are more general than others, and thus the codes are related vertically. The hierarchical system is one type of relationship that can be shown among categories. Qualitative researchers have a broad view of what may constitute a relationship. Many types of relationships have been identified and classified. Figure 3.5 presents Spradley's Universal Semantic Relationships, which were published in 1979.

In summary, before data can be analyzed and used, qualitative data must be coded. The coding process ensures that the data are managed methodically, and that the researcher can access all the ma-

Title	Form of Relationship
▪ Strict inclusion	X is a kind of Y+
▪ Spatial	X is a place in Y; X is a part of Y
▪ Cause-effect	X is a result of Y; X is a cause of Y
▪ Rationale	X is a reason for doing Y
▪ Location for action	X is a place for doing Y
▪ Function	X is used for Y
▪ Means-end	X is a way to do Y
▪ Sequence	X is a step (stage) in Y
▪ Attribution	X is an attribute (characteristic) of Y

FIGURE 3.5. Spradley's Universal Semantic Relationships

terial they contain. As in quantitative research, coding is a way of marking information for later use, and there are three levels at which it should be done:

- Identifying all pieces of data and respondents
- Identifying units of analysis (sections and subsections within the data)
- Identifying features of the data for analysis[6]

Diagramming

This is the process of making a sketch, drawing, or outline to show how something works. It is also used to clarify the relationship between the part of a whole. The use of diagrams is very effective in presenting qualitative data. There are many types of diagrams, such as a "network" diagram, which shows direct links between variables or events over time. Many types of matrices (classifications usually based on two or more dimensions) can be utilized to present qualitative data analysis.

Grounded Theory Approach

Grounded theory approach is essentially phenomenological. It aims to derive concepts inductively from raw qualitative data (taped/transcribed interviews, videoed/annotated observations, annotated documents) and to develop them into theories. Relationships between these hypotheses are explored systematically in order to provide coherent patterns of understanding about the research situation. Thus, theories (hypotheses) spring from concepts, which in turn arise from observations. They have been "grounded" empirically in the data and can be supported by actual, demonstrable evidence. Figure 3.6 presents the stages of the grounded theory process.

The grounded theory approach is systematic and can be envisaged as the series of stages. Theory is to be developed during the research process; so the research question needs to be open enough to allow this to happen. Instead of the hypothesis/null hypothesis required by the positivist approach, qualitative research should start with a clear statement of the research situation. Using this, a work schedule is drawn up, and the data are collected. Three types of coding are then employed to extract meaning from the data: *open coding, axial coding,* and *selective coding.* The objective is to produce theories that are grounded in empirical data, are conceptually dense (i.e., related to the data through many justifiable generalizations), and are well integrated (i.e., have common themes and support one another).

- *Open coding* involves looking through the data in order to identify concepts.
- *Axial coding* consists of a set of procedures whereby data are put back together in new ways after open coding, by making connections between categories. This is done by utilizing a coding paradigm involving conditions, context, action/interaction strategies, and consequences.
- *Selective coding* aims to integrate and interrelate the hypotheses that have been produced.

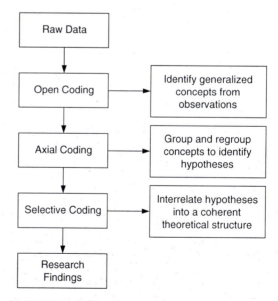

FIGURE 3.6. The Grounded Theory Process

Grounded theory has several advantages in that it is capable of handling all kinds of qualitative data. Further, it is flexible enough to suit a wide range of situations and variations in personal style. Finally it is inductive in concept; so it makes no presumptions about the data or the research situation.[7]

Computer-Aided Analysis

Computer-aided analysis is, traditionally, qualitative data analyzed by hand using some form of filing system. The availability of computer packages (that are specifically designed for qualitative data and analysis) has significantly reduced the need for the traditional filing technique. Among the most popular qualitative data analysis packages, currently, are NUDIST, ATLAS, and Ethnograph. Qualitative data analysis programs can facilitate most of the techniques that have been discussed in this chapter (e.g., storing and coding, attaching memos, finding relationships, and producing graphics).

One useful tool available in computer packages is Boolean operators, which can be used in performing complex searches that would be very time-consuming if done manually. Boolean operators are words that are used to create logical combinations such as AND, OR, NOT, IF, THEN, and EXCEPT. For example, a researcher can search for the co-occurrence of codes, which is one way to begin identifying relationships among the codes.[8]

CHAPTER REVIEW

This chapter revealed that there are a number of definitions for qualitative research and that the more market oriented was that qualitative research provides definitive market information regarding the opinions and behaviors of the subjects in the market research. It further stated that the role of qualitative research included defining problems, generating hypotheses, identifying determinants, and developing quantifiable research designs.

Six types/techniques for qualitative research were presented. These included (1) in-depth interviews; (2) focus groups; (3) direct mail and electronic surveys; (4) observation; (5) documents; and (6) projective techniques. Selective qualitative data analysis approaches were presented and included the following: coding, diagramming, grounded theory, and computer-aided analysis. It was pointed out the qualitative research allows for in-depth probes to ascertain rationale for behavior, to identify attitudes, and to solicit the basis for opinions. And, finally, it was concluded that collection of data is wide in scope and that both written and videotaped documentation may be utilized in the research process.

KEY CONCEPTS/TERMS

Analysis
Closed ended
Coding
Conformability
Credibility
Dependability
Documents
Enumeration
Ethnography
Focus groups

Interviews
Laddering
Nonverbal communications
Observation
Open ended
Projective techniques
Structured
Transferability
Unstructured

DISCUSSION QUESTIONS

1. Three definitions of qualitative research were presented in the chapter. Select the one you believe best serves the purpose of marketing research and discuss why you feel this way.
2. State three reasons why coding is important in the qualitative research process and why.
3. What do you believe are the greatest advantages of qualitative research? And, what do you feel is the biggest disadvantage?
4. How would you explain the difference between "priori codes," a priori codes, and inductive codes?
5. What does the grounded theory process begin with (the first step) and where does it end (the last step)?
6. What are "NUDIST" and "ATLAS" in the realm of qualitative research?

CASE 3.1. CARLSON COMPANIES, INC.

This chapter has focused on the variety of business development strategies that management can select from to help in their company's growth. The case example that follows presents a company that has utilized multiple strategies, including acquisitions, franchising, joint ventures, and new concept development. The company has also successfully utilized both horizontal and vertical integration strategies from an organizational perspective.

One of the most fascinating companies from a business development perspective is Carlson Companies. Its growth strategies include, but are not limited to, acquisitions, cooperative agreements, franchising, joint ventures, management contracts, partnerships, ownership, and global expansion in multiple hospitality industry sectors. In this case example, we will see how a multibillion dollar conglomerate of hospitality-related business grew to be one of the largest players in the industry through strategic deployment of a variety of business development and financial strategies.

It all began with a $55 loan and an entrepreneurial spirit that transcended the years and were keys in establishing Carlson Companies, Inc., as the Gold Bond Stamp Company in 1938.

Today, Carlson Companies is one of the largest privately held corporations in the United States, with operations in more than 140 countries. Gross system-wide sales under Carlson brands reached $35.0 billion.

Carlson Companies is a leader in providing services and solutions to two distinct customer groups: corporate customers, who depend on Carlson's expertise in integrated marketing services, business travel management, and hospitality services for business travelers, and consumer customers, who know Carlson through its worldwide restaurant, hotel, cruise, and leisure travel agency brands.

The company's brands include Regent International Hotels; Radisson Hotels Worldwide; Country Inns and Suites by Carlson, T.G.I Friday's, Italianni's, AquaKnox, Star Canyon, Timpano Italian Chophouse, Samba Room, and Taqueria Canonita restaurants; Radisson Seven Seas Cruises; Carlson Wagonlit Travel (co-owned with Accor of Paris); Travel Agents International; and Carlson Marketing Group.

Marilyn Carlson Nelson became the Chairman and CEO of Carlson Companies in March 1998, building on a legacy of business leadership, entrepreneurship, and community involvement that her father had nurtured since the beginning of the company.

The Carlson Companies story began with Curtis L. Carlson. The son of a Minnesota grocer, Carlson was a born entrepreneur who organized his own network of newspaper carriers as a teenager and who worked his way through college.

While selling products to Twin Cities grocers, Carlson became familiar with the trading stamp, which a handful of department stores had been giving to their customers since the 1800s.

Carlson recognized that the trading stamp provided an enormous opportunity for grocery stores, drugstores, gas stations, and other independent merchants to distinguish themselves from their competitors. Eager to capitalize on the idea, Carlson borrowed $55 from his landlord and began doing business from his dining-room table, calling the fledgling operation the Gold Bond Stamp Company.

After a slow start and meager gains during World War II, the Gold Bond Stamp Company hit it big in the early 1950s, when Carlson and his aggressive sales force persuaded the nation's largest supermarket chains that they needed trading stamps to draw and maintain customer loyalty. In fact, during the 1950s and 1960s, Gold Bond and a sister company—Top Value Stamps—helped revolutionize the way retail goods and services were marketed. Redeemable for a vast array of first-class merchandise, the trading stamp became the shopper's friend around the globe.

During the 1960s, the Gold Bond Stamp Company expanded into the hospitality industry with the purchase of the original Radisson Hotel in downtown Minneapolis and the construction of new Radisson facilities throughout Minnesota.

In the 1970s, the company acquired dozens of additional businesses, including the highly successful T.G.I. Friday's and Country Kitchen restaurant chains and internationally renowned Ask Mr. Foster travel agencies.

In 1973, in order to better reflect its diversified status, the Gold Bond Stamp Company changed its name to Carlson Companies, Inc. Four years later, Carlson Companies achieved its first billion dollars in annual sales as one of the fastest growing privately held corporations in the world. Today, Carlson Companies is one of the largest travel and hospitality services companies in the world.

The Carlson Companies story is one of continuous progress. It is the spirit of a business that started small, grew, and has positioned itself to grow to greater heights in the century ahead.

Milestones

1938—Curt Carlson founds and develops Gold Bond Stamp Co. in downtown Minneapolis, Minnesota.

1953—Super Valu food stores become the first large supermarket chain in the nation to use Gold Bond trading stamps. Almost overnight, Gold Bond became a household word in the United States.

1955—Gold Bond begins sales in Canada, eventually making it the largest trading stamp company in that country.

1960—Joins with Grand Union—Performance Incentives Co. acquires 50 percent interest in Radisson Hotel in downtown Minneapolis.

1961—Starts advertising agency—Adams, Martin, and Nelson.

1962—Contract Service Associates (CSA) officially forms; acquires remaining interest in Radisson Hotel in downtown Minneapolis.

1962-1963—Carlson buys out majority of partners in Minneapolis Industrial Park.

1963—Company name changed to Premium Service Corp. (PSC); Gift Stars coupons included on various grocery and grooming aid products.

1964—Acquires Red Scissors Coupons (Premium Associates).

1965—Acquires Aloha Stamp Co., acquires Holden Stamp Co., acquires Security Stamp Co., acquires 51 percent interest in Canning Co., Trinidad, West Indies.

1966—Builds Pacific International Building (four stories), Honolulu, Hawaii (six-story addition in 1968); Gold Star and Gift Bond trading stamps introduced in Japan.

1967—Company launches national Gift Stars coupons on packs of Old Gold cigarettes. Gift Stars coupons redeemable with Gold Bond stamps at Gold Bond Gift Centers.

1968—Gold Bond Stamp Co., in a joint venture with Mitsubishi, the Japanese industrial giant, introduces Gold Star and Gift Bond trading stamps throughout Japan; acquires Robinson Seidel—Twin Cities incentive company—part of which was a travel agency; acquires remaining 50 percent of Performance Incentives Co.; number of trading stamps issued nationally by all companies reaches peak year; acquires Frontier Stamp Co. (including Family Park Shopping Center, Flintwood Shopping Center, and Park Central Shopping Center—all in Lubbock, Texas); acquires majority interest in May Brothers Co., food wholesalers, Minneapolis; starts Direct Mail Division; acquires Gold Crown Stamp Co.

1969—National launch of LMC Coupons on packs of Chesterfield cigarettes. LMC Coupons is joint venture with Liggett and Myers. LMC Coupons were redeemable with Gold Bond Stamps at Gold Bond Gift Centers; builds and opens Radisson Mart, connected to the Radisson Hotel, in downtown Minneapolis.

1970—Opens Haberdashery Restaurant-Pub in the Radisson Hotel, Minneapolis.

1971—Gold Bond purchases Melior Stamp Co. in Belgium; acquires John Plain/Pick-A-Gift/John Plain Incentives—a direct mail and incentive company.

1972—Acquires majority of outstanding stock in May Brothers Co., Minneapolis; establishes Carlson Properties, Inc., to handle real estate development.

1973—Company changes name to Carlson Companies, Inc.; opens Haberdashery Restaurant-Pub at 7 Corners in Minneapolis.

1974—Opens Haberdashery Restaurant-Pub in downtown St. Paul, Minnesota; acquires majority interest in Superior Fiber Products, Superior, Wisconsin.

1975—Acquires Gold Strike Co., Salt Lake City, Utah; acquires T.G.I. Friday's, Inc.

1976—Acquires Gold Star Stamp Company, Montreal, Canada; acquires K-Promotions, Inc., Milwaukee, Wisconsin; acquires Northern Federal Building in downtown St. Paul.

1977—Acquires Country Kitchen International, Inc., Minneapolis; Carlson Companies achieves $1 billion in annual revenues.

1978—Acquires Naum Bros. (catalog showrooms), Rochester, New York; acquires NSI Marketing, Canada; acquires Omega Sports, Maryland Heights, Missouri; acquires WaSko Gold Products, Corp., New York, New York.

1979—Acquires First Travel Corp. (including Ask Mr. Foster and Colony Hotels).

1980—Premium Group changes name to Carlson Marketing Group, Inc. (CMG); company establishes Hotel and Resort Group, which includes Radisson Hotels, Inns and Resorts, and Colony Hotels and Resorts.

1981—CMG acquires E. F. MacDonald Motivation Company, Dayton, Ohio.

1982—Carlson Companies achieves $2 billion in annual revenues.

1983—Acquires P. Lawson Travel, Ltd., Toronto, Ontario, Canada; T.G.I. Friday's Inc. goes public, with 25 percent or 4.5 million shares sold out on first day (December 8, 1983).

1984—Launches associate (franchise) program for Ask Mr. Foster travel agencies; acquires Cartan Tours, Inc., Rolling Meadows, Illinois; acquires Valley Travel, Phoenix, Arizona; Radisson launches franchising program.

1985—Radisson purchases 25 percent interest and assumes management of new Radisson Mark Plaza Hotel, Alexandria, Virginia; Radisson signs international partnership agreement with Msvenpick Hotels International; Carlson Companies achieves $3 billion in annual revenues.

1986—Radisson enters an international partnership agreement with SAS International Hotels; acquires 50 percent interest of Harvey's Travel Ltd. in Atlantic Canada.

1987—Radisson Hotels Corp. signs international partnership agreements with Park Lane Hotels International and Commonwealth Hospitality, Inc., of Canada; Carlson Companies achieves $4 billion in annual revenues.

1988—Carlson officials set goal of $9 billion in revenues by 1992; Radisson Hotel Corp. renamed Radisson Hotels International; acquires Gelco Travel Management Systems; Radisson enters Eastern Europe market with Radisson Béke Hotel in Budapest, Hungary.

1989—CCI moves most of its operations to the new World Headquarters at Carlson Center, Minneapolis; CMG acquires Promo Marketing (consumer promotions), Montreal, Canada; Radisson opens new Worldwide Reservation Center in Omaha, Nebraska; Carlson Companies acquires all outstanding T.G.I. Friday's, Inc., stock to make it a private company again; Carlson Companies achieves $6.2 billion in system-wide revenues.

1990—CMG acquires Forum Organization Pty. Ltd. (motivation and marketing services), Australia/New Zealand; CMG acquires FKB Group, London (ten marketing and sales promotion companies in the United Kingdom), plus AVDM in New York City; Ask Mr. Foster Travel name changes to Carlson Travel Network; Company achieves $8.1 billion in system-wide revenues.

1991—Carlson Travel Network launches co-branded Visa bank card worldwide; Radisson Slavjanskaya Hotel Moscow opens in Russia as first American-managed hotel in the Commonwealth of Independent States (formerly U.S.S.R.); Country Lodging by Carlson expands into Canada; CMG (formerly E. F. MacDonald) moves Dayton, Ohio, employees to Minneapolis in consolidation; Carlson Companies achieves $9.2 billion in system-wide revenues—one full year ahead of goal.

1992—Radisson Diamond cruise ship sails on maiden voyage; CMG acquires CMI, a San Francisco–based incentive travel/business meetings management company; Carlson Travel Network wins General Electric account—largest single travel account in history and creates "travel agency of the future"; Carlson Travel Network Associate network surpasses 1,000 locations.

1993—Carlson Travel Network opens GE Travel Center in Phoenix, the world's single-largest dedicated reservation office; Carlson Companies achieves $10.7 billion in system-wide revenues.

1994—Radisson Plaza Hotel La Paz opens in La Paz, Bolivia (first Radisson hotel in South America); CMG forms joint venture with Hermann Marketing of St. Louis, Missouri (corporate logo merchandise); Carlson Wagonlit Travel (CWT)/P. Lawson Travel launches associate program in Canada; T.G.I. Friday's, Inc., opens new concept—Front Row Sports Grill in the Ballpark in Arlington, Texas; T.G.I. Friday's, Inc., opens first Italianni's restaurant, Miami, Florida; Carlson Travel Group and Paris-based Wagonlit Travel sign alliance to form Carlson Wagonlit Travel, one of the world's largest travel management companies; Radisson Diamond Cruise and Seven Seas Cruise Line merger creates Radisson Seven Seas Cruises.

1995—Carlson Hospitality Group and Radisson Hotel International renamed Carlson Hospitality Worldwide and Radisson Hotels Worldwide; CWT implements more than $2 billion in U.S. Army contracts, which entails hiring more than 400 employees and opening 250 new locations; CWT opens seventh travel academy in Phoenix, Arizona; T.G.I. Friday's, Inc., opens sixteenth restaurant in England. Friday's Hospitality Worldwide now operates, franchises, and licenses more than 340 T.G.I. Friday's, Italianni's, and Front Row Sports Grill restaurants in 248 cities and 18 countries; largest Carlson Wagonlit Travel Associate, Murdock Travel in Utah, joins associate program; T.G.I. Friday's opens in Beijing, China.

1996—CWT acquires corporate travel business of Jetset Travel Pte Ltd. in Singapore; Radisson SAS hotels open in four cities in Italy (Milan, Brescia, Bergamo, Lodi) and five in Norway (Bergen, Kristiansand, Stavanger [2], Trondheim); Country Inns and Suites by Carlson opens 24 new properties; Friday's Hospitality Worldwide opens Friday's American Bar in Makati/Burgos, Philippines (first international location); Carlson Hospitality Worldwide and Four Seasons Hotels, Inc., create partnership for the future development, management, and marketing of Regent International Hotels around the world.

1997—Marilyn Carlson Nelson named Chief Operating Officer—CCI; Radisson Hospitality Worldwide acquires Radisson Seven Seas—the world's third-largest luxury cruise line; Carlson Travel Group splits into two separate operating companies: Carlson Wagonlit Travel (CWT) and Carlson Leisure Group (CLG); CLG acquires Travel Agents International (TAI), becoming the largest travel agency franchiser in North America; Carlson Hospitality Worldwide debuts new-generation business support and reservation system, Curtis-C; T.G.I. Friday's, Inc., opens its first restaurant in Moscow; CLG acquires Inspirations, PLC, in the United Kingdom, marking entry into airline business through its subsidiary Caledonian Airways; CMG acquires Aegis Group, a U.K. performance improvement company; CMG acquires Incentive Dimensions, a San Francisco–based incentive travel, event management, and production company; Friday's Hospitality Worldwide reaches $1 billion in domestic sales.

1998—CMG acquires S&H Citadel, one of the top five performance improvement firms in the United States, with annual revenues in excess of $100 million; Friday's teams up with Earvin "Magic" Johnson's company, Johnson Development Corporation, to develop T.G.I. Friday's restaurants in underserved U.S. urban communities.

1999—System-wide gross sales hit $31.4 billion.

2000—Founded Results Travel Agency Franchise.

2001—Acquired Cruise Holidays Franchise units.

As Carlson's milestones and timeline demonstrate, a complete array of business development strategies and techniques have helped shape this very large and fast-growing company.[9]

Case Discussion Questions

1. Why do you believe Carlson Companies has been successful in deploying so many different business development strategies?
2. What do you perceive as the weaknesses and strengths of Carlson's Companies' managerial strategies?

CASE 3.2. AMERICAN EXPRESS CARD MEMBER SERVICES

This case example could easily be included in the chapter on customer service and quality. However, it would be difficult to offer outstanding customer service and a quality experience without an excellent communications process, both within the organization and between the organization and customers. Listening to your employees and to your customers personifies good communications. For this reason, American Express is the case example for communications.

At American Express, quality service is defined by excellence in communications. The excellence in communications extends from the credit card application process to the disputed charge inquiry—all along the way exceptional written and verbal communications by well-trained professionals. To American Express, quality equals outstanding customer and employee communications processes.

American Express has long believed that quality should be the goal of its business worldwide. The chairman of the company also carries the title of Chief Quality Officer to help convey this goal to the entire organization. American Express goes beyond the signals by supporting their quality performance with substance, all focused on one goal—better customer service.

Basic substance begins with superior training (at their "quality university") and full support of senior management. American Express publishes an annual quality management report. Its focus is to emphasize that the corporation is in the customer service business. Employees are routinely expected to go beyond the normal procedures to provide outstanding customer service. Those who do are recognized by a corporate awards program.

Like many service organizations, American Express has numerous customer bases to address. The two largest are their cardholders and those who use their worldwide travel services. Necessarily, a lot of time is devoted to seeing that the relationship between these two provides synergy instead of becoming a source of conflict.

American Express recognizes and successfully satisfies an immense and diverse group of customers around the globe. It focuses on their customers' needs for timeliness, accuracy, responsiveness, and immediate resolution at the first point of encounter.

Customer satisfaction is constantly monitored, and when new customer needs emerge, new services are implemented to meet these needs. These new services come from one principal source according to company executives, who stated: "Virtually every new service introduced by American Express during the past ten years came directly from listening to the suggestions and expressed needs of the customers themselves." In addition to listening to their customers, American Express employees are asked to spend 10 percent of their time striving to improve their job of delivering quality service. The result is many internal and procedural changes culminating ultimately in better service to the customers.

American Express sincerely believes that the key to success begins with not only pride and motivation of the employee but also with ongoing research into both job enhancement and customer needs identification. It utilizes sophisticated research techniques and the latest technology to quantitatively and qualitatively assess the needs of the customer. From these assessments, delivery of service improvements and new services are developed for its card membership. Ultimately, American Express wants its customers to feel that it is the only company they want to do business with.

The common elements of their success formula include getting employees involved to redefine their jobs so they can better serve the customer; a passion for listening to the customers' needs; responding with action; prompt implementation of new services; addressing the needs accurately and with targeted marketing messages; reinforcing their quality image in how they promote and market their brand; and having the basic quality systems fully operating at all customer contact points.

American Express often "begins again," as exemplified by the innovative services introduced year after year. Many of these things we now take for granted—because American Express is there doing it for us. Things like cash when and where we need it; replacement of lost travelers' checks; global assist programs, which help their card members with virtually any need, anywhere on earth; Gold Card holder account statements and categorizations at year end that help in preparing tax returns; a product/service guarantee program that makes returns simple and workable; very high credit; translation services; lost luggage assistance; and the list could go on for pages.

In essence, American Express quality service levels and innovative new service offerings have improved an entire industry as competitors strive to keep up with the leader. Leadership, quality service, customer satisfaction, and outstanding communications are what make American Express a winner.[10]

Case Discussion Questions

1. Listening, especially to your customers, is one of the most effective steps a hospitality industry firm can undertake to improve its service and product delivery. Describe the process you would employ to take these findings to action or implementation.
2. Do you believe it is a good practice to actually have a "chief quality officer" in a hospitality industry corporation or should quality be the focus of all?

NOTES

1. M. Hammersley, *The Dilemma of Qualitative Method: Herbert Blumer and the Chicago Tradition* (London, UK and New York: Routledge, 1990), p. 1.

2. A. Strauss & J. Corbin, *Basics of Qualitative Research: Grounded Theory Procedures and Techniques* (London, UK: Sage, 1990), p. 19.

3. S. Wells, "Wet Towels and Whetted Appetites or a Wet Blanket: The Role of Analysis in Qualitative Research," *Journal of the Market Research Society,* vol. 33, no. 1 (2004), pp. 39-44.

4. G. Mars & M. Nicod, *The World of Waiters* (London, UK: Allen and Unwin, 1984), p. 33.

5. N. Johns & D. Lee-Ross, *Research Methods in Service Industry Management* (London, UK: Cassell, 1998), p. 129.

6. Ibid., pp. 130-131.

7. http://www.analytictech.com/mb870/introtoGT.htm; www.analytictechnologies.com.

8. Johns & Lee-Ross, *Research Methods in Service,* pp. 137-138.

9. www.carlsoncompanies.com.

10. R. Nykiel, *Points of Encounter* (New York: Amacor, 1999), pp. 73-74.

Chapter 4

Quantitative Research

CHAPTER OBJECTIVES

- To define quantitative research.
- To identify the major types of quantitative research.
- To point out the advantages and disadvantages of quantitative research.
- To discuss the various approaches to conducting quantitative research.
- To present the areas where quantitative research is applied in the business environment.
- To address the key forms and techniques associated with the approaches, techniques, and definitions of quantitative research.

In Chapter 3, qualitative research methodologies and applications were discussed. In this chapter, the other basic approaches to quantitative research are examined. Focus is on the definition, advantages and disadvantages, the various types of quantitative research and related designs, the components of a research plan, and applications in the services sector.

DEFINITION

There are numerous definitions of quantitative research. In an overview form, quantitative research is about quantifying relationships between variables. A more scientific approach to defining quantitative research comes from Huysamen: "descriptions of quantitative research typically discern a cycle of successive phases of hypothesis formulation, data collection, analysis and interpretation."[1] Using a deductive approach, quantitative research seeks to establish facts, make predictions, and test hypotheses that have already been stated. And, from a marketing perspective, quantitative research is most useful in gathering measurable information that can be tracked over time. Almost all definitions go on to point out the differences between or contrast quantitative research with qualitative research. This is helpful to the marketer because the comparisons help delineate not only the advantages and disadvantages but also the applications most appropriate for various research purposes.[2]

ADVANTAGES AND DISADVANTAGES

There are strong proponents of both qualitative and quantitative research methods. Each has presented their respective arguments, usually focusing on the advantages of one over the other or the disadvantages of one of the basic forms of research. Our goal is to be objective and present the facts, allowing the researchers to draw their own conclusions based on their needs and perspectives.

Handbook of Marketing Research Methodologies for Hospitality and Tourism
© 2007 by The Haworth Press, Inc. All rights reserved.
doi:10.1300/5927_05

Qualitative research is said to have two primary advantages. The first is that it allows (the moderator or interviewer) for interaction with respondents. This freedom allows for in-depth probing of issues and yields great detail in responses. The second advantage is that it also allows for interaction between respondents (group members). This interaction often stimulates discussion that uncovers issues unanticipated during the design phase. The primary disadvantage of qualitative research has been said to be its unreliability as a predictor of the population. As a result of the advantages and restrictions, qualitative research is deemed more appropriate when used to generate ideas and concepts and to uncover consumer perceptions and attitudes.

Quantitative research has two distinct advantages. The first (if designed and conducted properly) is that the results are statistically reliable. That is, quantitative research can reliably determine whether one concept, idea, product, package, and so on, is better than the alternatives. The second distinct advantage is that the results are projectable to the population. The primary disadvantages of quantitative research are that the issues are only measured if they are known prior to the beginning of the survey (and, therefore, have been incorporated into the questionnaire). As a result of the aforementioned advantages and constraints, quantitative research is more appropriate when the issues to be tested are known and the language used by the consumers to describe these issues is known. Finally, quantitative research is essentially evaluative, not generative.[3]

Figure 4.1 provides a comparison of the major distinctions between quantitative research and qualitative research.

Both quantitative and qualitative methods are said to be systematic. In fact, having a system following a process is a defining principle of research. Broadly speaking, quantitative research is thought to be objective, whereas qualitative research often involves a subjective element. It is thought that in gaining, analyzing, and interpreting quantitative data, the researcher remains detached and objective. Often this is not possible with qualitative research where the researcher may actually be involved in the situation of the research.

Quantitative research is inclined to be deductive. In other words it tests theory. This is in contrast to most qualitative research which tends to be inductive. In other words it generates theory.

N. Johns and D. Lee-Ross
Research Methods in Service Industry Management (1998)

If the data cannot be structured in the form of numbers, they are considered qualitative data. Note that qualitative data can sometimes be handled in such a way as to produce quantitative data; for example, the researcher can analyze the responses, negative or positive, so as to produce a figure/percentage of negative responses.

Therefore, objectivity, deductiveness, generalizability, and numbers are features often associated with quantitative research. When a researcher selects an approach for a study, it should be a reflection of which approach is most suitable for the topic under consideration.

TYPES OF QUANTITATIVE RESEARCH

In quantitative research, the aim is to determine the relationship between one thing (an independent variable) and another (a dependent variable or outcome variable in a population. Depending upon the sources (authors and researchers) there are two, three, or four types of quantitative research. While all sources agree

Quantitative	Qualitative
Both are systematic in their approach	
Deductive	Inductive
Generalizable	Not generalizable
Numbers	Words

FIGURE 4.1. Comparative Distinctions Between Quantitative and Qualitative Research

that designs may be descriptive or experimental, some add quasi-experimental and others add correlational (ex post facto), and still others include all four. For purposes of explanation, the focus here is on the major two types, descriptive and experimental, followed by a brief discussion of the others. Figure 4.2 depicts the types of research designs.

Descriptive

Descriptive designs are designed to gain more information about a particular characteristic in a particular field of study. A descriptive study may be used to develop theory, identify preferred current practice, justify current practice, make judgments, or identify what others in similar situations may be doing. There is no manipulation of variables and no attempt to establish causality. Usually, this type of research involves studying the preferences, attitudes, practices, concerns, or interests of some group of people. Two critical issues in descriptive design, both necessary for validity, are the ability to generalize from the sample (which must be large) and the reliability and validity of the observations (measurements).

Experimental

This type of research also looks for a cause-effect relationship between two or more variables. The difference between this type of research and causal-comparative research is that the researcher has control over the independent variable in experimental research. The paradigm for scientific method in research is the true experiment or randomized control (RCT). Experimental designs are set up to allow the greatest amount of control possible so that the variables selected/data may be examined closely. The three essential elements of experimental design are manipulation, control, and randomization. In manipulation, the researcher does something to at least some of the participants in the research. In control, the experimenter introduces one or more controls over the experiment. And, in randomization the experimenter assigns participants to different groups on a random basis. The classic example is the before-after design or pretest posttest design. This is perhaps the most commonly used experimental design. Comparison of pretest scores allows the researcher to evaluate how effective the randomization of the sample is in providing equivalent groups. The treatment is fully under control of the researcher. The dependent variable is measured during the study (before and after the manipulation of the independent variable).[4]

Quasi-Experimental

Quasi-experimental designs were developed to provide alternate means for examining the situations that were not conducive to experimental control. The designs have been developed to control as many threats to validity as possible in situations where at least one of the three elements of true experimental research is lacking (i.e., no randomization, control group).

Correlational

This type of research attempts to determine whether, and to what degree, a relationship exists between two or more variables. Once a relationship is established, it is identified by a correlation coefficient, a number between

Descriptive or observational
▪ Case
▪ Case series
▪ Cross-sectional
▪ Cohort or prospective or longitudinal
▪ Case-control or retrospective
Experimental or longitudinal or repeated-measures
▪ Without control group
○ time series
○ crossover
▪ With a control group
Quasi-experimental
Correlational
Causal-comparative

FIGURE 4.2. Types of Research Designs

−1.00 and +1.00. If a correlation is positive, it means that as one variable increases, the other also increases. If a correlation is negative, as one variable decreases, the other also decreases. Correlational studies are not universally accepted as a form of quantitative research. As already noted, they are also known as ex post facto studies. This literally means "from the fact." The term is used to identify that the research in question has been conducted after the description of the independent variable has occurred naturally. The basic purpose of this form of study is to determine the relationship between variables. The significant difference from experimental and quasi-experimental design is that causation be established due to lack of manipulation of independent variables. "Correlation does not prove Causation."[5]

Causal-Comparative Research

Causal-comparative research is also called ex post facto research. This type of research seeks to discover a cause-effect relationship between two or more different programs, methods, or groups. The researcher in this type usually does not have control over the causal factor or independent variable because it is studied after the fact. The effect is called the dependent variable.

RESEARCH DESIGN ELEMENTS

Independent/Dependent Variables

Quantitative approaches allow for the collection of large amounts of data and often allow for faster collection and analysis than qualitative approaches. Management/marketers need to know certain environmental/organizational elements (variables) are linked. In other words, they need to be able to predict the effect of one variable upon another. This concept is known as "prediction." In order to link the elements and be able to predict, it is necessary to identify the underlying features, namely the independent and dependent variables. Remember, the proposition is always that when the independent variable changes, the other independent variables change with it in a dependent way.

Hypotheses

Hypotheses or testable propositions are specific research questions devised based on a review of the initial data. A distinguishing feature of quantitative research techniques is the methods used to see whether these hunches are plausible or valid.

Questionnaire Design and Attitude Measurement

In order to test a prediction, a plan for collecting data needs to be developed. This is known as research design. Figure 4.3 provides an outline of the research design process.[6] In this process, questionnaire design is extremely important in that if not clear and readily understood by the respondent, the response can be inaccurate. A survey is basically a question and answer dialogue between the questionnaire and the informant. Therefore, the questions themselves must be carefully thought out, relevant, and cautiously worded. If these steps are not religiously undertaken, the questionnaire design may well impact the quality of the response and the rate of return or response rate. A questionnaire must also have a means of classifying respondents in a way that is appropriate to the study. It is recommended that personal or threatening questions should be asked last, at the end of the questionnaire. This may help to improve the rate of return.

Obtaining answers relevant to hypotheses becomes the overall objective of the research.

N. Johns and D. Lee-Ross
Research Methods in Service Industry Management (1998)

Some general rules of thumb include being sure about the sequence and wording of the actual questions. Further, the questionnaire should accurately reflect the conceptual framework of the research. In the case of attitudinal research, questionnaires should apply an analytical framework of attitudinal measurement within the context of the subject matter of the research. And, finally, the questionnaire should permit detailed analysis of the sample and subsamples categorized in a way that permits comparisons, and scales composed so that they permit further analysis.

The Pilot Study

A pilot study is an exploratory phase that aims to identify and eliminate problems before the full survey is carried out. An accepted way to do this is to give a newly formulated questionnaire to a small group or sample of the individuals who could be involved in the research project. As a result of the pilot study, the questionnaire can be edited and reformatted for testing the larger sample. Unsatisfactory questions can be ruled out and misinterpretations can be reworded or clarified. Figure 4.4 provides a summary of reasons for pilot testing.

Rates of Response

Respondents must be given every encouragement to complete questionnaires. These encouragements consist of reminders and a variety of incentives including, but not limited to, gifts, vouchers, cash, charity pledges, prizes, and so forth. Researcher persistence has proven to increase the rate of return as well as reminder letters, using actual stamps versus prepaid postage/envelopes, and recorded delivery reminders. Figure 4.5 illustrates an approximate schedule for a reminder letter.

The precise shape, size, and speed of response vary with the situation, but the graph's overall characteristics remain fairly constant for most surveys. Response rates should be plotted against time, as shown in Figure 4.5, and reminders sent out when the curve begins to flatten. As a

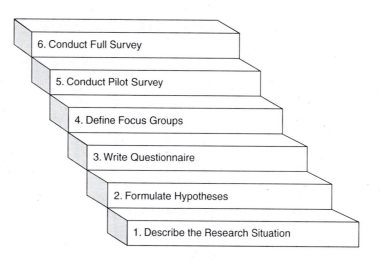

FIGURE 4.3. Research Design Process

- ✓ Check questions for relevancy
- ✓ Check if respondents understand all the questions in a sample group
- ✓ Check the logical flow/sequence of all the questions
- ✓ Check for questions which may have a double meaning or that may confuse respondents
- ✓ To provide an estimate of the referred rate
- ✓ To ascertain the best time to conduct the survey
- ✓ To check for ways of changing open-ended questions to be closed or multiple choice
- ✓ To estimate the length of time required to complete a questionnaire or an interview

FIGURE 4.4. Summary of Reasons for Pilot Testing

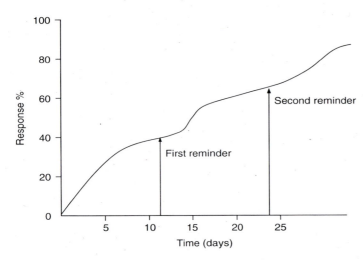

FIGURE 4.5. Reminder Letter Time Sequence

general rule, a good time for the first reminder is around 10 days after the initial questionnaire has been sent out, followed by a second reminder on day 18. To encourage responses, the initial letter and reminders should emphasize three things: the importance of the study, the importance of cooperation, and the need for a speedy response. Should the respondents e-mail addresses be available, reminder e-mails also help to increase response rates. In some instances, the online survey also increases response rates, but be aware that a significant percentage (30 to 40 percent) of the overall population may not have sufficient knowledge of or access to a computer.

QUESTIONNAIRES: DESIGN, STATISTICAL ANALYSIS, AND SCALES

It is important to understand the relationship between statistical techniques and questionnaire design. Questions can be linked with statistical techniques if the questionnaire design is compatible. In order to achieve linkages as well as to be able to analyze the data, it is necessary to understand the basic types of quantitative data.

There are four basic types of quantitative data: nominal, ordinal, interval, and ratio data. Each has different mathematical properties that affect analysis. Briefly, here are descriptions of each type of quantitative data:

- *Nominal data* are the least conducive to statistical analysis as they only describe things. Nominal data are the simplest to conceptualize. In this procedure all that can be done with data is to count them, usually from observation. This means that the only findings will be the number of times something occurs. For example, autos either turn right, left, or go straight ahead at an intersection of two streets. Codes cannot be used for mathematical calculations because they only indicate the different behaviors. An "average" of the numbers in a data set would be meaningless. Examples of nominal data are gender, socioeconomic status, physical appearances, and so forth.
- *Ordinal data* are data that are reported when respondents are asked to rank order preferences. Ordinal data are ranked estimates of magnitude.
- *Interval data* are data that are measured on a scale which has intervals between its values. Thus, the difference between any two points one scale reading apart is one, the difference between two points two scale readings apart is two, and so on.
- *Ratio data* are measured upon an absolute scale that starts at zero. This means that the scale readings are exactly proportional to the values being measured.

Ratio data always have the characteristics of interval, ordinal, and nominal data as well. Interval data have the characteristics of ordinal and nominal data (e.g., 7, 6, 5, 4 would also rank themselves in this order). Ordinal data possess the characteristics of nominal data, but, as mentioned earlier, nominal data possess none of the other mathematical properties. Nonattitudinal data, such as temperature and height, can be measured with certainty using interval or ratio scales. This information is often termed hard data and lends itself to rigorous statistical analysis.

Question structure and design. The actual structure of the questions affects both the way respondents will view them and their ultimate analysis. Measurements can be undertaken by using different types of rating scales. Three of the more common ones are comparative rating, Likert, and semantic differential scales:

- *Comparative rating scales* are strictly ordinal in character. It is impossible to know the exact numerical interval between each rating, as all are individual value judgments. It would be methodologically wrong to treat the data as anything other than ordinal, because this is what the questions are designed to elicit.
- *Likert scales* are the commonest type in general use for measuring attitudes or perceptions. In market research, there may be preference to have an even scale, so that respondents must lean toward one view or the other. Likert scales are frequently treated as interval scales in analysis, since the scale values 1 to 5 appear to be evenly spaced, one unit apart. However, there is no guarantee that the magnitudes of the feelings expressed by respondents are spaced like this, and there may be considerable variation between different individuals in this respect. Treating the data as interval in nature is at best an approximation, and it is much safer to treat the data as ordinal.
- *Semantic differential scale* values are assigned in much the same way as Likert scales. However, the format makes it possible to position respondents' judgments on a preset bipolar scale. Opposing poles can be chosen by the researcher rather than the respondent. Figure 4.6 presents examples of a comparative scale, Likert scale, and semantic differential scale.[7]

SAMPLING

A total population is usually too large and too expensive to survey and to analyze, so researchers usually devise a method technique to take a sample. This is called sampling. The size of the actual survey sample is usually dependent upon three things: the confidence level to which the researcher wishes to work, the acceptable error range in the final result, and the way the attribute that is being measured is distributed within the survey population. If these three things are known, the sample can be calculated using the formula in Figure 4.7.

Scale	Example
Comparative rating	Most attractive to least attractive (1 = most and 5 = worst) Travel by: airplane 3 automobile 1 bus 5 rail 2 ship 4
Likert scales	Quality of service: Very good = 5 Good = 4 Neither good nor poor = 3 Poor = 2 Very poor = 1
Semantic differential scale	Destination Mexico: Expensive 1 2 3 4 5 Cheap Friendly 1 2 3 4 5 Unfriendly Busy 1 2 3 4 5 Relaxing

FIGURE 4.6. Scales and Examples

Allowable error is based upon expenditure and is chosen entirely arbitrarily, based upon the requirements of the eventual findings. There are several ways to select samples. Simple random selection attempts to ensure that every unit in the population has an equal chance of being picked. This usually means sampling from a sampling frame. Stratified sampling is used when the population is known not to be homogeneous. Another more practical technique is known as random interval sampling. Here, the population is first divided by the size of the required sample to provide the interval (X). The sample is developed by selecting every Xth name on the list, beginning at a randomly selected starting point.

$$N = \left(\frac{Z \times S}{E} \right)^2$$

N = sample size
Z = number of standard deviations required to give the desired confidence level
E = acceptable error
S = standard deviation

FIGURE 4.7. Sample Formula

When a sample is not representative of a population, selection bias is a possibility. A high compliance (the portion of the people contacted who end up as subjects/respondents) is important in avoiding bias. Compliance rates of 70 percent plus or minus are usually okay. Sample size can be approached in a variety of ways. You can approach this crucial issue via statistical significance, confidence intervals, or "on-the-fly."

Statistical significance is the standard approach but somewhat more complicated. Using confidence intervals or confidence limits is a more accessible approach to sample size estimation and interpretation of outcomes.

The precision with which you measure things has a major impact on sample size. The worse your measurements, the more subjects you need to lift the signal. Precision is expressed as validity and reliability.

What to Measure

In any study, you measure the characteristics of the subjects and the independent and dependent variables defining the research question. Many things can impact the dependent variable (or outcome). These things are the independent variables such as training, sex, the treatment in an experimental study, and so on. With all experiments, the main challenge is to determine the magnitude and confidence intervals of the treatment effect.

APPLICATIONS IN THE SERVICES SECTOR

As previously indicated, quantitative research is most useful in gathering information that is measurable and can be tracked over time. This includes customer satisfaction surveys, employee morale surveys, brand awareness, image studies, and product usage studies, to name a few. Types of quantitative research surveys with service industry applicability are highlighted in Figure 4.8.

Advanced statistical methodologies such as regression analysis, conjoint analysis, and discrete choice modeling can be used to gain additional insights into research results. Quantitative research results usually include comprehensive reports and presentations to top management.

COMPONENTS OF A QUANTITATIVE RESEARCH PLAN

Prior to undertaking a quantitative study, it is important to prepare a research plan. Doing so forces the researcher to think through the methodology and to anticipate problems, issues, and

↳ Customer satisfaction studies
↳ Buyer retention studies
↳ Pricing research
↳ Customer/market segmentation
↳ Competitive benchmarking
↳ Employee attitudes and opinions
↳ Consumer attitudes and opinions

FIGURE 4.8. Types of Quantitative Research Surveys

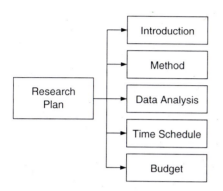

FIGURE 4.9. Components of a Research Plan

I. **Introduction**
   A. Defining a problem
   B. Literature review
   C. Hypotheses
II. **Method**
   A. Population and subjects
   B. Instruments
   C. Design and procedures
III. **Results**
   A. Data and statistics
      1. Types of measurement scales
      2. Descriptive statistics
         a. Types of descriptive statistics
         b. Calculation for interval data
   B. Inferential statistics
      1. Level of significance
      2. Tests of significance
         a. t test for independent variables
         b. t test for dependent variables
         c. ANOVA
IV. **Discussion**
   A. Interpretation of results
   B. Generalization
   C. Discussion of implications
V. **Conclusion and recommendation**
   A. Based on practical significance to draw conclusion and make suggestions

FIGURE 4.10. Basic Outline of a Quantitative Research Plan. *Source:* Adapted from Gay, L. R. (1996). *Educational Research: Competencies for Analysis and Application.* Upper Saddle River, NJ: Merrill.

opportunities. A written plan facilitates evaluation of the proposed study and provides a guide for conducting the study. The five major components of a research plan are presented in Figure 4.9.

The introduction should include a statement of the problem, a review of related literature, and a statement of hypothesis. The method should include the subjects, instruments/materials, if appropriate, and design procedure. The data analysis should provide a description of the statistical technique or techniques that will be used to analyze study data. And, finally, the budget should list all tentative expenses specifically as well as any submitted externally to a funding agency. The budget should include items such as personnel, clerical assistance, travel, postage, and other expenses, equipment, fringe benefits, fees, and so forth. Figure 4.10 presents an outline/summary of the basic format of a quantitative research plan.

CHAPTER REVIEW

Quantitative research is about measuring a market and quantifying that measurement with data. Most often data relate to market size, market share, customers, penetration of the market, and growth rates/trends. Quantitative research can also be used to measure customer attitudes, satisfaction, commitment (loyalty), and a range of other useful market data. Quantitative research is particularly applicable to measuring data over time. At the core of all quantitative research is the statistical sample, and great care and planning are required with respect to selecting the sample, designing the questionnaire, and ensuring the quality of the analysis.

Also, in this chapter, the various types of quantitative research—descriptive, experimental, quasi-experimental, and correlational—were reviewed. Further, a discussion of numerical data and statistical parameters, including the type of sampling and the concept of the standard deviation, was provided. The advantages, disadvantages, and applications related to quantitative research were also discussed.

To do good quantitative research, certain essential elements should be present. These include a well-designed questionnaire, a randomly selected sample, and a sufficiently large sample. Further, the data from questionnaires and interviews are best analyzed statistically. The results of the analyzed data (analyses) can provide useful and important management information that is measurably reflective of the population surveyed.

KEY CONCEPTS/TERMS

Association
Bias
Cases
Causality
Codes
Comparative research
Control
Correlation(al)
Data
Deductive
Design
Descriptive
Experimental
Generalizable
Hypotheses
Inductive
Interval data
Manipulation
Measurement
Nominal data
Ordinal data
Pilot test
Population
Questionnaires
Randomization
Ratio data
Rates of response
Reliability
Sampling
Scales
Survey
Validity

DISCUSSION QUESTIONS

1. What are the advantages of quantitative research?
2. What are the major types of quantitative research?
3. Why is quantitative research inclined to be deductive?
4. Why is a pilot survey important?
5. How would you define the terms validity and reliability?
6. What are the four major types of quantitative data?

7. What are Likert scales?
8. What are five types of quantitative research surveys used in marketing?
9. Why is it important to have a research plan?

CASE 4.1. STARWOOD HOTELS AND RESORTS WORLDWIDE, INC.

Hotel industry REITs (Real Estate Investment Trusts) have developed a number of investment models to take advantage of their unique tax situation. These models include paired-share REITs, such as Starwood Hotels and Resorts Worldwide and Patriot American Hospitality. In the second example, REIT structure, two organizations tie together through an intercompany agreement in which they share certain senior members of management and board members. An example is the REIT formed between CapStar Hotel Co. and American General Hospitality Corp. They created a REIT called MeriStar Hospitality Corp. and a C-Corporation called MeriStar Hotels and Resorts. The last model is a REIT in which companies form a strategic alliance with no formal agreement. This is exemplified by the FelCor Suite Hotels, a hotel investment company, and Bristol Hotel Co., a hotel management company. In this model the real estate is separated from day-to-day management elements. This allows for hospitality companies such as Six Continents, which owns Holiday Hospitality and holds a 32 percent stake in Bristol, to free up capital for other transactions through a lease-back arrangement with FelCor.[8]

In this case example, focus is on Starwood Hotels and Resorts Worldwide and on how the REIT concept has played the major role in its financial management strategies.

Starwood is one of the world's largest hotel and leisure companies. The company conducts its hotel and leisure business both directly and through its subsidiaries. The company's brand names include Sheraton, Westin, The Luxury Collection, St. Regis, W, and Four Points by Sheraton. The company's revenue and earnings are derived primarily from hotel and leisure operations, which include the operation of the company's owned hotels; management fees earned from hotels that the company manages pursuant to long-term management contracts; the receipt of franchise fees; and the development, ownership, and operation of vacation ownership resorts, marketing, and selling VOIs (vacation ownership investments) in the resorts and providing financing to customers who purchase such interests. The company's hotel and leisure business emphasizes the global operation of hotels and resorts primarily in the luxury and upscale segment of the lodging industry. Starwood's financial strategy involves acquiring interests in or management rights with respect to properties in these segments. The company's portfolio of owned, managed, and franchised hotels totals approximately 800 in 80 countries (2001). This portfolio is comprises 165 plus hotels that Starwood owns or leases or in which Starwood has a majority equity interest (substantially all of which hotels Starwood also manages), 265 plus hotels managed by Starwood on behalf of third-party owners (including entities in which Starwood has a minority equity interest), and 315 plus hotels for which Starwood receives franchise fees. Additionally, the company is currently selling VOI inventory at more than a dozen resorts.

In 1990, Barry Sternlicht formed Starwood Opportunity Fund, using money from private investors with most of the investment being made in apartments. After success with the first fund, Starwood Opportunity Fund II was created. Properties were bought at deep discounts. In 1994, Starwood acquired Hotel Investors Trust, one of the largest hotel REITs in the United States and one of only two grandfathered under the so-called paired-share structure that allowed the same investors to own stock in a hotel operating company, Hotel Investors Corporation. The names of the two parts of the REIT were changed to Starwood Lodging Trust and Starwood Lodging Corporation. Over the next few years, Starwood continued to acquire individual and small groups of properties. Significant purchases included three Westin Regina resorts in Mexico—the company's first international properties (1997) and the Flatley Company/Tara Hotels—15 full-service hotels purchased in August 1997 for $470 million. Late in 1997, Starwood acquired ITT Sheraton for $13.3 billion; the sale was approved by shareholders early in 1998. At that time, the company bought four former Ritz-Carltons in Aspen, New York City, Washington, DC, and Houston for $334 million; they were converted into Luxury Collection properties for a limited time. Early in 1998, on the completion of the Westin purchase, the companies' name was changed from Starwood Lodging Trust and Starwood Lodging Corporation to Starwood Hotels and Resorts and Starwood Hotels and Resorts Worldwide, respectively. Late in 1998, the launch of W Hotels was announced. In January 1999, Starwood relinquished its grandfathered paired-share REIT status and became a C-Corporation and the Trust became a subsidiary of the corporation. In 1999, Starwood sold the gaming interests it had acquired in the ITT Sheraton deal to Park Place Entertainment.

Starwood's acquisition of ITT Sheraton and Westin Hotels and Resorts in early 1998 gave birth to the hotel corporation as it is known today, which encompasses six global brands including Sheraton, Westin, St. Regis, Luxury Collection, Four Points, and W Hotels.

As one of the largest hotel and leisure companies focusing on the luxury and upscale full-service lodging market, Starwood has the scale to support its core marketing and reservation function. Its scale contributes to lowering its cost of operations through purchasing economies in such areas as insurance, energy, telecommunications, employee benefits, food and beverage, furniture, fixtures, and equipment and operating supplies.

Starwood has strong brand leadership based on the global recognition of the Company's lodging brands. Starwood was designated as the "World's Best Global Hotel Company" by *Global Finance* magazine in their September 2000 issue. Starwood benefits from a luxury and upscale branding strategy that provides a strong operating performance.

Starwood Hotels and Resorts Worldwide, Inc., through its St. Regis, Luxury Collection, Westin Hotels and Resorts, Sheraton Hotels and Resorts, Four Points Hotels by Sheraton, and W Hotels subsidiaries, is one of the better positioned hotel companies in the world and has a good mix of product (Exhibit 4.1).

Sheraton, the largest brand by far, has nearly 400 properties. Growth for this brand is by franchising and management contracts. Four Points by Sheraton with about 140 properties, many of which were Sheraton Inns and Hotels, is the big franchise brand for Starwood. It will continue to grow by franchising. Westin with approximately 120 properties is being overhauled to return it to its four- to four-and-a-half-star heritage. Franchising will continue but on a limited basis; most growth will be in management contracts. St. Regis/Luxury Collection with about 45 properties and almost 10,000 rooms is targeted for the first or second position in any given market and will not be franchised. With only a handful of properties now, fairly rapid international growth is on the horizon. Luxury Collection is not targeted for growth, although there may be additions to the brand from among properties seeking its international sales and distribution clout. W Hotels, the newest chain, is growing rapidly. Most of these properties are owned by Starwood, although there are a number of management contracts. No franchising is planned at this time.

Starwood's strategies include refining the positioning of the company's brands to further its strategy of strengthening brand identity, and rebranding certain hotels to one of Starwood's proprietary brands to further solidify its brand reputation and market presence. Other major strategies include the following:

- Continuing to expand the company's role as a third-party manager of hotels and resorts
- Franchising the Sheraton, Westin, and Four Points by Sheraton brands to selected third-party operators, thereby expanding the company's market presence, enhancing the exposure of its hotel brands, and providing additional income through franchising fees
- Expanding the company's Internet presence and sales capabilities to increase revenue and improve customer service
- Continuing to grow the company's frequent guest program, thereby increasing occupancy rates while providing the company's customer with benefits based on loyalty to the company's hotels
- Enhancing the company's marketing efforts by integrating the company's proprietary customer databases, so as to sell additional products and services to existing customers, improve occupancy rates, and create additional marketing opportunities
- Optimizing the company's use of its real estate assets to improve ancillary revenue, such as restaurant, beverage, and parking revenue from the company's hotels and resorts
- Continuing to build the new "W" hotel brand to appeal to upscale business travelers and other customers seeking full-service hotels in major markets
- Developing additional vacation ownership resorts near select hotel locations
- Becoming the first hospitality company in the world to embrace Six Sigma, the internationally recognized program that dramatically accelerates and maximizes business performance—an initiative that is expected to deliver significant long-term financial benefits

Based on these goals, Starwood has established supporting business strategies. Starwood intends to expand and diversify the company's hotel portfolio through minor investments and selective acquisitions of properties, domestically and internationally, that meet some or all of the following criteria:

- Luxury and upscale hotels and resorts in major metropolitan areas and business centers
- Major tourist hotels, destination resorts, or conference centers that have favorable demographic trends and are located in markets with significant barriers to entry or with major room demand generators such as office or retail complexes, airports, tourist attractions, or universities
- Undervalued hotels whose performance can be increased by rebranding to one of the company's hotel brands
- Portfolios of hotels or hotel companies that exhibit some or all of the criteria listed here

Also, Starwood selectively chooses to develop and construct desirable hotels and resorts to help the company meet its strategic goals.

Starwood's financial strategies are viewed within the context of a three-year timeframe (1999-2001) for purposes of this case example. Analytical focal points include review of the balance sheet; analysis of the income statement; ratio analysis and competitive comparisons; ROI and market value, and net income, cap rate, and market value. It should be pointed out that these are examples of financial performance for a historic three-year period and may or may not be representative of current or future performance.[9]

The balance sheet is considered a statement of financial position (Exhibit 4.2). The balance sheet presents a snapshot of the investments of a firm (assets) and the financing of those investments (liabilities and shareholders' equity) as of a specific time. The balance sheet shows the following balance or equality:

Assets = Liabilities + Shareholders' Equity

When defining an asset as a potential resource that provides a firm with a future economic benefit, the right side of an asset in the balance sheet presents the method of how to raise the financial resource.

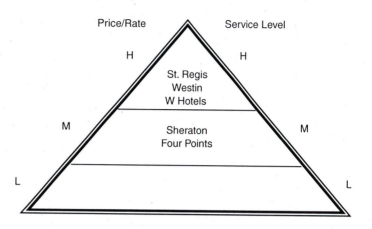

EXHIBIT 4.1. The Starwood Brands

In Millions of U.S. Dollars	1999		2000			2001		
		%		%	Δ%		%	Δ%
Cash & Equivalents	436.0	3.37%	189.0	1.49%	56.65%	157.0	1.26%	-16.93%
Accounts Receivable	468.0	3.62%	538.0	4.24%	14.96%	432.0	3.47%	-19.70%
Total Inventory	167.0	1.29%	238.0	1.87%	42.51%	219.0	1.76%	-7.98%
Prepaid Expenses	92.0	0.71%	120.0	0.95%	30.43%	89.0	0.71%	-25.83%
Other	0.0	0.00%	0.0	0.00%	#DIV/0!	0.0	0.00%	#DIV/0!
	1,163.0	9.00%	1085	8.55%	-6.71	897	7.20%	-17.33%
Total Current Assets								
P, P & E	8,920.0	69.01%	9,376.0	73.84%	5.11%	9,675.0	77.64%	3.19%
Accum. Depreciation	-1,133.0	-8.77%	1,487.0	-11.71%	31.24%	-1,840.0	-14.77%	23.74%
Net P, P & E	7,787.0	60.25%	7889	62.13%	1.31%	7835	62.88%	-0.68%
Goodwill	2,872.0	22.22%	2,881.0	22.69%	0.31%	2,825.0	22.67%	-1.94%
Long Term Investment	442.0	3.42%	412.0	3.24%	-6.79%	400.0	3.21%	-2.91%
Other Long Term Assets	661.0	5.11%	430.0	3.39%	-34.95%	504.0	4.04%	17.21
Total Long Term Assets	11,762.0	91.00%	11612	91.45%	-1.28%	11564	92.80%	-0.41%
Total Assets	12,925.0	100.00%	12697	100.00%	-1.76%	12461	100.00%	-1.86%
Accounts Payable	205.0	1.59%	186.0	1.46%	-9.27%	225.0	1.81%	20.97%
Accrued Expenses	1,112.0	8.60%	1,074.0	8.46%	-3.42%	1,030.0	8.27%	-4.10%
Short Term Debt	988.0	7.64%	585.0	4.61%	-40.79%	332.0	2.66%	-43.25%
Other Current Liabilities	0.0	0.00%	0.0	0.00%	#DIV/0!	0.0	0.00%	#DIV/0!
Total Current Liability	2,305.0	17.83%	1845	14.53%	-19.96%	1587	12.74%	-13.98%
Total Long Term Liabilities	4,643.0	35.92%	4,957.0	39.04%	6.76%	5,227.0	41.95%	5.45%
Other Liabilities	2,287.0	17.69%	2,044.0	16.10%	-10.63%	1,891.0	15.18%	-7.49%
Total Liabilities	9,235.0	71.45%	8846	69.67%	-4.21%	8705	69.86%	-1.59%
Preferred Stock	0.0	0.00%	0.0	0.00%	#DIV/0!	0.0	0.00%	#DIV/0!
Common Stock	4.0	0.03%	4.0	0.03%	0.00%	4.0	0.03%	0.00%
Paid-In Capital	4,785.0	37.02%	4,796.0	37.77%	0.23%	4,861.0	39.01%	1.36%
Retained Earnings	-856.0	-6.62%	-592.0	-4.66%	-30.84%	-609.0	-4.89%	2.87%
Other Equity	-243.0	-1.88%	-357.0	-2.81%	46.91%	-500.0	-4.01%	40.06%
Total Equity	3,690.0	28.55%	3851	30.33%	4.36%	3756	30.14%	-2.47%
Total Liabilities & Equity	12,925.0	100.00%	12697	100.00%	-1.76%	12461	100.00%	-1.86%

EXHIBIT 4.2. Analysis of Balance Sheet of Starwood

As seen in Exhibit 4.3, Starwood raises 30.1 percent of its financial resource with liabilities and 69.9 percent with shareholders' equities. In analyzing the Starwood's balance sheet for three years, there aren't any significant changes. Slight changes can be found in current assets, current liabilities, and long-term liabilities. Cash and equivalents decreased almost half in 2000, while inventory increased by 40 percent. Also, Starwood might select the transfer of short-term liabilities to long-term liabilities. The ratio analysis about balance sheet is discussed in more detail later.

The income statement presents the results of the operating activities of a firm for a specific time period (Exhibit 4.4). The income statement indicates the net income or earnings for that time period. Net income is the difference between revenues and expenses.

Revenue of 2001 decreased approximately $378 million to $3,967 million from $4,345 million in 2000 and net operation income decreased approximately $413 million to $615 from $1,028 million in 2000. The decline in operation results when compared to 2000 reflects the impact of lower revenue per available room primarily attributable to the September 11 terrorist attacks.

Ratio Analysis

Ratio analyses help managers or outside users of financial statements to monitor the performance of the firm's operation or to evaluate its efforts to meet a variety of goals. Ratios are used to communicate financial performance. However, different ratios reveal different conditions or abilities of an operation.

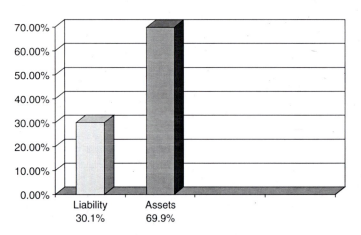

EXHIBIT 4.3. The Composition of Financial Resources

"Current ratio," the most common liquidity ratio, can express the ability of a hospitality establishment to meet its short-term obligation. Therefore, as you see in Exhibit 4.5, Starwood's current ratio is relatively low compared to other competitors and industry averages, compelling the need for Starwood to push up its current ratio.

Debt-equity ratio, one of the most common solvency ratios, indicates the hospitality establishment's ability to withstand adversity and meet its long-term debt. Exhibit 4.6 shows that Starwood's debt-equity ratio is higher than Marriott's[10] and the industry average, but lower than Hilton's;[11] it means that Starwood is at a high leverage level. Starwood raised a large portion of its

In Millions of U.S. Dollars	1999	%	2000	%	%	2001	%	%
Revenue	3,391.0	88.56%	3,659.0	84.21%	7.90%	3,343.0	84.27%	-8.64%
Other Revenue	438.0	11.44%	686.0	15.79%	56.62%	624.0	15.73%	9.04%
Total Revenue	3,829.0	100.00%	4,345.0	100.00%	13.48%	3,967.0	100.00%	-8.70%
Cost of Revenue	2,313.0	60.41%	2,433.0	56.00%	5.19%	2,365.0	59.62%	-2.79%
Gross Profit	**1,078.0**	**28.15%**	**1,226.0**	**28.22%**	**13.73%**	**978.0**	**24.65%**	**-20.23%**
General & Admin Expense	220.0	5.75%	403.0	9.28%	83.18%	411.0	10.36%	1.99%
Depreciation/Amortization	452.0	11.80%	481.0	11.07%	6.42%	526.0	13.26%	9.36%
Unusual Income/Expense	3.0	0.08%	0.0	0.00%	-100.00%	50.0	1.26%	#DIV/0!
Total Operating Expense	2,988.0	78.04%	3,317.0	76.34%	11.01%	3,352.0	84.50%	1.06%
Operating Income	**841.0**	**21.96%**	**1,028.0**	**23.66%**	**22.24%**	**615.0**	**15.50%**	**-40.18**
Interest Expense/Income	-484.0	-12.64%	-420.0	-9.67%	-13.22%	-358.0	-9.02%	-14.76%
Gain/(Loss) Sale of Assets	191.0	4.99%	2.0	0.05%	-98.95%	-57.0	-1.44%	-2950.00%
Other, Net	-15.0	-0.39%	0.0	0.00%	-100.00%	0.0	0.00%	#DIV/0!
Income Before Tax	**533.0**	**13.92%**	**610.0**	**14.04%**	**14.45%**	**200.0**	**5.04%**	**-67.21%**

EXHIBIT 4.4. Analysis of Income Statement of Starwood

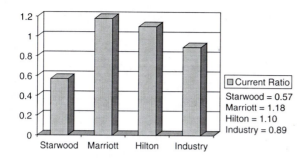

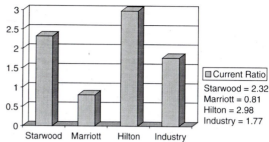

EXHIBIT 4.5. Ratio Analysis. Current assets are 897 and current liabilities are 1,587.

EXHIBIT 4.6. Debt of Equity. Total debt is 8,705 and total equity is 3,756.

assets from creditors. On the basis of those ratio analyses, Starwood's financial strength would not be considered good at this point in time (2001).

Accounts receivable turnover and inventory turnover ratios are both relatively low. The accounts receivable turnover ratio measures the speed of conversion to cash from credit. High accounts receivable turnover means that accounts receivable is managed well. The inventory turnover ratio shows how quickly the inventory is moving. All things fixed, generally, the quicker the inventory turnover the better, because inventory can be expensive to maintain. A high inventory turnover ratio is the result of a well-managed inventory. Starwood's ratios are low compared to other competitors and industry averages:

	Starwood	Marriott	Hilton	Industry
Receivable Turnover	8.30	14.60	5.19	12.73
Inventory Turnover	10.29	93.07	11.16	42.42
P/E Ratio	52.30	50.32	31.85	39.92

ROI and Market Value

ROI is calculated by dividing EBITDA by equity. The ROI of Starwood is relatively higher than Marriott:

	1999	2000	2001
Starwood	39.24%	46.19%	37.18%
Marriott	14.89%	24.55%	19.15%
Hilton	57.38%	73.81%	48.20%

The debt-to-equity ratio of Starwood is a lot higher than for Marriott. One could conclude that Starwood uses leverage efficiently.

Market value of Starwood increases every year:

	1999	2000	2001
Net Income	$1,141	$1,509	$1,293
Cap Rate	31%	40%	34%
Value	$3,681	$3,792	$3,802

This shows that Starwood raised and allocated capital fairly well. One goal of financial strategy in a company is to increase shareholders' value by increasing ROI and by increasing market value. Currently, the ROI and market value of Starwood have been growing in support of that goal during the three years referenced earlier.

Case Discussion Questions

1. Based on the data presented in this case example which company (Starwood, Marriott, or Hilton) would you invest in and why?
2. Do you think the concept of a REIT has been good or bad for the hospitality industry and why?

NOTES

1. N. Johns & D. Lee-Ross, *Research Methods in Service Industry Management* (London, UK: Cassell, 1998), p. 15.

2. http://www.sportsci.org; www.sportscience.com.

3. http://writing.colostate.edu/references/gentsans; www.coloradostateuniversity.com.

4. Johns & Lee-Ross, *Research Methods,* pp. 58-59.

5. S. Wright, "Correlation and Causation," *Journal of Agriculture Research,* vol. 20 (1991), pp. 557-585.

6. Johns & Lee-Ross, *Research Methods,* p. 77.

7. Ibid., p. 84.

8. S. Barney, *The Lodging Stocks* (New York: Salomon Smith Barney, 2002), pp. 45-54.

9. www.starwood.com.

10. www.Marriott.com.

11. www.Hilton.com.

Chapter 5

Integrative Research

CHAPTER OBJECTIVES

- To provide a definition of the integrative research approach.
- To discuss the advantages and disadvantages of integrative research.
- To delineate the major types of integrative research approaches.
- To provide the academic versus applied perspective of integrative research.
- To discuss issues related to the integrative research approach.

Up to this point, the various types of qualitative and quantitative research methodologies have been delineated. The advantages and disadvantages of the methodologies have also been reviewed. Further, the most applicable areas to which both qualitative and quantitative research are best suited have been examined. This brings us to the concept of integrative research.

DEFINITION

Frequently in the business sector, multiple research approaches are utilized with respect to the same situation. For example, a focus group and questionnaire might be combined with customer comment cards, the results from the analysis of the data used to support or negate suspected trends. When two or more different research techniques are utilized to obtain multiple data about the same situation it is defined as an integrative approach. The parameters for integrating research techniques are wide and can include combinations of two or more qualitative methodologies or qualitative methodologies and quantitative methodologies used in tandem.

ADVANTAGES AND DISADVANTAGES

The combining of two or more different research techniques allows for more in-depth probes as well as serves as a verification cross check. The integrative approach also allows management to change specific situations during the research to ascertain whether the original or modified situation is better or worse, faster or slower, and so on. Integrative approaches are pragmatic in outlook and are attractive from a practitioner point of view. While viewed favorably by industry, academicians challenge the integrative approach from the point of view of academic rigor. Quantitative work is usually conducted within a hypothetic-deductive, positivistic framework, which is viewed as incompatible with the phenomenological stance of qualitative research. Academicians sometimes question whether the results from integrative research compromise academic knowledge because of both the narrow study situations and the nonapplicability to other systems.

Handbook of Marketing Research Methodologies for Hospitality and Tourism
© 2007 by The Haworth Press, Inc. All rights reserved.
doi:10.1300/5927_06

Further, the practice of integrating research and action is deemed questionable on the basis that it is difficult to clearly identify how much of a project is research and how much is action.

As indicated, in business, especially in the service industry that deals with the everyday environment, the mixture of quantitative and qualitative techniques is viewed as supportive and pragmatic. Managers tend to be skeptical of too rigorous of an approach because questions tend to be narrow in focus and the focus is often perceived to be on the process versus the application of meaningful/actionable results. Figure 5.1 summarizes the advantages and disadvantages of the integrative approach.[1]

Given the aforementioned perspectives on integrative research, we are now ready to look at the variety of forms of integrative research. For discussion purposes, the framework is limited to three major/basic types: triangulation, case studies, and action research. Figure 5.2 depicts these three types.

TRIANGULATION

In its simplest definition, triangulation means "making triangles" from two known points to an unknown one. In research, triangulation typically involves the comparison of data from two different techniques in order to check the accuracy of each set of results. This can frequently involve the comparison of quantitative and qualitative data. In principle, there are two basic reasons for integrating qualitative and quantitative research methods into a single project. First, a qualitative study may be used to provide insight into a specific situation prior to proposing hypotheses and designing a questionnaire. Second, it is also possible to follow a quantitative study with a qualitative one, where the objective is to build upon the survey findings by examining the sample in greater depth. Either of these rationales can be okay to use in a triangulative approach, but neither represents triangulation per say. The essence of triangulation is that the techniques are used in a parallel sense, so that they provide overlapping information.

Triangulation is commonly employed in business research projects. The use of overlapping, mutually supporting research techniques is often the most effective way to assess the feasibility of a new marketing strategy, or to evaluate a new management initiative. Evaluations of this kind usually need to survey a large sample of people, in order to provide an overview of the research situation. They usually also include an element of in-

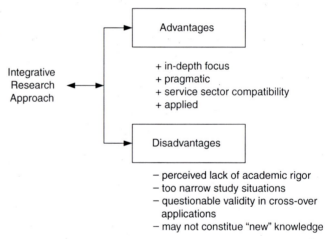

FIGURE 5.1. Advantages and Disadvantages of the Integrative Approach

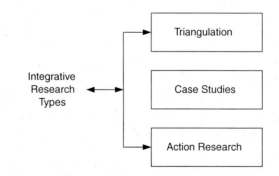

FIGURE 5.2. Basic Types of Integrative Research Approaches

terviewing, which allows the researcher to check the survey findings. This enriches the data available for the evaluation and also allows the survey findings to be verified through an independent research approach.

The first step in triangulation is to compare the survey sample with that used for the interviews. Any other data that have been gathered would be meaningless without the comparison. The second step is to check correspondence between the information provided by interviewees and that obtained from the survey. Third, an outline picture of the responses should be drawn up. Next, the qualitative findings are then compared with the pictures. It should be noted that triangulation frequently calls for interpretation and further data gathering.

Triangulation is not restricted to comparing quantitative and qualitative results. It may also utilize different qualitative techniques to provide a more meaningful view of a research situation. Observation can be used to verify or challenge information provided during interviews. Triangulation can be used to check the truth of informants' statements. It can provide useful insights and even suggest new lines of enquiry. Finally, triangulation may be used to check interviews or observational findings.[2]

CASE STUDIES

The common denominator between the academic and the business sectors is that case studies provide both sectors examples of others' successful and unsuccessful strategies. Academia utilizes case studies for many purposes. These include, but are not limited to, providing in-depth information on a subject organization and/or strategy, assisting in teaching the analytical thought process, and providing a methodological approach to identifying, locating, and deciphering information as part of the research process.

Case study research employs multiple sources of information to focus on and study a single limited situation through one particular recent time period. Case study research is a focusing approach. As it proceeds it zeros in on an even smaller portion of the research situation (the subject case) in even greater depth and detail than triangulation. The case study method aims to view a research situation from as many sides as possible in order to build up a rich data picture about the situation. Case studies are premised on a very thorough collection process of pertinent data utilizing a variety of research methods in combination with each other. For example, personal interviews, analysts' reports, industry sector quantitative and qualitative (performance and ranking) data, extensive secondary research, and, where desired, primary research may all be utilized in compiling data for a case study. In fact, in order to build up a rich source of data, each stage of the case may involve a different research technique. Like triangulation, it is the utilization of multiple and different methods that benefits the study. The case study process is flexible, often developing as it proceeds. Case study research is particularly useful where areas of perceived complexity exist. Again, since complexity is a recognized feature of many service organizations, case study research is often used in actual service situations.

Case study research is most compatible with service sector situations and is a most applicable research tool.

N. Johns and D. Lee-Ross
Research Methods in Service Industry Management (1998)

Case study research begins with a clear strategy to allow for the research to proceed, but flexible enough to permit research strategy to change or be adapted. Figure 5.3 presents a case study research design.[3]

As depicted in Figure 5.3, the case study research design involves multiple research techniques. Figure 5.4 delineates the phases of the case study research design.

Survey

An advantage of the survey phase is the "distance" it places between the researcher and the subjects. It is felt that there might be a tendency for "blind spots" to develop if the researcher is too close to the subjects. The survey phase is intended to identify and clarify the main features of the case situation and to suggest ways for the focusing process to go forward. However, this "distance" also has its disadvantages. A survey can reduce its data to a few numbers, providing a broad overview, but little or no detail. The interview and observation phases of the research can provide this detail but may bring the researcher into close contact with the subjects, possibly jeopardizing objectivity.

Observation

The second phase of the research strategy is observation. Observation represents a simple way to build an overview of what is occurring within the case situation. Participant observation is a term also used and is described as looking at a range of activities and their interconnections, rather than focusing on a single activity. Observational data can be used to assist in building up hypotheses about a case. Observation is a relatively straightforward and unsophisticated way of gathering data, while permitting for very close study of the complexities of a case. Observation allows for a wider view of a situation than many other methods. Finally, it should be noted that observation may affect behavior of research subjects, due to the presence of the researcher. Semistructured interviews are used to gather information. Results can be compared with the findings of a questionnaire survey. Semistructured interviews consist of a mixture of precoded and short-answer, open-ended questions. They can elicit biographical data about the respondents, such as age, gender, and marital status, as well as attitudinal and behavioral details.

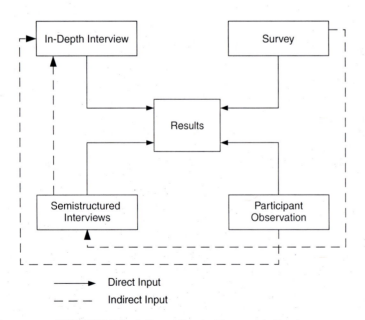

FIGURE 5.3. A Case Study Research Design

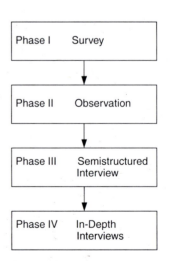

FIGURE 5.4. Phases of a Case Study Research Design

Some interview questions may be based on responses to the questionnaire, and others centered on the researcher's observations. Open-ended questions allow respondents to supplement the data they gave with opinions and attitudes. Demographic questions allowed direct comparisons to be made across subgroups and make it possible to check the representativeness of the sample. The data obtained in this way are overlapped with both survey and observation findings. They could therefore be used to check results that may have been obtained previously, substantiating and explaining data from the first two phases of research strategy. Semistructured interviews also provide further attitudinal information and are used to contextualize and explain data from the other sources.[4]

In-Depth Interviews

The final phase of the focusing procedure uses in-depth interviews. These can be structured as "guided conversations" in which the researcher steers respondents around specific topic areas in whatever order seems appropriate at the time. The objective is to ensure a free response so that the informant can discuss issues or add anything important. In this responsive situation, a particular replay can be reexamined during the interview itself, in the context of the interviewee's other replies. In this way, in-depth interviews are able to provide a high level of contextual understanding.

In-depth interviews reduce the "distance" between interviewer and interviewee. Many times interviewees are more willing to reveal details about themselves and their organization because they do not perceive the interview situation as threatening. Like the semistructured interviews, in-depth interviews may note demographic details of respondents, so that their findings can be correlated with the other results.

ACTION RESEARCH

The term action research simply means that the researcher is actually working within the research situation itself, through the perceptions of members of the organization (managers, employees, etc.) in order to enhance operational practice. This in contrast to the triangulation and case study methods, where the researcher is an external agent viewing a research situation from an outside viewpoint. There are advantages to action research as a result of the stimulating research situation. It may also foster questions with respect to methodology and research ethics. One of the most common forms of action research is when a business contracts with a consultant to look upon a research situation from within the business. In some instances, action research can include a team of researchers deployed within an organization. In other circumstances, the team may consist of a single researcher/facilitator and selected members of the organization to form a team. This latter approach allows the researcher to provide advice and make suggestions and, in general, facilitates the situation.

The action research process begins with the orientation of team members focusing on the philosophy of the research approach. The action research process involves rounds of planning, data collection, and analysis. At each completion of a round, a rigorous review is undertaken resulting in a fine-tuning and/or modifications, additional probes, and so forth, of the next round. Each round produces a progressively focused and richer picture of the research situation.

Action research is usually utilized in situations that are limited in terms of time, scale, and areas covered. The research phenomenon is generally described from the perspective of the research team, rather than the researcher/facilitator. One benefit of this approach is that it incorporates the "external" expertise of the researcher and makes full use of the "internal" team's knowledge. Hypotheses are generated through the action research team's discussions of the data collection and rounds, allowing for reflection and modification before proceeding. In essence, repetitive observations produce hypotheses, test hypotheses, and modify hypotheses. This process also produces or identifies new lines of inquiry. Figure 5.5 depicts the action research process.

Action research is often favored by service industry managers for three primary reasons. First, action research is familiar to managers and does not require an in-depth knowledge of research methodology. Second, it is practical and the results are usually very actionable. And, third, it allows for management as well as members of the business to be empowered to make changes and to develop their own working culture during the process. These benefits, combined with the ability of the individual and team, tend to produce a

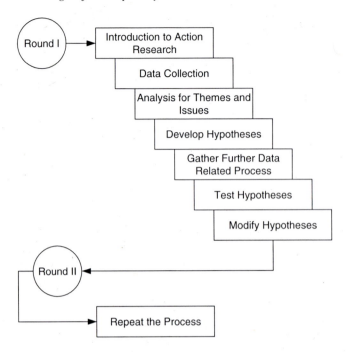

FIGURE 5.5. The Action Research Process

work environment of open disclosure, depersonalized debate, and a resolution of conflict and tensions. From an organizational behavior prospect, the action research approach makes it possible to bring together different members of the hierarchy of the organization in a positive and productive way. Thus, learning, professional development, and cultural and behavioral change are often outcomes of the research.

In action research, it is important that the team leader or facilitator perform both administrative and research-related tasks. These include planning the research and integrating it into the organization's schedule, identifying and motivating the research team, developing a planned series of meetings and taking minutes, and also carry out data collection and analysis. In most instances, the research goals and techniques are more or less imposed from the outside (of the team) by the organization's senior management or by a combination of the external consultant and senior management. In the academic situation, the goals are likely dictated by the sponsoring funding entity.[5]

ACADEMIC VERSUS APPLIED ACTION RESEARCH

The academic perspective is usually focused on the hypotheses and process and the corporate focus is usually on the actionable or that which can be implemented. Academicians believe action research is difficult to justify in terms of rigor. This is due to the fact that the research situation is potentially tainted as a result of the researcher actually being immersed within the situation itself. It is believed that action research and the involvement of the researcher may inhibit wider perception. Action research also shares with the case study method a focus on problems of wider applicability and external validity.

Action research can conform to claim academic rigor and acceptability. Twelve criteria may make this conformation and acceptance possible. These are as follows:

1. There must be some implications beyond the findings and actions required by the project itself.
2. Action research findings must be both usable in everyday life and explicitly concerned with theory.
3. It is not enough to draw generality from the action research findings themselves. The basis upon which the action research project is planned and executed must also be explicitly related to theory.
4. Theory should emerge from action research as a synthesis of the inductive findings with what has already been published on the research subject area.
5. Theory building should be incremental, moving from the specific to the general in small steps.
6. Presenters of action research findings should be clear about the requirements of the research "customer" and should present the findings in accordance with this aim.
7. Action research should be conducted with a high degree of method and orderliness, in which the phases of the work can be clearly perceived.
8. The process of exploring/analyzing the data should be either replicable or demonstrable through argument or analysis.
9. The eight contentions outlined previously are necessary but not in themselves a sufficient condition for the validity of action research.
10. Data collection and reflection should be focused only upon research aspects that could not be captured by any means other than an action research model.
11. Opportunities for triangulation, which are not available through other research models, should be exploited fully but also used to enhance the incremental development of theory.
12. The history and context of the action research project must be taken as critical for the likely range of validity and applicability of the findings.

In the real business/corporate world, there is little interest or need seen for academic rigor or many of the aforementioned criteria. As previously stated, the focus is on results that can be implemented, and not on process. In fact, action research remains a most attractive management research choice and instrument for assisting in progressive change. Action research is viewed as combining research with action steps and thus reducing costs and improving organizational effectiveness and efficiency. This is perhaps best exemplified by the practice of quality teams within a continuous quality improvement (CQI) program where both effectiveness and efficiency (in service delivery) are the end products.

ISSUES

A variety of issues and concerns arise with respect to the integrative research approach and related techniques. Many believe that the case study research technique restricts itself to a narrowly defined study situation. Narrowness is often stated to include a limited environment and geographic area, and too short a time frame for the data-gathering process itself. Further, another shortcoming is that findings usually cannot be generalized by the case study method alone. Action research also may result in an unintended evaluation of management itself, especially if it identifies past practices in the process. This in turn may have an unintended effect on the organization itself.

As previously indicated, action researchers by definition are involved in the process/situation that they are researching, which at times may make it difficult for them to claim objectivity. In situations where external consultants are utilized as facilitators or researchers, there are two other issues that can arise. First, is the consultants' presence intimidating to the team and/or their perspectives already biased? Second, if they are not well versed in the organization service offerings they can provide disastrous recommendations. Often there is also a philosophical issue related to the ownership of action research. The board or top management buys off on the research and pays for it, which is a presumption that the organization needs external help or is not functioning properly. Often middle management and employees participate in it only because they have to, and often this will result in a negative perspective taking hold at the outset of the situation research.

CHAPTER REVIEW

In this section, the concept of the integrative approach to research was explored. The following three major types/techniques of integrative research were discussed: triangulation, case study, and action research. Each differs in terms of outcome and methodology. First, it was stated that triangulation compares the results obtained by two different methods of research. These two methods/techniques are carefully selected so that they overlap in a parallel way. The method is designed in order to reduce bias and error as much as possible. Second, it was indicated that case study research uses different techniques in order to focus progressively on the research situation. The techniques chosen may overlap, which in turn also allows for triangulation. The strength of the case study method is in its ability to uncover complexity within a research situation. And, third, in action research, the concept of teams composed of the research subjects themselves planning and carrying out the research was discussed. It was pointed out that the role/scope of the researcher may be far reaching or it may be restricted to merely facilitating the project. It was also pointed out that an external consultant is often employed to take on the role of facilitator. Finally, in the case of action research, it was indicated that difficulties may be encountered, such as where the researcher's own role must be identified and the boundary between research and intervention clarified. It was pointed out that integrative research and the three major techniques (previously defined) are the preferred tools (key) for the development of research in the service sector.

KEY CONCEPTS/TERMS

Action research
Boundary
Case studies
Complexity
Facilitator
In-depth interviews
Mythology
Observation
Phenomenological
Semistructured
Triangulation

DISCUSSION QUESTIONS

1. What would be an example of integrative research?
2. How would you define integrative research?
3. What are three approaches to integrative research?

4. What are some of the advantages and disadvantages of integrative research?
5. Why is integrative research more acceptable in the services sector than in academia?
6. What are the three issues related to the integrative research approach?

CASE 5.1. STOUFFER HOTELS AND RESORTS: COMPETITIVE STRATEGY

In the fall of 1988, the top management group of the Stouffer Hotel Company (SHC) was trying to decide how much to bid for the Stanford Court, a world-famous San Francisco hotel.[6] Acquisition of the Stanford Court would give SHC representation in a market that was important both because of its size and because it was a major "gateway" for travelers to and from Hawaii and the growing Pacific Rim region. Adding the Stanford Court was also seen as a significant next step in carrying out Stouffer's strategy, adopted several years earlier, of becoming a national chain of first-class hotels. The cost of the acquisition was, however, expected to be high. SHC was only one of several known or potential bidders who were attracted by the Stanford Court's reputation and its prestige location on Nob Hill.

SHC President William N. Hulett had appointed a task force to investigate the proposed acquisition. The task force concluded the bidding for the 402-room property would reach at least $90 million, and possibly as much as $100 million. Even the lower of these amounts would be considerably higher than the hotel's value according to traditional industry standards. Moreover, although the Stanford Court was a well-known and highly rated hotel, its occupancy rate had declined in the past three years as new upscale competitors entered the San Francisco market. To rebuild the hotel's market share and its profitability would require further investments in refurbishing as well as increased marketing expenditures. Whether the total prospective investment could be justified was a subject for debate by SHC's management group.

Company Background

Stouffer was founded by Vernon Stouffer in the late 1920s as a family-style restaurant in Cleveland, Ohio. During the period 1930-1960 Stouffer evolved into a chain with five to six restaurants in each of six Midwestern and northeastern cities. Also during this period, Stouffer entered the frozen food business stimulated by the success of one restaurant manager who sold frozen items to his customers. Over the years, Stouffer's frozen food business grew steadily and by the 1980s it was one of the leading brands in the U.S. market.

During the 1960s Stouffer began to open suburban restaurants. As a "side line" to these restaurants, the company also began to develop, acquire, or franchise motels and motor hotels with restaurant facilities. The first of these, the Anacapri, was purchased in Fort Lauderdale, Florida, in 1961 as a winter haven for snow-weary Clevelanders including the Stouffer family and their employees. Other Stouffer motels of this era were mostly franchised operations in which Stouffer's primary interest was that of operating the restaurants. The independent franchisees owned and managed the hotels.

In 1967 Litton Industries acquired Stouffer. Litton was a highly diversified industrial company that had pioneered in microwave technology. Litton's primary interest in Stouffer was centered on frozen foods as an avenue for exploiting microwave cooking, then in its infancy. Certainly, Litton showed little interest in hotels, adding only one new property to the chain between 1967 and 1973.

In 1973 Litton sold Stouffer to Nestlé S.A., one of the world's largest food producers (Nestlé's worldwide sales in 1988 amounted to 40.7 billion Swiss Francs, equivalent to about $27 billion). Nestlé, with headquarters in Lausanne, Switzerland, produced and marketed coffee, chocolate, dairy, and other consumer products worldwide. Like Litton, Nestlé was originally interested in Stouffer primarily on account of its frozen foods. Despite this, according to James M. Biggar, CEO of Nestlé Enterprises, Inc. (Stouffer's parent company), Nestlé had provided resources for growth in the hotel business. These were, however, a "mixed bag, ranging from two franchised facilities with 900 rooms each down to a 70-room establishment."

The development of the present-day Stouffer Hotels and Resorts chain began in 1981 when Jim Biggar sought out and hired Bill Hulett as president. Hulett had spent the previous 21 years with Westin Hotels, rising through the ranks from a busboy at the Davenport Hotel in Spokane to a position as corporate VP of Westin at age 36. Hulett had managed the St. Francis Hotel in San Francisco, the Mayflower in Washington, DC, the Ilikai in Honolulu, and the Westin Wailea Beach Resort in Maui, all first-class hotels. Recalling his decision to accept Nestlé's offer, Hulett stated that he would not have joined the company on any basis other than one of eventually developing a "first-class chain, one of which Stouffer and Nestlé could be proud." (A long-time Nestlé advertising theme was "Nestlé's Makes the Very Best.") His first step in this direction was the acquisition, in December 1981, of the Mayflower.

During his first two years as president, Hulett moved gradually but deliberately toward his goal of converting Stouffer into a chain of upscale hotels. In addition to the Mayflower, new units were opened in the suburbs of Columbus, Ohio (1981), and Boston (1981). A resort hotel, the Cottonwoods (near Scottsdale, Arizona), was acquired in 1982. By mid-1983 all Stouffer hotel franchises were terminated and several company-owned hotels were sold. In retrospect, Hulett said in 1989, "it would have been easier to start from scratch, and to use a new name for the hotels." Using the name Stouffer, according to Hulett and Senior Vice President—Marketing Ronald Nykiel, meant that the company had to overcome its "less than luxury" past reputation in the hotel industry as well as avoid confusion between Stouffer hotels and Stouffer's frozen foods. (To reduce confusion between the hotels and the food products, a new logo was designed for Stouffer Hotels.)

Strategic Repositioning

By 1983 Hulett's efforts to upgrade the quality of Stouffer Hotels was producing encouraging results in terms of growth and profitability. He, therefore, proposed, and Nestlé approved, a full-scale program aimed at repositioning SHC as a major competitor in the first-class segment of the U.S. lodging industry. The key elements of the repositioning strategy were as follows:

- Expansion of SHC into a national chain. Prior to 1983 the company had only one property west of the Mississippi River. The new strategy called for nationwide expansion including, eventually, representation in nearly all of the country's largest metropolitan areas. A target of 50 hotels was set for 1990.
- No future use of franchising as a method of operation. Whenever possible, Stouffer would be at least a part-owner of its properties in addition to managing them.
- Future Stouffer Hotels would be designed to meet the needs and preferences of "upscale, frequent travelers"—those with incomes of $75,000 or more, who took at least 12 trips annually. A mix of downtown, suburban, airport, and resort hotels would be developed to satisfy the demands of these travelers for both business and pleasure trips. Existing properties, where necessary, would be renovated to fit the new Stouffer positioning.
- New hotels should have a minimum of 300 rooms and a full range of facilities including restaurants, meeting facilities, etc.

Hulett explained the thinking behind the new strategy: Franchising is incompatible with a chainwide first-class product and reputation because of the difficulty of controlling quality. Our past franchisees wanted upscale Holiday Inns, not truly first-class operations. Also, to do well in the first-class market, we felt we must become a national company. Frequent travelers, he explained, visited cities throughout the United States. If one of these customers could stay in a Stouffer Hotel in most or all of his or her destinations, good service in each location would lead to the development of "brand loyalty." In a similar fashion, he said, meeting planners who were satisfied with their experiences in one Stouffer property would be more likely to choose Stouffer Hotels for meetings in other locations, too.

Reflecting the new strategic emphasis, what had been the hotel division of Stouffer was converted into the Stouffer Hotel Company in 1983. This move by Nestlé, according to Hulett, signaled a recognition of the size and growth potential of the business, and made it easier for him and his associates to develop and champion their own business plans and capital-spending proposals.

To carry out the strategy of repositioning and national expansion, SHC invested heavily in acquisitions and new hotel development. Thomas Stouffer, then Senior Vice President—Development, worked closely with Hulett to identify opportunities for growth during this period. Between early 1983 and mid-1988, the number of Stouffer Hotels increased from 18 to 32, while total room capacity grew from 5,258 to 12,936 (see Exhibit 5.1). New hotels in the western United States included three Hawaiian resorts: Wailea Beach (1983), the former Westin property Hulett had opened in 1978, Poipu Beach, and Waiohai Beach (both 1987). Airport Concourse hotels were opened in Denver and Los Angeles in 1986. At the opening of the Denver hotel, which coincided with the company's annual management conference, Mr. Helmut Maucher, Managing Director of Nestlé S.A. said: "This spectacular hotel exemplifies the vision we have for Stouffer Hotels and Resorts to grow into a major force in the top end of the hotel industry." This was reaffirmed when Nestlé approved a significant addition to the Stouffer chain via the acquisition of four former Wyndham hotels (Grand Beach in St. Thomas, Orlando, Dallas, and Austin) in 1987. SHC took the Wyndham hotels over from real estate developer Trammell Crow via a controlling joint ownership venture and management contract agreement. The addition of the four Wyndham hotels, along with the opening of three others in 1987, represented a 40 percent increase in SHC's room capacity in that year. The most recent addition in the chain, Stouffer Harborplace, was in the redeveloped section of downtown Baltimore; it opened in March 1988.

Name	Opening Date	Rooms	Rating AAA	Mobil	Stouffer Ownership 100%	Partial	Mgt. Only
1. Oak Brook, IL (Suburban Chicago)	4/66	170	4		X		
2. Valley Forge, PA (Suburban Philadelphia)	6/73	289					X
3. Concourse (Washington, D.C. Airport)	4/74	388					X
4. Pine Isle Resort, Georgia	7/75	250	4	4*	X		
5. Greenway Plaza – Sub Houston, TX	8/75	390	4		X		
6. Center Plaza – Downtown Dayton, OH	7/76	287	4		X		
7. Westchester (Suburban New York)	12/77	364	4	4*	X		
8. Tower City Plaza – Downtown Cleveland, OH	9/78	500	4		X		
9. Five Seasons – Downtown Cedar Rapids, IA	2/79	278	4				X
10. Hamilton – Suburban Chicago, IL	5/81	409	4				X
11. Dublin – Suburban Columbus, OH	9/81	215				X	
12. Bedford Glen – Suburban Boston	9/81	286	4	4*		X	
13. Battle Creek, Michigan (Downtown)	11/81	245					X
14. Mayflower – Downtown Washington, D.C.	12/81	724				X	
15. Cottonwoods Resort – Scottsdale, Arizona	8/82	170	4		X		
16. Waverly – Suburban Atlanta, GA	4/83	521	4			X	
17. Riverview Plaza – Downtown Mobile, AL	6/83	375	4	4*			X
18. Rochester Plaza – Downtown Rochester, NY	7/83	364	4				X
19. Concourse – St. Louis, MO (Airport)	7/83	400	4		X		
20. Wailea Beach Resort – Maui, Hawaii	11/83	350	5				X
21. Madison – Downtown Seattle, Washington	5/84	554	4	4*		X	
22. Winston Plaza – Downtown Winston-Salem, NC	6/84	318					X
23. Concourse – Denver, CO (Airport)	1/86	400	4			X	
24. Concourse – Los Angeles, CA (Airport)	8/86	750	4			X	
25. Austin – Sub Austin, TX	1/87	478	4	4*		X	
26. Dallas – Sub Dallas, TX	1/87	542	4			X	
27. Grand Beach Resort – St. Thomas V.I.	1/87	290	4			X	
28. Orlando Resort – Orlando, FL	1/87	778	4			X	
29. Nashville – Downtown Nashville, TN	8/87	673			X		
30. Waiohai Beach Resort – Kauai, Hawaii	8/87	430	4			X	
31. Puipu Beach Resort – Kauai, Hawaii	8/87	138				X	
32. Harborplace – Downtown Baltimore, MD	3/88	622				X	

EXHIBIT 5.1. Stouffer Hotels in Operations in the United States as of Late 1988 (Listed in Order of Opening or Acquisition Dates)

As shown in Exhibit 5.1, SHC had management contracts, but no equity position, for 4 of the 17 Stouffer Hotels that were added from 1983 on. SHC was part-owner of the other 13 hotels, with equity positions ranging from 12 to 75 percent. The other equity investors in these hotels were usually limited partners, insurance companies, or other institutional investors, in contrast to some hotel management companies. SHC required long-term (typically 20-year) contracts for the properties that it managed. SHC's profits were derived from (1) its management fees (less the corporate expenses of providing management services) and (2) its shares of the operating profits of hotels in which it held equity positions. SHC's management fees averaged around 4 percent of revenues and were charged to all Stouffer Hotels, regardless of ownership.

In addition to developing and acquiring new properties, SHC invested substantial amounts in remodeling and refurbishing older properties during the 1980s. A $2.2 million enhancement program at the Cottonwoods Resort was completed in late 1988, for example. The program included new furniture, carpeting, and wall coverings in all guest rooms, redecoration of meeting facilities, and exterior repainting. A similar enhancement program at Stouffer's Dublin (Ohio) hotel was scheduled to begin in 1989 at a cost of $2.4 million. The 500-room Tower City Plaza hotel in downtown Cleveland had been undergoing renovations since 1986: total investment in this program, which was scheduled for completion by fall 1991, was expected to amount to $36 million.

Organization

Paralleling the growth of SHC's physical facilities during the 1980s, the company's headquarters organization was expanded and strengthened. The structure of the organization in 1988 is shown in Exhibit 5.2.

As a former hotel general manager, Hulett was a strong believer in giving broad authority and responsibility to the manager of each Stouffer property.

Each hotel general manager was responsible for hiring and firing and for the performance of his or her property. The general managers earned base salaries of $60,000 to $100,000 and could also earn bonuses of up to

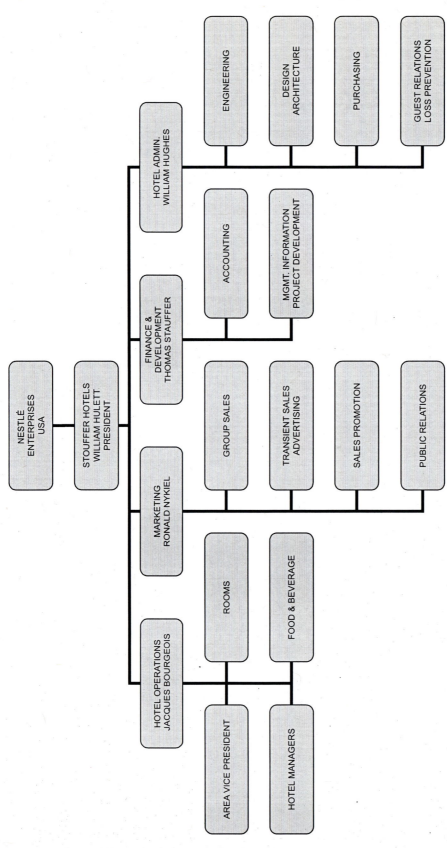

EXHIBIT 5.2. Simplified Organization Chart, Late 1988

50 percent of base salary. The bonus amounts depended in part on a hotel's gross operating profit (GOP) performance in relation to a Stouffer management goal that was set for each year. If actual performance fell below 85 percent of the goal, *no* bonus was earned. In addition to actual versus goal GOP, each manager's performance was evaluated in terms of the hotel's Guest Satisfaction Index (described in a later section).

Stouffer's "Products"

The focus of SHC's strategy during the 1980s was to develop "first-class" hotels. Stouffer properties varied in terms of location, architecture, and other factors. All of them, however, offered the kinds of facilities and services that were thought to be preferred by the high-income frequent travelers who comprised Stouffer's target market. Ronald Nykiel explained that common denominators for first-class hotels included the following:

- An initial investment of at least $100,000 per room
- Multiple dining and meeting room facilities
- A high level of personal service
- A high ratio of staff to rooms, in order to support high-service levels on a 24-hour basis
- High-quality, attractive décor
- A full range of guest amenities including multiple telephone extensions, television sets, etc.

Other hotel chains that offered first-class facilities and services in the U.S. market included Four Seasons, Westin, Hyatt, Intercontinental, Ritz Carlton, and several recent foreign entrants such as Mandarin Oriental, Nikko, and Meridien.

In addition to providing first-class facilities and high level of guest service, Stouffer had adopted several policies in recent years that were designed to enhance guest satisfaction:

- Delivery of room service orders was guaranteed within 25 minutes; otherwise the order was free.
- In November 1988, Stouffer discontinued all surcharges on guests' long-distance calls except those billed to rooms. Previously, a $0.75 surcharge had been levied on credit-card, collect, and 800 number calls. Comments by guests on Stouffer's Guest Comment Cards showed that those surcharges were a major source of irritation to customers. In announcing the new policy, Hulett stated, "There are times when revenues, even substantial ones, should take a back seat to pleasing your guests; in our judgment this is one of those times." The reduction in revenue attributable to this new policy was estimated at $1.3 million annually.
- "Club Floors" were installed in most of Stouffer's hotels beginning in 1984. The club floors could be entered only via a special elevator key. Each had a concierge and a private lounge where complimentary continental breakfast and evening hors d'oeuvres were served.
- Express check-in and check-out service was introduced in mid-1988. Under this program, members of the Club Express program and guests staying on Club Floors could register simply by signing a card; other information needed for registration was obtained from a computerized reservation record or guest history file. On the morning of a guest's scheduled departure, a billing statement was brought to the guest's room, and no check-out was required unless there were questions about the bill, which was mailed to the guest's address within 24 hours.

Pricing

Consistent with the positioning of its hotels as first-class facilities with a full range of guest services, Stouffer's published or "rackrate" prices were at or near the top of the range among comparable hotels in each market. Some examples illustrate the point:

Location	Stouffer Hotel/Room Rate	Competitors/Rates
Washington, DC	Mayflower $139-234	Ritz Carlton "$220 and up" Four Seasons $225-255 J.W. Marriott Natl. Place $224
Dayton, OH	Central Plaza $109-139	Marriott $102-125 Radisson $76-86
Denver, CO	Concourse (Airport) $119-159	Hyatt Regency $102-122 Brown Palace $149-214
St. Thomas	Grand Beach $295-875	Frenchman's Reef $260-425 Sapphire Beach $265

Like other hotel groups, Stouffer varied its room rates based on supply and demand conditions, using a "yield management" system. Thus, the rate quoted at a given time for a given future date would depend on a hotel's current reservation status and on expected future reservations based on historical patterns.

Stouffer also offered various discounts on room rates to specific groups. These included the following:

- Corporate rates—typically 10 percent below published rates
- Travel industry employee rates
- "Preferred rates" for high-volume accounts (negotiated)
- Promotional rates—for senior citizens, government agencies, etc.

Marketing Stouffer's Hotels

Hulett realized that repositioning Stouffer would require a significant expansion of the company's marketing program. In 1983, SHC's national advertising expenditures amounted to $1.4 million, a sum that was dwarfed by the spending of Hyatt ($7.6 million), Marriott ($3.3 million), Hilton ($10.1 million), and other large hotel chains. (In addition to these national advertising outlays, each of the competing chains had local advertising budgets; Nykiel estimated that individual Marriott hotels spent, in total, another $3 million+.)

To strengthen Stouffer's marketing Hulett recruited Ronald A. Nykiel, who was Executive Vice President—Marketing of the Ramada chain, in mid-1983. A veteran hotel industry executive, Nykiel previously worked at Marriott and Holiday Inns.

Nykiel described his early experiences at Stouffer as a "David and Goliath story." When he joined Stouffer, he explained,

> our consumer awareness level, on an unaided basis, was zero. So my first objective was to try to change that. I also had another objective: to change the image of Stouffer, which was closely associated with frozen foods, and reposition us in the consumer's mind as being something very different. . . . But I was being outspent 10 to 1, and to take a product that looks like a frozen food box and have people think of it differently, and be aware of it, was quite a challenge.

As SHC expanded, marketing expenditures increased substantially, as shown here:

Year	Corporate Expenditures	Hotel Allocations to National Programs	Total
1983	$3,287	0	$3,287
1984	5,950	0	5,950
1985	5,458	$2,717	8,175
1986	5,732	3,672	9,404
1987	7,264	5,386	12,650
1988	7,438	6,468	13,906

Ron Nykiel explained that Stouffer's marketing budget included both amounts allocated by the corporate office itself and amounts allocated by individual hotels in national programs. The "corporate" expenditure figures shown were partly funded by a charge of 1 percent of revenue that was paid by the hotels; this charge was in addition to the management fees (4 percent of revenue) that the hotels paid to headquarters for general management services. The "hotel allocation" figures were allocated from the individual hotels' advertising and promotion budgets to national programs that were administered by headquarters. A third source of funding for Stouffer marketing (not shown) was joint advertising campaigns with American Express and Avis; these programs were paid for in part by Stouffer's "partners."

To illustrate how the funding of Stouffer national marketing activities worked, in 1987, national marketing expenditures were $12,650,000. Of this amount, $5,386,000 was allocated by hotels to national programs. Corporate outlays amounted to $7,264,000, of which $3,860,000 came from the 1 percent charge that was levied on hotel revenues (see Exhibit 5.5, later in this section, for revenue data) and $3,404,000 came from SHC headquarters' own operating budget.

The SHC marketing program included several elements:

- Media advertising (slightly over 50 percent of the total budget)
- Salaries and expenses of headquarters staff (about 10 percent)
- Sales promotion programs (about 10 percent)
- The costs of five regional "National Business Research Offices" that developed sales leads for group business (just under 15 percent)
- Creative services and public relations programs (about 15 percent)

Stouffer's national media advertising program was limited by the company's relatively small budget. To make the most of this budget, Nykiel adopted an extreme version of "target marketing." He explained:

> If you're traveling, the first thing you might do in the morning is to get a newspaper and look at the weather forecast. So one thing that we did was to negotiate a deal with *USA Today* to sponsor their weather page on a daily basis. This happens to be the most widely-read single page of any paper in the country. This deal was expensive, but I persuaded some of the other Nestlé companies to share the cost with us.
>
> We can tailor our *USA Today* ads for each of 28 regions in the U.S. each day. So for the areas that feed into Los Angeles, we'll run a Los Angeles ad, and so on.
>
> Then, building on our approach in *USA Today,* we negotiated an agreement with the *Wall Street Journal* to provide them with business travelers' weather forecasts. We do this only in the journal's editions for 20 major markets, and we can vary our ads among 16 different regional printings.

Other print media used by Stouffer for national advertising included the following:

- The back cover of the pocket edition of *Official Airline Guide,* a monthly condensed airline schedule used by frequent flyers and by corporate travel planners
- *Frequent Flyer* magazine
- The airline magazine provided on board most U.S. airline flights, such as "Vis a Vis" on United Airlines
- The protective covers used by airlines on general magazines (*Time, Business Week,* etc.) that were carried on many airplanes, supplied by Inflight Advertising, Inc. (Stouffer had an exclusive contract for advertising on the covers themselves.)
- Travel industry trade magazines and directories, including the *Hotel and Travel Index*
- Magazines that reached meeting planners, such as *Sales and Marketing Management*

In addition to advertising in print media, Stouffer had a long-term exclusive contract for hotel commercials during the in-flight video programs that were broadcast on some airlines. Stouffer video commercials also appeared on the weather broadcasts supplied by Cable News Network to some hotels and airline club rooms. Stouffer had not advertised on commercial television; according to Nykiel, the target customer for Stouffer Hotels was typically not a heavy TV viewer.

Nykiel believed that Stouffer's advertising since 1983 had been highly effective in achieving its objectives. Consumer awareness of Stouffer Hotels was measured annually in a large-scale survey. Results of the survey showed that unaided brand awareness had increased from 0.1 percent in 1983 to 8.6 percent in 1987 and 32.5 percent in 1988. Aided brand awareness (measured by showing consumers a list of hotels and asking which ones they recognized) rose from 1 percent in 1983 to 80 percent by 1987 and 92 percent in 1988.

Stouffer supplemented its national advertising with several promotional programs, some of which were conducted in partnership with other travel industry firms. The "Club Express" program, Stouffer's frequent guest program, was initially confined to American Express credit card holders. (Nykiel estimated that almost 70 percent of hotel charges in the United States were made on this card.) The program rewarded frequent Stouffer guests with American Express gift certificates. By 1988 the Club Express program was no longer specifically linked to American Express. Club members could, by staying a specified number of times at Stouffer, earn any of several awards:

- A United States Savings Bond
- A merchandise certificate from Brooks Brothers or the Sharper Image
- Free car rentals from Avis Rent-A-Car
- Free weekend "Breakations" (see later)

U.S. Savings Bonds were also awarded to other Stouffer guests under the "Share in America" program. A $50 bond (cash value $25) was given for three nights of patronage.

Another Stouffer promotional program was designed to increase hotel occupancy on weekends. Almost all hotels had substantially lower occupancy rates on Saturday and Sunday (typically 20 to 30 percent) than on weekdays (typically 70 to 100 percent). As a result, most hotel chains or individual hotels offered various kinds of weekend "packages" at reduced rates. Nykiel recalled the development of Stouffer's "Breakations" program in 1986:

> Everyone (in the hotel business) is doing research on how to fill up empty rooms on weekends . . . we wanted to come up with a different way of packaging the idea. We recognized that there were more and more households with both husband and wife working, where the consumers have high incomes but limited time. So we did some focus group research among consumers of this type and tried various names out on them . . . we came up with the term "Breakation." It's meant to appeal to the consumer who thinks, "I need a break, I need a vacation, but I don't have time for a real vacation." The word was so well rated in subsequent tests, we couldn't believe it.

Breakations were standard one- or two-day weekend "packages," including room and some meals. "Resort Breakations," at Stouffer Resort Hotels, were three- to five-day packages that also included rental cars as well as tennis, golf, or other activities. The Breakation packages ranged in price from $59 for one night at a downtown or suburban hotel up to $10,000 for the five-day "Ultimate Resort Breakation" in St. Thomas. The latter included transportation by helicopter to an uninhabited island for a day, as well as a day on a private yacht and a helicopter trip to a casino in Puerto Rico.

The promotional programs produced substantial revenues for Stouffer: sales of Breakations, for example, amounted to over $10 million in 1988. Overall, it was estimated that sales attributable to promotional programs represented about 10 percent of total occupancy and revenues.

Local Marketing

Each Stouffer hotel conducted its own local marketing activities in addition to those at the national level. Sales representatives were located at each hotel, with as many as nine reps being employed at a large downtown hotel or resort hotel. The sales reps called primarily on individuals responsible for handling travel arrangements or planning meetings for corporations, consulting firms, trade associations, and so on, in their areas. Sales reps were compensated on a salary basis with bonuses averaging about 10 percent of salary depending on performance. All of them had, by 1988, completed a five-day in-house training program that was designed and conducted by Stouffer managers.

The primary objective of local hotel sales reps was to develop group business. Group bookings, which accounted for nearly half of Stouffer's room revenues, included a wide range of customer types: corporate conferences, seminars, wedding receptions, and so on. The sales reps' activities were supported by the efforts of National Business Research Offices located in New York, Chicago, Los Angeles, and Washington, DC. Stouffer reps based in the NBROs called on prospective corporate clients and passed all promising leads on to the individual hotels.

Nykiel felt that the quality of Stouffer's field selling efforts needed to be improved. Historically, he said, hotel selling had been largely an "order-taking" function. But the increased competition in the industry, he believed, called for a more creative approach.

Managing Service Quality

Maintaining a high level of service quality was a key element of Stouffer's positioning as a chain of first-class hotels. Jacques Bourgeois, Senior Vice President—Hotel Operations, expressed the view that the foundation for excellent service was

> formed by a vision focused on a total commitment to quality. Companies that consistently deliver superior service display that commitment in everything they do, large and small. They imbue their employees with the desire to excel at every task, at each encounter with every guest. A standard of excellence must be maintained without exception or exemption. Brutal persistence in pursuit of quality is the only sure path to consistent service excellence. Success in such a constant effort requires selecting the right people, training them thoroughly and empowering them in a real-world way. Management must then make sure that every policy, every procedure, every action is geared to guest satisfaction.

Bourgeois emphasized that strong leadership from each hotel's general manager was essential for achieving high-quality service. Each general manager was responsible for his or her own hiring and firing. The general managers were also responsible for implementing programs such as "The Spirit of Hospitality," a two-day orientation program developed in early 1988 by the Educational Institute of the American Hotel and Motel Association. By late 1989, it was planned that virtually every Stouffer employee, from general managers to housekeepers, would complete the Spirit of Hospitality program.

A quarterly publication, *Service Leaders,* was distributed to all Stouffer employees beginning in mid-1988. *Service Leaders* included interviews with and articles by headquarters executives as well as current news illustrating the hotels' efforts to improve service or outstanding performance by individual employees.

Stouffer's policy was to offer a better package of compensation and employee benefits than competing hotels in each area. The company also believed in "empowering" employees. Service problems, in Bourgeois's opinion, often could be traced to lack of responsiveness on the part of an individual employee—usually because he or she lacked authority to deal with a situation. To minimize such problems, Stouffer encouraged employees to put higher priority on resolving a customer's problem than on rigid adherence to standard policies or procedures. According to Bourgeois: "Common sense and flexibility are key factors in such situations. A Stouffer premise here is that a hotel is judged to be 'a quality place to stay' by its users, not its operators."

To measure guests' evaluations of service quality, Stouffer relied heavily on the Guest Response System, introduced in early 1988. The Guest Response System was the responsibility of Senior Vice President—Hotel Administration Bill Hughes. Comment cards, placed in each guest room, were mailed to company headquarters. About 2 percent of the guests staying at Stouffer hotels submitted completed response cards. The response cards were tabulated every month manually by office employees at headquarters, under the direction of Barbara Waldier, Manager of the Office of Guest Relations. Overall, according to Hughes and Waldier, guest comments had averaged "88 percent good or excellent, 7 percent average, 5 percent fair or poor" since the adoption of the Guest Response System.

The evaluations received on Guest Comment Cards were used as one component of a Guest Satisfaction Index (GSI) that was prepared monthly for each hotel by the Office of Guest Relations. Other components of the GSI included unsolicited letters and calls, an annual survey of guests who stayed at each hotel, and a yearly on-site inspection of each hotel. The on-site inspections were conducted by an outside contractor who sent inspection teams to observe and evaluate each hotel. The inspections covered Reservations, Front Desk, Housekeeping, Room Service, Restaurant and Bar, Club Floor, Airport Pick-Up, Concierge, Hotel Courtesy, and Physical Plant.

Ratings of each hotel, based on Guest Comment Cards, were compiled and published monthly. An example of the monthly rating summary for one hotel is given in Exhibit 5.3. Along with the monthly rating summaries, hotel general managers received a monthly commentary on service performance from Bill Hughes. An example of the monthly commentary is shown in Exhibit 5.4.

Any guest ratings of "D" or "F" (Fair or Poor) that were received on the Guest Comment Cards required a personal telephone call from the hotel's general manager. In addition, each hotel's front desk had a special "hot line" telephone that any guest could use to speak directly with the general manager in case he or she could not satisfactorily resolve a problem. The general managers carried paging devices that were activated by "hot line" telephone calls.

On the positive side, Stouffer rewarded employees for outstanding guest ratings. Any employee who was favorably mentioned by name, for example, received an extra vacation day.

Customer Evaluations

Nykiel and Bourgeois were pleased with the evaluations given to Stouffer hotels in several recent consumer surveys. In a 1988 Gallup survey of business travelers, for example, 61 percent of Stouffer guests rated it above average on overall satisfaction. Comparable figures for competitors were Embassy Suites 72 percent, Hyatt 64 percent, Westin 63 percent, and Marriott 61 percent.

The results of a large-scale subscriber survey by *Consumer Reports* included the following "overall satisfaction indexes" for "luxury hotels":

Four Seasons	92
Embassy Suites	85
Intercontinental	83
Stouffer	82

Westin	82
Marriott	81

Stouffer's Denver and Los Angeles airport hotels were ranked first and second among U.S. airport properties in a survey of readers of *Andrew Harper's Hideaway Report,* a travel newsletter.

Measuring Performance

Key indicators of Stouffer's operating performance are summarized in Exhibit 5.5. The performance measures shown in the exhibit include most of those that SHC executives monitored on a monthly basis, for each hotel and for the chain as a whole. Some of these performance measures could be compared directly with hotel industry "norms" that were available from published sources.

		Excellent	Good	Average	Fair	Poor	None
Front Desk:	90.15%						
Accuracy	88.79%	137	60	7	1	11	33
Courtesy	91.30%	132	54	10	3	1	49
Checkin	90.39%	125	65	11	1	2	45
Checkout	90.19%	102	41	9	2	3	92
Guest Services:	85.45%						
Valet	86.49%	40	28	5	2	2	172
Bell	87.02%	55	47	5	1	3	138
Concierge	81.72%	22	25	7	2	2	191
Laundry	84.10%	13	21	5	0	0	210
Phone Messages	81.51%	41	36	6	2	8	156
Phone Wake Up Call	90.36%	75	30	5	1	3	135
Coffee/Newspaper	84.03%	85	14	6	3	16	125
Guest Room/Bathroom:	84.73%						
Decor	82.93%	71	95	25	4	3	51
Cleanliness	86.22%	103	71	15	4	6	50
Comfort	83.82%	91	79	20	10	4	45
Supplies	88.03%	118	57	23	5	1	45
Condition	80.80%	83	75	21	12	10	48
Housekeeping	86.64%	101	70	12	5	5	56
Room Service:	84.28%						
Menu	80.20%	38	45	20	4	3	139
Value	77.55%	29	49	17	8	3	143
Promptness	86.79%	63	28	13	2	3	140
Service	90.72%	71	32	4	1	2	139
Food	85.95%	52	46	9	2	2	138
Restaurant/Lounge:	82.92%						
Value	72.91%	37	87	41	17	10	14
Promptness	84.95%	113	55	16	7	11	4
Service	86.53%	124	42	20	10	6	4
Food	82.99%	82	87	18	8	6	5
Beverage	82.40%	65	89	20	7	3	22
Atmosphere	87.46%	95	82	12	1	3	13
Recreational Facilities:	.00%						
Golf	.00%	0	0	0	0	0	249
Tennis	.00%	0	0	0	0	0	249
Pool	.00%	0	0	0	0	0	249
Other	.00%	0	0	0	0	0	249
Other	.00%	0	0	0	0	0	249
Hospitality:	85.38%						
Hospitality	89.72%	131	72	8	4	3	31
Public Areas	88.72%	108	92	12	0	1	36
Price	78.42%	48	101	26	8	7	59
Atmosphere	.00%	0	0	0	0	0	249
Returning	83.71%	95	79	15	6	10	44
Stayed Before		YES: 121		NO: 89		NO RESPONSE: 39	
Overall Rating:	85.89%	98	87	11	7	4	42

EXHIBIT 5.3. Sample Monthly Comment Card Summary for Hotel (Period Selected Totals)

TO: General Managers

FROM: W. H. Hughes

SUBJECT: MARCH GUEST COMMENTS

Front Desk – Pinelsle and Madison lead this category for the month, Pinelsle with a very respectable 96.91%, nearly perfect. Dublin has also done a good job scoring 94.25%. Concerns exist at Rochester with check-in and reservation accuracy, and Grand Beach continues to have problems with check-in and courtesy. LAX is still working on this area and has gained 2% over last month. Front Desk remains the strongest category company—wide with a chain average of 90.58% YTD.

Guest Services – For the month Pinelsle, Madison, Orlando and Greenway Plaza, with bell service being the strongest line item for all. Westchester is scoring poorly in the Concierge and laundry area, while Los Angeles has problems with phone messages and wake-up calls.

Guest Room/Bathroom – Harborplace, Denver and Wailea are in the top in this area. Nashville previously had many problems in the housekeeping area has worked its way up through the ranks to fifth position, an outstanding effort over last year. Sixteen hotels are below company average in this area. I suggest these hotels take a look at each line item of this category and include in your action plan. Poipu and Mayflower remain in need of renovation, while Westchester needs to look at engineering and maintenance issues. Use your comment cards for your punch list, you'll have an excellent start.

Room Service and Restaurant/Lounge Areas – Continue to slowly improve. Congratulations to Nashville 89.98% for the month in room service, along with Madison 89.64%, Bedford 89.62%, Hamilton 88.03% and Waverly 87.87%. In this area 17 hotels are below the company average of 83.11% for the month and 13 below 82.47% YTD. Value and promptness 67.03 and 69.63% are big issues in the restaurant/lounge area at Center Plaza and Rochester; while Dallas suffers from slow service, 69.05%.

Hospitality – Madison leads for the month with 92.73%, followed by Pinelsle, Nashville the Waverly and Harborplace. YTD its Harborplace, Pinelsle, Austin, Oakbrook and Orlando. In this category two or three properties at the bottom are resorts, Poipu and Grand Beach; price seems to be an issue at both, 68.48% Poipu and 64.13% Grand Beach. The likelihood of return is also low.

EXHIBIT 5.4. Sample Monthly Commentary on Guest Ratings

The two performance measures that Stouffer executives found most useful were average occupancy rate and average house rate (the average room revenue per night, after allowing for all discounts and complimentary guests) Hotel managers often had to make trade offs between these two dimensions of performance. occupancy could be increased by offering bigger discounts from posted prices (rack rates), but this practice depressed the average house rate. Conversely, holding the line too tightly on prices would typically lead to lower occupancy.

Another important measure of performance was gross operating profit (GOP) as a percentage of revenue. GOP was measured separately for the Rooms and Food and Beverage departments, and in total for each hotel (the total GOP included other departments, such as gift shops). GOP was defined as revenue *minus* purchases and the operating costs (mostly labor and purchased materials) of providing room or food and beverage services. Annual figures for the most important categories of hotel operating costs are shown in Exhibit 5.5: these included administrative and general expenses, advertising and promotion, maintenance, and utilities. As noted earlier, a significant portion of the hotels' advertising budgets was allocated to national programs and administered by headquarters.

The GOP earned by each hotel had to cover its nonoperating expenses: debt service, insurance, and property taxes. Nestlé did not disclose Stouffer's net profits after deduction of these nonoperating expenses. Bill Hulett pointed out that, in addition to operating profits, gains or losses in real estate values comprised a significant element of any hotel company's overall performance. It was not uncommon for a hotel company to develop

	1980	1981	1982	1983	1984	1985	1986	1987	1988
Number of Hotels (Beginning of year)	13	13	18	18	22	22	22	24	31
Number of Rooms	3,567	5,124	5,258	7,311	7,850	7,845	8,713	12,358	12,936
Avg. Occupancy Rate - %	64.8	57.1	57.2	57.3	61.1	60.0	60.3	63.0	63.2
Avg. Transient Rate - $[a]	49.83	57.74	65.17	69.50	76.17	83.09	85.10	87.45	92.60
Avg. House Rate - $ [a]	48.18	49.20	62.03	66.48	72.51	78.67	80.03	82.22	88.34
Total Revenue - $000	99,248	109,968	138,208	168,509	227,231	248,971	279,916	386,114	453,603
Rooms Revenue - $000	40,935	47,493	64,679	83,643	120,755	134,749	151,718	217,356	259,897
Food & Beverage Revenue - $000	53,093	56,371	65,819	76,908	96,691	102,510	114,162	147,938	169,345
Other Revenue[b]	5,220	6,104	7,710	7,958	9,785	11,712	14,036	20,820	24,361
Gross Operating Profit [c]									
Total, As % of Total Revenue	24.3	20.4	15.4	16.4	23.1	25.5	24.1	23.9	24.7
Rooms, As % of Room Revenue	77.7	76.0	74.4	80.7	75.3	76.1	76.7	75.8	75.7
F&B, As % of F&B Revenue	24.7	20.8	18.7	20.1	21.5	23.4	21.7	21.6	21.0
Operating Expenses									
% Total Rev.[d] - Admin. & General	7.6	8.3	10.5	11.2	9.9	9.8	10.8	11.1	10.7
Advertising & Promotion	3.5	5.6	6.9	7.4	6.9	6.9	7.3	7.8	8.0
Maintenance Expense	4.1	4.8	5.3	5.2	5.0	4.9	4.8	4.9	4.6
Utilities Expense	4.6	5.0	5.9	5.8	5.4	5.2	4.8	5.0	4.8
Total Labor Cost - % of Sales[e]	35.1	37.8	39.3	39.1	37.7	36.6	36.9	36.8	36.7
Per Available Room – Day									
Gross Revenue - $	75.72	65.04	76.08	76.66	83.31	87.21	89.09	91.98	97.42

Notes:

Data for some years include hotels subsequently closed or sold. All financial data include results for hotels opened during the year.

[a]Transient rate is average for "regular paying guests." Average house rate reflects reduced revenues due to complimentary rooms and rooms sold on long-term contract basis, e.g., for airline crews.

[b]Revenue from gift shops, etc.

[c]Gross operating profit = revenue minus purchased goods and direct labor expenses for rooms and food and beverages.

[d]Operating expense at hotel level includes allocated headquarters expenses for marketing and central reservation system, but not other headquarters expenses.

[e]Labor cost includes costs of personnel also covered under other operating expense categories.

EXHIBIT 5.5. Operating Performance—All U.S. Hotels, 1980-1988

a property, sell it for a profit, and retain a contract for management. Stouffer had followed this approach in several of the hotels it added during the 1980s. Thus, gains from property sales and ongoing management fees had to be taken into account in evaluating results. Consequently, the operating performance measures in Exhibit 5.5 did not reflect Stouffer's "total performance." (Some hotel companies *did* incorporate real estate gains in their reported financial data, making comparisons among firms difficult.)

The Stanford Court

The Stanford Court was located on Nob Hill, several blocks away from the central Union Square district of San Francisco. The 402-room hotel occupied a building atop the hill that was constructed in 1913 on the former site of railroad magnate Leland Stanford's mansion. Nearby were the traditional premier hotels of the city, the Mark Hopkins and the Fairmont. The famous San Francisco Cable Car line passed by the front doors of all three hotels.

Opened in 1972, the Stanford Court had been managed ever since by James Nassikas. Nassikas had earlier become well known as the General Manager of the Royal Orleans Hotel in New Orleans. With the financial backing of several investors, Nassikas supervised the renovation of the building (which had historical landmark status) and its decoration. The size and configuration of the building, however, meant that its guest rooms were relatively small, as were the lobby and meeting room facilities.

Nassikas's management style was intensely personal: a 1985 newspaper article described him as a "24-hour-a-day hotelkeeper," noting that he was personally involved in virtually every detail of the hotel's operations.

By 1988, the Stanford Court had earned the Mobil Travel Guide's highest rating, the Five-Star Award, for 15 consecutive years. It also received outstanding evaluations in a *Wall Street Journal* survey of corporate executives and in other published hotel ratings. Room rates at the Stanford Court were in line with the hotel's high-service level and its ratings: published rates in 1988 ranged from $155 to $245.

From the late 1970s until the mid-1980s, the Stanford Court's high ratings were accompanied by equally outstanding rates of occupancy and revenue per available room. Eventually, however, the continued growth of the San Francisco market attracted new entrants. By 1987, it was estimated that San Francisco was attracting 2.8 million overnight visitors annually, and the number had been growing steadily since 1983. Area hotel capacity grew even faster, reaching 25,400 rooms in 1988, with a reported average occupancy rate of 73 percent.

Among the recent additions to the lineup of hotels that competed with the Stanford Court were the following:

- *The Mandarin Oriental* (160 rooms, opened 1987), located in the city's financial district. This hotel, managed by the Hong Kong–based Mandarin chain, was highly regarded for its service standards. Published room rates ranged from $200 to $300.
- *The Meridien* (675 rooms, opened 1983), located near the recently built Moscone Convention Center. Published room rates (double occupancy) ranged from $180 to $220.
- *The Nikko* (525 rooms, opened 1987), located near Union Square. Room rates for this Japanese-owned hotel were $179 to $210.

In addition to these new properties, several other San Francisco hotels had recently been extensively renovated or were scheduled to be renovated in the near future. The Westin St. Francis (1,200 rooms, $175 to $270) had been renovated in 1987. The Four Seasons Clift (329 rooms, $160 to $270) was slated for renovations in 1989, as were the Grand Hyatt (693 rooms, $180 to $240) and the Stanford Court's Nob Hill neighbor, the Huntington (143 rooms, $180 to $240). Two new hotels were expected to open in 1989—the Park Hyatt (360 rooms) at the Embarcadero Center and the San Francisco Marriott (1,500 rooms) near the Convention Center.

The newer competing hotels typically offered larger rooms, more extensive meeting facilities, and amenities (such as health clubs) not available at the Stanford Court. For this reason, SHC executives anticipated that some renovations would be needed at the Stanford Court. The cost of these renovations was estimated at $5 million.

By 1988, the impact of increasing competition on the Stanford Court's business was apparent. Average occupancy fell from 66 percent in 1986 to 59 percent in 1988. In response to this, the hotel's management had accepted more group bookings at discount rates. As a result, the average house rate per room-night had declined significantly. The hotel had, however, maintained a "low marketing profile"—advertising outlays in 1988 amounted to only $172,000. About half of the advertising budget was devoted to national media such as *The New Yorker* and *Travel & Leisure* magazines, while 40 percent was spent for California publications and 10 percent for travel industry directories.

By the mid-1980s, Nassikas had withdrawn from the day-to-day management of the Stanford Court. According to Stouffer executives, a "caretaker" style of management prevailed with little attention being given to marketing or service improvements.

How Much to Bid?

Hulett saw the Stanford Court as a significant prospective addition to Stouffer Hotels. At the same time, he recognized that the price of the acquisition would be high. Thomas Stauffer, SHC's Senior Vice President—Finance and Development, had prepared estimates of the rates of return (pretax) that could be expected on the project at various acquisition costs. Even if SHC could acquire the Stanford Court for $90 million, the expected rate of return would be 4 percentage points lower than Nestlé's normal "hurdle rate" for investments. Hulett wondered whether the strategic value of the acquisition was sufficient to justify it.

Stouffer Hotels and Resorts: Strategy for the 1990s

In March 1990, the top management group of SHC was reviewing the company's progress during the 1980s and its prospects for the 1990s. Jim Biggar, CEO of Nestlé Enterprises, Inc., had hired William N. Hulett as president of SHC in 1981. Since then, Hulett and his management team had (in the words of one newspaper story) transformed it from a "sleepy, Midwestern" firm into "one of the world's fastest growing luxury hotel companies." SHC's performance during the 1980s had, indeed, been impressive and Hulett characterized the company as "the Hyatt of the 1990s." But there were important choices to be made regarding directions for future growth. One issue was how much emphasis to place on international expansion. In May 1989 SHC had ventured outside the United States for the first time by entering into a joint venture in which it managed and partially owned the seven-hotel Presidente chain in Mexico.

Within the U.S. market, Stouffer managed (and, in most cases, owned either wholly or in part) 34 hotels in downtown, suburban, and resort locations. While there were still many metropolitan and resort areas in which Stouffer was not represented, it was not clear whether or not the company should continue to expand by adding additional hotels similar to those already in place. Several of SHC's competitors had successfully developed "multiple brands" of hotels that were designed to meet the needs of specific customer segments. These included budget hotels, all-suite hotels, and long-stay apartment hotels. Hulett and his colleagues were well aware of these developments, but they had thus far chosen to focus solely on developing or acquiring first-class, full-ser-vice hotels that included a broad range of facilities for business and pleasure travelers. This was in concert with Nestlé's mission to have only quality brands. SHC executives were also aware of the increasing competition among hotels in the United States, due in part to the recent entries of several foreign chains into the market. More intense competition among hotels, especially among higher-priced establishments, meant higher costs for acquiring suitable hotel properties or developing new ones. It might also lead to lower operating margins via escalating promotional budgets or increased price discounting. Perhaps a more diversified "product line" or a greater presence in foreign markets would give Stouffer some relief from these competitive pressures. Before exploring alternative directions, however, Hulett wanted to evaluate SHC's prospects in the 1990s under its present strategy.

Developments During 1989

In addition to the Presidente joint venture in Mexico, Stouffer had added two hotels to its lineup in the United States during 1989. In December 1988, the company was the successful bidder, at $93 million, for the Stanford Court Hotel. Stouffer assumed responsibility for the Stanford Court in January 1989. Commenting on the acqui-sition, SHC President William Hulett stated:

> Our purchase of the Stanford Court, one of the country's foremost hotels by any measure of quality and public acceptance, culminates the transformation and nationwide expansion of Stouffer that was set in motion seven years ago. This prestigious property epitomizes our commitment to the highest standards of quality and anchors our positioning in the top ranks of America's hotel companies.

> The other 1989 addition to the chain was the 560-room Stouffer Esmerelda Resort Hotel, located in Indian Wells, California, which was developed and built by SHC and opened in September.

During the year, SHC announced plans for the development of a new 600-room hotel in downtown Chicago. This property, to be named the Stouffer Riviera, was scheduled to open in mid-1991. It was a joint venture of SHC and Denka Fudosan, U.S.A., a subsidiary of Denki Kagaku Kogyo, a Japanese chemical company. Ac-cording to a Stouffer press release, the partners would invest a total of $82 million in the Riviera project.

In January 1990 SHC had announced plans to develop a $50 million, 400-room hotel adjacent to Atlanta's Hartsfield International Airport. Stouffer's partners in the Atlanta project were London and Edinburgh Trust PLC and Balfour Beatty Developments, both from London, England. Even more recently, in February, Stouffer had been selected to develop a new hotel on an island in San Diego harbor, a 400-room, $85 million project. Another new 367-room Stouffer resort hotel was under construction in St. Petersburg, Florida, with a projected cost of $88 million.

Stouffer's Performance, 1981-1989

Exhibit 5.6 summarizes trends in Stouffer's performance during the years 1981-1989 and the budgeted fig-ures for 1990. These trends had been presented by Bill Hulett, in a series of charts, to a meeting of Nestlé top management in early 1990. As shown in the exhibit, the results for 1989 showed improvement over 1988 in all dimensions. (The administration and selling expenses shown in Exhibit 5.5 are those incurred by SHC itself; the administration and general and advertising and promotion expenses shown in Exhibit 5.6 are those reported at the *individual hotel* level.)

Ronald Nykiel said that the Stanford Court's performance during its first year as a Stouffer hotel had not been entirely satisfactory. The process of "Stoufferizing" the hotel had proceeded slowly, he said, but was continuing. Occupancy rates at the Stanford Court, as at other San Francisco hotels, had been depressed since the dra-matic and intensively publicized earthquake that struck the Bay Area in October 1989.

Year	Occupancy %	Avg. Transient Rate-$/Room	Gross Oper. Rev.-Mil $	Gross Oper. Profit-Mil $	Management Fees-Mil $	Corporate Adm. & Sell. Exps.-Mil $
1981	57.1	57.74	110	22	4.4	5.3
1982	57.2	65.17	138	21	5.4	8.0
1983	57.3	69.50	169	28	6.5	8.6
1984	61.1	76.17	227	52	8.6	11.9
1985	60.0	83.09	249	63	9.4	11.2
1986	60.3	85.10	280	68	10.5	11.8
1987	63.0	87.45	386	92	14.7	13.8
1988	63.2	92.60	454	112	17.8	14.6
1989	63.8	99.07	508	118	19.6	17.6
1990*	65.9	109.12	563	152	22.7	17.8

*Budget

EXHIBIT 5.6. Trends in Stouffer's Performance, 1981-1990. *Source:* Company Records.

Stouffer's marketing programs were expanded in 1989: total expenditures increased from $13.9 million to $16.1 million, and the 1990 marketing budget called for a further increase to $16.9 million.

Industry Developments During 1989

The hotel industry continued to be intensely competitive during 1989, although there were some indications that the rate of expansion in room capacity was diminishing. According to estimates by Laventhol and Horwath, demand for lodgings grew by 3.8 percent in 1989 while room supply grew by 2.5 percent. New hotel construction declined by 16 percent, to a level 32 percent lower than in the peak year of 1987, reflecting the impact of the changes in the tax laws.

While reduced new hotel construction suggested that supply and demand would eventually come into a better balance, industry observers continued to express concern about an "overhang" of excess supply that was attributed to earlier tax shelter–oriented development. The average rate of occupancy for the industry as a whole in 1989 was estimated at 63.8 percent, up from 62.3 percent in 1988. Price increases were modest in 1989, and discounting of rates was widespread; the average percentage discount (actual revenue per night versus rack rate) was over 20 percent in most regions.

Stouffer occupancy for 1989 for hotels and resorts in full operation for the year was 64.4 percent. The figures in Exhibit 5.6 reflect all hotels and resorts including Grand Beach (partially operational last quarter 1989 due to Hurricane Hugo), Esmeralda (opened in the fall of 1989), and the Stanford Court (11 months of 1989).

While U.S. investors' interest in hotel projects had diminished, foreign capital was increasingly available for expansion by domestic developers and domestic chains, with the big Japanese banks, among other financial institutions, having committed to strong investments in the U.S. lodging market. Two factors were driving this commitment: the desire to participate in the expanding travel market, calculated to be the largest in the United States by the end of the 1990s, and the desire to earn a premium on real estate investments that could be made in the United States at interest rates 1 to 3 percentage points higher than the cost of funds at home. Resort investments of this type were particularly prominent, but foreign-based chains and foreign capital were now beginning to be well established also in second-tier cities such as those of the industrial Midwest.

Reduced availability and rising costs of qualified and motivated staff continued to present problems for the industry. Moreover, one consequence of projections that travel would become the nation's largest industry by the end of the 1990s was that the unions' efforts to organize hotel workers on a regional market basis were intensifying. At the end of 1989, there were rumors that spring would see an islands-wide strike in Hawaii. Congress was considering a number of bills that would raise staff costs, including bills dealing with employer responsibilities for health care and day care.

Stouffer's Prospects in the 1990s

Since the repositioning and national program was begun in the early 1980s, SHC had pursued a highly focused strategy. All Stouffer Hotels were designed to appeal to the same target customer: the high-income, frequent business traveler. All of the hotels added since 1983 were first-class or deluxe in terms of facilities, appearance, and service. This strategy had produced outstanding results: the chain's average occupancy rate had

Metro Area	Stouffer	Four Seasons	Ritz Carlton	Westin	Hyatt	Marriott
New York						
Manhattan	-	1	1	1	1	1
Airports						1
Los Angeles						
City	-	1	-	3	3	2
Airport	1				1	2
Chicago						
City	-[a]	2	-	1	2	1
Airport/Suburbs	1	-	-	1	6	4
Philadelphia	1	1	1	-	1	1
San Francisco						
City	1	1	1	1	3	2
Airport	-	-	-	1	1	1
Detroit	-	-	-	1	-	3
Boston	1	1	1	1	1	8
Houston	1	2	1	2	2	8
Washington, DC	2	1	2	1	8	12
Dallas	1	1	-	1	2	5
Miami	-	-	-	-	2	3
Cleveland	1	-	1	-	-	2
St. Louis	1	-	1	-	1	2
Atlanta	-	-	2	1	3	6
Pittsburgh	-	-	-	1	1	2
Baltimore	1	-	-	-	1	2
Minneapolis	-	-	-	-	1	3
Seattle	1	1	-	1	1	1
San Diego	-[b]	-	-	-	1	2
Tampa	-	-	-	-	2	1
Denver	1	-	-	1	2	3
Phoenix	-	-	1	1	1	-
Cincinnati	-	-	-	1	1	-
Milwaukee	-	-	-	-	1	1
Kansas City	-	-	1	1	1	2

[a]A new 600-room Stouffer hotel was planned for downtown Chicago in 1991.

[b]A new 400-room Stouffer hotel was planned for San Diego in 1990.

EXHIBIT 5.7. Representation of Stouffer's and Selected Chain Competitors (Top 25 U.S. Metropolitan Areas—Number of Hotels). *Source:* Compiled from *Hotel & Travel Index,* Winter 1989-1990 (Seacaucus, MJ: Reed Travel Group, 1989) and American Hotel Association, *Directory of Hotel and Motel Systems* (Washington, DC, 1990).

climbed from 57.3 percent in 1983 to 64.4 percent in 1989. This was achieved as industry occupancies declined from 67.5 percent to 63.2 percent during the same period.

Bill Hulett believed that there was still considerable room for SHC to expand by continuing to pursue its existing strategy. He observed that the U.S. hotel business had become "polarized" during the 1980s, with the greatest growth coming at the extremes of the price/quality spectrum—economy hotels such as Red Roof, Motel 6, and Days Inn and upscale hotels like Stouffer and Four Seasons. With only 34 hotels in the United States, he suggested, there were still numerous opportunities for Stouffer to expand. Hulett estimated that by the year 2000, SHC could profitably grow to at least 75 properties and possibly 90. The majority of these were expected to be in the United States, with 10 to 12 in Mexico, 4 to 6 in Canada, 8 to 12 in Europe, and 6 to 8 in Asia. (Exhibit 5.7 compares Stouffer's representations with that of other hotel chains in the 25 largest U.S. metropolitan areas.)

Hulett commented on the "segmentation" strategies that some hotel companies were pursuing:

> Marriott and some others have adopted segmentation approaches, with several different hotel formats or brand names, out of necessity. They have saturated their markets with their original formats and now must look for new types of customers. The problem with this approach is that you risk confusing your customers.

Case Discussion Questions

1. What do you perceive to be the three major reasons Stouffer was able to outperform the industry during the five-year period referenced in the case?
2. Did Stouffer's operational, marketing, and development strategies appear to be interlinked? How?

NOTES

1. N. Johns & D. Lee-Ross, *Research Methods in Service Industry Management* (London, UK: Cassell, 1998), p. 142.

2. www.telecomprogramatsunit.com.

3. www.novauniversity.com.

4. www.ryersonuniversity.com.

5. www.webnetworksservices.com.

6. Case 5.1 is based on information contained in the following works: R. Buzzell, *Stouffer Hotels and Resorts Competitive Strategy* (Boston, MA: Harvard Business School, 1990), adopted from case study N9-590-096, revised 1/4/91, pp. 1-15; R. Buzzell, *Stouffer Hotels Case Study* (Cambridge, MA: Harvard Graduate School of Business, 1989), pp. 1-14; R. Buzzell, *Stouffer Hotels and Resorts: Strategy for the 1990s*, N9-590-097, revised 1/9/91, pp. 1-5. All quotations are from these documents.

PART II:
MARKET ANALYSIS AND ASSESSMENT

Market research and analysis when applied to the development process may undertake the form of a study. The three terms most associated with studies are market area study, project feasibility study, and site selection study. The broadest concept is the market area study that seeks to profile a given market and assess its economic vitality, general market characteristics, and potential (supply and demand) for the product/service under consideration. Once the overall market potential has been evaluated, a project feasibility study is undertaken, which looks at the feasibility of a specific venture from a supply and demand and financial perspective. Next comes the site selection study that evaluates and assesses specific sites for the given project. Often, a number of sites may be evaluated in the site selection process. There well may be considerable overlap between the studies, and frequently researchers and developers refer to the feasibility study with upfront references to the market and inclusion of the site recommendation(s). Analysis of supply and demand is the focal point of a feasibility study as it provides the key assumptions for market and financial models and proper scope.

We begin this part of the text by looking at how to analyze research findings and data in Chapter 6. First the locational analysis and site selection process is examined. Individuals, real estate agents, and developers often seek to sell a parcel of land or seek a joint venture partner to buy into a proposed development. Companies are usually approached by these entities with a specific site. If there is interest, the site is thoroughly reviewed (site selection study) to determine its general compatibility with a specific project or type of development. Assuming there is an interest the next step is usually to conduct a market study of the area to see whether the market is appropriate and in need of the proposed development. This step is often merged with the conducting of an actual project feasibility study which then would include the site selection and market area study findings. In Chapter 7, the locational analysis and site assessment process is discussed. In Chapter 8, the focus is on the design and components of a feasibility study including site evaluation and market area analysis. In Chapter 9, a process for market assessments for development planning is presented. And, in Chapter 10, assessing focal points and intuitive judgment techniques are explored.

Chapter 6

Analyzing Research Findings and Data

CHAPTER OBJECTIVES

- To discuss why the analysis of both qualitative and quantitative data is extremely important in research and in the application to market and marketing strategy.
- To delineate the difference between raw data, data prioritization, and data analysis.
- To provide an understanding of the concept of frequency.
- To recap the measures of central tendency, the median or the mode, and the mean.
- To explore the concept of normal distribution and asymmetric distributions.
- To discuss the concepts of the normal curve and standard deviation.
- To present some standard tests for quantitative data.
- To look at different techniques for the analysis of data.

In previous chapters, a review of qualitative and quantitative research methodologies was presented as well as integrative methods. Each of these topics focused on the various techniques and approaches involved with data collection. In this chapter, the focus is on the data analysis process. Data in raw form usually is not appropriate for managerial or scientific decisions. A sound data analysis process takes raw data and organizes it, classifies or categorizes it, and prioritizes it. The analytical process raises questions and provides directions. Is more research and data collection necessary to support potential findings? What stands out in the process that strongly supports the original probes? Are there sufficient data to draw a conclusion or provide sought after answers? And, can recommendations be made and be supported by the data and analysis of the findings?

While researchers often focus on the analysis and verification of quantitative research data, qualitative research findings also require analysis and verification. In this chapter both and related approaches to the analysis of research findings and data are discussed.

ANALYSIS OF QUALITATIVE RESEARCH FINDINGS

Qualitative research findings require analysis just as much as qualitative data before any reliable conclusions or recommendations can be stated. In fact, in certain circumstances qualitative research findings taken at face value can be misleading and can even lead to faulty recommendations and disastrous decisions.

Assessment

It is important to recognize that the qualitative research findings can be influenced by numerous variables. These include the actual structure of the research process/technique itself; the

Handbook of Marketing Research Methodologies for Hospitality and Tourism
doi:10.1300/5927_07

wording of written or oral questions; the makeup of the subjects/participants; the personality and attitude of the researcher (when interface with the subjects occurs, that is, focus groups, interviews, and so forth); the timing and environment in which the research was conducted, and so on. An assessment of every aspect leading up to the findings is essential in qualitative research. Poorly worded questions, illogical order, an unprofessional or poorly prepared focus group discussion leader, and one dominant personality can have substantial impact on the initial research findings.

Process Review

Another key step to support usable and sound findings is a pre- and postreview of the actual process(es) utilized in conducting qualitative research. One key consideration here centers on an assessment of the compatibility of the process selected with the topic and scope of the research. Another focal point of the process is the environment in which the research was performed. Environment includes the actual space and related conditions (focus group) as well as the overall environment at the time of the research. The key point with respect to timing is relative normality versus the abnormal. In dealing with behavioral and attitudinal assessments it is important to duly note any significant external events that could impact the subject participants' responses. For example, people's attitudes toward air travel were dramatically impacted post 9/11. Many political, social, and even individual circumstances can have an impact so strong that it would be prudent to reschedule or redo the research at another time.

Control

There are numerous control issues that need to be taken into consideration since each may influence the qualitative research findings and related analysis. Special attention needs to be applied at the outset or planning of the research to assure that the subjects selected are representative of the audience or population related to the research. During the process (focus group), is one of the subjects tainting the whole group due to a personality trait or dominance? Has the group discussion leader gone beyond the parameters of the research guidelines with probes or other inquiries? Has the facilitator overcontrolled the respondents and contaminated the research findings? Is the analysis of the data being undertaken and provided on a timely basis? Were there adequate observational opportunities during the research process to allow for further probes or key follow-up inquiries? And, was the analysis process objective, open, and timely?

Interpretation

It is also a good practice to allow for multiple interpretations of the findings related to qualitative research. What do the findings mean to the totally objective individual? What do the findings mean to the researcher? What do the findings mean to the professional in the field or management? How do these compare? Are they compatible and predictable interpretations? Should management be different and how will this be addressed and how could it influence the others? Is the nature of the research technical and do the findings require a depth of expertise in the topical area just to do the interpretation and analysis? Is it possible that more than one analytical conclusion or position can be reached on the same set of research findings? Is the interpretation and analysis of the findings sound enough to stand on its own and not require quantification? It is important to understand that the outcome of the qualitative research analysis process is only as competent as the individual(s) doing the analysis.[1]

Prioritization

Another key consideration in the analysis of qualitative research findings is the weight or relative importance of one finding over another. Normally, when analyzing qualitative research findings and subsequently when presenting the findings, the most important or significant comes first. The researcher must be careful not to push his or her own findings up or down the priority list of findings. Likewise, it is the researcher's/analyst's responsibility to properly position key findings even in the face of a management perspective that differs. An example of this was some focus group research conducted by a leading research organization for a major hotel chain a number of years ago. The qualitative research undeniably supported a 360 degree change in merchandising in the chain's gift shops. On the surface and during the initial briefing, management was very skeptical. The chain (at the time) had 80 percent male guests and gift shops were stocked to the ceilings with male-related merchandise. One senior executive stated: "We are meeting our customers' needs—that is why these gift shops are there and are profitable." The researcher and analyst had stated just the opposite—the chain's gift shops were not addressing their customers' needs and could be extremely popular. It became most evident that the researcher and analyst better quickly prioritize their findings in this area, get them on the table quickly, or they were going to lost not only their audience but also their credibility. Fortunately, they did just that. They stated: "We were also astounded by the responses provided by your customers and probed a little bit further." The researcher and analyst then ran a five-minute video tape of customer after customer expressing the same feelings and desires related to the merchandise in the gift shop—both completely the opposite of the management's perspective. The findings revealed a deep guilt about being away from their family and very strong desire to purchase gifts for their spouse and children in those gift shops that contained almost all male-related merchandise. Even with this visual evidence management remained skeptical and suggested that the research was bogus. The researcher and analyst countered with an offer to resolve the dilemma by setting up a test. Four company/management selected gift shops would be merchandised and stocked (85 percent +) with female and child gift related items. Hours would be changed to coincide with meeting adjournments and food and beverage service outlet closing times. The marketing and promotional messages would be changed to reflect this new set of customer needs and suggested behavior. The results would be presented to management and would determine the research firm's compensation and future relationship with the chain. The results from these test locations were as astounding as the initial research findings. The test gift shops showed an average of 500 percent increase in sales and an even greater percent increase in profits. Needless to say, management quickly reprioritized its gift shop related plans.[2] This brings us to the next key point with respect to qualitative research findings and analysis.

Actions

Qualitative research findings and related analysis should conclude with action steps or recommendations. These recommendations can be very different in nature, but should be considered a key part of the qualitative analytical process. Yes, it is fair to say one such recommendation may be to take no action at all. This simply means that the research findings may have confirmed or validated that an existing situation is fine or that without further research (qualitative or quantitative) no steps should be undertaken. Additional research, quantification, or experimentation are all valid actions or recommendations that can be made at the conclusion of the analysis process. Other actions can be specifically recommended change processes or new policies, products, services, and so forth. The point is research that sits on a shelf serves neither the researcher, academician, management, nor the customer/market. For research to have meaning and usefulness it needs to be supportive of some form of action, a next step, or recommendation, even if it is no action. Figure 6.1 summarizes the groups or steps for qualitative analysis.

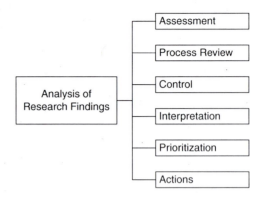

ANALYSIS OF QUANTITATIVE DATA

Quantitative data allow for statistical analysis that can help verify or provide confidences in the data. The first step in the quantitative analysis process is to count and rank the responses on the basis of frequencies. The second step is to calculate percentages. This section begins with a recap of these two initial steps and proceeds to look at other statistical processes and concepts related to the anal-

FIGURE 6.1. Analysis of Qualitative Research Findings

ysis of quantitative data. These processes and concepts include raw data, frequency, measures of central tendency, normal distribution, asymmetric distributions, spread of the distribution, variances, the standard deviation, inferential statistics, bivariate statistics, testing techniques, regression analysis, multivariate analysis, multiple regression, factor analysis, cluster analysis, and discriminant analysis.

Quantitative analysis begins with counting the number of times (frequencies) responses are given in the same category. One example would be using a scale of 1 to 5 and would be to count all in each category or number of responses in each, that is, the number of 5s, 4s, 3s, and so forth. The second step would be to then rank responses in order of their frequency. For example, 50 percent of the respondents selected 5, 23 percent selected 4, and the balance selected 3. Therefore, the responses were between 5 and 3 (this is defined as the parameters) and the response with the highest frequency was 5. These data can now be depicted on graphs and diagrams.

Raw Data

Quantitative data start with raw data. Raw data simply means nothing has been done to extract any meaning from the numbers. Here, the first step is to count the respondents who answered a specific way. Having a simple 5-point scale the researcher usually counts the responses in each number category. For example, on a 5-point scale where 5 is the strongest agreement with a statement and 1 represents disagreeing strongly, the researcher can readily identify both the number and percentage of respondents who select 5, 4, 3, 2, and 1 as their choices. Both the number of respondents and percentage of respondents who answered a specific way provide the researcher and/or the manager with useful indicators.

Frequency

One of the first steps in the analysis of quantitative data is to count how often a particular response or score appears. In Figure 6.2 scores are presented for two groups along with the frequency and percentage that relate to each. For example, in group A, 5 subjects received a score of 9. Thus the frequency of occurrence of 9 is 5. This efficient way of organizing data is referred to as the "frequency distribution."

A frequency distribution gives a clearer picture of the aspects of each set of scores and of the relationship between two sets (groups). The scores of group A tend to be higher and the percent-

Group A			Group B		
Score	Frequency	%	Score	Frequency	%
1	0	0	1	0	0
2	0	0	2	2	10
3	0	0	3	2	10
4	1	5	4	2	10
5	2	10	5	2	10
6	3	15	6	2	10
7	3	15	7	3	15
8	4	20	8	3	15
8	5	25	9	2	10
10	2	10	10	2	10
Total	20	100	Total	20	100

FIGURE 6.2. Sample Scores, Frequencies, and Percentages

age receiving these scores is likewise higher than group B. Group A's scores are also broader in range than group B's, which tend to be clustered around the narrow 2-3 range. It is common practice to indicate the midpoint of each class (group) of scores as it provides the numerical value of all scores in that group for the purposes of additional analysis.

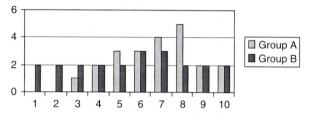

FIGURE 6.3. Sample Histogram

Data can be organized and presented graphically by representing the interval frequencies in graphic form, as a histogram or bar chart. Also, data can be plotted at the midpoint of each bar creating what is termed a frequency polygon. Histograms and frequency polygons both provide clear impressions of the main features of the data. Figure 6.3 illustrates a histogram related to the scores in Figure 6.2 and Figure 6.4 illustrates a frequency polygon of the same information. Preference of

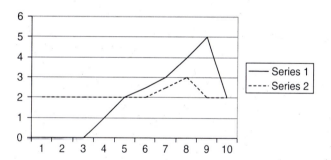

FIGURE 6.4. Sample Frequency Polygon

presentation is up to the researcher and how the researcher believes the data will best be understood and or best make the point desired.[3]

The next step in the statistical treatment of data focuses on ways to summarize the data. One treatment referred to as "central tendency" is a measure of the most representative score for the whole set. The spread of scores on either side of the central value is referred to as the "dispersion" or variability of the data. Both must be measured. Other features of the distribution may also be significant, such as the maximum and minimum values, as well as whether the data fit a symmetrical curve. Central tendency and dispersion are the most important descriptive parameters for the purposes of describing results and drawing inferences.

Measures of Central Tendency

The central tendency of a set of quantitative data can be expressed as the "mean." The mean is calculated by adding together every score and dividing this total by the number of scores, using the equation

$$\bar{x} = \frac{\Sigma x}{N}$$

where $\bar{x}$ is the mean, x represents the other scores, the symbol Σx indicates the sum of all the scores, and N represents the number of scores.

The median is defined as the value that has as many scores ranked above it as below it. For example, in the "A" set of scores presented in Figure 6.5, the median score is 80, because there are four scores above it in the rank order and four scores below it. If there is an even number of scores, as in the "B" set, the median is the midpoint between the two middle scores (see Figure 6.5) or in this case 78.[4]

The mode is the most frequently occurring value within a set of scores. It is found by simply inspecting the data. Figure 6.6 presents two sets of scores, A and B, and identifies the mode. It should be noted that a set of data can have only one mean and only one median, but may have more than one mode (see set B in Figure 6.6) if several values have the same highest frequency.

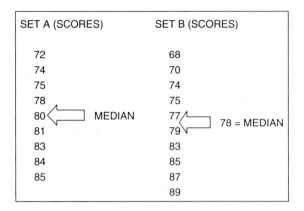

FIGURE 6.5. Sample Ranking of Scores and the Median

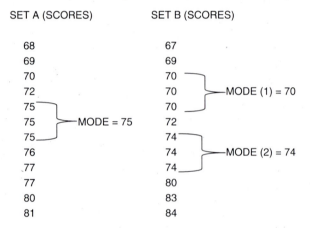

FIGURE 6.6. Sample Sets of Scores and the Mode

The mean, median, and mode can be calculated from either raw scores or a frequency distribution. The mean is calculated from frequency data by multiplying the scores by their frequencies, totaling the values thus produced, and dividing by the total number of cases. The equation for this is as follows:

$$\bar{x} = \frac{\Sigma fx}{N}$$

where x represents each score, f is frequency, Σfx is the sum of scores times frequencies, and N is the number of cases.

The median can be obtained from the frequency distribution as follows. All the scores are ranked in order from the lowest to the highest. For example, if there were 100 scores in total, the middle position in the series falls between the fiftieth and fifty-first scores. The median is, therefore, the midpoint between the fiftieth and fifty-first scores. The mode can be read directly from the frequency distribution, as the most frequently occurring value.

When data in a series are fairly symmetrically distributed about the central tendency, the mean, mode, and median have similar values and one could reasonably use the value which is easiest to compute, that is, the mode. However, if further analysis of the data is required, the mean is the preferred measure of central tendency. The mean summarizes all the data from which it is derived, so a change in any one score changes its value. This makes it a more reliable index of the underlying features of the data. The mean also has mathematical properties that make it suitable for more advanced statistical analyses. However, if scores are asymmetrically distributed about the central tendency, the mean will differ significantly from the mode and the median. It may, therefore, be less appropriate as a measure of central tendency for some purposes.[5]

The Normal Distribution

Figure 6.7 shows what is referred to as the normal distribution curve. The distribution has two parameters, the mean and the standard deviation. The standard deviation is a measure of central tendency. The standard deviation is always a positive number, whereas the mean can also assume negative values. The normal distribution is one of the most commonly observed and is the starting point for many processes. It is usually found in events that are the aggregation of many smaller but independent random events. Satisfaction scores, quality ratings, individuals' test scores, and so forth, are just a few examples of the data types that tend to have normal or close to normal distributions.

The areas of each bar on a histogram (see Figure 6.3) are proportional to the frequency of the observations within the interval represented by the bar. In an exactly parallel manner, the area beneath a normal distribution bonded by two vertical lines represents the portion of the cases falling within the limits. The normal distribution has useful properties that help in the description of data and support the formulation of many statistical tests.[6]

Asymmetric Distributions

An asymmetric distribution of scores is skewed. It may be skewed either positively or negatively. If skewed positively the right-hand tail is extended and if it is skewed negatively the left-hand tail is extended. Skewness separates three measures of central tendency. The mode always remains at the center point of the distribution, irrespective of its shape. The mean moves in the direction of the extended tail, and the median falls somewhere in between the mode and the mean, as shown in Figure 6.8.

Spread of the Distribution

The spread is the dispersion of scores on either side of the central value. Dispersion is how the scores of an interval/ratio variable are spread out from lowest to highest and the shape of the distribution in between. The most commonly used dispersion statistics are the range and the

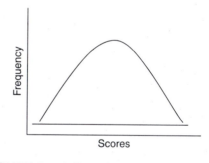

FIGURE 6.7. A Normal Distribution Curve

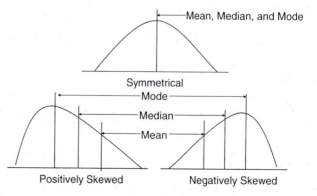

FIGURE 6.8. Distributions—Symmetrical and Asymmetrical

standard deviation. The range is an expression of how the scores of an interval/ratio variable are distributed from lowest to highest. It is the distance between the minimum and maximum scores in a sample. The range has a narrow informational scope. It provides the width of a distribution of scores, but tells nothing about how they are spread between the maximum and minimum scores. As previously indicated, the standard deviation describes how scores are spread across the distribution in relation to the mean score. It provides a standard unit of comparison or a common unit of measure for comparing variables with very different observed units of measure. Its computation centers on how far each score is from the mean or how far it deviates. Deviation score is the difference between the mean and the observed score for one observation. Two important properties are signed numbers (+ or –) and the sum of deviation scores, which must equal zero.

The *variance* is defined as the *sum of the squares of differences between data points and the mean.* It is a useful measure of dispersion because it reflects the distance of every observation from the mean of the scores, rather than just two arbitrarily chosen points. The reason for squaring the differences is that about half of them are negative, and for normal distributions the simple sum of the differences always approaches zero. The formula for calculating the variance is as follows:

$$\text{Variance} = \frac{\sum (x - \bar{x})^2}{N}$$

where x represents each score value, $\bar{x}$ the mean value, and N the number of scores. Thus the variance is in effect the *mean squared deviation* of all data from the sample mean.[7] The most widely used measure of dispersion is the standard deviation. In order to calculate the standard deviation begin by sorting givens and calculate the mean and deviation scores. The sum of the deviation scores should result in zero. Square the deviation scores and sum them to obtain the variation or "sum of squares." Next divide the variation by $n - 1$ to get the variance. Finally, take the square root of the variance to get the standard deviation. The elements of the standard deviation are arrived at as follows:

- You square deviation scores to remove negative signs and to obtain a sum other than zero.
- You divide the sum of the squares by $n - 1$ to adjust for sample size and sampling error.
- You take the square root of the variance to obtain directly interpretable units of measure (units instead of squared units).

Scores

The value of a score, *X,* can be expressed in the following three ways: first, as a raw score the observed value of *X* in its original units of measure such as inches; second, as a deviation score, the difference between a raw score and a mean, also in its original units of measure; and, third, as a standardized score, as a number of standard deviations (SDs) from the mean.

Standardized scores or *Z-scores* express a raw score as a number of standard deviations (SDs) from the mean score. You divide the deviation score by the standard deviation to produce a measure of *X* in the standard deviation units.

Inferential Statistics

Inferential statistics are used to draw inferences about a population from a sample. Descriptive statistics often do not provide all the necessary information about a research situation. Service industry researchers often need to draw inferences from data about market share, customer satisfaction, brand preference, motivation, training, and the like. Consider a simple experiment in which twenty subjects who performed a service task after four hours of training scored 10 points lower than twenty subjects who performed after one week of training. Is the difference real or could it be due to chance? How much larger could the real difference be than the 10 points found in the sample? These are the types of questions answered by inferential statistics.

There are two main methods used in inferential statistics: estimation and hypothesis testing. In estimation, the sample is used to estimate a parameter and a confidence interval about the estimate is constructed. In the most common use of hypothesis testing, a "straw man" null hypothesis is put forward and it is determined whether the data are strong enough to reject it. Inferential statistical analysis is used when ideas, hypotheses, or predictions need to be tested. Inferential statistics can relate to a pair of variables (bivariate) or to a larger number (multivariate). Obviously, the mathematical complexity of the calculations increases with the number of variables that are involved.[8]

Bivariate Statistics/Statistical Tests

A statistical test calculates the possibility that observed results are due to the proposed hypothesis. Two general types of statistical tests are available for research. Parametric tests assume that the data being analyzed are taken from a normal distribution. Nonparametric tests do not assume data to be measured on an interval scale and the test populations are taken to be comparable in terms of variance (as in parametric tests). Nonparametric tests can be used with ordinal data, with skewed distributions, and for samples with widely divergent variances. Parametric tests are considered more powerful and can detect more subtle differences between sets of scores. It is important to point out that there is always the possibility that parametric approaches could produce inaccurate results.

Statistical tests can be employed for a variety of situations. A statistical test calculates the possibility that observed results are owing to the proposed hypothesis (i.e., that a particular dependent variable is influenced by an independent variable). If the test suggests that differences between groups may be due to the independent variable, the results are said to be significant. Statistical tests also seek to put a figure to significance, expressing it as a level of confidence or a percentage of likelihood that the hypothesis is correct. The acceptance level for most research work is 95 percent. The level of confidence is calculated by converting the difference between two sets of scores into a standardized measure of deviation known as the test statistic. The test statistic is then converted into probability, using published tables analogous to the normal distribution tables. The lower the level of significance, the more convincing the outcome of the survey or experiment.[9]

Testing

Three tests researchers may utilize include the *t* test, the *Z* test, and their nonparametric equivalent, the Mann-Whitney test. The *t* test is employed to establish whether there is any significant difference between the means of two sets of scores. It does this by calculating a *t*-statistic, which effectively consists of the difference between the two means divided by the mean of the two standard deviations. The *Z* test, or normal distribution test for independent samples, may also be used to compare the mean scores of two independent samples. Like the *t* test, it compares the means and standard deviations of the two samples, but it converts them to a *Z* value, from which probability can be derived using normal distribution tables. The *Z* test and *t* test are similar in outcome, but the *t* test is better suited to samples of thirty or fewer. The samples for a *Z* test need not be exactly the same size, but it is assumed that the two sets of scores come from normal populations with equal variance.

The nonparametric Mann-Whitney test makes no assumptions about the normality or variance of statistical data. Its rationales and procedures differ from t and Z testing. The Mann-Whitney test is conducted by taking all scores from the two test samples and combining them into one large group. The scores are ranked from lowest to highest. If the scores on one sample are ranked on average lower or higher than the other, it may be suspected that the two samples were not derived from the same population. The test determines the probability that a given separation between the ranks of the two samples could have arisen by chance.

While statistical tests with complex formulas appear overconvincing, researchers need to remember that they can never prove beyond all doubt that the differences between two groups are not caused by chance alone. It should also be remembered that hypotheses must be realistic and be based on experience in order to reflect any organizational situation accurately.[10]

Correlation

Correlation aims to relate one variable to another. It does so by calculating the extent to which one variable increases as the other is increased. A numerical value known as the correlation coefficient can be calculated to describe the relationship between two variables. The most common measure of correlation is the Pearson's coefficient of correlation (usually represented by the letter r). One way correlation studies may be presented is through the use of a scattergram. A scattergram provides an impression of how variables are correlated with each other. The correlation coefficient conveys two pieces of information. First, it is a measure of the spread of points about an imaginary line. The closer the points are to this line the larger the value of r. Second, if the r is squared it indicates how much of the variation in the y scores can be explained by knowing x.

In Figure 6.9 the sample scattergram shows an r value of 0.9. Thus, 81 percent ($0.9^2 \times 100$) of variation in y can be predicted by knowing x.

Another useful analytical tool for correlation analysis applied to nonparametric data is Spearman's rank correlation procedure. This is based on two sets of data and their rank orders. If they are the same, the rank correlation coefficient (known as Spearman's *rho* or p) is $+1.00$. Values in between indicate a partial correlation.

Regression Analysis

The goal of regression analysis is to determine the value of parameters for a function that cause the function to best fit a set of data observations that the researcher provides. Regression analysis carries correlation one stage further. It determines whether two sets of data fit a straight line graph using a standard mathematical formula: $y = ax + c$. In linear regression, a function is a linear (straight line) equation. Regression can demonstrate a relationship between two variables, but like correlation it cannot prove causality.[11]

Multivariate Analysis

Multivariate analysis is a generic term for any statistical technique used to analyze data from more than one variable. Multivariate procedures represent a type of inferential analysis that deals with several variables at the same time. These procedures include testing by analysis of variance, multiple regression, factor, cluster, and discriminant analysis. As we indicated, Z and t tests are based upon the difference between mean

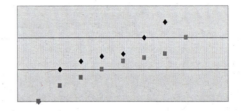

FIGURE 6.9. Sample Scattergram

scores of two data sets. Group differences can also be detected by the analysis of variance (ANOVA). This procedure has the advantage in that several data subsets and several variables can be examined at once. A difference between the responses from any one subgroup and those of the population as a whole is indicated by a difference in variance, which can be converted to a single test statistic, the F value. However, further testing (e.g., t testing) is necessary to find which and how many subgroups are significantly different from the rest.

The value of F is calculated by first ascertaining the values of the two or more subgroup means and the total population mean. Next, the differences between each subgroup mean and the population mean are calculated, squared, multiplied by the number of scores in that subgroup, and then added together. The total of these values is divided by the number of *degrees of freedom* (the number of subgroups minus 1), providing the *between variance.*

The difference between each score and its own subgroup mean is then calculated and squared. The sum of these values is divided by the degrees of freedom (i.e., the total number of scores minus the subgroups) to produce the *within variance.* The F ratio is calculated by dividing the between variance by the within variance and compared with a "chance" value of F, obtained from published F tables.[12]

Multiple Regression

Modeling data and seeking a relationship between a dependent variable and an independent variable is termed multiple regression. It differs from simple linear regression in that it allows for more than one independent variable to be considered.[13]

Factor Analysis

Factor analysis is a term that relates to simplifying data by identification variables in the data set. The variables are grouped together into a smaller number of factors resulting in patterns within the data. There are two stages to factor analysis: principal components analysis (PCA) and rotation. PCA groups the variables through correlation. Higher correlation variables between any pair of variables are taken to indicate a relationship between them. The PCA procedures, therefore, consist of calculating all possible correlation coefficients and identifying and grouping the relationships. Rotation is a mathematic procedure in which the list of principal components is compared with regular geometric arrangements of factors. The objective is to identify the exact geometric position of each variable relative to each factor. There are two types of rotation, orthogonal rotation and oblique rotation. Orthogonal rotation assumes that the factors are all at right angles to one another. Oblique rotation assumes that the factors are angled in other ways, and calculates the correlation between them.[14]

Cluster Analysis

Cluster analysis seeks to identify groups of respondents who give similar responses to two or more variables. Data points are plotted against the two variables as if they were coordinates in planar space. Spatial distances between each point are then calculated using Pythagoras's theorem. Computer output will show a tree of special relationships called a dendogram. The dendogram helps identify which points are close to one another and which are far apart and assigns them to clusters. Figure 6.10 illustrates a dendogram cluster.[15]

Cluster analysis often needs to use more than two variables. If three are employed, the computer would have to calculate interpoint distances in three-dimensional spaces. Figure 6.11 illustrates clusters formed by plotting points against two variables.

Discriminant Analysis

Like factor analysis, discriminant analysis seeks to relate variables together into similar groups called discriminant factors. The primary difference between discriminant analysis and factor analysis is grouping. In factor analysis, variables are related together on the basis of their correlation coefficients. In discriminant analysis, variables are placed in groups on the basis of their ability to discriminate within the data. Discriminant analysis is used less than factor analysis in service research situations.[16]

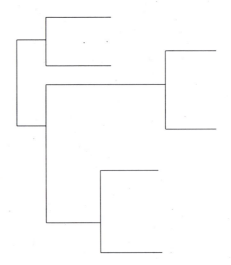

FIGURE 6.10. Sample Dendogram

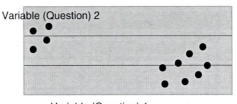

Variable (Question) 2

Variable (Question) 1

FIGURE 6.11. Cluster Plotting

PERSPECTIVES

There are differing perspectives on qualitative research findings and quantitative research data. Some believe that academician-quantifiable data are the best (if not the only) research output to be scientific and reliable. Others believe that qualitative findings are of equal value and more appropriate for their use. In the services sector, both perspectives can be found among research professionals. Many of the qualitative research methodologies discussed in Chapter 3 are extremely valuable and their findings are utilized to make key strategic decisions. Likewise, many of the quantitative research methodologies presented in Chapter 4 and the related analytical techniques reviewed earlier have a valuable and significant role in the corporate sector. In the latter sections of the book, we will explore the applications of these methodologies and analytical techniques.

Intuitive Judgment

It is important to note that in the services sector, research is often viewed as an indicator or provider of direction. In this role, the recommendations of researchers (even if based on the analysis techniques presented) can be and often are overruled by the seasoned manager's intuitive judgment. This may involve everything from brand and product decisions, to price points, to critical development decisions.

CHAPTER REVIEW

This chapter began by looking at the analysis of qualitative data. Focus was on how a researcher can become overwhelmed with information. A six-step process for analyzing qualitative research findings was suggested. The process included assessment, process review, control, interpretation, prioritization, and actions as the six key steps. The focus then turned to the analysis of quantitative data, indicating that this process begins with counting the number of times (frequency) responses are given. The concepts of ranking, raw data, histograms, and the frequency polygon as basic ways to organize and view data were presented. Next, measures of central tendency, the median and mode, and the concepts of normal/symmetrical and asymmetrical distributions were discussed. Additional concepts presented and discussed related to quantitative analysis and included the spread of the distribution, variance, standard deviation, and scores. In the latter part of the chapter, a number of statistical techniques and tests, including inferential statistics, bivariate statistics, the *t* test, the Z test, and Mann-Whitney test, were examined. It was concluded that the level of confidence acceptable for most research is 95 percent. Also, correlation, scattergrams, regression analysis, multivariate analysis, multiple regression, factor analysis, cluster analysis, and discriminant analysis were examined. Finally, the discussion concluded with intuitive judgment and the perspectives of the academician/scientific approach and that of the corporate or applied approach to qualitative and quantitative findings.

KEY CONCEPTS/TERMS

ANOVA
Asymmetric distribution
Bar chart
Bivariate statistics
Central tendency
Cluster analysis
Correlation coefficient
Discriminant analysis
Dispersion
Factor analysis
Frequency
Histogram
Inferential statistics
Multiple regression
Multivariate analysis
Nonparametric tests
Normal distribution
Observation analysis
Parameters
Probability
Raw data
Regression model
Scattergrams
Skewed distribution
Spread
Standard deviation
t test
Testing
Variance
Z test

DISCUSSION QUESTIONS

1. Why is it important to assess and prioritize qualitative research findings?
2. Explain the concept of frequency.
3. What is the difference between normal distribution and asymmetrical distribution?

4. What are the three standard statistical tests? How are they conducted?
5. What are the measures of central tendency and why are they important in data analysis?
6. Discuss how scores could be positively or negatively skewed.
7. When would inferential statistical analysis be utilized by a researcher? Discuss an application of the concept.
8. Discuss the two pieces of information conveyed by the correlation coefficient.
9. Why do you think the academician is more focused on the process and science of analysis and why is the corporate manager prone to focus on the findings (results) of the research process?

CASE 6.1. CHICK-FIL-A—ASSESSMENT, PRIORITIZATION, AND ACTION

Assessment of the research in the fast-food industry reveals a plethora of studies on high turnover rates and resultant customer dissatisfaction. This case example looks at how one fast-food chain listened to its employees, assessed the research, established priorities, and acted. The end result was higher employee job satisfaction, the lowest turnover rate, and high customer satisfaction. In the hospitality industry, a good climate helps to reduce turnover. And in industry sectors such as food service, this becomes especially important as turnover rates run very high.

Your assessment, prioritization, and actions must be on target when your hourly employee turnover rate is 100 percent less than your competitors and the industry sector. You know your strategies are working when many of your new investors come from within the ranks of your own employees. Both of these astonishing facts are true for the fast-food Chick-fil-A chain.

Chick-fil-A Inc. is one of the largest held restaurant chains and the third largest quick service in the nation with nearly 1,000 locations in thirty-four states and in South Africa. Chick-fil-A serves nutritious food products in malls, freestanding units, drive-through outlets, Chick-fil-A Dwarf House, and Truett's Grill full-service restaurants, and through licensed outlets in college campuses, hospitals, airports, businesses, and industrial sites. Their mission statement is to be America's best quick-service restaurant and to satisfy every customer. Their sales in 2006 reached more than $2 billion. Amazingly, the restaurant chain maintains a "closed-on-Sunday" policy for all types of Chick-fil-A restaurant concepts, in keeping with the Christian faith of the founder and his family.

Chick-fil-A has the following three simple business rules:

1. *Listen* to the customer.
2. Focus on getting *better* before trying to get bigger.
3. Focus on *quality.*

In national surveys conducted by leading market research firms, Chick-fil-A's core menu products have consistently ranked number one in their respective categories for "product quality."

Good-quality food ratings do not necessarily equate to high employee satisfaction and low turnover rates without some other strategies. The fast-food industry research revealed these high turnover rates and employee job dissatisfaction for years. What did Chick-fil-A do to substantially reduce turnover and improve job satisfaction? First, their assessment of the research findings involved "listening" to their employees. In essence, the industry quantitative research pointed out the problems and in-depth interviews (qualitative research) identified potential solutions. These potential solutions were evaluated and a number of actions were identified and prioritized for implementation. The results were then put into place. For example, one unique human resource strategy that contributes to Chick-fil-A's low employee turnover rate is allowing hourly employees to determine their own work schedules (within reason). Other human resource strategies include encouraging employees to grow and reach their potential by providing $1,000 scholarships to all restaurant employees. These scholarships may be used at the college or university of the employee's choice. Chick-fil-A's philanthropic efforts include a children's summer camp program and supporting foster homes.[17]

Analyzing research findings and data involves much more than a quantification and/or verification of numbers, data, or trend lines. It involves taking this information and assessing how it can be applied to improve products and services and/or prevent or resolve issues and problems. Translating research findings and data into actionable steps is what assessment and analysis should focus on in the applied environment.

In summary, Chick-fil-A employees have multiple managerial strategies that have resulted in an extraordinarily low turnover rate and resultant cost savings and performance enhancements. Its human resource strategy to retain and reward its employees and its flexibility in relating to employee needs have proven to be a success.

Case Discussion Questions

1. Correlations support the fact that satisfied and motivated employees contribute directly to higher-quality performance and a better customer service experience. Name two or three ways you could apply research and analysis to improve employees' satisfaction with their jobs.
2. What are some of the reasons or research and analysis steps missed by others (other than Chick-fil-A) with higher turnover rates?

NOTES

1. R. Hiebing Jr. & S. Cooper, *The Successful Marketing Plan* (2nd ed.) (Lincolnwood, IL: NTC Business Books, 1996), p. 18.

2. R. Nykiel, *Marketing Strategies* (New York: CORMAR Business Press, 2002), p. 88.

3. www.loyolauniversitychicago.com.

4. www.statisticsglossary.com.

5. www.insightexpress.com.

6. www.davidmalane.com.

7. www.psychologyuniversity.com.

8. www.davidmalane.com.

9. N. Johns & D. Lee-Ross, *Research Methods in Service Industry Management* (London, UK: Cassell, 1998), p. 107.

10. Ibid., p. 111.

11. www.pennsylvaniastateuniversity.com.

12. Johns & Lee-Ross, *Research Methods in Service,* p. 116.

13. J. Myers, *Segmentation and Positioning for Strategic Marketing Decisions* (Chicago, IL: American Marketing Association, 1996), pp. 32-33.

14. www.cornelluniversity.com.

15. www.multivariantanalysismethods.com.

16. Myers, *Segmentation and Positioning,* p. 184.

17. S. Cathy, *It Is Easier to Succeed Than Fail* (Nashville, TN: Thomas Nelson, 1989), p. 47.

Chapter 7

Location Analysis and Site Evaluation

CHAPTER OBJECTIVES

- To provide an understanding of how to assess the life cycle stage of land values.
- To delineate the guidelines for site acquisition.
- To present criteria for site identification and selection, including access, egress, traffic patterns, regulations, and zoning.
- To view the obstacles and opportunities related to locations.
- To provide an understanding of the relationship and compatibility between site, development concept, and market opportunity.

Many people believe that it doesn't take a rocket scientist or scientific approach to identify a good location for a development project. The acquisition of land and investment in a facility require substantial capital. Not conducting a comprehensive locational analysis and site evaluation can be devastating. There are numerous examples of investors who failed to check things as simple as future relocation of exit ramps or changes in traffic patterns, or to do simple soil tests that could have warned them that their development, facility, or concept was doomed to failure. Even the pros sometimes find surprises. For example, a group of investors funded a major new hotel at a western U.S. city airport only to find out a few weeks before the hotel opening that the city planned and actually had started to construct a new airport fifty miles away, and more significant was closing down the old airport. The entire financial structure of the hotel was based on twenty years with the airport feeding the hotel over 85 percent of its business. Needless to say, five years later when the new airport opened and the old shut down, all the financial and market assumptions were no longer valid. There are numerous examples of buildings that had to be vacated due to soil problems, which were not properly identified prior to construction. The risks associated with not doing a thorough locational analysis and site evaluation are just too great to skip the process.

TIMING

In most cases with most investments, timing plays a very significant role as well as has a bearing on price paid or received. This is true in everything from investing in stocks, to acquiring a professional athlete's contract, to buying and selling real estate. Where and when to purchase are the critical questions in land acquisition and site selection. Like the stock market timing doesn't always work. However, with research and analysis the odds of losing can be minimized given no external disasters. In land, the greatest appreciation usually occurs in those properties that are already experiencing robust growth in value. Buyers should not be dissuaded merely because a property is expensive compared to the cost of a property in a less expensive area.

Handbook of Marketing Research Methodologies for Hospitality and Tourism
© 2007 by The Haworth Press, Inc. All rights reserved.
doi:10.1300/5927_08

Often there is a delayed reaction in property values reflecting property potential, particularly where events such as abnormally low interest rates or lack of supply cause robust growth in average value. On a local basis, news of a new major roadway or of a large employer relocating to the area may cause real estate values to appreciate rapidly. If the news holds true, real estate values are likely to continue to rise after the roadway is completed or the major company has relocated. Development usually causes more development, which in turn feeds appreciation. The caution of course is that the events justify the initial increases. If they do not, there is likely to be a flattening or correction in values. In essence, the price should not unduly deter the buyer, as it is appreciation that ultimately determines rate of return, regardless of the initial price paid. Properties in areas experiencing the greatest appreciation are likely to continue going up in value in the future. Properties purchased in hopes that they may soon experience strong appreciation are riskier investments than those properties whose appreciation trend is already established.

The economics of the end use of the land influences the price potential. In essence, the land cannot appreciate beyond the economics of the end use. Price needs to allow for the end user to make a reasonable profit. Land enters its maturity phase when prices reach the plateaus of what the end user can afford to pay. Land usually continues to appreciate in the maturity phase but at a much slower rate because it cannot appreciate beyond the land owner's ability to pay. When urban and/or close-in (with respect to the city) land goes beyond the end user's ability to pay or the price is too high to justify the planned use, the land is passed by and the end user looks further out (from the city). Historically, this is one of the driving forces behind suburban development. There are a number of items that can influence and even change end-user economics including rezoning or innovative multiuse planning. In these instances, value may actually be added to the land over and above the normal appreciation due to location.

In researching land and in site selection, analysis of price and price trends plays a significant role. Normally, quality property is preferable to bargain priced parcels. Lesser priced land is usually a higher risk and/or encumbered with developmental constraints. The rule of thumb is that the nearer the property is to the point of final use in the appreciation curve, the less the risk, assuming the property was bought right to begin with. The reason for this is that property purchased near the point of final use provides greater leverage value because of the increased likelihood that the next sale will be a cash sale.[1]

LAND ACQUISITION CONSIDERATIONS

Land Value Trend Line

Property appreciation is not readily measured by an average annual rate of growth since the growth rate will vary dramatically depending on the relationship of the land to its use cycle. Land receives value in relation to its potential use. The three stages are the dormant stage, the growth stage, and the maturity stage, as depicted in Figure 7.1.

Just as the value varies by stage so does the risk factor. Purchasing land in the dormant stage is risky because the land may appreciate very little while in the dormant stage. When growth pressures approach the property, buyer speculation will fuel a bid-up in land prices in anticipation of near-term user needs. As user needs are met, land approaches the prices required to support the economics of the end user. And, since land value cannot exceed the economic capability of the end user, the land enters the maturity phase. It is during this later phase that land continues to appreciate, but at a much slower than during the growth phase. Many believe land should appreciate at more or less 20 percent compounded annually to be an attractive investment. Land in the maturing phase is, therefore, generally not suitable as an investment in itself.

Criteria for Purchasing Land

As indicated at the outset of this chapter, land acquisition is a sizable investment and needs to be approached with an understanding of all the critical factors. One way to help place the many research facts into a more meaningful perspective is to have a definitive end purpose in mind for it. The appropriateness of the land/ property in fulfilling the end

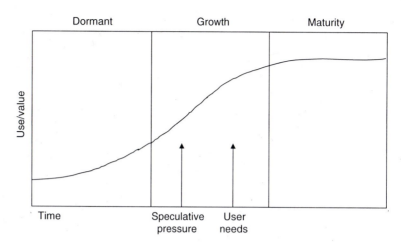

FIGURE 7.1. Land Value Trend Line and Stages

purpose can then be determined and the opportunities and obstacles evaluated at an early date. Often, the intended end purpose/use of the property may differ substantially from that envisioned by the current owner. It may even require zoning or some alteration of the physical characteristics of the property.

Reasons Not to Purchase

Remote land—not ready for immediate development—should not be considered for purchase for many reasons. In this situation, there are too many imponderables such as changing growth patterns, no growth, environmental constraints, unfavorable legislation, utilities, and so on. It is better to buy where the action is to reduce risk. However, in buying where the action is be sure not to overpay, underutilize the site (also includes no lesser quality than surrounding development), or undermarket or undermerchandise the land. The goal is to create value. Another don't is not to purchase land prematurely as economic downturns or changes in local economy may seriously hamper plans. Land should not be improved too soon, as improvements accelerate carrying costs and lesser holding flexibility. Further, as different sectors of a market are likely to perform or behave differently, it is prudent not to purchase parcels all in the same economic sector. It is better to spread the risk with a mix of property suitable for development in several income ranges.

Locating the Land

Basic research to find a good site (land) includes everything from driving the area, to utilizing a broker, to developing a model. Local brokers usually are one good source for identifying available land, assessment/tax data, zoning information, and sales/price trends, and other good sources are builders with land inventories. Obviously, professionals in land development, appraisers, and the tax assessor's office are also excellent sources of data. Other good sources include mortgage bankers, real estate investment trusts (REITs), financial institutions/banks, savings and loans, real estate and tax attorneys, accountants, civil engineers, soil engineers, architects, and appraisers.[2]

More sources of information that can help in locating desired land include municipal officials, utility companies, planning agencies, and traffic management officials. Usually, the city and state planning departments can provide detailed information on existing and potential highways, major thoroughfares, freeways, interstates, and mass transportation routes. The Chamber of Commerce is also a good source of information on business activity. Finally, newspapers and other local media can serve as another source of data.

Many times a great deal of the aforementioned data can be obtained by a buyer in the solicitation of land proposals from landowners or by obtaining a copy of recent feasibility studies for projects that required public records. For many seasoned professionals, their instinct combined with factual data proves the best approach. This requires spending a few days in the area, driving to potential locations to obtain a "feel" as to whether the land and surroundings will "fit" with actual concept/future development in mind. Also, by thoroughly driving the area prospective sites may be uncovered as well as new "hot" spots. Often, these discoveries end up to be the actual land desired.

LAND SELECTION GUIDELINES

Frequently, a field researcher will gather an overabundance of data from numerous sources. It is a good idea to collect as much as possible and to sort by data relevancy to the proposed land use concept/development. Guidelines for land selection should include a measure of the regional and local economic vitality. This is achieved by analyzing the trends in new industry development, corporate and regional office relocations to the area, and improvements to the transportation network, net new retail space, and its rate of growth. Researchers should also zero in on the housing and residential activity in terms of both growth and quality. And, finally, an objective assessment of the political environment and attitude toward business is essential.

Selection guidelines should include an evaluation of crime statistics as well as plotting "hot spots" and growth corridors or pockets. In the later phases of this land selection process the qualification, quantification, and, most of all, compatibility factors need to be major overall focal points.

To assist the researcher to approach the selection process, it is recommended that a "flow" or stepped process be utilized. These steps are depicted in Figure 7.2 and include regional analysis, community analysis, and site identification.

Regional Analysis

A considerable amount of information can be ascertained from the beginning with a regional analysis perspective. At the very least, the researcher will develop a sense for which communities within the overall area have the greatest promise and which communities have or are beginning to plateau. This is essential in assuring the investment made in the land purchase and related development has the best chances at appreciating. As a rule those communities most suited for future development will have good geographic characteristics, good water tables, adequate utility services, and hopefully an identifiable pattern of growth. Historical development patterns are helpful especially if they indicate saturation or overdevelopment, which is likely to stagnate values. More current assessments of growth corridors or "hot spots" may reveal where future development will be needed in the near-term future. Knowing the direction of the growth and timing of land inventories is essential to good decision making in land acquisition.

Another important factor is to look at income distribution through the census tracks and/or zip code analysis. These data provide a good indication of buying power and end-user economic capabilities. The key indicator here is the direction in which income is moving. Also, one needs to take into account what are the most likely positive and negative areas for development. Figure 7.3 represents typical areas of positive potential and those that may potentially be negative.[3]

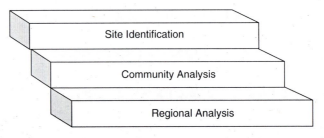

FIGURE 7.2. Steps in the Land Selection Process

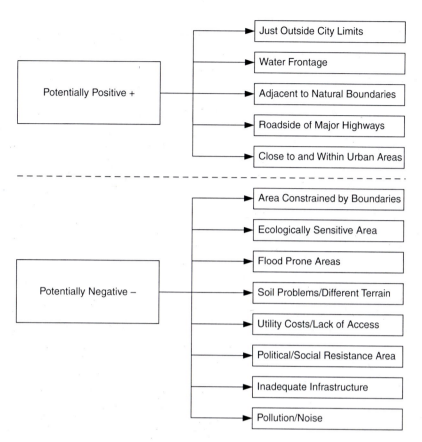

FIGURE 7.3. Potentially Positive and Negative Areas for Development

Community Analysis

After completing the regional analysis/perspective, the researcher usually will have eliminated many areas and narrowed the potentially positive growth areas down to a moderate number. Now the consideration becomes the site selection research process to narrow the choices to a specific community and/or communities. Here the focal point or key criterion is greatest appreciation potential. It is always more difficult to get a feel for every community in a given area/region in terms of ultimate positive potential. Narrowing the choice of communities down to one, two, or maybe three will help in this process. Ultimately the quality of the purchase will depend to a substantial extent on the depth of knowledge about the community.

Another key consideration is to project what the likely competitive positioning and related reaction the development will have/cause with respect to the competition. How will the development fit with respect to existing competitors and with those already in the pipeline? A key consideration should be market share. The developer needs to be sure the project will achieve its desired market share. Will the project achieve fair market share or will it outperform the market? How long will it take to achieve its market share objective? These are key questions that will have direct impact on the value and appreciation of the investment.

Competition is always a constraint to absorption, or complete sale or occupancy of a project.

Up to a point competition may actually help a new project's performance. If the competition has already created a traffic flow to the area and it is perceived as the "district" or "vicinity" for like businesses/projects, this may have an initial positive impact. Often, being on the same corner or intersection has its advantages over being an individual project in a location by itself.

The key indicator of demand and ultimately success for a new development is absorption rate. Absorption rate is how fast the project is filling up or is being occupied. One mistake a developer can make is to purchase a site and develop the project too far out (geographically). In this case while the land may be purchased for a really low price, it is most likely the absorption rate will be too slow to make the project meet the economic expectations. It is essential for the buyer to have a good grasp of both the historical absorption rates for the area as well as the appreciation rates in order to make the best business/development decisions.[4]

Site Identification

The very successful and experienced developers will tell you that one major consideration in site selection is visibility. Visibility has a great influence on sales, rentals, traffic, and so forth. A site with good visibility has the competitive advantage of self-advertising. Research has shown that sites/developments with good visibility outperform other like projects without this advantage. Good visibility means more awareness and recognition and lower advertising and merchandising costs. All of the advantages of good visibility contribute to a reduction in absorption costs. All developments/projects should make visibility a primary goal in the planning of the actual development. One reason traffic count is important is that it is a measure of good visibility and self-advertising value. This is one reason that being by a freeway or interstate highway is often an advantage in the sense of high visibility. This type of location also extends the geographic market as a result of the convenience of the freeway or interstate highway to the consumer.

Today, accessibility is important to consumer satisfaction because easy accessibility adds to convenience.

The easier we make it for today's time-stressed consumers, the greater our competitive advantage and the more likely they will purchase. Likewise, the physical appearance or first visible impression of the project or development is what will dictate the consumers' initial reactions to trial or purchase. Figure 7.4 provides a checklist for site selection.

Recording the basic data provides quick access to key phone numbers, addresses, and the like. Next is the process of the physical analysis of the site itself. Figure 7.5 provides a checklist for this analysis.

The physical analysis is not only important with respect to the basic decision process but also can/will be of immense help in the planning and architectural phases of any future development. The more copious the notes and data gathered, the less cost is incurred later in the process. Many of the items on the checklist may require further exploration as a number of these can potentially negate the development process. With the basic data and physical analysis completed it is time to proceed to the next critical checklist on accessibility factors. Figure 7.6 provides a checklist for accessibility.

It is important to note that there are a number of items on the checklist for accessibility that require some extensions. For example, driving times should be noted during rush hour and off peak, and when assessing a frontage road, ask if it will be necessary for the developer to upgrade or modify the road due to the proposed concept/development, and how much that will cost. Next is researching the utilities factors. Figure 7.7 provides a checklist for utilities related to site selection.

✔ Basic Data

Date: _____

Owner: _____

Address: _____

Phone: _____ Fax: _____

Site Location: _____

Crossroads: _____

Landmarks: _____

City: _____ County: _____

Firm/Broker: _____

Address: _____

Phone: _____

Current Use: _____

Income Producing: Yes ❏   No ❏

Current Zoning: _____

Proposed Zoning: _____

FIGURE 7.4. Checklist for Site Selection Basic Data

Completing the utilities checklist will help the buyer ascertain what the attitudes of the utility services and municipality are toward land developers. These can range from almost completely cooperative to hostile. It should be noted that any potential problems with utilities are usually very time-consuming and often complex to resolve. Delays in this area will directly add to costs. Attitudes are important because they provide a key reading on likely problems, delays, or other impediments to site acquisition and project development. Attitudes may be viewed within the context of the overall political, social, and environmental areas. Figure 7.8 provides a checklist for factors related to these aforementioned three areas.

The checklist for political, social, and economic factors should never be taken lightly by the researcher. There are numerous examples for potentially great development projects that never occurred due to politics, social factors, or environmental issues. In many of these cases, the nature of the problem or severity of the issues was not understood and the results were very costly.

One final checklist should be completed in order to put the prospective project (land acquisition and development) into perspective. Figure 7.9 presents a checklist for a comparative evaluation.

It is not only a good idea to employ these or other checklists during the research and data collection process, but also a good time-saving practice for the researcher to organize the file system (paper or electronic) to follow the same flow. This will lead to faster sorting and recall of key items.

Zoning and Other Regulatory Considerations

Zoning codes and constraints need to be a specific area of focus prior to any land or site transactions. Zoning in almost any form represents a constraint on the use of property. Zoning codes

✓ Physical Analysis

Size of property _____ net; _____ gross
Frontage feet _____ Other frontage _____

Planning problems due to: Describe
  Site configuration _____
  Access _____
  Topography _____
  Easements _____
  Water courses and storm drainage _____
  Objectional off-site features: Noise, unsightly development which would require special planning
  solutions _____
  _____

Planning opportunities due to: Describe
  Lake, river, stream, pond _____
  Attractive, mature trees _____
  Attractive views _____
  Attractive neighboring uses _____
Is site self-advertising? _____
Topography _____
Type of soil _____ Soil report available? Yes ☐ No ☐ Summary of report _____
_____
Will much earth movement, fill, or compaction be required? Yes ☐ No ☐ Cost _____
Will excessive foundation costs result from soil and topographical conditions? _____
_____

How much land may be lost due to:
  Vertical slopes _____
  Flood areas _____
  Unusual site configurations _____
  Setbacks and easements _____
Physical improvements Yes ☐ No ☐ Approximate value _____ Condition _____
Can improvements be utilized? Yes ☐ No ☐   Is demolition necessary? Yes ☐ No ☐
Cost _____
Does site possess any outstanding attributes? Yes ☐ No ☐ What potentials do these attributes
contribute? _____
Are there major constraints identified with property? _____
_____

Does property have any of the following constraints:
                                              Explanation
Floods   Yes ☐ No ☐   _____
Earthquake faults   Yes ☐ No ☐   _____
Objectional air traffic Yes ☐ No ☐   _____
Unsightly views   Yes ☐ No ☐   _____
Noise   Yes ☐ No ☐   _____
Unsightly neighbors   Yes ☐ No ☐   _____
In-flight pattern   Yes ☐ No ☐   _____
Fire hazards   Yes ☐ No ☐   _____
Slide danger   Yes ☐ No ☐   _____

FIGURE 7.5. Checklist for Physical Analysis

need to be thoroughly checked for cost-additions requirements such as dedicated street widening, sidewalks, utility rights-of-way, flood control, and so forth. Furthermore, all potential fees that might be imposed will need to be checked. These fees may be for such items as a sewer tap fee, park fee, water fee, flood district fee, bedroom tax, and so on. It should be noted that zoning codes may also restrict the type of structure that can be developed. Unzoned properties or properties that will require rezoning may present special challenges and risks. The bottom line is that the researcher and/or buyer must have a comprehensive understanding of the zoning regulations and process. Special consideration should be taken when the buyer or developer wishes to change the zoning or is contemplating a planned unit development (PUD). Figure 7.10 provides a checklist of such considerations.[5]

✔ Accessibility

	Driving Time	Miles
Distance to commercial hub	_____	_____
Distance to employment center(s)	_____	_____
Distance to airport	_____	_____
Distance to entertainment	_____	_____
Distance to freeway(s)	_____	_____

Type of construction and condition of frontage road _____

_____

Ingress/egress restrictions _____
Will frontage road accommodate proposed traffic? Yes ❏   No ❏   Modification ❏
Private road _____ State highway _____ County road _____
U.S. highway _____ Other _____
Any costs to acquire or improve access? _____
If private road, is there legally guaranteed right-of-ingress/egress to property? _____

_____

Any proposed highway and freeway plans that would affect property? _____

_____

Bus service: Good ❏   Fair ❏   Poor ❏
Other rapid transit available _____ Distance _____
How frequent is service? _____ Cost _____
Tolls: Bridges _____ Freeways _____

FIGURE 7.6. Checklist for Accessibility

✔ Utilities

Gas at site: Yes ❏   No ❏   Distance from site _____
Size _____ Cost to extend _____ Any problems with
use? _____ Service Fee _____
Electricity at site: Yes ❏   No ❏   Distance from site _____
Must relocate? _____ Go underground off site? _____ Cost _____
Any problems with use? _____ Service fee Yes ❏   No ❏
Water at site: Yes ❏   No ❏   Distance from site _____
Size, pressure _____ Cost to extend _____ Any problem
with use? _____ Water furnished by _____ Are costs
refunded to developer? Yes ❏   No ❏   Formula _____ Service fee _____
Water wells: Yes ❏   No ❏   Depth _____ Capacity _____
Any problems with use? _____ Depth of groundwater _____
Sewer at site: Yes ❏   No ❏   Distance from site _____
Size _____ Depth _____ Cost to extend _____
Service fee _____ Will pumping station be required? Yes ❏   No ❏   Cost _____

FIGURE 7.7. Checklist for Utilities

Another caution with respect to planning boards and politics is to look for signs that might result in a good project being turned down. These signs include the impact of the project on the character and lifestyle of the community, the desirability of growth itself, and simple political risk (especially in election years).

Environmental and Physical Factors

It should be noted that environmental assets inherent in a particular site/property also may require a substantially different type of land utilization and developmental approach than would otherwise be appropriate for the same location.

Physical factors such as the size and shape of the property itself are likely to be the most significant factors in site selection after location. Larger sites provide for the potential to plan a self-contained environment independent of off-site physical factors. In addition, the larger the site, the more the need to provide diversity of product to achieve absorption. Special attention should

✔ **Political – Social – Economic**

Is community discouraging growth through:
Moratoriums _____
Excessive processing time, indecision _____
Excessive fees _____
Environmental impact restrictions _____
Refusing services _____
Will there be vocal antigrowth citizens' groups to contend with? _____
Is there danger of zoning rollbacks? _____
Are there conflicting policy guides and jurisdictions which make it difficult to ascertain requirements and to secure approvals? _____

Are elections forthcoming which would place heavy political influence on governmental and municipal policies? Yes ❑ No ❑   Would these influences be positive or negative? _____
Are there planning policies or studies in the works which would affect the master plan and create an interim vacuum of indecision or no decision? _____

Are there any new taxes or tax hikes on the horizon which would have a material effect on feasibility? ____

Are there building code restrictions which would economically discourage certain types of construction? __

Are there fire department restrictions which would economically discourage certain types of construction and planning?_____
Are there traffic department policies which would economically discourage development?_____
_____ or reject development plans? _____
Are there pollution policies which would discourage or halt development plans? _____
Is environmental impact report required? _____
Are there rent controls? _____ Possibly in the near future? _____
Federal Housing Administration (FHA) loan outlook:
Area _____
Site _____
Sales or rental range _____
How many commitments will they give? _____
Do they have recent studies available? _____
Veterans Affairs (VA) loan outlook:
Area _____
Site _____
Sales or rental range _____
How many commitments will they make? _____
Do they have recent studies available? _____
Local bank advice _____
Local savings and loan advice _____
Local builder's association advice _____
Local title company advice _____
Local engineer's advice _____
Local mortgage banker-broker advice _____
Building department discussion _____
Planning department discussion _____
Availability of subcontractors, suppliers, and workforce _____
Local appraiser's evaluation of market _____
Realtor's advice _____

FIGURE 7.8. Checklist for Political, Social, and Economic Factors

be given to any potential problem areas such as soil conditions, terrain, tree cover, water table level, and the availability and capacity of utilities.

Opportunities and Obstacles

In evaluating a site, its limitations become apparent as well as its potential for the highest and best use. All opportunities and obstacles should be listed and studied prior to any financial commitments. The identified opportunities and obstacles are especially important with respect to

✔ Comparative Evaluation

How does property compare with other comparable properties in area? _____

Is property higher or lower in price than comparables?   Higher ❑   Lower ❑
Why? _____

Is there a particular potential for adding value to this property through creative financing, planning, subdivision, or rezoning that others may have overlooked?_____
_____

Is there a current or emerging new development pattern, trend, fad, or cycle which will change the potential of the property from what others have recognized it to be in the past?_____
_____

What development is land suitable for at this moment? _____

In 2 to 3 years? _____ In 5 years? _____

Would the land be an attractive investment, from inflation and speculative interests alone, if no value were added through planning, packaging, or rezoning? _____

What was cost of comparable land 1 year ago? _____

2 years ago? _____ 4 years ago? _____

Where is the price in relation to the ultimate end-user price? _____

At what time will the property justify the ultimate end-user price? _____

If property is currently at the end-user price, what can realistically be anticipated for inflationary-appreciation gain per year? _____

Considering terms and price, how long can the organization afford to hold the land before developing or selling it? _____

Tax advantages associated with property:
   Interest deduction _____
   Property tax deduction _____
   Tree removal _____
   Depreciation of trees _____
   Depreciation of equipment _____
   Depreciation of buildings _____

Major constraints associated with property _____

Major opportunities associated with property _____

How does investment in property compare with other opportunities available to the organization? _____

FIGURE 7.9. Checklist for a Comparative Evaluation

✔ Consideration for PUD

What is the planning department's informal position on the proposed rezoning? _____
_____

How does the proposed property relate to the regional plan? _____
_____

Will an environmental impact report (EIR) be required? _____
_____

What is the political environment with respect to the property? _____
_____

Are the community facilities available and adequate to support the new use under the rezoning? _____
_____

Where does the community stand with respect to the project?   ❑ Favorable   ❑ Lack of support

Is there anyone else or any other group that is likely to oppose the project? _____
_____

FIGURE 7.10. Checklist for Considerations for a Planned Unit Development

price, marketing strategy, and the feasibility analysis and other assumptions. Obstacles will provide limitations and opportunities will identify the potential upside. Both may cause a reevaluation of the developer's initial plans. When plans have to be modified, the earlier it is done, the better. It should be noted that potentials and constraints of a property may be the result of on-site circumstances and/or off-site circumstances. The circumstances may be physical, political, economic, legal, or environmental. In conducting the site analysis, a list should be recorded of any major factors or problems that could act as constraints on the property. Looking back at the history of the property may help to identify some constraints and looking forward at the overall development environment may help identify future constraints.

CHAPTER REVIEW

Knowing the right time and right site is the end product of a comprehensive locational analysis and site evaluation. This chapter provided the focal points and guidelines for conducting a comprehensive analysis. The many items that need to be taken into consideration in the analysis and selection process were pointed out. Some of the items included access and egress, environmental considerations, traffic patterns, competition, regulations, and zoning. Also presented was the consideration of obstacles and opportunities related to the site itself/location. Finally, the importance of the "fit" or relationship between the concept/development, the site, and the market opportunity was delineated. Compatibility of these three key components is essential for successful site selection, acquisition, and development.

KEY CONCEPTS/TERMS

Access
Appreciation
Boundaries
Broker
Codes
Competitive assessment
Configuration
Constraints
Depreciation
Easements
EIR (environmental impact report)
Egress
Flood plan
Frontage
Growth corridor
Land value
Patterns (traffic, air traffic, etc.)
Point of final use
PUD (public urban development; public utility district)
REITs (real estate investment trusts)
Regional analysis
Regulations
Restrictions
Site identification
Soil report
Topography
Traffic counts
Upside potential
Visibility
Zoning

DISCUSSION QUESTIONS

1. Why is it important to ascertain the stage in the life cycle of a prospective location?
2. What role does visibility play with respect to site selection?
3. How could configuration preclude site acquisition?
4. Why are access and egress important to site selection?
5. What are three obstacles to site selection?
6. Why is it important to understand the relationship between site, development concept, and market opportunity?

CASE 7.1. FOXWOODS RESORT CASINO—A MEGAFORCE

Site Location

Most people do not recognize the Foxwoods Resort Casino as the world's most profitable and highest volume operation in its field. One reason for this success is its extraordinary location—midway between New York City and Boston or, if you prefer, in the center of 70 million people. Foxwoods is no more than a two-hour drive from most of the major population centers in the northeastern United States. The site selection could not have been better. Its majestic location on a hillside in the plush green woods of Connecticut adds even more to this industry leader's position in the marketplace.

Casinos generate substantial cash flow. Total ownership garners more cash (profits) than a joint venture or minority position. This case example looks at a very substantial cash generator and profitable enterprise.

Foxwoods Resort Casino, like many gaming entities, could form a good case example in a number of management strategy areas such as communications, human resources, risk management, and marketing, to name a few. However, Foxwoods offers a more interesting financial example for a number of reasons. Not only is Foxwoods the largest and financially most successful gaming enterprise, it's also one of the largest nongovernment entities to have positively affected a state's and region's economy. Before presenting a snapshot of its financial significance, let's briefly look at the history/development of this unique facility.[6]

Milestones

February 1992—The original Foxwoods High Stakes Bingo and Casino opened on February 15. The casino at that time offered a 46,000-square-foot gaming area with 170 table games including roulette, poker, and blackjack. Although Foxwoods did not have any slot machines, it offered poker and the aforementioned range of table games. The facility, including the bingo-hall expansion, cost $60 million, totaled 250,000 square feet, and contained a retail boutique, museum, three restaurants, and a piano bar. The casino was built next to the original 2,100-seat bingo hall, which opened in 1986 and is now part of Foxwoods. The enterprise employed about 2,300 people, nearly all from Connecticut and Rhode Island.

January 1993—The tribe and state negotiated an agreement, which allowed the tribe to operate slot machines at Foxwoods. The tribe agreed to pay the state 25 percent of its slot machine win (called net win) each year. The agreement provided that the tribe's obligation to make such payments would cease if the state legalized the operation of slot machines anywhere else within Connecticut, or if any other entity in the state operated slot machines. The agreement provides the state with 25 percent of the slot revenues, or a minimum of $100 million annually.

November 1993—A $240 million expansion increased Foxwoods' size to 1.3 million square feet. Now known as Foxwoods Resort Casino, the total facility included five large gaming rooms with mixed slots, keno, racebook, table games, a theater complex, twenty-three retail shops, a beauty salon, and health spa. Four full-service restaurants were now operating, with a fifth restaurant located in the newly opened Two Trees Inn, owned by a limited partnership in which the tribe is an investor. An ice-cream parlor, a deli, and a pizza stand were also completed. The two hotels offered a total of 594 rooms. The expansion increased the number of table games to 234 and slot machines to approximately 2,650. Frank Sinatra helped Foxwoods celebrate the formal opening of the new facility with five performances in the new showroom/theater offering 1,400 seats, and with a large screen video theater with a seating capacity of 375.

April 1994—After federal recognition of the nearby Mohegan Tribe of Indians of Connecticut, the Mashantucket Pequot Tribe amended its slot revenue agreement with the state. The new agreement provided that both tribes' obligation to make slot payments would now terminate upon the legalization or operation elsewhere in the state of any kind of commercial casino gaming. Each tribe agreed to make payments of 25 percent of their slot machine win, or 30 percent in any year that the annual payment for such tribe falls below a minimum threshold of $80 million.

June 1994—Completed a $65 million expansion, adding another 300,000 square feet. Bingo moved to a new location, which offers 3,000 bingo seats and which can be converted into an entertainment center capable of holding up to 5,000 for headline performances and boxing events. The old bingo hall became a slot room, which increased the casino's slot total to 3,864. At this time Foxwoods' gaming area offered nearly 230 table games and a variety of entertainment options for the whole family. The casino gaming area measured 190,000 square feet.

October 1995—The success of Foxwoods' operations and management capability was recognized in October when a selection committee, appointed by the governor to review proposals for the development of a casino facility in Bridgeport, Connecticut, selected the tribe's proposal over a proposal submitted by an affiliate of Mirage Resorts, Inc. Authorizing legislation for this development was defeated by vote of the Connecticut General Assembly on November 17, 1995.

March 1996—Foxwoods opened the first full-service, nonsmoking casino on the East Coast. This was the second phase of a two-level 140,000-square-foot casino expansion project. The first phase, which opened on December 22, 1995, contains a state-of-the-art Racebook, an expanded poker room, and a 30-table high-limit gaming area. Foxwoods now offered its patrons 4,244 slots and 308 table games, as well as many other entertainment options.

July 1997—Foxwoods opened the first three levels of the Grand Pequot Tower. This first phase added 50,000 square feet of casino space including 958 slots and 60 table games and an additional 2,500 parking spaces. Two gourmet restaurants, Fox Harbour and Al Dente, along with the Intermezzo Lounge, opened in August 1997. The high-limit gaming area and Club Newport International opened along with some remaining floors of the Grand Pequot Tower Hotel in November 1997. The Veranda Café, a twenty-four-hour coffee shop/café, opened in December 1997 along with the 25,000-square-foot Grand Pequot Ballroom. Additional conference facilities opened in April 1998.

Fall 1998—Foxwoods opened a 20,000-square-foot state-of-the-art spa and salon along with the Villas at Foxwoods. There are twenty-three luxury suites with premium amenities located on floors 22 and 23 of the Grand Pequot Tower.

December 1999—*Casino Players Magazine* lists Foxwoods as number one in nearly half of all the categories evaluated for casino resorts in the United States and Caribbean. The resort casino averaging 40,000 guests per day is also ranked number one on a composite basis.

February 2002—Foxwoods celebrates its tenth anniversary.

June 2006—Foxwoods unveiled a plan for a $700 million expansion to be completed in summer 2008.

Overview

The Mashantucket-owned Foxwoods is the largest single casino in the Western Hemisphere, and the most lucrative in America. What is key to their success and the marketing methods they use are the issues for this case study.

With nearly 6,000 slot machines and 350 table games, Foxwoods Resort Casino offers the best in resort amenities; gaming in a relaxing atmosphere; live entertainment with headliners from around the world; and fine dining at Mashantucket, the ancestral home of the Mashantucket Pequot Tribal Nation.

In addition to the massive amounts of money generated by gaming, the tribe runs a successful pharmaceutical division, operates high-speed ferries through its Fox Navigation, and owns the Mystic Hilton, the Spa at Norwich Inn, and Randall's Ordinary Restaurant in North Stonington. The tribe also built and operates the $194 million Mashantucket Pequot Museum and Research Center, the largest American Indian museum in the country. It serves not only as a popular tourist attraction, but also as an educational resource for scholars.

The aftermath of the September 11 terrorist attacks might seem like the worst possible time to double the casino's capacity. A well-publicized gaming downturn, after all, led to layoffs throughout the Las Vegas economy at the time. Where the destination resorts of the Vegas Strip reported dramatic declines in fly-in visitors (as much as a 30 percent drop in work hours), American Indian casinos across the country held up very well, because they draw on day-trippers from the regional market. Foxwoods Resort Casino rebounded quickly. The shift from airplane to automobile showed up strongly over the Thanksgiving holiday, in which a record 87 percent of travelers drove versus flew. At the same time, Indian casinos reported a surprisingly good turnout. Gamblers at Connecticut's two American Indian casinos lost $120 million in November, boosting the two tribes' year-over-year slot machine win by 16.2 percent. The war on terrorism and uncertainty about the economy didn't deter players from leaving $63 million at Foxwoods Resort Casino in November 2001. Considering the economy and the world situation, these numbers are extremely impressive. The fact that the market has sustained a 16.2 percent increase shows how deep a market it is, and it tells a good story about the ability of Connecticut to garner revenues. Moreover, when casinos in Las Vegas faced business declines, Foxwoods continued to grow and gain market share.

The real financial story is Foxwoods' contributions to the State of Connecticut and the entire region. Prior to Foxwoods, the coastal area of Connecticut and many inland towns were extremely economically depressed. Manufacturing had moved out or closed down leaving ghostlike blocks of empty buildings, stores for lease, and a general economic state of poverty along with high unemployment. Tax revenues were negatively impacted and state services left much to be desired. Schools were strapped for resources and roads were badly in need of repair.

As indicated, Foxwoods agreed to contribute 25 percent of its slot machine win each year to the state. As a result the state began to receive hundreds of millions of dollars from Foxwoods. In addition, Foxwoods' growth was accounting for one out of every two new jobs in the state by the late 1990s. Foxwoods, along with the Mohegan Sun Casino, was also a significant contributor to lowering the state's high unemployment rate (approaching 10 percent at its worst) to 3 percent.

There is more to this story than Foxwoods' financial impact. As a result of Foxwoods' direct monetary economic contributions, there was a multimillion-dollar plan, which spurred on new business, new service establishments, and a whole new economy. Connecticut's economy turned around and became very healthy. Its schools are now rated as some of the best in the country. Its roads—once in a state of disrepair—are now rated the best in the country. Land values have dramatically increased throughout the state. And the surrounding areas in Rhode Island and Massachusetts have also enjoyed a positive spillover effect.

Being the largest and most profitable casino in the nation with the best amenities, Foxwoods has more than a very strong position in the industry. Its financial performance has contributed greatly to the rebirth of a state and regional economy.[7]

Case Discussion Questions

1. What must Foxwoods do to maintain its financial leadership position?
2. Do you believe it was a good idea to share its profits with the state? Why or why not?

NOTES

1. M. Halpin, *Profit Planning for Real Estate Development* (Homewood, IL: Dow Jones Irwin, 1977), p. 22.
2. Ibid., p. 24.
3. R. Nykiel, *Marketing Your Business* (Binghamton, NY: Best Business Books, 2002), p. 28.
4. Halpin, *Profit Planning,* p. 26.
5. Ibid., p. 27.
6. Milestones based on information from www.foxwoods.com.
7. R. Nykiel, *Hospitality Management Strategies* (Upper Saddle River, NJ: Prentice Hall, 2005), pp. 98–102.

Chapter 8

The Design and Components of a Feasibility Study

CHAPTER OBJECTIVES

- To define the difference between a feasibility study and a market area study.
- To provide a logical process by which to locate needed data and to suggest a method to organize the collected data.
- To present the major components of a feasibility study.
- To discuss the economic and market components of a feasibility study.
- To provide time parameters for data and trend analysis of selected data within a feasibility study.
- To view the concept of supply and demand analysis.
- To walk through the process of actually conducting a feasibility study.

DEFINITIONS

Understanding the design and components of a feasibility study can be difficult as various study terms are frequently interchanged. At the outset, a clarification of terms will be helpful.

A *market study* is defined as a broad macroeconomic analysis that looks at the general market conditions of supply, demand, and pricing or the demographics of demand for a specific market or area for a project. It may include or may not include analysis of construction and absorption trends.

While a market study will generally include a conclusion relating to supply and demand and project the probability of the market area's ability to absorb additional construction, market studies neither include property-specific projections of income nor do they address the financial feasibility of the project. To determine these factors, a feasibility analysis is required.

A *feasibility study* is an analysis undertaken to investigate whether a project will fulfill the objectives of the investor(s). The probability of a specific real estate project is analyzed in terms of the criteria of a specific market or investor.[1]

A well-prepared feasibility study usually includes all the elements within a market study and additionally will provide projections of total project cost, achievable income, probable operating expenses, cash flow/needs, and rate of return to the developer/investor(s).

A *site selection and locational analysis study* is defined as a study of a specific site located within a prespecified market to ascertain the site's compatibility for a proposed project (real estate development).

Handbook of Marketing Research Methodologies for Hospitality and Tourism
© 2007 by The Haworth Press, Inc. All rights reserved.
doi:10.1300/5927_09

This study examines the market to see whether the site(s) is appropriate for the proposed project and what the maximum use and potential is for the land selected. It further looks at potential site-related problems that could impact project costs, timing, and so forth (Figure 8.1).

The purpose of this chapter is to delve deeper into the feasibility study. It will be necessary to also focus on the

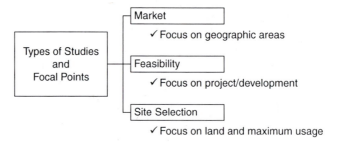

FIGURE 8.1. Focus of Studies by Type

market study and site selection study within the overall scope of the discussion on feasibility studies.

Site and Property–Specific Market/Feasibility Study

By far the most common type of report, a site and property–specific market study analyzes supply and demand for a given property type proposed to be built on a given site. The report includes a complete analysis of macroeconomic and microeconomic conditions that impact the proposed development. The site is analyzed to determine its suitability for the type of development proposed. If plans have been developed for the proposed improvements, we also scrutinize the design, composition, and layout of the proposed facility and make suggestions pertaining to modifications, additions, or subtractions that might improve the design. The report also includes a detailed analysis of the competition in the area, including pricing, occupancy, lease-up information, pertinent physical information, and a rating of each competing property. Most important, the report will analyze supply and demand within the area we define as the primary market area (PMA) for the proposed development. The report concludes with a "go/no go" recommendation based upon our analysis of supply and demand. If a financial feasibility analysis is included, the analysis will also review the relationship between cost and future economic benefits and will conclude with a final "go/no go" recommendation. It is important to note that a proposed development might receive a "go" recommendation based upon market supply and demand but receive a "no go" recommendation after analysis of financial feasibility.

Conducting a Feasibility Study

Conducting a feasibility study and market research requires understanding of the following:

- the difference between a feasibility study and a business plan;
- major components of a feasibility study;
- key market analysis as well as organizational and financial questions in the feasibility study;
- techniques for conducting market research; and
- where to obtain information needed to conduct market research.

This chapter focuses on two vital issues: how to conduct a feasibility study and how to do market research.

MARKET FEASIBILITY STUDIES OVERVIEW

A feasibility study is designed to provide an overview of the primary issues related to a business idea. The purpose is to identify any "make or break" issues that would prevent the business from being successful in the marketplace. In other words, a feasibility study determines whether the business idea makes sense.

A thorough feasibility analysis provides a lot of information necessary for the business plan. For example, a good market analysis is necessary in order to determine the project's feasibility. This information provides the basis for the market section of the business plan.

Since putting together a business plan is a significant investment of time and money, you want to make sure that there are no major roadblocks facing a business idea before making an investment. Identifying such roadblocks is the purpose of a feasibility study.

A feasibility study looks at three major areas:

1. Market issues
2. Organizational/technical issues
3. Financial issues

Again, this is meant to be a "first cut" look at these issues. For example, a feasibility study should not do in-depth long-term financial projections, but it should do a basic break-even analysis to see how much revenue would be necessary for meeting operating expenses.

Market feasibility studies provide information critical to evaluating the potential of new markets, based on a complete review of the market dynamics, products/services, customers, competition, distribution, pricing, and promotional efforts. This information can be used to evaluate short- and long-term market potential, the cost of market entry, return on investment, and strategies related to market entry such as distribution, pricing, and promotion.

Since each industry and market is different from all others, a process may include techniques like telephone interviews, mail surveys, industry expert interviews, and customer response systems. Once the information is obtained, an analysis of the information provides direction for making effective and efficient decisions.

Studies

Although each industry and market is unique, generally, market feasibility studies profile seven areas:

Market dynamics—general information on the market.
Products/services—What products or services are available?
Customers—Who currently purchases the products or services?
Competition—Who provides the products and services?
Distribution—How do the products and services get to the customers?
Pricing—What pricing levels are used with the products and services?
Promotion—How are the products and services promoted and sold to the customers?

Studies primarily use secondary information sources such as trade periodicals, databases, government statistics, news publications, and industry association reports to uncover basic information about an industry or market. Often the most productive information is found by digging beneath the surface to uncover information about the market directly from customers and competitors. Surveying and interviewing industry experts, customers, and competitors provides this enhanced information, which is focused to relate specifically to a proposed or potential project.

Benefits

It is difficult to conceive of an investment in the services sector that would take place without a feasibility study being required by the investor and/or lender. The benefits of a feasibility study include providing these decision makers with an understanding of the size and potential of the market (and/or feeder markets) to support the demand for the project. The feasibility study also provides identification of pricing strategies and managerial objectives needed to be successful. The study provides a current and future assessment of competition. In addition, a comprehensive feasibility study will uncover the communities' attitudes toward the development, sources of potential employees, and suppliers. It will also provide key program/project components to be included in the facility through the supply and demand analysis and competitive assessment. It will provide the financial expectations for the project. Without these answers (information) an investment decision would be made in a vacuum. For these reasons, it is obvious that a comprehensive feasibility study should be undertaken well in advance of any project. The higher the level of investment and complexity of the project, the further out in time the study should be undertaken.

Processes and Profiles

Not all service industry sectors can be categorized into a single template for a feasibility study. Likewise, each market has its own individual characteristics and dynamics. Given the individuality of sectors (services) and markets, it is good practice for each project/development to have a tailored feasibility study process. This means emphasis and depth of research can be focused on the greatest areas of need related to each individual project. In some instances, many questions may need to be addressed with primary research. Other situations may lend themselves to rely more on secondary research. Feasibility studies may utilize research techniques such as telephone interviews, mail surveys, focus groups, customer response systems, model creation, and so on. Once the process and related research steps are undertaken, analysis of the data and findings can begin.

There are a number of areas that almost all processes and techniques must look at with respect to any project or development. Some of these areas that are usually profiled include the dynamics of the market, competition, supply and demand, and the major economic/financial issues.

Components

While the design process and research techniques may be individualized for most projects, the overall components of feasibility studies are fairly consistent in overall context and flow. Overall, a feasibility study examines three major areas: (1) market analysis or issues, (2) competition, and (3) project development and financial assessment.[2] With respect to the latter, a feasibility study financial assessment examines at a first-cut level whether the proposed project will work or not work through a break-even analysis and preliminary financial projections (usually three to five years out in time). Figure 8.2 recaps the major components of a feasibility study.

Market Analysis

In this section an assessment of the primary and secondary market areas is undertaken. Growth trends and areas of specific correlation such as trends in retail sales (shopping), office space, traffic statistics, and so forth, are included. Also, if the project has other markets as sources of demand, the feeder markets are analyzed to identify their significance and rank order of importance. Any other significant patterns or major facts about overall supply (competition) are also collected and analyzed. Demographic and psychographic information is also collected and assessed. When a thorough market analysis is completed, large amounts of data need to be condensed and organized in a logical flow for the reader.

Information generated in the market analysis section is critical to all other sections.

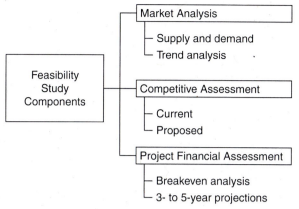

FIGURE 8.2. Major Feasibility Study Components

A written summary will usually provide a synopsis of market area data including geographic boundaries of the primary and secondary market areas; rank order identification of the major feeder markets; key lifestyle, demographic, and socioeconomic highlights; breakdown of the appropriate market segments (potential users/customers) including current size and future growth rate projections; identification of overall competition and related trends; recommended strategic direction for the project (size/scope/positioning within the market and by price/rate, etc.). Many of these overall market analysis components will be further delineated later in the chapter and in the case examples.

Competitive Assessment

The competitive assessment provides extremely important data with respect to the supply and demand for overall products and/ or services that compete directly and indirectly with the proposed project/development. Most feasibility studies go into as much depth as possible on the top five competitors (those nearest to the project/development concept/positioning). All other potential competitors in the total market are also profiled. Utilizing a competitive market positioning grid to present the top five competitors as well as a positioning map (see Chapters 10 and 12) is most useful to the readers of the study. Next, all competition (projects/developments) currently under construction and proposed for the future should be identified on a market area map. For each project under construction or planned for the future, a competitive profile should be prepared with reference to how much this affects supply and demand as well as the positioning of the proposed project/development. In addition, where possible, the sources of business, pricing/rates, and mix of business (market segments) for each competitor should be analyzed and profiled. More details on the competitive assessment will be presented later in this chapter and in the case examples.

A breakeven analysis is a good first step to test project viability.

Financial Assessment

In this section three major areas are presented. First, based on the market analysis and competitive assessment the concept or scope of the development is either confirmed as appropriate or modified to provide the best fit with respect to scope (size), quality level (positioning), and price/rate level. Other modifications or recommended project/development adjustments may relate to mix, facility size, concept, space allocations/plan, design, and so forth. Second, cost estimates may require refinement or adjustments. The adjustments can relate to recommended scope, construction and design changes, and any other cost and revenue assumptions that have changed. Third, adjustments may be required with respect to the financial feasibility of the project/development. Based on the market analysis, competitive assessment, and cost adjustments related to project design changes, a three- to five-year pro forma should be prepared. The pro forma should detail the probable revenue, expenses, profits, cash flow, and pretax return on investment. Detailed breakdowns of expenditures and sources of revenue should be included. A sensitivity and breakeven analysis should also be prepared. Naturally, all underlying assumptions should be duly noted. This allows for the readers (management) to assess the basis for the conclusions.

CONDUCTING FEASIBILITY STUDIES

Feasibility studies may be contracted out to external research consultants/firms or conducted by employees of the firm that is investing in the project. Developers seeking others to participate in the project investment or management will usually seek external nationally known firms that provide an independent perspective on the project. In reality, the external nationally known firms are simply contracted consultants to the developer. Reading the disclaimer of the external firms will always reveal the famous words "not responsible." When contracting with any external firm, there are a number of criteria against which the firm should be compared. Figure 8.3 provides a brief checklist of some of the key criteria and questions that should be asked of the potential contractual party(ies).

Numerous other questions can be added based upon the actual project/development. The aforementioned inquiry areas should provide a good reading on the firm, its researchers, and the degree to which they will need to find new information and/or how much current applicable information they may have already collected in their files from other projects in the market. These factors should be taken into consideration when viewing their proposed cost and timing estimates.

With respect to internal employees it may be beneficial to utilize a team approach for all the obvious reasons. The team should be able to complete the feasibility study faster than an individual. It should also be made of individuals whose strengths vary, that is, a marketing-oriented member, a financially oriented member, and so on. This balance and mix of talents helps to assure multiple perspectives and reduces the number of pieces of information that might be missed in the collection and assessment phases of the study.

___ 1. Size and scope of the firm
___ 2. Previous experience in this specific type of project study
___ 3. Previous experience in this specific market
___ 4. Work undertaken previously for competitors or others in the same market
___ 5. Background of specific individuals who will actually do the fieldwork
___ 6. Detailed work plan/time required
___ 7. Detailed total cost for the study and related expenses
___ 8. Contingencies and the amounts/percentages
___ 9. Samples of previous studies
___ 10. References from previous clients
___ 11. Information required from client
___ 12. Presentation format (oral, written, computer based, number of reports provided, etc.)

FIGURE 8.3. Checklist for External Researchers

Critical Information for Collection and Analysis

Whether the external or internal team approach (or mix of the two) is undertaken, some critical information needs to be collected and analyzed, including, but not limited to, the following categories and items. Figure 8.4 recaps these focal points.[3]

Market

- Market size in units, volume, sales, by segment
- Market activity—growth/decline/stagnant
- Market entry/exit—competitors entering or leaving the market
- Projected market or industry changes—demand, movement within the market

Products/Services

- Products/services available—top five in depth and all others
- Key products/services attributes such as sizes, ratings, facilities, and so forth
- Factors impacting future products/services
- Ranked importance of key product/service attributes of top five competitors and all others

Customers

- Current customers—number, names of significant suppliers of demand
- Satisfaction with current products/services—top five competitors
- Satisfaction with current top two competitors
- Willingness to switch or consider new product/service offerings

Competition

- Primary competitors—number, names, market significance
- Market share of direct competitors and alternatives
- Market focus—price leadership, volume leadership, technology leadership
- Competitive intelligence—competitor plans and activities
- Competitive evaluation—customer perception of the competition, strengths/weaknesses, rank order market position

Distribution

- Distribution channels—direct sales, through intermediaries, mix of business
- Geographic coverage—demand in the market, fringe areas, feeder markets, and so on
- Push versus pull market strategy recommendation
- Satisfaction with sales relationship such as sales force, intermediaries—competitive ranking

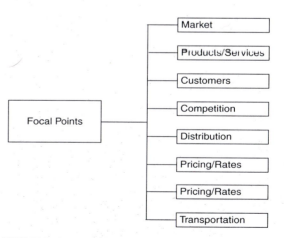

FIGURE 8.4. Focal Points for Conduction of a Feasibility Study

Pricing/Rates

- Price/rate levels and structures for products/services
- Customer price sensitivity
- Average prices/rates by market segments
- Prices/rates compared to national and regional averages

Promotion

- Advertising/promotional media and methods—assessment of top five competitors
- Focus or goal of advertising/promotion plans
- Attracting new sales—major conventions, trade shows, citywide events, and so forth
- Estimated competitive expenditures in market, nationally, and internationally

Transportation

- Proximity to major transportation routes such as airports, rail stations, major interstates
- Road and traffic patterns, areas of congestion
- Proposed new transportation and its impact on the project/development
- Assessment of customer convenience to transportation to proposed project

Finding and Organizing the Information Collected

There are numerous approaches to expedite the conduction process. For example, most Chambers of Commerce can provide maps, updates on community developments, key market statistics, economic data, and other market area contacts and resources that can be very helpful. If the city/market has an economic planning department this is well worth another interview stop. Naturally, if you haven't done so prior to traveling to the market to be researched, go to the Internet with a fresh stack of paper in your printer and you will be able to download documents, research, and economic reports. Also, this will provide you a list of data to inquire about and be sure to seek up-to-date copies. By stopping off at the city planning department and tax assessor/collector you will likely obtain key information to help you extrapolate performance measures of the competition and potentially any public or filed documents (i.e., previous feasibility studies) on competitive projects. Likewise, stopping at local offices of the major banks in the commercial loans business may prove a good source for previous project/development financial information.

It is important to drive the market to understand the patterns of traffic to the project/development site from all major transportation centers (airports, rail stations, interstates, and major thoroughfares). Observe not only the traffic patterns but also the viewable environment and access to the site. The viewable environment is significant as it sets the initial impression or perception that encompasses the project/development. This perception will eventually influence design, rates, pricing, and perhaps even actual volume of business. In observing access to the site, look for any aspects in the lay of the land that present opportunities and/or potential obstacles to the development of the project/development.

Visit all major competitors and make detailed notes on your observations. Place yourself in the role of a consumer as you assess facilities, services, and the overall professionalism of the staff. Take note of opportunities to outdo the competitors. Assess employee attitudes and performance. Look for competitive strengths and weaknesses. These notes may be highly significant to the design and marketing terms for the project. Assess all other aspects of the infrastructure surrounding the project/development. Remember to record names and phone numbers and to get the business cards of key contacts in the market. These may be useful for follow-up questions or other future market probes.

Depending on the skills of the researcher(s) and degree of confidentiality about the project/development, some additional probes to be considered include interviewing competitive facilities' managers, walking and touring the competitors, posing as a customer to obtain pricing/rates, and assessing sales forces and other competitive operational aspects/details. Also view the respective site and market area later at night to determine how or if its character changes. Many areas will appear fine during business hours but take on a less attractive nature after dark.

The quality of demand is highly significant to price/rate sensitivity.

Look at the quality of demand and ascertain whether it is in line with the quality of your customer base. Visit the Convention and Visitors Bureau (CVB) and analyze the current nature of conventions and what is on the calendar for future years. Will the CVB bring in visitors and business that will be of help to the project/development? What is the quality of retail, entertainment, and other area attractions, and how will they help the project/development?

Another way to conduct the feasibility study is to organize your activities in relationship to three focal points. First, looking *within* at the project/development itself. This will provide a thorough understanding of the development and help relate it to the information collected. Second, looking *around* is where you focus on the competition and market infrastructure. And, third, looking *ahead* is where trends, future developments, future competition, and alternate scenarios can be recorded. Figure 8.5 summarizes this investigative approach.

Analysis of the Information Collected

Once the fieldwork and follow-up data identification are completed, it is time to analyze the information. In conducting the analysis divide the data by the focal points, as presented earlier in Figure 8.4. After the aforementioned initial sorts of the information/analysis, label key findings in concert with the actual feasibility study outline, that is, market demand I. A-1, competitive pricing/rates III. B-4, and so on. This two-step process will expedite sorting through mounds of information and data analysis output. It will also facilitate writing the study as well as creating a presentation if necessary.

Either of the two collection and conducting methods may be used or one can be tailored based on the nature of the feasibility study and timing requirements. With respect to input, analysis, and recording key information much of the data will come from direct questions to key contacts. It is useful to have a preprepared script or list of interview questions when conducting a feasibility study. Figure 8.6 provides some key questions related to the market section of the study.

There are many more specific questions the field researcher might wish to add to this list. The key point is that the market analysis should be conducted first because it is critical to the success of the project/development. If adequate demand cannot be sub-

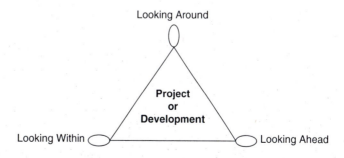

FIGURE 8.5. The Investigative Process

1. What is the current and projected level of demand?
2. What is the target market (primary and secondary) and what is the demographic characteristics of the target market? How many or what percentage are in the market?
3. What are the major feeder markets?
4. How many and what level (quality, price) competitors are in the market?
5. What is the current supply and projected supply in the market?
6. What is the opinion on the location (site) for the project/development of those in the market and those coming to the market?
7. Are there any other sites more appropriate in the market? Are they available?
8. What is the mix of product/service offerings in the market by price/rate and/or quality level?
9. Is there a specific type of product/service not in the market that should be?
10. Why is the market appropriate for investment for your product or service offering(s)?

FIGURE 8.6. Sample Key Market-Related Questions

stantiated (both qualitative and quantitative demand) then the project is not feasible and there is no need to proceed to other areas of the feasibility study. Assuming the market is acceptable, it will be very important to document what price/rate the market will support. This along with the growth rate in supply and demand will form the key assumptions for the financial projections. It is always better to be conservative and realistic in these assumptions. Also, in preparing the financial assumptions, a thorough review on not only revenue assumptions but also detailed cost estimates will be required. The costs include preopening expenses; start-up costs including capital goods, land, the building(s), FF&E (furniture, fixtures, and equipment), and so forth; operating costs (rent, utilities, wages, etc.); revenue projections; where applicable, sources of financing; and a profitability analysis. The profitability analysis, be it a breakeven analysis or a detailed long-term model, pro forma, and so on, is the ultimate bottom line for the proposed project/development. Key focal points here include identification of revenue levels to cover costs (mixed and variable), the breakeven point, and cash flow.

In essence, the total composite of all sections of the feasibility study should result in a clear picture of how the project/development will look from all perspectives—positioning in the market, financial performance, and so on. It will be very important to present this information and analysis in both a written and oral format to convey the results clearly.

SAMPLE DESIGN AND COMPONENTS OF A FEASIBILITY STUDY

This section presents a sample feasibility study design and select key components using a fictitious city and a proposed hotel project. The sample is not intended to be representative of a feasibility study for all areas of the hospitality industry, as individual segments and enterprises possess their own sets of variables, assumptions, peculiarities, and requirements. The sample should be considered illustrative only and not representative of every feasibility study.

A feasibility study is an investigative, objective, and logical process wherein marketing data and financial projections are determined, analyzed, and integrated for the purpose of rendering an accurate decision as to the financial advisability of undertaking the particular project in question. As such, it should be presented in an organized executive style. A suggested format for presentation follows.[4]

Section One—Introduction

The introduction should be brief, no more than two pages, with one page the more desirable length. The language should be crisp, incisive, and to the point, as the persons who will make the final decision have time pressures and want the facts fast. The six questions that should be answered in this section are as follows:

1. The type and size of the proposed project/development and the location
2. Why the study was undertaken
3. The scope of the evaluation
4. How the evaluation was conducted
5. Who conducted the evaluation
6. The time period within which the evaluation was conducted

Section Two—Summary and Conclusions (and Recommendations if Requested)

The results determined and conclusions drawn from the study should be presented first for impact and emphasis. If the host organization requests recommendations as to decisions, interpretations, and/or procedures, these are placed appropriately in this section. The body of the report that follows should provide supporting documentation and detail and be presented in a sequence that parallels the remarks made in this section. This allows for depth and ease of information location for any interested party.

Section Three—General Characteristics of the Market

This entails a *brief* general description of the location, its population, important business activities, economic and population growth rates, and other relevant characteristics that relate *directly* to demand for the project/development. Also included, especially for studies in foreign countries, would be any special political and/or financial considerations that might affect the project.

This section should be as concise as possible. Many miscellaneous general tables are undesirable; a good area map is useful, with concentric circles showing population densities.

Remember a study is on a specific project/development, not formulation of a city's new urban-planning program or a thesis on over-researched market data. A typical description of a general economic environment of a major North American city follows.

An Example of a Market Characteristic Report:
Section Three—General Economic Environment

Superior City is a newly emerged suburban city and is one of the largest of its type in North America. It is the capital of a well-to-do and stable political subdivision, a commercial and industrial area that has been well planned, and is the center of a populous, flourishing, and cultural metropolitan area.

The population of 1.9 million represents an increase of a quarter of a million persons in the last ten years. Estimates from various sources indicate that the population may reach 3 million by 2010. The percentage gain in population in the last decade has been higher than that of any other North American city of over 1 million persons. Once predominantly Anglo-Saxon, Superior City today has multiple nationalities, with approximately 40 percent of the population being of European ancestry. Although second to the Capital City in population, Superior City ranks ahead of Capital City in many important economic aspects. A summary of these follows:

	Superior City	National rank	Capital City	National rank
Population	1.9 million	2	2.2 million	1
Total effective buying income	$4.03 billion	1	$4.02 billion	2
Per capita income	$2,155	2	$1,828	17
Per household income	$8,127	2	$7,001	13
Total retail sales	$2.54 billion	1	$2.51 billion	2
Food and beverage sales	$112 million	2	$135 million	1

Superior City is the country's most significant new retail market and is the center of secondary manufacturing. One-third of the nation's buying power is within 100 miles of Superior City. Manufacturing production within a thirty-mile radius is greater than in any other area in the nation of comparable size. Personal disposable income is 26 percent above the national average.

Over 5,000 manufacturing plants account for an annual production of goods valued at more than $20 billion, twice the value of fifteen years ago. There is considerable variety in this production. Although some plants are large and employ many, others are highly automated.

Section Four—Supply and Demand Analysis

A macroeconomic rather than a microeconomic approach is normally preferable when determining future hotel room demand in a given market. Macroeconomic means looking at your market in the broad sense and anticipating what changes will occur in the future. Microeconomic projections for transient room usage involve individually quantifying and then totaling the increasing demand from all various sources in units of "room nights"; for example, so many room nights will be sold per 1,000 tourists, visitors, convention delegates, and so on. Obviously, the assumptions required for the latter type of projection are such that small errors in the parameters employed lead to major errors in the total forecast.

Also, building a market by microeconomic techniques runs the risk of missing one or more important segments of demand. Unless correlated back to a macroeconomic approach, demand may be understated and the influence of quality differentiation ignored. The macroeconomic approach, as outlined later, affords more realistic projections from historic trends in hotel occupancies for a particular city and is a much less expensive research process.[5] An example outline for preparing a report for this section follows:

I. Definition and description of the local hotel market
    A. Inventory of all acceptable transient accommodations, subgrouped to indicate "most competitive," "fairly competitive," and "somewhat competitive"
        1. Number of rooms
        2. Published rates
        3. Map showing groupings of hotels by areas within the city
    B. New hotel construction within the last ten years
        1. Name of hotel and its location
        2. Date of completion
        3. Number of rooms
        4. Quality and extent of facilities
    C. Overall hotel occupancy
        1. Historical trend for the total city market for the last ten years
        2. Current year occupancy

II. Identification of principal competitive hotels as to the following:
   A. Location
   B. Number of rooms
   C. Average room rate
   D. Occupancy
   E. Quality of facilities and services offered
   F. Composition of trade, that is, tourist and/or commercial
III. Analysis of principal sources of demand
   A. Business travelers
      1. Growth in airport traffic and other transportation facility traffic
      2. Growth in employment and occupied floor space in primary central business district office buildings
      3. Analysis of other available parameters indicating potential growth in demand from business travelers
   B. Local convention business and meetings
      1. Number of conventions
      2. Number of delegates
      3. Types of conventions
      4. Sizes of conventions
      5. Seasonality of convention activity
      6. Observable growth in convention trade
      7. Public convention facilities currently available
      8. Convention facilities offered by competitive hotels
      9. Facilities required at planned hotel to serve desired convention business
   C. Area tourism
      1. Number of tourists
      2. Seasonality
      3. Spending characteristics
      4. Purpose of visits and length of stays
      5. Extent to which tourists are potential customers for proposed hotel
      6. Projected growth in tourism
   D. Other significant sources of demand, if any, such as nearby universities, hospitals, national parks, sports arenas, and so forth

The following ten associations and agencies are common to most metropolitan areas, and they can be of great assistance in providing information on the preceding items:

   1. Visitors and Convention Bureau
   2. Hotel/Motel Association
   3. Port Authority
   4. Chamber of Commerce
   5. Transportation Companies
   6. Customs Officials
   7. State, Province, or National Department of Tourism
   8. Building Owners and Managers Association
   9. Hotel Index
   10. AAA Guide to Hotel/Motel Accommodations

Many other sources exist, and it is up to the researcher to find those which will provide information not available from any of the previous sources. Obviously, local hoteliers have extensive knowledge of their own market area. Some are glad to share their viewpoints when approached forthrightly with an explanation of what you are seeking and why. Yet the interviewer must be careful to evaluate their responses, recognizing the vested interests that exist. Last, confidential treatment of information is often required. The importance of honoring such conditions is obvious.

Continuing with the previous outline:

IV. Estimated additional rooms required to meet demand through the next five years
   A. First-class rooms needed for now to result in 75 percent occupancy at competitive facilities. The 75 percent occupancy rate is normally used for it is a point of healthy balance between supply and demand, and a condition under which an owner can usually attain sufficient profit to justify his or her investment. Example:

   Let us assume that Superior City has 1,500 competitive rooms in 6 hotels averaging 80 percent occupancy during the last year. These 1,500 rooms @ 80 percent occupancy = 1,600 rooms @ 75 percent occupancy, as determined by 1,500 rooms × 80 percent occupancy = 1,200 rooms occupied.

$$\frac{1,200 \text{ rooms occupied}}{75\% \text{ occupancy rate}} = 1,600 \text{ rooms available}$$

   B. Composite growth rate in demand sources. Example:

   Assume evaluation of data indicates that the three primary generators of hotel room demand will increase at varying growth rates, as shown in the following list. The extent to which each classification of traveler will occupy the proposed hotel's facilities is also estimated from the research findings. A 9.3 percent annual composite rate of growth (CRG) in demand is then calculated as anticipated growth rate (AGR) × estimated proportion of trade (EPT):

Source of demand	AGR (%)		EPT (%)	CRG (%)
Business travelers	9	×	65	5.85
Convention delegates	7	×	10	0.70
Tourists	11	×	25	2.75
Composite demand			100	9.30

Summarizing this example:

$$\left(\begin{array}{c}\text{Current first-class room}\\\text{inventory (1,500)}\end{array}\right) + \left(\begin{array}{c}\text{Number of additional}\\\text{first-class rooms}\\\text{needed now (100)}\end{array}\right) = \text{Current demand level (1,600)}$$

$$\left(\begin{array}{c}\text{Current demand}\\\text{level (1,600)}\end{array}\right) \times \left(\begin{array}{c}\text{Anticipated growth}\\\text{in demand (9.3 percent)}\end{array}\right) = \begin{array}{c}\text{Total number of rooms}\\\text{needed in future years}\end{array}$$

Therefore, future room requirements in Superior City are as follows:

Year	Total rooms required @ 75 percent occupancy	Cumulative new rooms required
2005	1,600	100
2006	1,750	250
2007	1,910	410
2008	2,090	590
2009	2,285	785
2010	2,500	1,000

    C. What new hotels are under construction or in planning?
       1. Name of new hotel
       2. Identity of developers and/or operators
       3. Location
       4. Size
       5. Target date for completion
       6. Probability of realization of planned hotels
    D. Will any existing competitive rooms be removed from the market or substantially downgraded during the next five years?
    E. Determining additional rooms needed in future years is based on the foregoing supply-demand analysis. Continuing with the aforementioned example:

> If a 400-room hotel is presently under construction and no other hotel projects are contemplated for Superior City, sufficient demand for another 400-room hotel is evidenced by late 2009, and construction could start in 2007 assuming two years are required for completion.

Obviously, this case is an oversimplification. There may be many projects under consideration, some of which are nearly certain to be completed; for others, the probability of realization will be difficult to determine. Furthermore, in cities with substandard facilities, a properly conceived and well-managed project may succeed regardless of the general market. Acknowledging such qualifications, this process still serves as a rational basis for decision making.

Section Five—Site Evaluation

An example outline for preparing a report for this section follows:

    I. General location considerations
       A. General layout of the city with a map or maps illustrating:
          1. The central business district and subcenters of business activity
          2. Primary transportation routes and facilities
          3. Specialty shopping district
          4. Concentrations of dining and entertainment establishments
          5. Location of major cultural and athletic facilities
          6. Other locational factors affecting hotel site suitability
       B. Anticipated future real estate developments and trends in the city which will enhance or detract from a site's desirability
    II. Sites considered—map locations

III. Descriptions of site(s) selected
   A. Physical characteristics
      1. Dimensions
      2. Existing improvements
      3. Estimated cost of site preparation required prior to commencement of construction
      4. Adequacy of land area for addition
      5. Soil conditions
   B. Other site data
      1. Current ownership
      2. Sign ordinances, especially for a motor inn project
      3. Cost
      4. Property taxes
      5. Zoning or height restrictions
      6. Access to and availability of adequate utility services
      7. Future street plans
IV. Identification of space devoted to:
   A. Guest rooms
   B. Food and beverage facilities
   C. Meeting and public areas
   D. Back-of-the-house functions (e.g., housekeeping, maintenance)
   E. Parking
   F. Other facilities

Marketing Plan—Scope of Facilities Based on Study Findings

These are the initial general criteria given the architect prior to preparation of conceptual plans:

   1. Sizing—number of rooms
   2. Quality and room mix
   3. Special design concepts

Section VI—Financial Analysis

A sample outline for preparing this section of the report follows:

  I. Estimated capital costs
 II. Pro forma income statement
III. Does indicated rate of return justify proceeding?
IV. Financial plan
   A. Evaluation of alternate methods of financing
      1. Own or lease
      2. If own, estimated amount of debt financing available from various sources
         a. Mortgage money
         b. Bonds or debentures
   B. Costs of borrowed money from various sources
   C. Equity capital requirements
      1. Sources of equity capital
      2. Relative percentage of equity participation by various principals involved
 V. Preparation of pro forma cash flow and capital budgeting statements

Financial Planning for New Hotel Developments

Project costs and how they are estimated. In the initial phases of project analysis, the developer and the hotel system's development division (when the two entities are separate) usually prepare preliminary cost estimates based on the proposed scope of the project.

At first, this is accomplished with minimum detail. The developer draws from his knowledge of local building costs and the hotel's development division draws from their own previous experience on projects of similar size and quality, adjusting for local building conditions and special characteristics of the proposed structure.

Each group's preliminary estimates are then compared, as shown in Table 8.1, and discrepancies are discussed so each party gains an understanding of the other's expectations, and a preliminary budget is agreed upon.[6]

Detailed capital budgeting. At completion of preliminary drawings, the developer and the hotel's development division initiate a more detailed capital budgeting projection. This is not a one-time effort, but rather one that is refined at regular intervals throughout the development program. Each revision is dated to avoid confusion as to the most current estimate.

Institution of rigid cost controls and periodic reviews of expenditures are essential to ensure that a new hotel is completed within economic limits. Cost estimating is a team effort involving corporate management with outside contractors and consultants.

TABLE 8.1. Comparative Preliminary Cost Estimates, Superior City Hotel (408 Rooms)

	Developer's Preliminary Estimate		Superior City's Preliminary Estimate	
	Total ($)	Per Room (Rounded $)	Total ($)	Per Room (Rounded $)
Construction costs	48,896,000	120,000	63,500,000	155,650
Architectural and engineering fees	1,400,000	3,450	3,800,000	9,300
Design fees and expenses	750,000	1,850	1,250,000	3,050
Bonds	250,000	600	250,000	600
Legal fees	350,000	850	350,000	850
Interim financing	2,750,000	6,750	3,8000,000	9,300
Taxes and insurance during construction	20,000	50	300,000	750
Title policy	150,000	350	150,000	350
Furniture, fixtures, and equipment	10,000,000	24,500	18,150,000	414,500
Preopening expenses	7,500,000	18,380	6,250,000	15,300
Parking garage	3,700,000	14,000	5,700,000	14,000
Overhead	250,000	600	250,000	600
Land	3,000,000	7,350	3,000,000	7,350
Total	81,080,000	198,750	106,750,000	261,600

For instance, the judgments of the architect and contractor are relied on heavily for estimating costs of site preparation, construction, and programming and supervision. Often the hotel company has their own design and supply sources and draws on its experiences to assist in estimating costs of furniture and fixtures, interior decoration, kitchen equipment, and the many stocks and supplies needed to open a new hotel. Operating management prepares a preopening expenses budget and determines working capital requirements.

Similarly, expert counsel, inside and outside the company, is solicited when projecting financial costs, insurance requirements, tax liabilities, and many of the other items that must be considered in the total budget.

An ability to estimate costs accurately and then control them throughout the developmental process is, as in almost every business, essential to profitability. It requires experience, good judgment, and conscientious attention to detail.

Estimating revenues and expenses. Table 8.2 illustrates the type of form used to prepare pro forma income projections for a proposed hotel operation. Without undue elaboration, each item is evaluated based on findings of the market research portion of the feasibility study and drawing from current experience at existing properties and the expertise of operating management.

Again, this is periodically refined right up to opening day, and then it becomes the first operating budget for the new hotel. From the earliest stages of development, operating management plays an important role in reviewing the development division's cost and revenue analyses.

Table 8.3 is a simplified preliminary cash flow statement in a case where the hotel operator is acting as a lessee. In cases where the operator has an ownership position, the cash flow statement naturally takes a different form and includes depreciation, interest payments, amortization of principal, income tax liability, reserves for capital replacement programs, and so forth. This table is also constantly updated and reviewed as new information becomes available.

Presentations

Written reports should be concise and in executive-briefing style. Any accompanying visual presentation materials such as maps, photos, displays, video, and so forth, should be of high quality with clarity and ease of reference for the viewers/readers. Finally, the researcher or presenter should be prepared to answer questions or provide information to back up any recommendations or summary statements. It is extremely important to adhere to the allocated time for the presentation. This again reinforces the point to present the conclusions and recommendations on a timely basis during the presentation. It is also suggested that the materials include the executive summary, the actual study, copy of the presentation, and any appropriate appendixes for those requesting in-depth backup data.

CHAPTER REVIEW

This chapter began with delineating the differences and relationships between market area studies, feasibility studies, and site-selection locational studies. Logical processes to ascertain what types of information are needed and where these data might be located were provided. Further, a number of processes for collecting, categorizing, and analyzing the information were suggested. A description and review of the major components of a feasibility study were presented, including market area analysis, competitive assessments, and project/development financial assessments. The latter suggested that a breakeven analysis and three- to five-year projections be included. Numerous sources for market, competitive, and economic data were provided. Approaches to data collection and actually conducting and presenting the study were also suggested.

TABLE 8.2. Preliminary Pro Forma Income and Expense Statement, Superior City Hotel (408 Rooms) ($1,000s)

Average Room Rate Occupancy

| | $200.00 | | | | $220.00 | | | |
| | 70% | | 75% | | 70% | | 75% | |
	Amount	%	Amount	%	Amount	%	Amount	%
Departmental gross receipts								
Rooms Dept.	$20,850	51.2%	$22,350	51.6%	$22,950	52.4%	$24,600	52.8%
Food and Beverage Dept.	17,500	43.0	18,500	42.7	18,500	42.2	19,500	41.8
Telephone Dept.	1,300	3.2	1,400	3.2	1,300	3.0	1,400	3.0
Other Operating Depts.	1,050	2.6	1,100	2.5	1,050	2.4	1,100	2.4
Total	$50,700	100.0%	$43,350	100.0%	$43,800	100.0%	$46,600	100.0%
Departmental gross profit								
Rooms Dept.	$14,800	71.0%	$16,090	72.0%	$16,520	72.0%	$17,960	73.0%
Food and Beverage Dept.	3,850	22.0	4,260	23.0	4,260	23.0	4,680	42.0
Telephone Dept.	(330)	(25.0)	(350)	(25.0)	(330)	(25.0)	(350)	(25.0)
Other Operating Depts.	320	30.0	330	30.0	320	30.0	330	30.0
Total	$18,640	46.1%	$20,330	46.9%	$20,770	47.4%	$22,620	48.5%
Other income	120	0.3	130	0.3	130	0.3	140	0.3
Gross operating income	$18,760	46.1%	$20,460	47.2%	$20,900	47.7%	$22,760	48.8%
Deductions from income								
Adm. and General Expense	$3,500	8.6%	$3,500	8.1%	$3,500	8.0%	$3,500	7.5%

TABLE 8.2. (continued)

Average Room Rate Occupancy

| | $200.00 | | | | $220.00 | | | |
| | 70% | | 75% | | 70% | | 75% | |
	Amount	%	Amount	%	Amount	%	Amount	%
Advertising and Business Promotion	1,160	2.8	1,300	3.0	1,160	2.6	1,300	2.8
Heat, Light, and Power	1,050	2.6	1,150	2.6	1,050	2.4	1,150	2.5
Repairs and Maintenance	1,220	3.0	1,300	3.0	1,310	3.0	1,400	3.0
Total	**$6,930**	**17.0%**	**$7,250**	**16.7%**	**$7,020**	**16.0%**	**$7,350**	**15.8%**
House profit	$11,830	29.1%	$13,210	30.5%	$13,880	31.7%	$15,410	33.1%
Store rentals	$600	1.4	$600	1.4	$600	1.4	$600	1.3
Gross operating profit	**$12,430**	**30.5%**	**$13,810**	**31.9%**	**$14,480**	**33.1%**	**$16,010**	**34.4%**
Fire Ins. and Franchise Taxes	200	0.5%	220	0.5	220	0.5	230	0.5
Property taxes and other capital	**$12,230**	**30.0%**	**$13,590**	**31.4%**	**$14,260**	**32.5%**	**$15,780**	**33.9%**
Real Estate Taxes	1,020	2.5	1,080	2.5	1,100	2.5	1,170	2.5
Estimated other capital expenses	**$12,210**	**27.5%**	**$12,510**	**28.9%**	**$14,216**	**30.0%**	**$14,610**	**31.4%**

TABLE 8.3. Preliminary Cash Flow, Superior City Hotel (408 Rooms) ($1,000s)

Year	Profit Before Rent	Fixed Rent*	Percentage Rent**	Cash Flow
1	10,000	7,620	134.0	104.0
2	11,250	7,620	196.5	166.5
3	12,500	7,620	259.0	229.0
4	13,000	7,620	284.0	254.0
5	13,500	7,620	309.0	279.0
6	14,050	7,620	336.5	306.5
7	14,600	7,620	364.0	334.0
8	15,200	7,620	394.0	364.0
9	15,800	7,620	424.0	394.0
10	16,450	7,620	456.5	426.5

*Fixed Annual Rent: $65,000,000

    First Mortgage of $6,500,000 @ 7.25%, 25 years = $5,640

    Amortization of FF&E Loan & Replacement

        Reserve = 10% FF&E Cost Estimate   = 1,800

    Land @ 6% of $3,000,000   =   180

                              $7,620

**Percentage Rent:

    Equal to 50% of Profit After Fixed Rent + $150,000

KEY CONCEPTS/TERMS

Absorption rate
Breakeven analysis
Capacity
Competitive analysis
Competitive position
Data collection
Demand generators
Effective buying income
Feasibility study
Financial analysis
Infrastructure
Inventory
Issues
Labor availability
Lifestyles
Locational analysis

Market area study
Market characteristics
Market dynamics
Office space
Per capita income
Pro forma
Retail
Selection
Site
Socioeconomics
Supply and demand analysis
Target market
Time frame
Traffic counts
Transportation systems
Trends
Utilities
Variances
Zoning

DISCUSSION QUESTIONS

1. How does a feasibility study differ from a market study or site selection study?
2. Discuss what type of information you would seek from the Chamber of Commerce.
3. How can a Convention and Visitors Bureau be of help to the researcher?
4. What are the major areas or focal points of a feasibility study?
5. How would you conduct a supply and demand analysis?
6. Describe and discuss two ways to categorize/analyze information collected.
7. What do you believe would result from "driving" the market?
8. What does the term "quality of demand" mean?
9. Why is the presentation phase of the feasibility study so important?

CASE 8.1. BEST SITES, GREAT LOCATION, A VERY POSITIVE FEASIBILITY STUDY—OOPS: WE DIDN'T KNOW!

In the mid-1980s an upscale hotel chain was seeking to enter the major airport markets in the United States. As an upscale product, the hotels represented a major capital investment and usually involved proportionately expensive real estate. The chain had recently sold one of its older hotels located near the airport. This older hotel was one of the chain's most successful; however, it no longer fit the new luxury strategy. As a result of this excellent market track record, the company sought an appropriate site for a "flagship" hotel in the same airport market.

One afternoon the development and real estate department received a call about a parcel of land with an incredible location adjacent to the entry road to the airport/terminal. In order to tie up the site, they quickly executed a ninety-day option on the land. A development team was quickly assembled to conduct a site analysis and "quick" feasibility study (since the company was already familiar with the market and had prior success in a less desirable location). Further, speed was of the essence due to an upcoming mayor's election that could unfavorably change the zoning on the land. The finance, development, real estate, and operating executives who made up the team developed a "pro forma" on the proposed 400-room luxury hotel. The team was most enthusiastic as they projected that the hotel would achieve an 85 percent occupancy and the highest average daily rate in the market in its first year of operation and break even in less than two and a half years. The design team already at work presented a dramatic contemporary design that would truly make this flagship hotel a landmark building. In a matter of weeks the president and CEO flew out to the site and shortly thereafter convinced the parent company to provide the substantial cash needed to immediately begin the project. All approvals were obtained, contracts put in place, and construction underway within a very short time frame. In fact, all this was done before the mayoral elections! Construction moved ahead of schedule and it was a matter of about eighteen months and the hotel was open and outperforming the projections. The company was so proud of this new hotel they decided it would be the site of their annual meeting. The chairman of the parent company was invited to be the keynote speaker. The meeting was a motivational success.

A few days after the meeting a newspaper article was sent to the president/CEO indicating that the newly elected mayor announced that a major new airport (located 50 miles from the existing airport) was to be built. After some brief research by the marketing department (never asked to be part of the initial development/site selection and feasibility study team), it was uncovered that the new airport had been in the planning for some five years. Also, the current airport would be destined to be an "industrial center/park."

The obvious point of this case example is that feasibility studies and research need to be very thorough and should not just look at history or present performance but also, and more important, "look ahead" to the future.

Case Discussion Questions

1. Why is it important to check with city, regional, or state planning offices?
2. What are some methods to employ doing field research to uncover data that can potentially impact a proposal development?

NOTES

1. From http://www.e-valueappraisal.com/marketfeasibility.htm; www.e-valueappraisalservices.com (June 2, 2004).

2. From http://www.agecon.uga.edu/~gacoops/info6.htm (June 2, 2004).

3. From http://www.perspec.com/MktFeas.htm; www.perspectivesconsultinggroup.com (June 2, 2004).

4. R. Nykiel & B. Nearn, *The Design and Components of a Feasibility Study* (Memphis, TN: Holiday Inns, Inc., 1975), p. 1.

5. Ibid., pp. 2-5.

6. Ibid., p. 8.

Chapter 9

Market Assessment for Development Planning

CHAPTER OBJECTIVES

- To provide a perspective on how market assessments are utilized in longer-range development planning.
- To delineate a model and sample process for data collection and analysis to support development planning.
- To discuss the interrelationships of development planning to various management strategies such as acquisitions, dispositions, refurbishments, repositioning, and new products/services development.
- To present key analysis focal points related to both market and products/services over the longer range associated with development and capital investment planning.
- To identify key components and influences upon products, markets, and services over selected time frames related to development planning.

In the services sector and particularly in the hospitality industry it is often necessary to plan on a longer-term basis. To grow brands and related service offerings requires both an internal assessment of the existing product/service offering portfolio and related markets as well as an external assessment focused on the future of both. Key questions need to be addressed directly related to capital investment. How old is the product/service offering? Is the positioning and type or level of product/service still appropriate for the market? How is the market changing? What are our current and future competitive positions in the market? What other markets should we be in? What is our competition, both traditional and nontraditional, doing in the market(s)? All of these plus many more questions become the focal points for market assessments for development planning. In this chapter, we discuss the assessment process related to development planning.

INTRODUCTION TO THE DEVELOPMENT PLANNING PROCESS

The development planning process focuses on two key strategic focal points—existing products/services and defining development approaches over time in specific markets.[1] This process and related research findings will ultimately result in a detailed growth and development plan for an organization. The process must take into consideration an internal assessment (looking within), and external assessment (looking around and looking ahead). Figure 9.1 depicts the process.

Looking Within

In development planning, looking within usually involves a detailed assessment of the entire portfolio of business assets and involves assessing and classifying each. Classification may involve the use of portfolio analysis techniques, financial models, simulations, scenarios, rank-

Handbook of Marketing Research Methodologies for Hospitality and Tourism
© 2007 by The Haworth Press, Inc. All rights reserved.
doi:10.1300/5927_10

ings, segmentation, and many other market research techniques. These assessments provide guidelines and prioritizations for capital spending, reallocation of resources (financial and human), and product/service development strategies. Key areas of focus also include an examination and analysis of return on equity, return on capital, return on net assets, alternative scenarios of asset mix, and related returns on net assets (RONA). Another area of assessment focuses on identification of "keeps" and "dispositions." Keeps are products or services that one wishes to retain and develop a plan for their longer-term usage. Dispositions are those assets that are targeted for sale, conversions, disposition, and demolition. Managing the mix of assets and planning for future improvements and/or new products/services, illustrated in Figure 9.2, provide a simple way to view such items.

Figure 9.2 provides an overview of a typical multiunit and/or multibusiness organization. It classifies or categorizes the organization's holdings into three actionable areas: assets for disposition, assets to keep, and assets for markets to further research. It quickly provides a reading on the overall health of the organization.

Another way to view units of a business is to develop a portfolio matrix consisting of the market or market segment growth rate and the organization's relative market share. This approach can be used for the total portfolio or for the total facilities within a given market. Figure 9.3 provides a framework for a portfolio analysis matrix.

This analytical tool quickly focuses the development planner on markets and businesses where further development is likely to be based in an environment for growth. Likewise, it provides a categorization of businesses where the markets/products may be structured or overbuilt.

Additional models and matrices are usually developed to look at return on investment (high to low ROI), growth (fast to slow), cash flow (high/positive to low/negative), and major problems (near term to long term; for asset/business and for unit). Another quantitative classification approach that assists in development planning strategy is exemplified by an internal deployment index. The index measures the relative extent to which the unit is either contributing to or drawing from the corporation's supply of cash. The value itself may be defined as the percentage of earnings generated by the business unit that was used by the unit. Figure 9.4 provides a synopsis of this

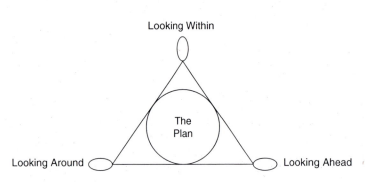

FIGURE 9.1. The Development Planning Process

	Asset Mix		RONA	
	2005	2010	2005	2010
• Inappropriate businesses/units and markets (dispositions)	13.2%	2.1%	2.4%	4.2%
• Businesses/markets with good performance/ potential (keeps)	38.5%	53.4%	8.8%	9.6%
• Businesses/markets undergoing strategic change (study)	48.3%	44.5%	2.8%	11.8%
Total Corporate Return on Net Assets			4.7%	10.4%

FIGURE 9.2. Mix Strategy and Analysis: Improvement on Asset Mix and Return on Net Assets

categorization approach and the related meanings associated with internal deployment percentages.

Utilizing the internal assessment and analytical processes presented up to this point provides a basis for the known related to existing products/services and markets. An organization that completes these categorizations and assessments now knows which businesses or units to get rid of (dispositions), which to keep, which to improve, and which markets to remain in and look for development opportunities. One could conclude that this structured approach is a logical and effective way to view looking within the company's business/unit portfolio. The end products of this internal research and analysis include a categorization of units with logical support for disposition, retention, and enhancement; a division of the units by market segment growth rate and relative market share; and a rank order of units by internal deployment/cash generation/cash usage. Another product of this internal assessment is a thorough review and categorization of product relevance in the markets and profile of all units with respect to condition, capital needs, age, and so forth. Further, where there is inadequate market share or products/units in need of replacement identified, an acquisitions list by market, products/units, and timetable can be established. In essence, the analysis of the internal data will help identify the degree to which meeting growth objectives must come from development-related strategies on a market-by-market as well as on an overall basis.

Looking Around

A sound long-term development plan must also take into consideration the competition. Therefore, the next logical step is to assess each market with respect to competitive positioning, current and planned. For each market and unit, a positioning map should be developed, which provides a quality comparison with your top five market competitors. Total competitive supply should also be obtained as well as be divided by market segment. If possible, announced and planned (even rumored) competitive supply should be assessed, and supply should be projected to coincide with the developmental time frames selected for the planning process, for example, next 24 months; 24 to 60 months; 60 to 120 months, and so on. This should also be done by product type and market segment. The competitive assessment is also the time to look around at what new or innovative ideas are being introduced by your competitors. These ideas may be design, operational innovations, marketing, develop-

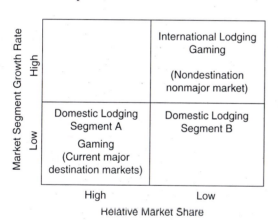

FIGURE 9.3. Sample Framework for a Portfolio Matrix

FIGURE 9.4. Sample Internal Deployment Matrix Outline

Units	Internal Deployment %	Meaning
#/Rank Order	Greater than 100%	Net cash user—cash for redeployment is negative
#/Rank Order	100%	Self-sustaining—cash for redeployment is zero
#/Rank Order	Less than 100%	Net cash contributor—cash for redeployment is positive

ment (physical product types and variations), human resources, and customer service or convenience oriented. Always assess whether you will have to do the same or better to remain in your competitive position in the marketplace.

Looking Ahead

After a thorough profile of your own product (units)/service and a comprehensive assessment of your major competitors it's time to map the road ahead by looking ahead at the key environmental factors that influence your market. These include macro trends as well as factors with strong correlations to demand for your products/services. Understanding what lies ahead becomes a basis for growth rate assumptions, prioritizing market opportunities, and preparing a baseline forecast.[2]

As pointed out, macro trends, such as growth in overall economic activity and general population growth, provide broad directional indicators. In order to fine-tune the directional indicators, it is essential to profile the demand generators or those specific trends or growth rates that correlate closely to and influence demand for your specific products/service. Some of these specific demand generators may have a higher correlation or more directly influence demand than others. One way to balance the variances between demand generators is to create a development point index (DPI). The DPI is weighted or provides for more points to be assigned to those factors that closely correlate or influence demand for your specific products/services. For example, a strong demand generator for an airport hotel would be airport activity (usually a one-to-one relationship); therefore, on a 10-point DPI, airport activity would receive a 10. Figure 9.5 provides an example of a demand generator data collection and related DPI.

In Figure 9.5, we see that for each market (in this case defined as Standard Metropolitan Statistical Area—SMSA), the major demand generators include air deplanements; convention activity; corporate activity, government activity; feeder market trends (which markets demand comes from); destination market (this means the actual market under study is the destination itself, that is, Las Vegas, Orlando); population/migration trend; performance (current measure of demand in the market being studied); fair market share; your product/service performance compared to the overall market and/or your percentage or share of the total market; and any other significant indicators of demand growth.

In the bottom half of Figure 9.5, we see that a weighted DPI has been assigned to each demand generator. In this example, airport activity is assigned 10 points and the population/migration trend is assigned 4 points. Also, bonus points have been assigned to further prioritize the value of each demand generator. The sum of all points is intended to reflect the potential of the market for future development. The compilation of all markets profiled then can be prioritized based on the highest DPI score to the lowest score.

Recommendations

Once the internal assessment and external research on the potential growth of the market area has been completed, it is time to prepare and present recommendations. These may be by market, product/unit type (most appropriate to the market's needs), and the preferred location within the market. Figure 9.6 presents a sample summary of development recommendations in the form of an easily readable grid. In this case we have used a lodging company with multiple product/service level properties and a 120-month (10-year) time frame.

Let's recap the development plan process up to this point. First, we defined where the company was today by assessing current product/units/service offerings. We analyzed each market and product with respect to our strengths, weaknesses, competitiveness, and market share. We assessed our top five competitors in depth. We then looked at ourselves in terms of our product life cycle to determine where we are heading. This formed a baseline forecast. We then looked ahead

_____SMSA

Air Deplanements:_____

Convention Activity:_____

Corporate Activity (national and regional headquarters): _____

Government Activity (federal white-collar employment): _____

Feeder Market Significance:_____

Destination Market:_____

Population/Migration Trend:_____

Performance:_____

Fair Market Share:_____

Other Indicators:_____

Development Point Index	_____ Points Total _____ Rank		
Indicator	**Points**	**Bonus**	**Points Earned**
Airport Activity	10	4	
Convention Activity	8	3	
Corporate Activity	10	0	
Government Activity	7	1	
Feeder Market Significance	10	0	
Destination Market	10	0	
Population/Migration Trend	4	0	
Performance Factor	8	2	
Fair Market Share	10	5	
Other	0	0	
Total	77	12	
TOTAL			

FIGURE 9.5. Summary of Demand Generators and Development Point Index

at macro trends and projected growth in demand generators. We organized this data by market area and utilized a DPI to establish priorities for market development. We then suggested an organized approach in which to present the findings of all the analysis and research in the form of a grid, which summarized the development recommendations by market, product type, and time frame. Figure 9.7 recaps the key areas in the development plan methodology or process.

DEVELOPMENT PLAN ORGANIZATION

Most strategic and long-term development plans are organized in a stepped process and include three major focal points or considerations: first, assessing what the environmental or competitive trends mean to the company; second, establishing where the company wants to go in the

_____SMSA

GRID

Development Timing	SMSA Recommended Product	Motel/Inn	Motor Hotel	Hotel
Immediate to 24 Months				
24 to 60 Months				
50 to 120 Months				
Always				

Location Type:	**Code**			
Airport	A			
Suburban	S			
City	C			
Highway	H			
Resort/Destination	D			

Comments:_____

_____

_____

_____

FIGURE 9.6. Sample Summary of Development Recommendations

future; and, third, establishing the long-range strategies or deciding how to get there. This encompasses and guides the five-step process involved with a development plan as presented in Figures 9.8 through 9.12.

The sample outline that follows can be adapted to any business, brand, or product/service offering. For purposes of consistency and linkage to other examples presented within this chapter, the outline assumes that the brand or product/service is both owned by the parent company as well as franchised. Further, the brand is part of the lodging industry.

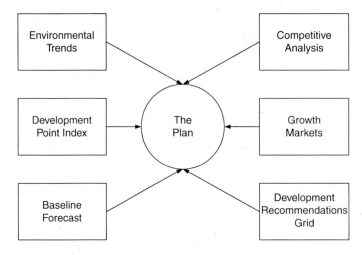

FIGURE 9.7. Development Plan Process/Methodology

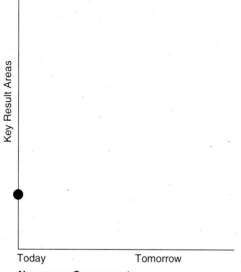

Necessary Components
- Historical Analysis
  - Strengths
  - Weaknesses
  - Voids

FIGURE 9.8. Step One: An Analysis of Our Current Position

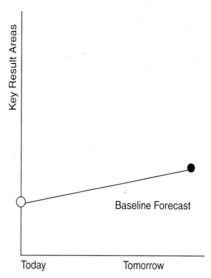

Necessary Components
- Environmental Outlook
- Creative Analysis
- Development of Baseline Forecasts Assuming Industry Growth and Inflationary Trends

FIGURE 9.9. Step Two: An Analysis of Where We Are Headed

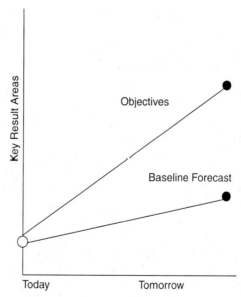

Necessary Components
- Identification of Strategic Issues
- Establishment of Objectives

FIGURE 9.10. Step Three: Formulation of Where We Want to Go

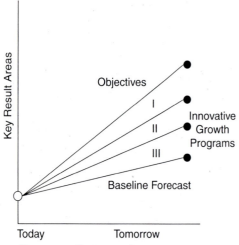

Necessary Components
- Formulation of Appropriate Strategies to Address Strategic Issues
- Development of Growth Programs to Translate Strategies into Definitive Plans

FIGURE 9.11. Step Four: Deciding How to Get There

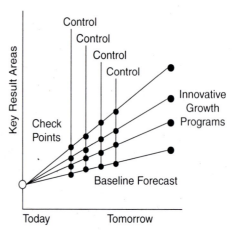

Necessary Components
- Tracing Achievement of Growth Programs
- Detailed (Annual) Planning

FIGURE 9.12. Step Five: Seeing That We're Getting There

SAMPLE DEVELOPMENT PLAN OUTLINE

Ascertain Current Position

I. Determine where the brand, individually and collectively, parent and franchise are today with respect to
   A. Market location
   B. Locational type
   C. Physical facilities
   D. Competitive position
   E. Quality of operation
II. Analyze the top SMSA markets to identify apparent growth markets within the parameters of these selection criteria

Evaluate Market Opportunities

III. Combine the results of I and II and lay the groundwork for strategic planning with emphasis on determining
   A. Markets where the total brand is underrepresented today
   B. Markets where the parent company is underrepresented today
   C. The key feeder markets
   D. Markets that have a distinctly unfavorable profile for future consideration
   E. Market/locational types (airport, city center, etc.) that appear to offer the best opportunity for development
IV. Prioritize opportunities
   A. Markets/opportunities strictly from a parent company point of view

B. Markets/opportunities strictly from a franchise point of view
C. Markets/opportunities where the parent company and franchise group can and should coexist

Product Analysis

V. Analysis of key consumer trends
   A. Determination of product quality level
   B. Determination of product service level
   C. Positioning upgrading, new parent company development, and franchising in line with quality and service levels specific in A and B
VI. Analysis of key competitive and environmental trends
   A. Implications of future trends for the company's long-term development of basic areas covered in research plan
      1. Demographic—population movement, income, lifestyles, etc.
      2. Transportation—airport and highway development trends
      3. Energy—availability and design/location implications
      4. Communications—viewed as both positive products/operations improvement and negative competitor moves and their related implications
      5. Business, government, and miscellaneous societal trends
   B. Competitive trends analysis
      1. Traditional competitive chains (brands) long-term strategy analysis
      2. Nontraditional competitive trend analysis—that is, other areas that compete for the same dollar and consumer

Implication

VII. Tie-in to five-year plan
   A. Prioritizing capital investment to be in concert with long-term development plan strategies identified by I to VI
   B. Plan for implementation
      1. Steps to be taken by parent company development
      2. Steps to be taken by franchise development
      3. Additional steps required

DEVELOPMENT PLANNING IN PERSPECTIVE

Development planning requires multiple research methodologies and techniques. The research data and findings are critical support to strategy selection and the resultant strategies often will impact the annual, capital, and strategic plans of an organization. Figure 9.13 presents a schematic of how the self-research probes, or looking within, looking around, and looking ahead, are interlinked to the development planning process and how the development plan is interlinked to overall corporate strategy.[3]

CHAPTER REVIEW

This chapter has provided a perspective on longer-term development planning and how market research and assessments along with internal analyses are utilized in the development planning process. Further, a model for data collection and focal points of research to support plan rationale were delineated. How the results of this research impact corporate strategies such as dispo-

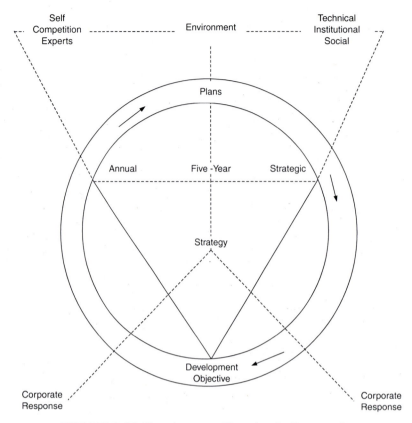

FIGURE 9.13. Development Planning in Perspective

sitions, acquisitions, ownership, and franchising was discussed. It was suggested that there are demand generators for most businesses/products/services that correlate to growth opportunities in any given market. A development point index, which weighted the demand generators and provided a method to score a given market, was presented. The point that the development planning process is interlinked with corporate strategy and specifically with the capital investment plan and strategic plans of a corporation was established. The three major focal points of the development planning process—assessing the environmental/competitive trends and what they mean to the corporation, establishing where the company wants to go, and establishing the long-range strategies or deciding how to get there—were stated. Finally, a five-step process related to a development plan as well as a sample development plan outline were presented.

KEY CONCEPTS/TERMS

Acquisitions
Additions
Book value
Competitive positioning
Concept relationships
Demand generators
Development point index
Dispositions
Emerging markets

Franchise markets
Growth markets
Joint ventures
Market penetration
Market share
Ownership
Patterns
Portfolio analysis
Priority markets
Product diversification
Service levels
Standard metropolitan statistical area
Strategic markets
Supply growth
Territory

DISCUSSION QUESTIONS

1. Why is it important and what results from an internal assessment or looking within?
2. What is involved in looking around at your competition in a development plan?
3. If you were asked to suggest a methodology to organize the data collection component of a development planning process, what would you suggest?
4. Why is it important to place a time frame that the development plan covers?
5. How would the development plan link to the capital investment plan?
6. How would the results of the development plan findings relate to the corporate strategic plan?
7. Select a hospitality or travel-related business and develop a list of demand generators in rank order of highest correlation to have a correlation factor. How would you structure your point index?
8. Which research process and marketing research tools would be beneficial to help identify customer satisfaction levels and methods to improve in this area?
9. Make a list of three product/service offerings and see whether you can identify their positioning, target market, and market segments.

CASE 9.1. SONIC DRIVE-IN—EXTERNAL FORCES REVIVE THE CONCEPT

Sometimes a business gets a whole new life and is invigorated by unforeseen external driving forces. Three major external driving forces had a dramatic impact on Sonic Drive-In. First a brief history of Sonic Drive-In will help provide an understanding of the concept and business. Then we will examine the three external driving forces that have positively influenced the chain and caused a reinvigoration of the growth process.

In 1953, Troy Smith, the founder of Sonic, was living in Shawnee, Oklahoma. Troy's dream was to own his own business. In fact, he had already tried his hand at running a restaurant . . . twice.

Troy's first venture was a tiny diner with twelve stools and four booths called the Cottage Café. It was barely large enough to make a living for his wife and two children. He sold it and bought a bigger place. Troy's Panful of Chicken was so successful that Troy tried opening more of them. Unfortunately, the fried chicken concept didn't fly in early 1950s Oklahoma, and Troy's Panful of Chicken faded quietly away. What didn't fade was Troy's desire to own a restaurant. His ultimate dream was to run a fancy steak house in Shawnee. And, for a while, he did.

The lot where Troy's steak house sat also had a root beer stand. Troy meant to tear it down to add more parking for the steak house. Until he got around to it, he figured the root beer stand could make him a little extra pocket change. In a twist of fate, the humble Top Hat Drive-In, as the root beer stand was called, proved to be more profitable, and outlasted the steak house.

The Top Hat was like other root beer stands of the era. It was a cash business, serving easily prepared hamburgers and hot dogs cooked-to-order. Customers would park on the lot and order at the walk-up window. They could eat on a picnic table or in their cars. The Top Hat was moderately successful.

Ever the entrepreneur, Troy continued to look for ways to improve the business. Yet, he could not have predicted that his improvements would earn him a place in American fast-food history.

While traveling in Louisiana, Troy saw homemade intercom speakers at a hamburger stand that let customers order right from their cars. A lightbulb went on in Troy's head. He contacted the innovator in Louisiana and asked him to make an intercom for the Top Hat. Troy hired some local electronics wizards, whom he called the "jukebox boys," to install the speaker system at his drive-in. He also added a canopy for cars to park under and hired servers to deliver food directly to customers' cars. "Carhops," as the servers were called, was a moniker from the early days of drive-in restaurants, when servers jumped onto the running boards of early-day automobiles driving onto the lot and directed them to their parking spots. Troy Smith now had the prototype of the future Sonic. The first week after the new intercom was installed, the Top Hat took in three times as much revenue than before the changes. It was 1954. The first Chevrolet Corvettes were rolling off the assembly line.

Space-age technology and "carhops" had come to Oklahoma.

Over in Woodward, Oklahoma, Charlie Pappe was managing the local Safeway supermarket. He wanted to get out of the grocery business and start his own restaurant.

While visiting friends in Shawnee, Charlie stopped by the Top Hat for dinner. Charlie had never met Troy Smith, but he was so impressed with the whole concept and operation that he went and introduced himself. Charlie opened the second Top Hat Drive-In on May 18, 1956, in Woodward, Oklahoma. Top Hat Drive-Ins were a big hit with both customers and businesspeople. By 1958, there were Top Hat Drive-Ins in Shawnee, Woodward, Enid, and Stillwater, Oklahoma. Although more entrepreneurs wanted in on their success, only four Top Hats were ever opened.

Troy and Charlie would have kept the Top Hat name, but lawyers informed them it was copyrighted. So, they opened up the dictionary and started searching for a new name. Echoing the common theme of those days, Top Hat's slogan had been "Service with the Speed of Sound[SM]." Indeed, the postwar world was changing fast. The country had seen the dawn of the Atomic Era and the beginnings of the Jet Age and the Space Race. When Troy and Charlie ran across "sonic," meaning "speed of sound," they knew they had the perfect name. The Stillwater, Oklahoma Top Hat Drive-In became the first Sonic Drive-In and still serves hot dogs, root beer, and Frozen Favorites[®]desserts on the same site.

The new name sparked more requests from aspiring Sonic operators. One of the reasons Troy Smith believes Sonic has been so successful through the years is that the drive-in operators are also part-owners, something he thinks makes a terrific difference.

The first Sonic franchise ever sold came with the first formal Sonic franchise agreement. The one-and-a-half-page, double-spaced franchise contract was drafted by Shawnee lawyer, O. K. Winterringer (who also happened to be Troy's landlord).

The royalty fee of one penny per bag was based on the number of Sonic sandwich bags sold through Cardinal Paper, one of Sonic's early vendors.

With each new franchisee, Troy would call Winterringer and another one-and-a-half page, double-spaced, contract based on the penny-a-bag royalty was drafted. Troy and Charlie helped new partners with the layout, site selection, and operation of their Sonic Drive-Ins.

In the early days, there was no national advertising and there were no territorial rights. If two prospects wanted the same town, Winterringer and Troy would talk to them and convince one to go somewhere else.

Charlie Pappe unexpectedly died of a heart attack in 1967 at the age of fifty-four. Troy Smith was left alone to run the burgeoning, fourteen-year-old company and its forty-one Sonic Drive-Ins. Troy invited two franchisees to take over running Sonic Supply (the supply and distribution division of Sonic). In the next six years, the trio built an additional 124 Sonics in a core group of states including Oklahoma, Texas, and Kansas.

In 1973, a group of ten key, principal franchise owners formed and restructured the company into Sonic Systems of America, later changing the name to Sonic Industries. They became the officers and board of directors and purchased the Sonic name, slogan, trademark, logos, and the supply company from Troy. They also offered each store operator the option to buy 1,250 shares of stock at $1 per share.

Sonic was now owned by its franchisees. Due to the number of shares offered, Sonic also became an over-the-counter, publicly traded, company.

There were now 165 Sonics in the chain.

In a period of tremendous growth, more than 800 Sonics opened between 1973 and 1978. By early 1975, Sonic Drive-Ins were present in thirteen southern and southwestern states. O. K. Winterringer established the Sonic School to formally train new managers. The public saw the first Sonic television advertising in 1977.

Interest in Sonic skyrocketed, but first the oil embargo of the early 1970s (major external driving force) and record inflation later in the decade took a big bite out of business. Profits fell 21 percent during 1978 and 1979. Despite the downturn, January 1980 saw the first Sonic National Convention. This demonstrated to franchise owners that company management was determined to weather the storm and increase cooperation between Sonic and its franchisees. Plans were unveiled for more evenly paced growth.

Unfortunately, the 1980 annual report showed sales and operating revenues down more than $5 million, with a net operating loss of $300,000. In response, Sonic consolidated store operations and development, and closed twenty-eight low-volume, company-owned drive-ins. Sonic was down, but not out. The key element to Sonic's comeback was its traditional franchise policy of owner-operators.

In 1984, Sonic was more like a collection of independent stores than a cohesive business entity. Less than 1,000 Sonics operated in nineteen states, yet there was no national advertising program or a national purchasing cooperative. This was the same year that Cliff Hudson joined the Sonic legal department. He was instrumental in making several major changes in the company before eventually becoming president and CEO in 1995.

Hudson was on a team that led Sonic's management in a successful leveraged buyout from its franchisee shareholders for $10 million in May 1986. He also spearheaded two pivotal changes in the company. The first of these was taking Sonic public in March 1991 and initiating a secondary stock offering in 1995, which raised enough cash to pay off the company's debt and add to its working capital. Second, franchises in seventeen key markets began purchasing together, giving significant cost savings to franchisees, and consistency and quality to customers. Advertising also increased to 1 percent of sales.

By 2000, Sonic's media spending approached $64 million, and during the same fiscal year, total system-wide restaurant sales exceeded $1.7 billion with an estimated market value of more than $600 million.

In 1994 and 1995, customers, franchisees, suppliers, and drive-in managers were invited to join a series of Dream Team meetings to discuss what Sonic was doing right and what Sonic could improve.

The meetings spawned Sonic 2000, a new multilayered strategy to further unify the company in terms of a consistent menu, brand identity, products, packaging, and service. As a result, the new "retro-future" Sonic logo was introduced, and the entire system adopted a consistent new look and menu, including a section dedicated to Fountain and Frozen Favorites™. The strategy resulted in Sonic's continued success. The chain is expanding, brand awareness has increased, and franchises are enjoying accelerated growth. Chain operations are now better unified for greater cost efficiencies.

Today, Sonic leads the fast-food industry in real sales growth, with higher same-store sales each year since 1987. As of February 28, 2002, there were 2,432 Sonic Drive-Ins in thirty states, making it the nation's largest drive-in chain.

The country and the fast-food business have changed a great deal since Troy Smith installed the first intercom system at the Top Hat Drive-In. Food fads have come and gone, but Sonic has differentiated itself through its business model, unique menu items, and, of course, friendly "Service with the Speed of Sound." Sonic has also benefited from a number of external driving forces, which has supported this growth.

It has been said that no one loves their automobiles more than North Americans. Combine that love of the car with growth of the baby boomer generation and you have one strong external driving force (no pun intended) that supports the basic concept offered by Sonic, a drive-in fast-food establishment.

We also see that in the early 2000s there was a shift back toward family values. This swing of the pendulum provided a second external driving force that supports the Sonic concept—the family eating together at a drive-in fast-food restaurant. You could also add to this the return of teenage drivers and "cruising" as yet another support for the Sonic concept.

The third external driving force was the result of the tragedy and terrorism attack on September 11, 2001, and the ongoing terrorism threats. This event caused more families and individuals to stay closer to home as well as drive versus fly. In fact, in summer 2002, auto travel by families as well as business travel by car (in all of 2002) accelerated substantially, while airline passenger counts declined or remained flat. For Sonic this meant yet another strong external driving force favoring its business concept.

These external forces combined with a number of internal forces and strategic management decisions have proven essential ingredients to Sonic's success. Factors that contributed to Sonic's strong growth and continued earnings success are discussed in the following sections.

Multilayered Growth Strategy

Sonic pursues a multilayered growth strategy to achieve targeted annual gains in earnings per share in the range of 18 to 20 percent. The following steps help diversify growth potential and strengthen profitability:

- Expanding the chain through the addition of both company-owned and franchised drive-ins
- Boosting brand awareness with steadily increasing media expenditures and new product news (which drives same-store sales and average unit volumes)
- Steadily growing franchise income due to accelerated franchise development and the company's unique ascending royalty rate
- Unifying chain operations for greater cost efficiencies

Highly Differentiated Concept

As the nation's largest chain of drive-in restaurants, Sonic is distinguished as the most highly differentiated quick-service brand through the following:

- A streamlined service delivery system
- Personalized carhop service that's fast, convenient, and a lot more friendly than the typical drive-through
- A unique menu with a variety of high-quality, made-to-order sandwiches and specialty items

Accelerated Expansion Program

Sonic subscribes to a lower-risk, higher-return development strategy that relies heavily on growth in the franchise side of the business. Recent program benchmarks include the following:

- A record 157 new franchise-owned drive-in openings during fiscal 2001
- A record total of 191 new drive-in openings (company- and franchisee-owned) during fiscal 2001—a significantly faster expansion than the range of 170 to 176 annual new drive-in openings over the past three years
- Sonic's accelerated expansion program continued during fiscal 2002, with 190 new drive-in openings

Strong Sales Trends

Sonic enjoys one of the strongest growth records in the restaurant industry, having posted more than 15 consecutive years of higher sales on a same-store basis. New product news and product innovations, along with higher media spending, continue to drive top-line gains:

- System-wide sales reached $2 billion in fiscal 2001, increasing 11 percent during the year and doubling from the $1 billion mark set just four years earlier
- System-wide same-store sales increased 1.8 percent in fiscal 2001, with gains accelerating to 4.8 percent and 4.9 percent in the third and fourth quarters of the year
- System average unit volumes advanced 2.5 percent for the year
- Total revenues rose 18 percent in fiscal 2001

Solid Financial Performance

Sonic's multilayered growth strategy continues to drive a strong bottom-line performance:

- Revenues increased at a compound annual rate of 17 percent during the five-year period that ended in August 2001

- Net income per share during the same period rose at a compound annual rate of 21 percent
- Return on stockholders' equity has increased for five consecutive years, reaching almost 22 percent in fiscal 2001

Sonic Drive-Ins, often viewed as a reflection of the nostalgic past (1950s-1960s), are also now viewed as meeting the needs of today's current market. It can be said that they will likely meet the needs of the future marketplaces as America's love of the automobile (SUVs) and desire for convenient food form some very strong external driving forces moving to support the Sonic Drive-In concept.[4]

Case Discussion Questions

1. "Retro" trends (reflections of past eras) are sometimes linked to a hospitality brand like Sonic. Select one such hospitality brand and discuss the benefits and/or pitfalls of a "retro" positioning strategy.
2. What future external driving forces do you see impacting the hospitality industry?

CASE 9.2. CARNIVAL CORPORATION—POSITIONING AND STRATEGY SELECTION

The case example which follows views a corporation's strategy to be the "biggest" player in its respective hospitality industry sector. It also demonstrates a strategy that extends to brand collection and individual market segments.

Introduction

Carnival Corporation, based in Miami, is the world's largest cruise ship operator with control of about a third of the global market. Carnival Cruise Lines is its best-known brand with sixteen ships. However, the company also owns/operates five other brands, namely Costa Crociere (seven ships), Holland America Lines (eleven ships), Cunard Lines (two ships), Seabourn Cruise Lines (six ships), and Windstar Cruises (four ships). Carnival serves 2 million passengers per year. Additional ships are planned for many of its brands over the next five to seven years.

Carnival Corporation generates over 90 percent of its revenue from cruise ships. The balance is generated through other travel/hotel-related operations. These include a 26 percent interest in Airtours, the second largest tour operator in the United Kingdom, and Holland America Westours, which operates Alaska tours and also owns fourteen hotels in the area.[5]

Carnival represents a corporate management strategy that focused on multiple products/brands positioning in the cruise industry. This case example delineates their different brands' positions with respect to quality, price, market, and lifestyle positioning. Further, its acquisitions strategy and product-positioning strategies allow it to exemplify a company that serves not only multiple market segments but also a vast array of geographic markets.

History

Carnival Cruise Lines was founded by Ted Arison in 1972. Arison realized that a market for cruise vacations existed even though the era of the transatlantic line had ended. He persuaded an old friend, Meshulam Riklis, who was the primary shareholder of American International Travel Service (AITS) to fund his purchase of a $6.5 million used vessel, the *Empress of Canada*. Carnival Cruise Lines was established as a subsidiary of AITS. Arison's vessel was renamed the *Mardi Gras* reflecting Arison's belief that a line could be established to attract young, middle-class tourists who wanted a short sea-going vacation in a warm climate with food, fun, entertainment, music, and gambling at reasonable prices. However, his dream almost ended at the beginning. The *Mardi Gras* ran aground off Miami on its maiden voyage. The company fared poorly, and in 1974, Riklis sold the operation to Arison for $1 million and the assumption of some $5 million in debt.

Things soon began to change; sales improved and by the end of 1975, the small line had enough money to buy another used ship. This vessel was the *Empress of Britain* and Arison renamed it the *Carnivale*. Again, the name reflected the fun, vacation-oriented concept of cruising, which Arison fostered. An additional used ship purchase was made in the late 1970s. Carnival's first new ship-building venture took place in 1978 when the *Tropicale* was built and delivered in 1981. Additional new buildings followed. Carnival Cruise Lines had become the largest cruise line in the world by 1987. That year it carried over 500,000 passengers and held about 20 percent of the North American cruise market.

Carnival continued to grow. The company went public in 1987 selling an 18 percent interest and raising some $400 million. This move marked a turning point for the company and allowed it to grow even faster. Newer ships were ordered. These included the *Fascination, Fantasy, Ecstasy, Celebration, Elation,* and others. The needs/wants of their customers were factored into the design process. More space, more amenities, advanced ship control and propulsion systems, improved safety and fire control, improved fuel economy, and new entertainment options were added. At the turn of the decade, it introduced the *Carnival Triumph,* at over 100,000 GRT (gross registered tons), which represented one of the largest ships ever built. It is considerably larger than Arison's first ship, which was 18,261 GRT. The *Carnival Triumph* carries some 2,750 passengers.

Carnival's growth was accompanied by acquisitions. The Carnival Cruise Lines product was aimed at the mass market. Cruises were predominantly to the Caribbean from the United States, customers were mainly American, and "fun" was the basis of the cruise. Carnival began an expansion program, through horizontal integration, to seek other markets and acquisitions helped them reach these markets. The names of their acquired subsidiaries were left unchanged. The company's name was changed to Carnival Corporation in 1994 to reflect their growing range of activities for various cruise market segments.

Acquisitions

Carnival attempted to purchase its primary competitor, Royal Caribbean Cruise Lines, in 1988. This move was not successful; however, they then turned their sights on the venerable Holland America Lines. Holland America was active in Alaska, owned fourteen hotels in that area under the Westmark brand as well as Holland America Westours, which provided tours in that region. They also owned/operated four sailing cruise ships under the Windstar name. Holland America competed with Carnival in the Caribbean as well. Windstar ships operated in the Caribbean as well as in the South Pacific. The purchase was finalized in 1989. It allowed Carnival access to the more upscale clientele of Holland America. The adventuresome passenger niche was served by Windstar (sail cruises). This move also positioned the company well in the growing Alaskan tour market, which was to become third, after the Caribbean and Mediterranean, in sought-after cruise destinations.

Carnival developed a joint venture with Seabourn Cruise Lines in 1992. This move would eventually lead to the buyout of Seabourn in 1999. Seabourn operates six small but upscale luxury vessels on worldwide routes. It is considered by many to be the highest quality cruise line in the world. Its purchase signaled the beginning of Carnival's entry into the luxury market.

Another move into the luxury market was made in 1999 when Carnival purchased the well-known Cunard Lines. This move added additional ships to their fleet including the world famous *Queen Elizabeth 2* and *Caronia.* Cunard vessels were well positioned in the luxury end of the market. Their vessels operated worldwide and the *Queen Elizabeth 2* remained the only vessel of the liner era to still offer regular transatlantic crossings from New York to Southampton and back for part of the year.

Carnival desired a stake in the growing European market. In 1996, they purchased a 26 percent stake in Airtours, the second largest tour operator in Britain. Together they purchased a 63 percent interest in Costa Crociere, the large Italian cruise operator that at the time held about a 28 percent market share in the European spring-fall market. Costa Crociere was fully purchased by Carnival in 2000.

Carnival Brands

The flagship of all Carnival brands, Carnival Cruise Lines, is Carnival's largest and most profitable subsidiary. It is also the most popular cruise line in the world. Its "fun ship" marketing philosophy has successfully defined their position in the mass-market sector.

The "fun ship" theme defines the company as a vacation alternative to land resorts. Carnival emphasizes the cruise experience itself rather than particular destinations. It also emphasizes the advantages of an all-inclusive vacation package. Carnival tries to avoid the stuffiness of the transatlantic liner era by offering a wide variety of shipboard activities. These include Las Vegas type shows, gambling, and other entertainment. Their ships are even designed to foster the spirit of "fun." This includes untraditional internal and external features that reflect theme atmospheres.

This practice established the ship as the destination where the fun was and ports as secondary attractions. This marketing effort was a complete reversal of the destination-based marketing of transatlantic era passenger ships.

The Carnival Cruise Lines fleets (sixteen cruise ships) range in size from 36,674 GRT carrying about 1,000 passengers to those in the 100,000 GRT category carrying about 2,700 passengers.

The company operates cruises ranging from three to sixteen days in duration to a variety of ports in the Bahamas, Caribbean, Mexican Riviera, Alaska, Hawaii, and the Panama Canal. Additional ports are regularly added. Vessels generally depart from the ports of Miami, Port Canaveral, Tampa, New Orleans, Los Angeles, San Juan, Ensenada, Vancouver, and Honolulu. Carnival also operates the world's first nonsmoking ship, the *Paradise,* that sails on alternating eastern and western Caribbean itineraries.

Carnival's average per person, per diem rate is about $195 (year 2000 U.S. dollars) without discount. Its cruises are strongly supported by those "fun" seekers whose average age is forty-three years old and who have an average income of about $50,000. Carnival's occupancy rate has stood at over 100 percent for the 1980-2000 year period, while the industry rate ranged from 70 percent to 88 percent. Their high occupancy rate has been accomplished through broad mass appeal with competitive all-inclusive pricing. Their wide range of onboard and shore activities further adds to the product offering. Carnival's "fun ship" marketing technique has brought cruising to the average American and changed forever the conservative, stodgy image of the passenger ships of the transatlantic era.

In 1986, Carnival offered its vacation guarantee. It states that if guests are unsatisfied with their cruise experience, they may debark at the first non-U.S. port of call and receive reimbursement for coach air fare back to the port of passenger embarkation. This move was undertaken partly to gain first-time cruisers and was a "first" in the cruise line industry.

The Mediterranean cruising area is the second-largest cruise vacation area after the Caribbean. Europeans have been experiencing a growth in leisure time since the early 1990s. In 1994, however, most European cruise lines were high-priced premium and luxury cruises; no cruise line offered the equivalent of Carnival's standard, low-priced cruise vacation. Carnival entered the European cruise business by completing a purchase of Costa Crociere in 2000.

Costa Crociere is a Genoa, Italy, based cruise ship operation that had its beginnings over 100 years ago. At that time, it operated cargo ships carrying olive oil. The company developed into one of the first cruise operators in the 1950s by operating trips from Miami. Costa is well known for its "cruising Italian style" theme. Their ships offered legendary Italian cuisine, Italian flair, and hospitality. Their largest ship, the *Costa Atlantica,* has twelve decks named after movies directed by the famous Italian director Federico Fellini.

It is estimated that Costa carries about 28 percent of the European cruise line trade during the spring to fall season. Two-thirds of the fleet operates in Europe; the others operate between Europe and the Caribbean. They own seven ships, ranging in size from 25,000 GRT to 84,000 GRT. Their customer base is mainly European, with an average age of forty-five years and annual income of $50,000 plus. Average per diem per person rates stand at about $245 (year 2000 U.S. dollars).

Holland America Lines was founded in 1873 as the Netherlands-America Steamship Company. This company primarily operated as a cargo and passenger carrying company. It was a major carrier of immigrants from Europe to the United States until well after the turn of the century. Unable to compete with the growing transatlantic air travel business, Holland-America suspended its transatlantic passenger trade in 1971 and turned to offering full-time cruise vacations.

The company operates eleven ships ranging in size from 33,930 GRT to 63,000 GRT and carrying about 1,200 to 1,500 passengers each. Their vessels sail to a wide spectrum of ports in Alaska, Mexico, Europe, Canada and New England, South America, and around the world. Holland-America also operated Windstar Cruises, a fleet of four specialty sail/cruise ships operating in Europe, the Caribbean, and Central America. Both fleets were purchased by Carnival in 1989.

Holland-America cruises offer a more upscale cruising experience than Carnival Cruise Lines. Typical undiscounted cruises cost about $350 (year 2000 U.S. dollars) per person per diem. Clientele are generally over fifty years of age and a large percentage travel in group tours. The ships are well known for their onboard art collections as well as educational programs.

Windstar Cruises was created in 1984 with the vision to offer an alternative to the typical cruise or vacation resort. The company was purchased by Holland-America and later by Carnival Corporation in 1989.

Windstar's theme is "180 degrees from the ordinary." This theme clearly defines it as a company providing a different cruise vacation. They operate four sail yachts carrying between 148 and 312 passengers to the Caribbean, Europe, and Central America. Guests are offered unique itineraries and the freedom to be as active or relaxed as they want to be. The company defines this atmosphere as "casual elegance." Passengers range from those in their twenties to those in their sixties. However, the average age is fifty-two and average income stands at about $120,000 plus.

The company offers a unique niche or specialty cruise vacation experience that has received awards from both *Conde Nast* and *Travel and Leisure* magazines.

Cunard Lines was purchased by Carnival Corporation in 1999. This purchase allowed it to serve the luxury cruise ship market.

Cunard Lines is one of the most famous brands in the history of passenger shipping. The company's founder, Samuel Cunard, began in 1839, by operating steamships for the British Admiralty in carriage of mail between the United Kingdom and North America. The company grew into a leader in the passenger ship trade. This company operated such famous liners as the *Queen Mary, Queen Elizabeth,* and *Queen Elizabeth 2.*

Cunard customers are typically traditional, well-off or wealthy, and generally over fifty years in age. About half of their passengers reside outside of North America particularly in Britain and Europe. They seek the elegance and tradition that Cunard Lines embodies. Typical per diem per person costs, undiscounted, range from just over $400 to $600 (year 2000 U.S. dollars) and up, depending on accommodations.

At the time of this writing, Cunard operates two ships. They are the *Queen Elizabeth 2* and the smaller 25,000-ton, *Caronia.* A new vessel, the *Queen Mary,* at 140,000 tons, is planned to be delivered in the next few years. Cunard ships operate on worldwide routes with emphasis on the Caribbean, Europe, and the Pacific. The *Queen Elizabeth 2* continues to operate regular transatlantic service between New York and Southampton for part of the year. It is the only cruise vessel that does so on a regular basis.

Seabourn Cruise Lines was fully purchased by Carnival Corporation in 1999. This exclusive fleet of "super yachts" has often been rated as the best cruise line in the world.

Atle Brynestad, a Norwegian industrialist, founded Seabourn in 1987. The concept, since its founding, was to provide the highest level of personal service equal to any hotel, resort, or restaurant ashore to its customers. Spaciousness and elegance is the rule and guests are pampered in accordance with their own personal tastes and lifestyles.

The company now consists of six ships (all but one is a "super yacht"). These vessels carry anywhere from 115 to just over 200 passengers. One vessel, a former Cunard Line ship integrated into the Seabourn fleet, carries about 760 passengers. These vessels operate worldwide, but focus on the Caribbean, Europe, South America, and Asia. Typical per diem per person rates stand at about $750 (year 2000 U.S. dollars). The average Seabourn passenger is affluent (average income is about $200,000 per year). About half of Seabourn's passengers are repeat customers.

Cruiser Profile

Cruise Lines International Association (CLIA) is an industry organization that promotes the cruise industry. It became the sole marketing organization of the industry in 1984 when the Federal Maritime Commission consolidated other industry organizations into CLIA. Its member lines make up about 95 percent of the total North America berths and about 81 percent of all the ships. They have developed a cruiser profile based on those who took cruises in the last five years (all North American bookings). Note that over 65 percent of all cruisers are North Americans. The cruiser profile is seen in Exhibit 9.1.

Characteristics	% of Cruisers
Married	78
Single	22
Vacation with Children	59
Don't Vacation with Children	41
Male	52
Female	48
25-39 Years of Age	30
40-59 Years of Age	42
60 Years or Older	28
Mean Age	50 Years
$20K-$39.9K Household Income	15
$40K-$59.9K Household Income	31
$60K plus Household Income	55
Mean Household Income	$79K

EXHIBIT 9.1. Cruiser Profile (Cruisers for the Last Five Years). *Source:* CLIA, 2000 Market Profile Study, www.cruising.org.

Segmentation of the cruiser of today can also be done by age, income, and by psychographic profile. Cruise Lines International Association 2001 studies have segmented prospective North American cruisers as (1) family folks with 31 percent of the market; (2) want-it-alls with 17 percent of the market; (3) adventurers with 12 percent of market; (4) comfortable spenders with 25 percent of market; and (5) cautious travelers with 15 percent of the market in North America. Profiles of recent cruisers (last five years) have also been developed.[6]

Exhibit 9.2 presents a description of the various cruise brands of Carnival Corporation and shows where they are positioned in the cruise vacation market in terms of pricing, product, and geographic area of operation.

Exhibit 9.3 shows how Carnival has positioned themselves in the marketplace on the basis of standard, premium, luxury, and niche or specialty segments of the population. Competitors in the cruise business are also noted.

It can be seen that Carnival has positioned itself in all major price/quality sectors through its various brands. Royal Caribbean, its chief competitor, is only represented in two areas. Carnival's major berth capacities lie in standard and premium (about 39,000 berths). In luxury and specialty sectors they hold about 4,500 berths. Royal Caribbean holds a total of about 33,000 berths in standard and premium.

One can also cite the geographic positioning of Carnival's various cruise lines. Exhibit 9.4 illustrates where Carnival's positioning lies in accordance with the top six travel destinations for cruisers. Destinations are ranked from highest to lowest (left to right) and are based on the CLIA 2000 Destination Analysis found in the CLIA 2001 market studies.

The aforementioned destination areas represent over 72 percent of the destination bed days in the industry. Carnival has positioned itself well for voyages in all the major destination areas.

Carnival's competition in the cruise vacation business relates to only four other companies. They are Royal Caribbean, Princess Cruises, and Norwegian Cruise Lines, which is now part of Star Lines. These four companies are estimated to control 64 percent of the total cruise vacation business. Carnival alone controls one-third of the business. It is clear that Carnival has been very successful in its brand acquisition and expansion strategy. Royal Caribbean, the second-rated company in terms of sales (about two-thirds of Carnival's), operates two brands. Celebrity is in the premium category and the Royal Caribbean name brand is in the standard priced sector.

Carnival Corporation has successfully expanded through multiple positioning strategies. Their brand positioning and acquisitions strategies have made it possible for them to serve the various price/quality segments of the cruiser population with varying products from mass market to niche and luxury. Furthermore, by positioning their various subsidiaries in the top cruiser travel destinations, they are able to serve almost all the popular destinations with more than one price/quality product.

Carnival's successful use of segmentation principles has allowed them to control about a third of the total cruise vacation market in this increasingly competitive field.[7]

	Carnival	Costa	H-America	Windstar	Cunard	Seabourn
Per Diem*	$190+	$245	$350	$400	$400-$600	$750+
Age	43	45	50+	52+	50+	55+
Income	$45,000	$50,000	$60,000	$120,000	$65,000	$200,000
Market Perception	Fun, Mass Market	Italian, Style, Service	Undisputed Value	Specialty, Adventure, and Uniqueness	Tradition, British	Affluence, Elegance

EXHIBIT 9.2. Market Positioning. *Note:* *U.S. Dollars for Year 2000.

Standard	Premium	Luxury	Specialty
Carnival	Holland America	Seabourn	Windstar
Costa	Celbrity	Cunard	Club Med
Norwegian Cruise Lines	Princess	Silversea	Disney
Royal Caribbean		Crystal	Orient
			Quark (icebreakers)
			Seabourn

EXHIBIT 9.3. Positioning in the Cruise Industry. *Source:* Adapted from B. Dickinson and A. Vladimir, *Selling the Sea: An Inside Look at the Cruise Industry* (New York: Wiley, 1997). *Note:* Overlap in categories is possible.

Caribbean	Med. Sea	Alaska	Europe	Bahamas	West Mex.
Carnival	Costa	Carnival	Costa	Carnival	Carnival
Costa	Cunard	Holland Am	Cunard	Holland Am	Holland Am
Cunard	Holland Am		Holland Am		
Holland Am	Seaborne		Seaborne		
Seaborne	Windstar		Windstar		
Windstar					

EXHIBIT 9.4. Geographic Positioning

Case Discussion Questions

1. Do you believe it is more or less advantageous for Carnival to retain the brand names of the cruise lines it has acquired?
2. While retaining its multiple brands and positioning strategies where do you believe Carnival could capitalize on its size?

NOTES

1. R. Nykiel, *A Strategic Plan for Business Development* (Memphis, TN: Holiday Inns, Inc., 1976), p. 1.
2. R. Nykiel, *Marketing Your Business: A Guide to Developing a Strategic Marketing Plan* (Binghamton, NY: Best Business Books, 2003), p. 9.
3. Ibid., p. 3.
4. www.sonicdrivein.com.
5. Nykiel, *Marketing Your Business,* p. 9.
6. Ibid. Nykiel, *A Strategic Plan,* pp. 1-21.
7. R. Nykiel, *Hospitality Management Strategies* (Upper Saddle River, NJ: Prentice Hall, 2005), pp. 42-48.

Chapter 10

Assessing Focal Points and Intuitive Techniques

CHAPTER OBJECTIVES

- To point out the importance of research focusing on the internal and external environment as well as the future.
- To provide a recap of the major types of marketing research with respect to products/services, consumers, competition, and the environment.
- To delineate the basic marketing research techniques widely utilized in today's marketplace.
- To present five essential marketing intelligence tools almost any business can utilize.
- To suggest a number of marketing research presentation tools to enhance the communication of research findings and related strategies.

At this juncture, a comprehensive assessment should be conducted that focuses on (1) self-analysis (the business itself), (2) competition, and (3) environmental factors that can impact your business/strategy (Figure 10.1).

Researching each of these areas is essential to developing the basis for a strategic marketing plan. In fact, before you can select strategies or deploy marketing weaponry to execute those strategies you must know your product or service, your target markets and their needs, and your competition. You also need to know what the road ahead looks like with respect to the business environment in which you will be operating. In essence, your marketing strategies must be based on sound research.

In this chapter you are provided a synopsis of basic types of research, selected marketing research techniques, and some analytical tools to help you categorize, prioritize, and present your research.

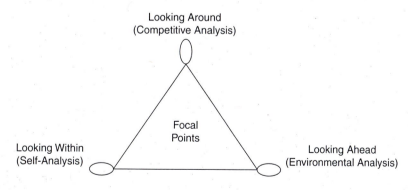

FIGURE 10.1. Focal Points

Handbook of Marketing Research Methodologies for Hospitality and Tourism
© 2007 by The Haworth Press, Inc. All rights reserved.
doi:10.1300/5927_11

TYPES OF MARKETING RESEARCH

Broadly speaking, marketing research can be either quantitative or qualitative. Quantitative marketing research seeks to quantify data using numbers, projections, forecasts, and so on. Qualitative marketing research seeks to identify, analyze, or profile consumers, looking at consumer attitudes, behaviors, and so on. Both quantitative and qualitative marketing research can be either primary or secondary. Primary research is research you conduct yourself; secondary research is research that someone else has conducted.

Marketing research can also be categorized with respect to the following:

- Markets
- Products or services
- Consumers
- Competition
- Environment

Let's briefly examine each of these marketing research categories in the following sections.

Market Research

Market research seeks to quantify and segment demand. Focal points of market research include the following:

- Market share (demand)
- Sales trends
- Market segments/quantification/trends
  - Primary target market
  - Secondary target market
  - Niche/special markets
- Distribution channels
  - Outlets
  - Penetration
  - Coverage
- Geographic markets/trends
- Media markets
  - Broadcast (television/radio)
  - Print (newspaper/magazine)
  - Electronic (internet)
  - Direct mail
  - Outdoor
  - Other

Product or Service Research

Product or service research usually focuses on your product's/service's strengths and weaknesses in relation to the products/services of competitors. This research focuses on the following:

- Products/services
  - Strengths
  - Weaknesses

- Development
- Life cycle
- Positioning
- Branding
- Packaging
- Pricing strategies

Consumer Research

Consumer research takes many different forms and covers a very broad range of customer and potential customer related issues. It may be quantitative or qualitative in nature. Consumer research many focus on the following:

- Demographics
- Geographics
- Psychographics
- Behavioral patterns
- Social attitudes
- Habits
- Benefits and needs

Since marketing frequently relies on the media as one method to reach prospective customers, present and future customers can be categorized by DMAs (designated market areas—geographic areas reached by clusters of television stations, as defined by the A. C. Neilsen Co.) or ADIs (areas of dominant influence—geographic areas defined by the circulation zones of major newspapers, as categorized by Arbitron, an audience research firm).

In summary, consumer research seeks to identify the usage patterns of customers and their preferences. Consumer research also seeks to classify consumers by age, income, education, and so on (demographics), as well as to discover their habits (psychographics) with respect to likes, dislikes, and so on, always seeking to quantify wherever possible. Consumer research explores everything from the purchasing habits to the attitudes and behaviors of consumers.[1]

Competitive Research

One of the keys to successful marketing strategy is understanding how your product or service compares to your top competitors' products or services. *Competitive research* compares your product or service to the products or services of competitors and tries to discover how consumers perceive and experience your product/service offering in relation to the competitors' products/services. Focal points of competitive research include the following:

- Pricing
- Value
- Quality
- Convenience to purchase
- Customer satisfaction
- Delivery

Environmental Research

Marketing must take into account not only what consumers and competitors are doing, but also what is occurring within and to the total industry environment. *Environmental research* focuses on external forces, major issues that will have an impact on your business, such as the following:

- Overall economic scenario
- Social issues
- Political issues
- Technological developments
- Legal implications
- Legislative issues

One key focus of environmental research is to look ahead at what form and shape opportunities and threats may take and how they will affect your activities. Frequently, competitive research and environmental research are linked. The output of these research assessments is often referred to by the acronym SWOT, which stands for strengths, weaknesses, opportunities, and threats. These strengths, weaknesses, opportunities, and threats can then be analyzed to provide support rationale for developing marketing strategies. Examples of focal points of a SWOT analysis include the following:

- Strengths
  - Company/brand
  - Value to the market
  - Product/service leadership
  - Brand awareness
  - Image
  - Technological
  - Operational
  - Marketing (distribution) share
  - Pricing
  - Financial
  - Customer loyalty/satisfaction
- Weaknesses
  - Consumption/sales trends
  - Product/service delivery
  - Technological
  - Operational
  - Marketing
- Pricing
- Distribution
- Promotion
  - Image
  - Awareness
  - Reputation
  - Financial
  - Obsolescence
- Opportunities
  - Brand extensions
  - New products/services

  - New markets
  - Incremental purchase
  - Exploiting competitive weakness
  - Excess demand (pricing)
  - New distribution channels
  - Technology
  - New trends
- Threats
  - Capacity to deliver
  - Labor availability
  - Cost to produce
  - Superior new competitor
  - Product/service obsolescence
  - Regulatory
  - Competitive pricing
  - Declining demand

In summary, research focuses on both quantitative and qualitative trends. Quantitative trend research seeks to identify significant increases or declines in customer preferences, methods of purchase, usage/frequency, and other factors impacting future demand. Qualitative trend research seeks to identify changes in consumer attitudes, interests, tastes, benefits sought, and so on. Trend research findings help marketers make strategic marketing decisions.

Selecting the appropriate research technique will expedite findings and applications.

MARKETING RESEARCH TECHNIQUES

Many types of marketing research techniques can be used to help you make sound marketing decisions. Which technique works best depends on many factors, such as the product/service offering, nature of the problem or opportunity, amount of resources available, time or urgency, budget, and so on. Basic marketing research techniques widely used include surveys, questionnaires, and focus groups. Of course, there are many other quantitative and qualitative research techniques employed, but the purpose of this section is to familiarize you with these basic techniques. Regardless of the research technique selected, the goal remains the same—to gain information and to apply the findings to improve the marketing and/or marketability of a product or service.

Surveys

A *survey* seeks to elicit consumer opinion, uncover facts, and gain insights on potential trends. Surveys may be conducted in a variety of ways, at various locations, among customers or potential customers, or even among competitors' customers. Surveys may be conducted in person, by phone, electronically, or by mail.

A survey is a structured document, usually seeking to quantify its findings in terms of percentages of those who agree or disagree with particular statements. It also seeks to measure the depth of agreement or disagreement, often employing a point scale, for example, "Circle 1 if you strongly agree, 5 if you strongly disagree"; 5-, 7-, and 10-point scales are commonly used. Surveys are also used to seek qualitative information, especially when open-ended questions are asked, e.g., "What else would you like to see or have?" and so on. Surveys may be conducted only once or periodically scheduled, such as an annual frequent-flier program preference survey. Multiple-period (semiannual, monthly, etc.) surveys often seek to spot improvements or declines in such areas as service levels or consumer preferences, thus providing a rationale for a marketing, operational, or development decision.

Questionnaires

Perhaps the most widely used research technique is *questionnaires*. These come in all types of forms and are used for multiple purposes. As data collection vehicles, questionnaires seek both factual information and opinion. Data that questionnaires are designed to collect include customer comments, customer profiles, product and service information, demographic and psychographic data, attitudinal information, consumer usage patterns and preferences, etc. The data collected may be used to measure performance, improve products or services, qualify prospects, build leads, create mailing lists, determine consumer price sensitivity, and analyze menus.

Like surveys, questionnaires can be conducted in person, by phone, by mail, or electronically. Questionnaires often are ongoing, such as customer satisfaction comment questionnaires, new customer/purchaser questionnaires, and so on. Also like surveys, questionnaires can use scales or point systems to yield quantifiable data or rank items in order of importance.

Frequently, the terms "survey" and "questionnaire" are used interchangeably. However, questionnaires tend to be briefer than surveys and are usually less complex in content.

Focus Groups

For additional analysis, focus groups may be recorded or observed via one-way mirrors. A *focus group* is a marketing research technique that combines personal-opinion solicitation in the form of group discussion with a structured set of questions. During a focus group session, a "moderator" conducts or facilitates the discussion using a script designed to elicit opinions from focus group members. Focus group members may volunteer their time or be compensated.

Focus groups by nature are more time-consuming for marketers to conduct and follow through on than surveys or questionnaires. Focus groups involve script writing, hiring a professional group leader, holding the focus group session itself, and then analyzing the focus group and its responses. In general, focus groups provide more in-depth qualitative findings related to attitudes and behaviors than do questionnaires or surveys. Sometimes focus groups come up with useful questions that can be placed on subsequent questionnaires or surveys.

There are a number of types of focus groups, ranging from single-area focus groups to regional/market-area focus groups to multiple focus groups. Single-area focus groups are focus groups drawn from one market; regional/market-area focus groups are single focus groups held in one or more regions of the country; multiple focus groups are more than one focus group held in multiple regions of the country. Also, there are product/service-user groups and nonuser focus groups. Focus groups may be made up of your customers, your competitors' customers, prospective customers, or any combination thereof.

FIVE ESSENTIAL MARKETING INTELLIGENCE TOOLS

As indicated at the outset of this chapter, prior to developing your strategic marketing plan you need to "look within," "look around," and "look ahead." These suggested five marketing intelligence tools will provide for key research findings or a "fail-safe" for any business:

1. *SWOT Analysis*—Recording and analyzing your capabilities or resources can improve your competitive position and performance. You develop this intelligence by looking within at your internal company data. Looking within and analyzing any capability or resource that may cause your organization to underperform or lose market share (weaknesses) may also be identified from this intelligence tool. Your external focus—looking around at competition and looking ahead at environmental trends—provides you with the marketing intelligence to spot opportunities and to justify new marketing strategies, and it may help identify trends that require changes to marketing strategy.

2. *Customer Satisfaction Index (CSI)*—Consistently measuring customer satisfaction is essential to marketing strategy. Developing a methodical marketing intelligence tool such as this index can provide you with an ongoing periodic scorecard on how your business is performing. Wherever possible, your CSI should be closely linked to performance evaluation and reward systems throughout every level of your organization.

3. *Customer Perceptions Audit (CPA)*—This is a marketing intelligence tool that provides objective (external) evaluation of how your business is performing and delivering throughout the entire prepurchase to postpurchase experience. A CPA is a step-by-step walkthrough of all "point of encounters" with the customer from the customer's perspective—pre- through postpurchase. Often "mystery shoppers" or external firms are used to perform the audit.

4. *GAP Analysis*—A GAP analysis as a marketing intelligence tool seeks to identify the difference between management's perspective of how the business is performing with respect to customer satisfaction and how the customer evaluates that performance. The difference is referred to as the "GAP." A good GAP analysis can be quantified/measured using an index. For example, on a 100-point index, management rates unit customer satisfaction at 85 percent and the customer rates the experience at 65 percent—thus a 20 percent "GAP" between management's perspective and the customers.

5. *Other People's Data (OPD)*—Not every business can afford to conduct extensive marketing research with limited resources. One solution is to employ the marketing intelligence tool called "OPD," which is secondary research that is conducted or compiled by someone other than yourself face-to-face with customers or potential customers. It may be industry or product category information. Many people (agencies, competitors, the U.S. government, etc.) are constantly conducting research (primary research) and reporting or sharing the findings with the public. Take advantage of this free or very inexpensive marketing intelligence tool.

MARKETING RESEARCH PRESENTATION TOOLS

There are many presentation tools that marketers can use to help individuals understand and analyze research findings. Some of these presentation tools are simple graphics such as triangles or pyramids, circles or maps, linear diagrams, boxes or rectangles, and grids or matrices.[2] Granted, some may view this as an oversimplification of the presentation process. However, the majority of research findings and models are visually presented using these simple forms. Let's look at a few research presentation tools that you may find helpful in presenting data/findings.

Pyramids

Pyramids are often used to depict size of markets, service levels, rates/prices, and product/brand positioning. Figure 10.2 presents a pyramid that profiles three brands by service levels and prices. This same presentation tool can be used to structure a profile of market and price strategies.

Other uses of the "pyramid" include segmentation, problem resolution, prioritizing, categorizing, targeting, and importance/weighting. In addition, subdividing the "pyramid" allows for benefits prioritization, strategy selection, positioning, cost/quality equations, etc. In these instances, the pyramid is referred to as a "product triad" (see Figure 10.3).

Circles

Circles are frequently used for "mapping" purposes, wherein you are comparing your product/service to the expressed needs and wants of consumers and/or in relation to the products/services of competitors (see Figure 10.4). A "positioning map" will help you focus on how well your product or service is doing in comparison to others in terms of quality and value, as perceived by your customers. In Figure 10.4, "quality" is plotted along the horizontal axis, "value" along the vertical axis. How your product/service is perceived by consumers is what locates you on the map. A positioning map can help identify your problems and opportunities in relation to the market and your competition. A positioning map can also be of great value in creating advertising or pricing strategies, or in determining the necessity for product or service-level enhancements.

Other uses of the circle include mapping of product/brand attributes, competitive relationships, inclusion and exclusion of services/benefits, needs assessment, and price-value relationships. In these instances, axis definitions and scales may be customized. In an "inclusion"/"exclusion" application, focus is on what is inside the circle, that is, within the scope of the business strategy, or what is outside the circle, or excluded from the current business strategy.

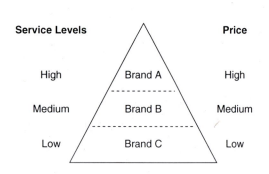

FIGURE 10.2. Sample Pyramid

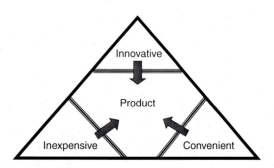

FIGURE 10.3. Sample Product Triad

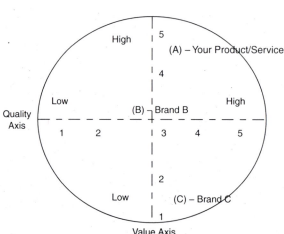

FIGURE 10.4. Sample Circle—Positioning Map

Linear Diagrams

Linear diagrams are frequently used to show "pathways" to targets, look at alternative strategies, develop networks and alliances, and aid in the decision-making process. One of the most popular linear diagrams is the "decision tree" (see Figure 10.5), most often used to view product/service extensions and expansions, market segment alternatives, product/service hybrids, and so on. Decision trees show various possible "branches" that you might take to reach an objective or outcome. Decision trees have applicability in the product or service development process, operations, and marketing. Their benefit is to clearly show the alternative of multiple routes to achieve goals and objectives.

Boxes/Rectangles

For many years, boxes and rectangles have proved to be useful presentation tools for marketers. One of the most well-known "box" creations is attributed to the Boston Consulting Group and is referred to as the "portfolio approach to strategy formulation." This leading management consulting firm recommended that organizations appraise each of their products on the basis of market growth rate (annual growth rate of the market in which the product is sold) and the organization's share of the market relative to its largest competitor. Each product is then placed in the corresponding quadrant of the Boston Consulting Group Portfolio Box (see Figure 10.6). By dividing product-market growth into high growth and low growth, and market share into high share and low share, four categories of products can be identified: stars, cash cows, question marks, and dogs. These categories can be summarized as follows:

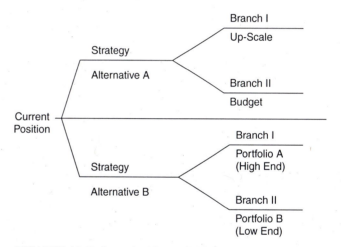

FIGURE 10.5. Sample Linear Diagram—Decision Tree

- *Stars* are those products in which an organization enjoys a high share of fast-growing (new) markets. Star products are growing rapidly and typically require heavy investment of resources. In such instances, the organization should mobilize its resources to develop stars in such a way that their market growth and market share leadership are maintained. If the necessary investment is made and the growth proves enduring, a star product will turn into a cash cow and generate income in excess of expenses in the future.
- *Cash cows* are those products that enjoy a high share of slow-growth (mature) markets. They

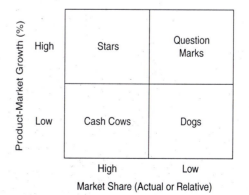

FIGURE 10.6. The Boston Consulting Group Portfolio Box

produce revenues that can be used to support high-growth products or underwrite those with problems.

- *Question marks* are those products that have only a small share of a fast-growing market. Organizations face the question of whether to increase investment in question mark products, hoping to make them stars, or to reduce or terminate investment, on the grounds that funds could be better spent elsewhere.
- *Dogs* are those products that have a small market share of slow-growth or declining markets. Since dogs usually make little money or even lose money, a decision may be made to drop them. Sometimes a business, for a variety of reasons, continues to sell dogs even though they are unprofitable. However, managers must remember that the resources that go into maintaining dogs are resources that business can't use for other opportunities.

The Boston Consulting Group Portfolio Box can also be used to analyze companies, brands, or markets.

Another box/rectangle tool is the G. E. Portfolio approach, which expands the Boston Consulting Group concept by adding the dimensions of market attractiveness and organizational strengths to the design. The Boston Consulting Group Portfolio Box and the G. E. Portfolio, as well as other boxes/rectangles, provide visual mechanisms that can help marketers understand data and formulate or select marketing strategies.

Grids

An extension of the box concept is the grid concept. Grids are excellent tools to help a business formulate marketing strategies and plans. The Marketing Strategy Grid, for example, is a dynamic tool that usually views both present and future market and competitive conditions (see Figure 10.7).[3] It allows you to gain perspective on your own product or service through an honest and frank evaluation. In order to objectively select the appropriate marketing strategies, you must understand the conditions (present and future) of the market you are in, where the market is going, and how your product relates to both the current and future conditions as well as the competition's products.

The Marketing Strategy Grid profiles the success of your product or service. A product's or service's position on the grid is a function of both the potential of the market and the competitive position within the market of the product or service. The horizontal axis of the grid denotes the potential of the market sector, while the vertical axis represents the competitive position of the product or service within the market sector. The possible rankings on both axes range from strong to weak. If you are ranking your business or products as a whole, your competitive position is a function of both quantitative and qualitative considerations, such as the amount and quality of competition; your competitive advantages as to amount and quality of competition; your competitive advantages as to distribution, share, image, pricing,

Present Time
(Market Potential)

Strong   Moderate   Weak

1	2	3	Strong
4	5	6	Moderate (Competitive Position)
7	8	9	Weak

Future Time
(Market Potential)

Strong   Moderate   Weak

1	2	3	Strong
4	5	6	Moderate (Competitive Position)
7	8	9	Weak

FIGURE 10.7. Marketing Strategy Grid

and so on; and your ability to meet the needs of target market segments. It is a good practice to develop two grids—one on your present competitive position, the second on your projected competitive position two to five years into the future. This will help you focus on the dynamics of your marketplace and competition.

Obviously, there is a meaning to the position on the grid in which a particular product or service is placed:

- Boxes 1, 2, and 4 denote a favorable, advantageous, or "go" situation. This situation occurs when both factors—market potential and competitive position—are either strong or moderate.
- Boxes 3, 5, and 7 denote a less favorable, less advantageous, or "caution" situation. A "caution" situation occurs when one factor is weak and one is strong, or both factors are moderate.
- Boxes 6, 8, and 9 denote an unfavorable, disadvantageous, or "no go" situation. This situation occurs when one or both factors are weak and neither factor is above the moderate level.

Given these definitions, the optimum position on the grid is the upper-left corner (the "1" box), where a strong market potential combines with a strong competitive position within the market. The worst position on the grid is the bottom-right corner (the "9" box), where a weak market potential combines with a weak competitive position within the market.

Since both factors being evaluated (market potential and competitive position) are dynamic, movement can take place within the grid framework—that is, the position of a particular product or service can vary over time. Horizontal movement involves changes in the potential of a market. Such changes are due to pressures in both the overall and local external economic and social forces. Vertical movement on the grid is possible from the lower six positions. These positions can be considered "action squares," because anyone with a product or service in these squares would want to take action to move up. Such vertical movement denotes changes in the product's/service's competitive position within the market and can be accomplished through strategies, product development, technological improvements, and so on.

The use of the grid concept is based on two key assumptions:

1. In order to best meet the needs of each market segment as well as to maintain a strong image and market share, we can assume that business and products/services will always seek the 1, 2, and 4 positions (favorable positions) on the grid whenever possible.
2. The position on the grid in which you place yourself assumes that no major improvement programs or other strategy changes will be undertaken soon, and few, if any, major changes will be made in marketing. As previously stated, you may wish to use two grids—one for the present and one for the future (usually within the next five years).

CHAPTER REVIEW

In this chapter, the significance of research, which focuses on the internal and external environments as well as the future, was pointed out. A recap of the major types of marketing research with respect to products/services/consumers, competition, and the environment was provided. Further, the basic market research techniques widely utilized in today's marketplace were described.

Five essential marketing intelligence tools (SWOT, CSI, CPA, GAP analysis, and OPD) were presented. These tools assist management in the identification and discovery of both problems and opportunities on an ongoing basis. The significance of communications of research findings and related strategy recommendations were discussed. A number of marketing research presentation tools to enhance the communications process were suggested.

KEY CONCEPTS/TERMS

ADIs (areas of dominant domain)
Boston Consulting Group Portfolio Box
Competitive and environmental research
Consumer research
CPA (customer perceptions audit)
CSI (customer service index)
GAP analysis
Marketing research
Marketing Strategy Grid
Qualitative
Quantitative
SWOT (strengths, weaknesses, opportunities, threats)

DISCUSSION QUESTIONS

1. Why is it important to conduct trend research?
2. What are the three variables that can influence a customer satisfaction index?
3. Why do you think customer perspectives and managerial perspectives usually are different? What causes the "gap"?
4. In determining your marketing strategies, why is it important to apply the marketing grid concept in both the present time and future?
5. How would your research be prioritized and techniques selected if your product or service was in the mature or cash cow stage?
6. Why is it important to research trends from the external environment perspective? How can these trends affect a business operation?

CASE 10.1. MAILING LESS AND MAKING MORE

A New England–based publishing company offered educational products from preschool to college market level. Products were sold primarily through direct mail. As postal rates began to escalate, the company was faced with dramatically rising costs to continue its mailings. This was coupled with two new competitors entering the market. A meeting was called to ascertain what could be done to reduce costs yet retain volume/market share. Traditionally, the company analyzed its sales of certain product lines by titles and by distribution warehouse volumes. The latter was tied to a state-by-state, city-by-city report. It seemed one of its most profitable product lines was its preschool through grade six children's book clubs. It was also the area the competitors had zeroed in on for their business. Mailings to the lists were escalated both in terms of number and intervals in between mailings (from four mailings to six and from four weeks apart down to two-week intervals). The results were the same—same sales trends, only an even higher cost.

Market research suggested that the answer might lie in a more refined approach to customer analysis. Management listened and decided to invest in new software and external research services. The new software would analyze sales by zip code for each mailing and the external research services were to profile the demographics and psychographics of the customer base. The results were eye opening. Over 80 percent of the "sales" were coming from less than 30 percent of the zip codes. Moreover, the demographic and psychographic profiles suggested that 20 percent of the zip codes would buy incremental products at even higher prices (quality-driven perceptions related to price and the "best" for their children). Moreover, these 20 percent of the zip codes were responding to the first three mailings. Needless to say, the company reduced its mailing costs (number of mailings and zip codes mailed to) and introduced a new line of books at a higher price point in selected markets. The results were increased revenues and reduced costs.

Case Discussion Questions

1. You have been asked to reduce expenditures by 15 percent. What steps would you take to generate the same level of revenues/business?
2. Select a product or service offering and ascertain the primary target market, any secondary targets, how many market segments the product targets, and how many market segments the product or service might potentially attract.

CASE 10.2. CAESARS PALACE—UNDERSTANDING THE FOCAL POINTS OF THE MARKET

The Las Vegas market is perhaps one of the best markets in which to view product positioning in the hospitality industry. The casino hotels, resorts, and complexes have followed and supported the concept of "comparison to the newest" for decades. This case example looks at a market leader for many years and the strategic steps it has undertaken over the past few decades to remain competitive and in the game with the new and spectacular mega casinos.

This case example focuses on Caesars Palace in Las Vegas, Nevada. It examines Caesars Palace's positioning technique through their development efforts. It also looks at how it is positioned compared to a couple of its primary competitors. The Bellagio and Venetian were selected based on hotel and casino size, elegance and grandeur, and perceived position in the market.

It is difficult to position Caesars Palace with its competitors. All three casinos and hotels have so much to offer their patrons. Each hotel and casino is impressive in its own right and brings elegance, opulence, and grandeur, among other things, to the table. Each has an impressive number of hotel rooms or suites, meeting space, restaurants, shopping areas, and entertainment.

However, Caesars Palace sets itself apart from the others because it has always been known and is still known as the "Golden Standard" of the hotel and casino industry. It continuously develops itself to maintain one of the top positions in the casino industry.

Caesars Palace hosts major and prestigious events contributing to its "headquarters" positioning. It also hosts only the most well-known entertainers.

Caesars Palace was built in 1966 for $25 million and over the years has had approximately $1 billion in renovations. The Bellagio was built in 1998 for $1.6 billion while the Venetian was built in 1998 for $1.2 billion.

Although Caesars Palace has been a premier hotel and casino since its inception in 1966, in the late 1990s it needed further expansion and renovation to maintain its dominance over the newer megahotels, such as the Bellagio and the Venetian.

In 1998, Caesars Palace spent $600 million on expansion and renovations. According to the Palace's president, this new construction and renovation restored the facility's leadership position in the market. This new construction increased the room number by 1,134, meeting and function space by 110,000 square feet, spa and fitness center space by 23,000 square feet, plus a 4.5-acre "Garden of the Gods" swimming complex, two new restaurants, and a 5,000-seat special event center. This renovation also enlarged and remodeled the front desk area, expanded the front entrance, and enhanced the baggage handling system.

Caesars Palace also planned a $475 million 900-suite all-suite wing, which would bring its room total to 3,350. This construction plan also included a 4,000-seat entertainment arena.

Although the events of September 11, 2001, temporarily postponed the all-suite wing construction, Caesars Palace continued with its construction of its 4,000-seat entertainment arena, the Colosseum. In addition to hotel and casino development, Caesars Palace positions itself through competitive pricing (Exhibit 10.1).[4]

While Caesars has made a massive investment to remain competitive to the newer megacasinos, it must continue to do even more. The Bellagio, Venetian, and whatever is on the horizon in the future have the strategic advantages of being newer or new in a market that inherently wants "to try the next thing." Caesars is to be complemented for its efforts to retain both its leadership positioning as "the" events and entertainment headquarters hotel.

Case Discussion Questions

1. Can you think of any other strategies Caesars' management might utilize to retain and/or regain its top position now and in the future?
2. Do you think "new" product has an advantage or disadvantage in the hospitality industry and why?

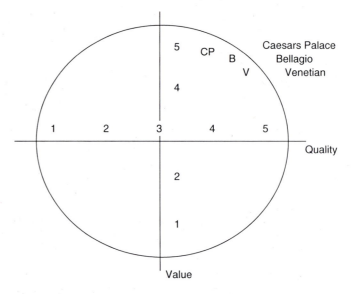

EXHIBIT 10.1. Caesars Palace Positioning Map

NOTES

1. R. C. Hiebing Jr. & S. W. Cooper, *The Successful Marketing Plan: A Disciplined and Comprehensive Approach* (2nd ed.) (Lincolnwood, IL: NTC Business Books, 1997), p. 48.

2. T. Richey, *The Marketeer's Visual Toolkit* (New York: AMACOM, 1994), p. 12.

3. R. Nykiel, *Marketing in the Hospitality Industry* (3rd ed.) (East Lansing, MI: AH&LA Educational Institute, 1997), p. 58.

4. R. Nykiel, *Hospitality Management Strategies* (Upper Saddle River, NJ: Prentice Hall, 2005), pp. 49-50.

PART III:
MARKETING RESEARCH APPLICATIONS

In Part I, we looked at research methodologies and techniques. In Part II, we focused on market analysis and assessment. In this part of the text the focus is on marketing research applications. The discussion begins with marketing research and testing in Chapter 11. This chapter presents the criteria for testing, demonstrates how to develop testing programs, and presents the focal points for testing and sources of information. Chapter 12 discusses applying research to marketing strategy selection, focusing on positioning and selection of marketing weaponry. Chapter 13 focuses on applying research to brand strategy and the dissection of the components of brand strategy. Chapter 14 discusses the application of research to pricing strategy. Here we examine key concepts and terms such as understanding demand, pricing options, breakeven analysis, and other pricing techniques. Finally, Chapter 15 looks at how to apply research to customer satisfaction strategy.

Chapter 11

Marketing Research and Testing

CHAPTER OBJECTIVES

- To present an assessment of the various marketing research tools.
- To identify why testing is important in marketing research.
- To provide a guideline of when testing should be deployed and when it may not be necessary.
- To delineate three different types of research and testing environments—exploratory, experimental, and in-market.
- To view examples of testing programs related to marketing—positioning, new products/ services, branding, promotion, advertising methods, and media.
- To present how to analyze and interpret the results and apply these assessments to decisions.

Testing research findings is especially important in the business sector where basing a decision on inaccurate or false data can result in losing millions of dollars. Evaluating the findings and resultant plans prior to large-scale implementation should be a rigorous and consistent process in all major marketing decisions. Marketing is both an art and a science; there is much chance for failure. There are no guarantees of success for new plans, products, or strategies. For example, it has been estimated that nine out of ten new product introductions fail in less than one year. Attempting to implement new marketing or promotional strategies on a broad scale requires a sizable outlay of dollars in today's marketplace. In order to enhance the success of new strategies as well as to improve the odds of any new product introductions, market research and testing are essential.

Both testing and research are a means of staying ahead of the competition and avoiding costly errors.

William Dillon
Marketing Research in a Marketing Environment (1994)

Research and testing can be challenging and complex disciplines. Many organizations find it more practical and efficient to draw upon the services of external professionals and firms. This chapter looks at when to test and when not to test. Three different types of research and testing environments—exploratory, experimental, and in-market—are explored. Later, the focus turns to testing in relation to positioning, new products, branding, promotion, advertising communications, and media.

Handbook of Marketing Research Methodologies for Hospitality and Tourism
© 2007 by The Haworth Press, Inc. All rights reserved.
doi:10.1300/5927_12

WHY, WHEN, AND WHEN NOT TO TEST

As we indicated earlier, the majority of new product introductions fail. The same is true for many small entrepreneurial adventures. Small ventures test the market in the most primitive way when they post a sign for the business and open up a shop or unit. Most do not do any formalized testing or in-depth research and most fail. With a research and testing program, the concept of risk management begins to play a role. Potential reasons for failure are identified and, if addressed properly, can significantly improve the odds for success.

It should be pointed out that not every strategy or tactical execution needs to be or should be tested. Testing every alternative every time is usually costly and time prohibitive. Therefore, most organizations establish some form of prioritization system. In order to do this, some key questions need to be answered and some key considerations need to be taken into account (see Figure 11.1). One of the first and best questions to ask is what is the risk of not having this information? This critical question, if answered objectively, will likely provide the answer and degree to which testing is required. For example, if one is spending millions of dollars on a new national global promotional or advertising campaign, it makes sense to spend a few thousand dollars to pretest the conception. On the other hand, if the expenditure is limited to adding another market or two to a media schedule, it is highly likely any testing investment could be justified.

Researchers and marketers need to ask another critical question before embarking on testing. What is the cost of obtaining reliable information? As simple as this question seems it remains a key checklist question because it may well cost so much to retain reliable data that the cost exceeds or dilutes the return on investment to a point that makes the new endeavor not worth doing. In some cases it may cost as much to develop and test a concept and campaign as it would to implement the concept or campaign without testing, in which case the decision may well be not to test.

Another key consideration related to the testing process is timing. One needs to know whether there are any time constraints. If test results will not be available in time to impact the decision-making process, then the value of testing must be questioned. One key related to timing is to avoid this situation by preplanning for research and testing at the earliest valid point in time. It also is important to keep in perspective the agility of your competitors. Will your testing or using on trial market result in their responding faster that you can implement a full-scale launch? If so, you may have to roll the dice and consider the risk of not testing to be first in the marketplace.[1]

Another consideration to be evaluated is how valid and translatable is the testing environment? Will you be able to take the research results and apply them to the specific marketing situation or need? This is especially important when attempting to test the reactions to advertising. Showing consumers a commercial in a research or test room and asking their reactions will not assess the effectiveness of the ac-

❑ Is the risk factor of not conducting research and testing tolerable?

❑ What is the cost of implementing the market execution? If high, conduct research.

❑ Can all variables, except the one test variable, be controlled?

❑ Is the research technique a match with the type of information desired from the testing?

❑ Do you intend to pursue the same path irrespective of the research? If so, do not do the research.

❑ Are you going to rely solely on the research for determining alternatives? If so, you should understand the risks of not using any other decision-making tools.

❑ What is the market scope of your testing? Is it adequate to provide the results you need? *Note:* national tests are too expensive and usually are not needed to obtain predictable or meaningful results.

❑ If you are going to implement the testing yourself, are you prepared to pay the consequences? *Note:* use a professional design and evaluate the results.

FIGURE 11.1. Checklist of Key Questions for Testing

tual advertising. You may be able to measure the communications value or awareness/recall but not the actual effectiveness with respect to purchase. Creative messages and copy can be imposed and fine-tuned through testing, but the impact/effectiveness is not likely measured.

RESEARCH AND TESTING ENVIRONMENTS

In general, there are three types of research and testing environments related to marketing research and testing. These areas are exploratory, experimental, and in-market.

Exploratory

Marketing objectives and strategies must address the consumers' needs. Communicating these objectives and strategies must relate to how the consumers think and behave, as well as take into consideration their attitudes. In many instances, exploratory research can help ascertain the most appropriate marketing tool to employ to best reach and communicate with the intended market/group of consumers. In trying to uncover the consumers' needs and best methods of communicating these needs, focus groups can play a critical and informative role.

Focus groups are an excellent way to generate ideas and obtain feedback from target respondents on complex attitudinal issues such as product concepts, advertising messages, positioning, and buying dynamics. A focus group provides for a guided discussion among a small group (eight to ten people) of target group respondents. The group is led by a moderator using an outline of topics to be covered (guide). When utilized early in the planning process, focus groups can help develop alternatives and provide initial qualitative feedback or alternatives. Marketers should remember that focus groups are qualitative in nature and provide an enlightened, but not quantifiable, insight into the target market.

Experimental

Experimental research is any kind of research that is not an in-market testing situation under "real" conditions. A focus group used extensively for exploration of the dynamics of consumer attitudes and behaviors is really a form of experimental research. Other forms of experimental research employed in marketing research and testing include mall intercepts; testing strategies (i.e., pricing) via telephone interviews; testing positioning concepts through mail surveys; and so on. In experimental research, you are generally forcing exposure of testing concepts onto your target market in an unnatural setting. This is done in order to control costs and work within time constraints. The research also needs to control the test environment in order to isolate and understand consumers' reactions and preferences related to product/service, positioning, and marketing mix tools. This also allows for only one variable (i.e., advertising message, product feature, positioning alternative, brand name, etc.) to be changed from one test exposure to the rest. This allows for the research to determine the difference(s) in consumers' preferences related to the change. If multiple variables were changed, the research would not know what attribute the consumer preferred. Marketers need feedback in very short time frames (days, weeks) for decision-making and strategy-implementation purposes. Experimental research permits this to happen by controlling the exposure to different marketing alternatives. Experimental research is also a more cost-effective form of gathering information than in-market testing.

In-Market Testing

The key to in-market tests is to "match" markets as much as possible. In-market testing should be a small-scale implementation of a specific marketing approach. With in-market testing you are controlling all variables except the one you are actually testing. The ability to actually read test results is heavily dependent upon the ability to match test markets as closely as possible. With respect to matching markets considerations would include, but not be limited to, sales trends, competitive situations, penetration and distribution options, media, and geographic and demographic issues. In-market testing is most appropriate when applied to new product/service introductions, prior to national or broad rollouts. Many entities use in-market testing prior to a national rollout of major packaging changes, reformulation of products, new menus, and positioning changes. In the marketing discipline itself, in-market testing can be used effectively for evaluating alternative media programs.[2]

DEVELOPING TESTING PROGRAMS

Each marketing plan issue or situation often needs tailored research and testing. Parameters and methods will often be dictated by costs and time constraints. We provide examples of typical research testing programs for major concepts such as positioning, product testing, branding, promotion, advertising messages/creative communications, and media.

Positioning

All marketing mix tools are developed and implemented to support a product/service/brand's positioning. Positioning is the heart of any market plan and strongly influences price. It is the link between the product or service and the consumer. Positioning concepts generally consist of complex attitude structures that require a sensitive means of testing. The reason to test positioning alternatives includes the evaluation of the connection between the target market relative to the product/service and competition. There are numerous significant issues related to positioning that testing can explore. These include the relevance of the positioning to the target, the importance of the positioning to the target, and the likelihood that the positioning would encourage trial. There are a number of ways to test positioning including focus groups, mall intercepts, and mail surveys. In many instances a "positioning" board or "concept" board is developed containing visual elements and copy points, which convey the benefits and positioning elements. Targeted consumers are shown the board and are asked to respond to a short survey that contains questions related to attitude and intention.

The limitation to the concept board approach is that the targeted consumers are likely to be very literal in the research setting. As some researchers have observed, the respondents begin to be copy writers rather than focusing on the positioning idea itself. One approach to counter this occurrence is the audio concept board. In this case, the positioning message is presented on an audiotape and the respondents have to take away what they heard. This makes the copy writing syndrome disappear, as there is no visual copy, so they must take away the key positioning from that which they heard. This allows for the short questions to be answered without the target respondents substituting their own copy into the process. This method is most effective for positioning with strong emotional appeal. This is the result of the audiotape setting the tone to impact the desired emotion more easily than does writing on a concept board.

Product/Service Testing

New product development usually dictates a higher level of expenditures for testing. Product/service concepts usually require a series of focus groups during which the concept is explored, formulated, and frequently reformatted. Concepts are refined through more consumer testing using the techniques previously discussed. There also are a number of software products which provide simulated test models that produce expected market shares when fed with market and benefit criteria. A good deal of new product/service testing is conducted to help determine the ideal set or bundle of benefits, both rational and emotional, that a new product or service offering should contain. Of course, the ultimate test of a new product or service is putting it into a real market situation.

Brand Testing

Consumers recognize products and services through their brand names. Brand testing helps determine what is likely to be the best brand name. A widely accepted methodology for brand testing involves developing alternative names for testing purposes. Normally, five or six names are used but not more than seven or eight. It has been proven that a number higher than this can cause respondent fatigue and result in the lack of name discrimination. The objective of branding research/testing is to narrow the list of alternative names and to identify the strengths and weaknesses of each alternative. Other factors need to be considered with respect to branding. Creative consideration is one example. Some names can be eliminated through branding research. This narrowing of the list allows for other factors to then be considered in the final decision-making process. When assessing brand alternatives, three areas of questioning are utilized. These include word association, ratings on product/service benefits, and preference scores.

- *Word association*—The objective here is to discover what connotations the name being tested elicits. Key concerns are related to these connotations being positives or negatives. It is important to note that both the name and connotations be viewed within the context of the actual product/service category.
- *Ratings on product/service benefits*—The objective here is to rate each name against the various product/service benefits to ascertain strengths and weaknesses. The more strengths associated with the name the better.
- *Preference scores*—In this instance, respondents are given a concept statement and are asked to identify their name preferences that best match the concept. Reasons for their preferences/choices are also obtained.

As selecting a good brand name is extremely important, all three types of measurements—word association, ratings, and preferences—are analyzed to determine the most viable names. This type of analysis is often conducted through telephone interviews or mall intercepts.

Promotion Testing

Promotion testing may take place at the developmental and/or execution stage. The key objective in testing promotions is to determine the effectiveness of the promotion in generating incremental sales and new trial business, or brand loyalty. On the front end, the developmental stage focus groups may prove an ideal method for obtaining ideas and feedback. This is particularly applicable to brand loyalty and frequency promotions. Mall or airport intercepts are valuable tools to help ascertain the stopping power and selling strength of alternative promotions in an advertising concept. At the execution stage, exit interviews or in-store/unit surveys are useful to determine consumer buying habits and profiles.

Advertising Messages/Creative Communications

Measuring advertising is often viewed as a controversial research topic. It is true that advertising is one of the most difficult of the marketing weapons to measure. Much of the difficulty rests in the fact that advertising has a long-term and cumulative effect and it is difficult to isolate a current advertising effort. There are many who frankly believe one cannot measure the effectiveness of advertising. Certainly, in many instances advertising can be correlated to sales trends. The only problem here is one has no way to know whether it was the advertising itself or the concept being conveyed in the message. This is especially true when advertising is used to support open promotions.

Copy Testing

Copy testing is a means of measuring the communication value of advertising. Copy testing is a diagnostic tool, not an evaluative method. It is most helpful in the creative development process. Copy testing focuses on determining whether the advertising can penetrate the general advertising clutter and make consumers stop and notice the advertisement. Copy testing is also used to determine whether a given ad communicates the intended message. There are many different techniques for copy testing and many are offered through syndicated services that also can provide norms to compare the test results with other products/services in the same category or format. The basic principle is common to most techniques. Respondents are shown the commercial or ad, often with other advertising clutter, and then asked questions pertaining to negative/positive diagnostics, feelings, and provide communications playback. Many times purchase intentions and persuasion scores can be built into the questioning. Copy testing can be utilized for both broadcast and print forms of advertising.

Media Testing

In media testing, the two key objectives are to evaluate the media mix and media weight. Testing will help answer some critical questions. Which media mix is the best? What media weight is needed? And, how many media dollars need to be spent? In-market tests are normally used for media weights and mix as it is difficult to apply forced-exposure experimental design. In in-market testing, market tiers are derived and then receive different weight levels of similar messages. The variable may also be media type, such as magazines versus television, and so on. Usually many combinations are used with markets with available dollars for testing being the limiting factor. The key is to control all variables except for media weight or mix. Typically, measurement tools such as sales analysis are employed. Survey research can also be utilized to determine awareness levels affected by different media plans. Telephone research is generally used for this purpose.

FOCAL POINTS AND SOURCES OF INFORMATION

A major responsibility of the market researcher is to manage the cost and assure the timelines of the research and testing. Fortunately, for many of the focal points of research and testing there are excellent sources of information as well as external expertise that can be of immense help. Figure 11.2 provides a quick reference guide to behavioral focal points and information sources.

There are numerous information sources to view and compare competitive spending information. It is a good idea to obtain these data on a regular basis (i.e., quarterly) to help ascertain spending trends and patterns. Media representatives from newspapers, radio stations, television stations, and outdoor advertising companies are excellent resources for the data. LNA (Leading National Advertisers) provides dates on national companies. Competi-

Focal Points	Information Sources

■ Behavioral Trends
  o Demographic/target market
  o Geographic trends
  o Social/consumer trends
  o Technological trends
  o Media viewing trends
  o Trial/retrial
	o U.S. Bureau of the Census data
	o Yankelovich Monitor and Yesowich Pepperdine, Russel and Brown Travel Monitor
	o The Popcorn Report
	o American Demographics Magazine
	o Syndicated Services
	o Market Survey

■ National Category Development Index (CDI)	o Sales and Marketing Management Survey of Buying Power
■ Company Brand Development Index (BDI)	o Internal Company Data
■ Brand Loyalty	o SMRB (Simmons Market Research Bureau) o MRI (Mediamark Research, Inc.) o Primary Research

FIGURE 11.2. Behavioral Focal Points and Information Sources

tive data information sources that are helpful in the marketing review analysis include Fairchild Fact Files, trade publications, industry 10-K reports, primary research, media and field representatives, and radio and television reports. Many additional sources of information are presented throughout the text and in the appendix.

CHAPTER REVIEW

This chapter indicated that knowing when and how to test is important to providing support for negating market-related strategies. Also presented were the dos and don'ts related to marketing research and testing. Three different types of research and testing environments—exploratory, experimental, and in-market—were presented. Various testing programs appropriate for positioning new products, branding, promotions, advertising messages, and media performance were viewed. Further, sources for evaluation and measurement of data and performance were identified along with the concept of indices—CDI and BDI.

KEY CONCEPTS/TERMS

Attitudes
BDI
CDI
Copy testing
Experimental
Exploratory
Fairchild Fact Files
In-market testing
LNA (Leading National Advertisers)
MRI (Mediamark Research, Inc.)
Media testing

Message
Positioning
Preference scores
SMRB (Simmons Market Research Bureau)
Testing
Word association

DISCUSSION QUESTIONS

1. Why is it important to test before strategy deployment and application in marketing?
2. Is it necessary to test everything? If not, what does not require testing?
3. What are the three different types of research and testing environments?
4. What is the difference between exploratory and experimental research?
5. How would you test with respect to positioning?
6. What are some methods utilized in testing advertising?
7. Why is it important to test media?

CASE 11.1. GREAT TESTING/POOR MARKET RESEARCH—AWARD/SALES DECLINE

There are times when testing can prove or predict an outcome. However, if the testing and research are not thorough or do not cover all the pertinent points, the results can prove misleading. This is a case example of the latter and involves the pretesting of a television commercial and advertising campaign. The case involves a major eye care provider, its agency, and related research.

Research revealed the need to address the many market segments that purchased eye glasses. Further research looked into the changing demographics and makeup of the population in the United States. The findings revealed the multiethnic diversity of the population in most of the company's major markets. It also revealed high growth rates for these segments. Competitive assessments revealed that no other eye care provider was addressing these segments in its advertising. Research further revealed that a number of the high-growth segments were disproportionately heavy television viewers.

The advertising agency was excited by these research findings and immediately went to work to develop a new campaign. In a few weeks, they had produced a number of possibilities presented on storyboards. The company liked the work and asked that some focus group and viewing testing be conducted. The agency developed a rough of the television version of the campaign and went on with the testing. The results of the focus group and viewing tests were extremely positive. Descriptors such as "couldn't be more on target," "that really relates to me," "it is about time someone recognized the buying power of my people," and so on were used. The agency was given the green light to produce the advertising campaign and received approval for an extensive media campaign. The launch date was set.

The commercials were developed just in time to be included in a major television advertising awards competition. The commercials won the top award in the category. The agency and company were delighted as this news came just two weeks into the new campaign. The advertising was viewed so favorably by consumers that they actually wrote or called the company, parent company, and agency. Almost all indicators were pointing to a huge success, except for one. This was the one that counted most—called "sales."

In the first few weeks of the campaign sales were flat. Many (especially the agency) attributed this to bad weather in some major markets. By the end of a month, sales were declining and the bad weather was becoming less of a factor. After six weeks (a lifetime in this sector of the retail industry) sales had plunged. Franchisees who initially called to praise the new campaign were now calling to kill it, despite its recent award/recognition.

What happened? Was the testing, focus group, and even award process faulty? What went wrong? The answer was quickly identified through sales analysis and competitive research. The sales analysis revealed that the only markets with sales increases were those where the local marketing co-ops and individual franchisees did not participate in the new campaign, especially the print version.

These markets were studied in depth as well as the markets where the greatest sales declines were recorded. Competitive research was conducted in the same positive and negative markets. This new wave of research revealed what was completely missed by all involved in the new campaign. While many felt very good about the wonderful commercial and advertising, they were primarily motivated to purchase competitors' products and services by discount coupons. Image and goodwill did not count. Price, discounts, and coupons were what moved sales. Unfortunately, poor or incomplete market research failed to ascertain a number of key points. First, while the new campaign was very strong (award winning) and consumers were very positive, it did not influence "how" they purchase or "what" incentives made them actually respond. While many or most answered "yes, this would make me feel like purchasing from this company," the reality was that "price" (coupons and promotions) was preferred to "image." Second, the very strong award-winning advertising actually caused a competitive reaction. In the first few weeks of the campaign, a number of other competitors' sales were down or flat. This performance led them to believe that the award-winning campaign by their competitor was working. The fastest response was to flood the market with heavy discounts/coupons including the strongest of all promotions—called "BOGOs" (buy one get one free). They also quickly tagged their television commercials with the same offer. The results were that they immediately took market share.

This case example points out that no matter how good or overwhelmingly positive the research test results come out, if not thorough in scope, there is always the possibility or probability that they can be misleading. Also, prior to acting upon the most favorable or flawless testing, one should also consider the implications in the real world—implications such as competitors' reactions and consumer behavior.

Case Discussion Questions

1. Why is it important to understand and take into consideration historic consumer behavior patterns when assessing marketing research findings?
2. How can you assure your research testing procedures are all-inclusive and cover all bases?
3. When should "judgment" override bona fide research findings or implementation recommendations?

NOTES

1. R. G. Hiebing & S. W. Cooper, *The Successful Marketing Plan: A Disciplined and Comprehensive Approach* (2nd ed.) (Lincolnwood, IL: NTC Business Books, 1996), pp. 391-392.
2. Ibid., pp. 392-393.

Chapter 12

Applying Research to Marketing Strategy Selection

CHAPTER OBJECTIVES

- To delineate the internal and external drivers of marketing strategy.
- To identify the specific research methodologies that assist in selecting marketing strategies.
- To provide an overview of the strategic marketing management process upon which service industry strategies are based.
- To discuss the applications of the various marketing disciplines and weapons.

Marketing strategy is determined, set, and orchestrated by internal and external drivers. Internally, the mission statement, goals, and objectives of the corporation set the parameters. Externally, competitive and environmental factors have a direct influence on the overall marketing strategy. The positioning of the brand and the execution of the brand strategy are usually functions of a strategic marketing plan and the orchestrated selection of marketing weapons. As in any disciplined business process, a number of steps are taken prior to developing a strategic marketing plan.

UNDERSTANDING THE ENVIRONMENT

We are in a transitory and ever-changing period for both business firms and marketing. This applies to every business, be it a new e-commerce venture, retail or service industry enterprise, small firm or mega-corporation. What worked in the past has no guarantee of working in the future as both external and internal change are taking place at an ever-accelerating pace. New technologies, new products and services, new delivery systems, and new competition change the playing field on a regular and frequent basis. Any one or a combination of these external and internal forces may suggest that it is time to redefine the business strategy or, if managing a new brand or enterprise, to define it for the first time.

Analyzing the market from customers' expectations and competitive perspectives reveals that a great deal of change is taking place. Internal changes are occurring, such as utilization of multidisciplinary management teams; managing up, down, and across; and field-based management versus headquarters-based, to name a few. There are changes in how business is being conducted, such as more outsourcing, more collaborative efforts (alliances and networking), an accelerated development process, use of fewer but more responsive suppliers, and so on. Businesses are asking to develop new competitive advantages, be more market and customer oriented, improve by benchmarking (measuring themselves against others), and where feasible offer customized products or personalized services. Focal points are also changing, such as

Handbook of Marketing Research Methodologies for Hospitality and Tourism
© 2007 by The Haworth Press, Inc. All rights reserved.
doi:10.1300/5927_13

looking globally versus locally, zeroing in on the value chain, and refining market targets. It is not surprising to find that customers are redefining value to include not just the traditional "quality at a fair price" but adding "speed and convenience" to the equation.[1]

In a dynamic marketplace marketing strategies must be based on research and analysis.

All of these dynamics in the marketplace are changing not only how business entities conduct business but also how they define it. Before beginning the marketing planning process, one must reflect on the company's core competencies and driving forces, with questions such as these: (1) Where does the business make a significant contribution to the customer's perceived benefits with the end product or service offered? (2) What do we do or what can we do that is difficult for our competitors to imitate? (3) Are we "market" or "product/service" driven and should we change? The answers form new core values and driving forces upon which the marketing strategy is based.

At this point, organizations reexamine or develop a new mission statement. To do so they need also to reexamine and record the philosophies of the firm; develop an overall positioning statement; and focus on the vision of the future—where they want to go and what they want to achieve. All of these activities require research and analysis.

FOCAL POINTS FOR MARKETING STRATEGY

Marketing strategy has many focal points. Obviously, the number one focus is on the target market. How the marketing message is presented with respect to the core market, price, positioning, and total value perception is what marketing strategy is all about. Further, in some industries, we have a more complex distribution channel upon which to focus. We have end users and various intermediaries and/or distributors in many sectors of the industry. An end user is the actual consumer of the product or service, whereas an intermediary can be wholesaler, retailer, or distributor. When intermediaries are involved, the need for multiple communications strategies is created. These different marketing messages are often required since the motivations and needs of the end user and the intermediary are not always the same. A business executive as an end user is looking for quality; crisp, on-time service; and reliability.

An intermediary such as a travel agent is looking for prompt full payment of commissions. Figure 12.1 provides some of the targets for marketing strategies. The perceptions that marketing strategies convey while directed at one focal point can very well influence multiple constituencies. Likewise, if a consumer marketing strategy is found to be distasteful or controversial, there could be major ramifications from shareholders, franchisees, and so on.

Marketing strategy and related research and analysis involves not only identifying targets, but identifying business opportunities.

Marketing strategy involves not only identifying the targets, but also identifying marketing opportunities. Opportunities are often discovered during the research phase. A marketing opportunity can be identifying an area of buyers' needs and interests and effectively communicating how your brand can fulfill that need. There are many potential sources of opportunity. For example, one might identify a marketplace in short supply and fulfill that need, for instance, an airline serving a new route. Another example could be supplying an existing product or service in a new or superior way, such as supplying rental cars in local communities by delivery, like Enterprise, or simply supplying a new product or service, such as was the case with Krispy Kreme or Starbucks, to a market. In some cases, breakthrough marketing strategies result in large market share gains or creating new market niches. Examples include finding new customers by a new strategy, such as a fast-food franchise locating within a super retail store (e.g., a McDonald's within a Wal-Mart). Other breakthrough strategies might be related to new sales approaches, such as selling through intermediaries for the first time or finding new pricing or financial solutions (e.g., the timeshare concept). Finally a breakthrough might involve something as simple as adding new product/service features.

Marketing strategy also has a very tactical side. As the industry and virtually all sectors within the industry fight for market share, winning marketing tactics are in demand. Figure 12.2 shows some winning marketing tactics; not all will work with every segment, but all have proven to be winners when applied properly.

THE NEW FIVE Ps

There are many different perspectives on marketing and marketing strategy, especially in our ever-changing environment. For nearly thirty years (from the 1950s to the 1980s), and still today, marketers have focused on the Four Ps identified by McCarthy and Kotler, as shown in the following list:[2]

1. Product
2. Price
3. Place
4. Promotion

In the 1990s, as we transitioned to a predominately service-oriented economy and marketing environment, marketing strategies shifted to focus on the Four Cs, as delineated by Lauterborn:[3]

1. Consumer wants and needs
2. Cost to satisfy (wants and needs)
3. Convenience to buy
4. Communication (creating a dialogue)

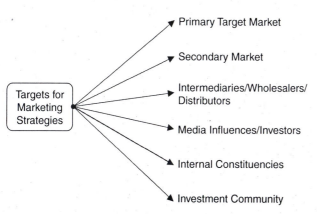

FIGURE 12.1. Targets for Marketing Strategies

Win Through:
- Ego Appeal
- Discounting
- Couponing
- Value-Added Offers
- Speed of Delivery
- Abundance of Availability
- Convenience of Purchase
- Targeted Awareness
- "Points of Encounter"
- Doing More for Your Customer

FIGURE 12.2. Winning Through Positioning

In the current decade, while marketing must still focus on the Four Ps and Four Cs, marketing strategies appear to have shifted and are now more and more based on the new Five Ps, as delineated by the author:

1. Preparation
2. Positioning
3. Perception
4. Proclamation
5. Power thrusts

Preparation

Preparation translates to "assessing your focal points" or "looking within, looking around, and looking ahead." It involves all the research steps and analysis described in Part II of this book, including deployment of the five essential marketing intelligence tools discussed in Chapter 10. Given the above process output (intelligence), a clear, concise, and most likely advantageous positioning strategy emerges.

Positioning

Overall positioning strategy takes into account the consumers' perspective. This should include the data collected with respect to the brand's attributes and relationship to competition with respect to value (quality, price, and convenience to and speed of purchase). Such information is derived from the positioning maps produced based on quality, price, and attributes. Combining these findings using an attributes and competitive rating scale (see Figure 12.3) provides a guide and parameters for positioning choices/options. Using these graphic tools should help to delineate the overall positioning strategy noting qualifiers and rationale.

There are many different positioning options, as previously delineated in Figure 12.2. There are other positioning tactics that have been successfully deployed for brands, products, and services. For example, "more for less" has been used by foodservice establishments and lodging facilities (such as all-suites). Other positioning tactics include more for more, more for the same, the same for less, and less for much less. Positioning techniques may be based on an attribute (e.g., largest) or multiple attributes (e.g., largest and easiest to work with). Further, firms have been known to utilize competitive positioning (e.g., we versus they; "our" first-class seating versus all the other airlines). The key to positioning strategy is to develop one that gives you the competitive advantage and translates into powerful marketing strategies. Some words of caution: "Overpositioning" is akin to overpromising. Focus, clarity, simplicity, and truth make positioning statements and strategy powerful and easily understood.

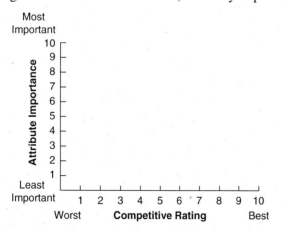

FIGURE 12.3. Positioning—Attributes and Competitive Ranking

Perception

The next three Ps of the new Five Ps, *perception, proclamation,* and *power thrusts,* are what marketing strategy is all about today. Successful businesses and brands today are those that succeed in creating "winning" perceptions for their products/services. We are living in a marketing environment that is perception driven. Consumers want to "ride the wave," "have the latest," "go counter to the masses," "want it all now," "seek the newest," and so on. These are perceptions that marketing strategy must convey from a message creation perspective. Creating a perception in tune with the target market is essential for successful marketing strategy in today's world. Perception can be directly linked to positioning; however, it must function as a "driver" or creator of a compelling call to purchase. In other words, the positioning strategy is the base and the perception message the call to action. Perception options are dynamic—they move with the pulse and mindset of consumers. For some the message is "new," and for others it is "retro." Figure 12.4 delineates some perception options; remember, these are always changing with today's consumers.

Proclamation

Linking positioning and perception messages requires reading the current and near-term future pulse of the market. Assuming the reading of the pulse of the market is correct and you have formulated your perceptions strategy, you now need to deploy the fourth P—proclamation. Proclamation is a declaration that the product/service or brand is worth looking at, trying, buying, or repurchasing. Proclamation may take on a different meaning depending upon where the product/service or brand is in its life cycle. For example, if the brand is new or unique, one can immediately proclaim, "We are the newest" or "We have the only . . ." This is a great position to be in, but most brands are not so fortunate. In some instances, you will only be able to declare, "Look—we are changing/improving," or perhaps you're at the stage of telling the market, "We changed/improved" or "We are like new." And hopefully, you are or will be at the point where momentum is demonstrating itself in sales and revenue gains and you're ready to declare, "We are new/the leader/the best," or whatever may be the positioning and brand strategy support, as a proclamation or declaration to the marketplace. Figure 12.5 delineates the phases and thrust (expenditure) levels usually associated with proclamation.

Power Thrusts

Now marketing strategy has moved to the active or launched phase. This is the time to deploy the fifth P—power thrusts. Remember, just because you have proclaimed you're on the move doesn't mean the consumer world will automatically listen. You will need to focus on a "breakthrough" or unique message and delivery thereof to be successful. Let's assume you have a very creative, unique, and on-target proclamation/message. This is still no guarantee you will be successful, as the marketing channels are very crowded with other messages. To be heard or seen you will need to have a multipronged approach that should involve as many of the marketing weapons as possible (advertising, promotions, public relations, etc.). These weapons will re-

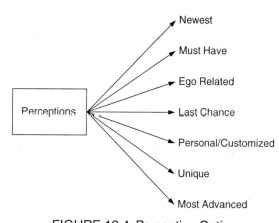

FIGURE 12.4. Perception Options

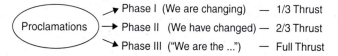

FIGURE 12.5. Proclamation Phases

quire synchronization to work most efficiently and effectively. This is the fifth P—power thrusts. Power thrusts are created from a variety of techniques such as "heavy up-front" and "waves" of advertising, overlapping direct mail and direct sales efforts, carrying promotional offers in the advertising, and hyping the offers with public relations. In essence, you are synergistically and methodically using your expenditures and marketing weaponry to create "waves" or "power thrusts" for your product/service or brand offering (see Figure 12.6).

SELECTING MARKETING WEAPONRY

Not every situation calls for deployment of all of your weaponry in concentrated periods of time or up front. If you have strong brand awareness or are in a market leadership position (box 1 on the Marketing Strategy Grid; see Figure 12.7) you may be better off selecting maintenance-level advertising or reminder messages or utilizing public relations to consistently trumpet your position. Selecting strategies often depends on your market's relative strength (overall consumer demand) and your competitive position. Let's now return to the Marketing Strategy Grid. Figures 12.7 through 12.15 depict a product/service or brand in a different position on the grid (boxes 1 through 9) and provide some potential accompanying marketing strategies that could be appropriate.

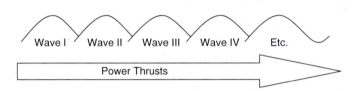

FIGURE 12.6. Power Thrusts

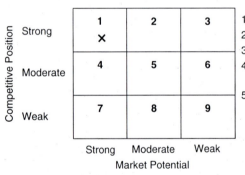

Strategies

1. Maintain position.
2. Cultivate core customers.
3. Maximize profits through pricing.
4. Keep competitively ahead by adding services or upgrading product.
5. Expand your product or service offerings or extend your brand.

FIGURE 12.7. Position #1: Strong Market/Strong or Best Product or Service

Strategies

1. Go for market share via competitive pricing.
2. If the market movement tends toward strengthening, improve to a #1 position.
3. If the market movement tends toward weakening, go after traditional marketing segments (build core market, consider alternative pricing strategy, etc.).
4. Create and capitalize on perceptions ("the only," ego related, etc.).

FIGURE 12.8. Position #2: Moderate Market/Strong Product or Service

Strategies

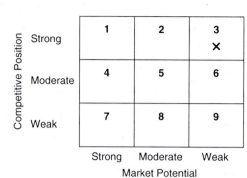

1. If the market movement tends toward strengthening, build market core now and retain loyalty of consumers.

2. Go after all market segments with multiple pricing strategies and/or product and service offerings.

3. Strongly emphasize cost control and targeted promotions.

4. Develop new "trial" business with promotional offers to build the customer base.

FIGURE 12.9. Position #3: Weak Market/Strong Product

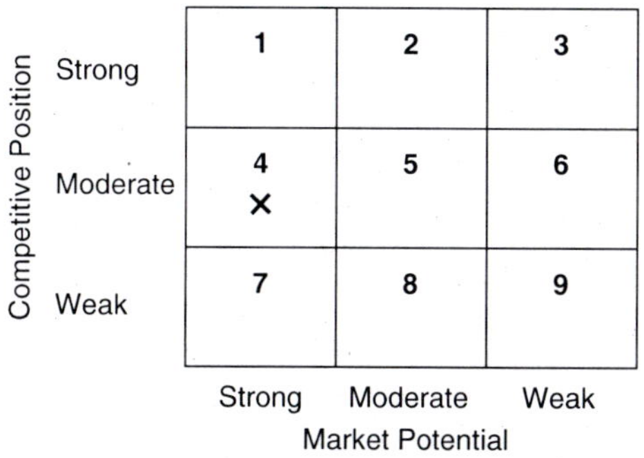

Strategies

1. Maximize profits by pricing slightly below the #1 competitor.

2. If the market movement tends toward strengthening, consider strengthening or upgrading your product/service to move closer to or into the #1 position.

3. Go after the "value-oriented" market segments.

4. Distinguish your product/service as an acceptable replacement for the #1 competitor.

FIGURE 12.10. Position #4: Strong Market/Moderate or Average Product or Service

Strategies

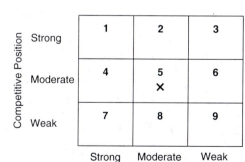

1. If the market movement tends toward strengthening, put the product/service in a stronger position with enhancements.

2. Expand the number of market segments you are attracting with specialized promotions.

3. Go after market share through competitive pricing.

4. Distinguish yourself as the value leader.

FIGURE 12.11. Position #5: Moderate Market/Moderate or Average Product or Service

Strategies

1. Maximize profits by pricing slightly below the #1 competitor.

2. If the market movement tends toward strengthening, consider strengthening or upgrading your product/service to move closer to or into the #1 position.

3. Go after the "value-oriented" market segments.

4. Distinguish your product/service as an acceptable replacement for the #1 competitor.

	Strong	Moderate	Weak
Strong	1	2	3
Moderate	4	5	6 ✕
Weak	7	8	9

Competitive Position / Market Potential

FIGURE 12.12. Position #6: Weak Market/Moderate or Average Product or Service

Strategies

1. Repackage, improve, or upgrade the most visible aspects of your product/service.

2. Once this is done, increase your prices to take advantage of strong demand periods.

3. Become the best at servicing the market segments your stronger competitors are not paying attention to.

4. Theme your promotions toward special or unique concepts and go for volume.

	Strong	Moderate	Weak
Strong	1	2	3
Moderate	4	5	6
Weak	7 ✕	8	9

Competitive Position / Market Potential

FIGURE 12.13. Position #7: Strong Market/Weak Product or Service

Strategies

1. If the market movement does not tend toward strengthening, look at special price schemes to build share.

2. If the market movement tends toward strengthening, make every effort to upgrade your product/service to move along with the market.

3. If the above is true, work promotions, sales, and advertising to convey your product's/service's availability and value orientation.

4. Consider marketing your product/service around a theme.

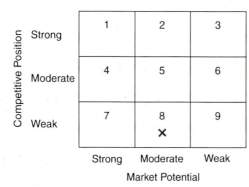

	Strong	Moderate	Weak
Strong	1	2	3
Moderate	4	5	6
Weak	7	8 ✕	9

Competitive Position / Market Potential

FIGURE 12.14. Position #8: Moderate Market/Weak Product or Service

Strategies

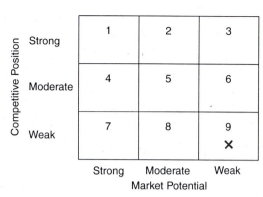

1. It is time to dispose of your product/service.

2. Consider alternative uses for your product/service that make sense in this poor environment.

3. Look for new markets for your product/service.

FIGURE 12.15. Position #9: Weak Market/Weak Product or Service

The marketing strategies accompanying these nine grid positions are only suggestions. There are many variables to consider, and each product or service may have a uniqueness unto itself that needs to be taken into consideration prior to selecting a strategy. The Marketing Strategy Grid is a tool designed to help you think about how to maximize your marketing strategies for the most productive results. In the final analysis, it is your judgment that will dictate the strategy selected; the Marketing Strategy Grid only helps to sharpen the judgment.

As previously discussed, one of the new Five Ps, power thrusts, is the deployment of multiple marketing weapons in overlapping "waves." For any business, product/service, or brand, understanding what each weapon in your marketing arsenal is capable of doing, and how and when to use it, is yet another component of marketing strategy. We will now focus on the weapons and choices/options for development and deployment, as shown in Figure 12.16.

In general, application of the marketing weapons can be viewed within the context of the overall approach. In some cases, the marketing strategy is to reach the masses—mass marketing. In other instances, it may be focused on target markets—target marketing. In the latter case, a segment, niche, or market cell may be the focal point. Not every weapon is appropriate for every strategy. In some strategy cases, there will be a need for rapid response, thus eliminating weapons that are time-consuming in preparation. In other cases, the marketing strategy will be anticipative, thus requiring a quick but thorough and timely launch. And in still other situations, time will need to be taken to execute need-shaping responses to have a competitive edge. In essence, the strategic option or objective desired will shape or dictate the appropriate marketing discipline and weapons to be deployed. Figure 12.17 delineates strategy application and appropriate marketing disciplines.

Most organizations in the hospitality industry utilize a mix of marketing disciplines to execute their overall marketing strategy. For example, a fast-food chain such as McDonald's uses network advertising to reach the mass-market target but also runs promotions at select market segments (kids, seniors, etc.). Likewise, a hotel chain such as Hilton utilizes national advertising in print media and broadcasts, along with promotions of its Hilton HHonors program (frequency rewards program) through various forms of direct marketing and the electronic media. Utilization of multiple disciplines is referred to as the "marketing mix." Successful application of the marketing disciplines results in winning marketing strategy.

Technology through information systems, market segmentation, transaction analysis, revenue analysis, customer profiling, and many other quantitative methodologies allows today's marketing managers to base strategic decisions on a sound basis of data. Yield and revenue management programs, cost-benefit analyses, market share reports, and simultaneous inventory management systems of reservations centers and units in the field, all contribute to sound selection of marketing strategies.

FIGURE 12.16. The Marketing Arsenal Weaponry

Strategy Application	Marketing Discipline
Simulate trade participation	✓ Trade promotion
Reward frequency and loyalty	✓ Frequency program
Create a sense of involvement	✓ Events
Reach a tightly targeted audience	✓ Addressable media
Establish credibility and build trust	✓ Public relations
Create lifestyle associations	✓ Advertising, events
Establish awareness and create images	✓ Advertising
Stimulate repeat purchases	✓ Sales promotion
Leverage social responsibility	✓ Mission marketing
Stimulate referrals	✓ Club or affinity group
Stimulate trial	✓ Sales promotion
Make a news announcement	✓ Public relations

FIGURE 12.17. Strategy Application and Related Marketing Disciplines. *Source:* Adapted from R. Hiebing Jr. & S. Cooper, *The Successful Marketing Plan* (Lincolnwood, IL: NTC Business Books, 1996), pp. 187-202.

Measuring Success

The application of marketing strategy is measured in numerous ways within the hospitality industry. Financial performance is evaluated, as is marketing performance. Today, market share, customer counts, customer retention (brand loyalty), customer satisfaction (through the CSI), and the various forms of revenue measurements are most common. The latter include REVPAR (revenue per available room; lodging), revenue per available seat (airlines and select foodservice establishments), revenue per person (airlines and foodservice), revenue per ticket (attractions), revenue per rental (car rentals), sales per square foot, and so on, as well as numerous other measurement techniques. Certainly for those building customer databases and viewing their potential total revenue generated per customer, the ultimate measurement of overall marketing strategy success is REVPAC or revenue per available customer. For a vertically or horizontally integrated company such as Carlson Companies, Cendant, and so on, REVPAC would take into account total revenue production from all sectors of the market by customer.

Strategic Issues

Marketing strategy is constantly being challenged not only by competitive and environmental forces but by a number of overall industry issues. Availability of labor (which influences CSI and revenue), security, shrinking margins, and more competition impact virtually all sectors. Some sectors, such as airlines, cruise lines, car rental, and the like, must also deal with regulatory changes, escalating fuel costs, and labor (strikes, availability, and competency). Rising sales and promotional costs, declining brand and customer loyalty, media fragmentation, and increased niche attacks present special challenges for marketing strategists. Also, increasing use of technological applications is affecting almost all areas of marketing research and marketing strategy.

Strategy selection is dependent upon overall strength of your market (demand) and your product's/service's competitive position. The premise of sound strategy is responding appropriately based on your positioning, anticipating the movement of the market (demand), and shaping your message to capitalize on the needs of the market in relation to your attributes. Marketing strategies need to be constantly revisited in a dynamic and ever-changing market. Your most valuable customers will quickly lose their loyalty to your products/services if you do not keep up with meeting their evolving needs. Marketing strategies may also differ based upon the target market selected or the stage of customer development. Figure 12.18 gives a recap of where we are in the strategic marketing planning process.

FIGURE 12.18. The Marketing Planning Process in Perspective

CHAPTER REVIEW

Understanding the consumer's perspective creates a marketing strategy that sells products and services. The marketing process must be thorough in its research and analysis of the consumer. Product development or changes in services offered should be in line with what consumers express as their needs. Marketing cannot succeed if the product or service offering is not in line with the consumers' needs.

The consumer's perspective centers on the needs fulfilled by a product or service. The marketing challenge is that not all consumers have the same needs. In fact, the same consumer can at different times have a very different set of needs. Much depends on the consumer's purpose or reason for using the product or service.

One key point to remember is that a consumer's perspective of products and services can and does change based on the perception created by marketing.

The nurture, care, and conveying of what a brand stands for and how it meets the needs of the consumer is what marketing strategy is all about. The nurture and care of the brand creates a perception by the consumer. This perception translates into action and to purchases. The perception created by packaging the brand helps to dictate the price consumers are willing to pay. Conveying how the brand meets the specific needs of buyers is one role of marketing strategies and promotional techniques.

KEY CONCEPTS/TERMS

CSI
End users
Focus group
Four Cs
Four Ps
Five Ps
Intermediaries
Market share
Marketing disciplines
Marketing mix
Marketing research

Marketing Strategy Grid
Marketing weapons
Mission statement
Perception
Perspective (consumer)
Positioning
Power thrusts
REVPAC
Value

DISCUSSION QUESTIONS

1. Give three reasons why research is important to marketing strategy.
2. Why is understanding your positioning important to marketing strategy execution?
3. If your product or service were located in box 4 of the Marketing Strategy Grid, what marketing tactics would you deploy?
4. Identify companies or brands that represent three different positioning strategy options.
5. Select two different companies or brands and discuss what you believe to be the marketing mix or marketing disciplines to best address their markets.
6. What do you believe will be the most significant issue to impact marketing strategy in the next decade?

CASE 12.1. STARBUCKS COFFEE—THE RISING STAR

Starbucks Coffee Company represents an excellent case example of a company that has successfully marketed an "experience."[4] Moreover, its marketing strategies provide examples of positioning, image development, merchandising, pricing, packaging, and market development. Starbucks' success has helped propel the entire industry segment.

The specialty/gourmet coffee segment has been rapidly growing since the early 1990s. According to the Specialty Coffee Association, specialty coffee beverage retail outlets (gourmet coffee shops) increased over tenfold in the past decade. Their locations are expected to double by 2015. The growth of this segment was started and accelerated mainly by Starbucks Coffee. Starbucks is the leader in this segment and is becoming one of the most well-known international brands in the hospitality industry, as with Hilton and McDonald's. In this case example, the current trends in the specialty coffee segment are briefly explained and then the business and marketing strategy of Starbucks is identified.

The thriving specialty coffee segment today differs much from what used to be. New, growing chain companies are now capturing the segment that used to be dominated by independent mom-and-pop-type shops. Several specialty coffee chains eagerly acquire other chains in order to be players in the segment, behind the market leader Starbucks. Specialty coffee shops frequently charge in excess of $3 for a cup of coffee or specialty coffee. The service style is limited service. The focus is on the quality and quick service of espresso, latte, and cappuccino. The serving of limited food items has given way to adding more items in an effort to be more competitive. It is common for chain companies to have their own roasting facility, where the quality of coffee is controlled and the profit margin is actually preplanned.

Starbucks opened its first shop in Seattle in 1971. Howard Schultz, the chairman, joined Starbucks in 1982 and introduced the Italian espresso bar concept in 1984. Becoming a public company in 1992, Starbucks accelerated the expansion of business with new capital. Starbucks has over 3,000 outlets in the United States and internationally and is rapidly opening new stores via joint ventures with local companies.

The company's retail sales mix (2000) by product type was approximately 73 percent beverages, 14 percent food items, 8 percent whole bean coffees, and 5 percent coffee-making equipment and accessories. The main beverage items are dark-roasted coffee, espresso, latte, and cappuccino.

Interestingly, Starbucks, unlike other chain companies in the foodservice industry, operates 85 percent of Starbucks outlets by itself. It does not franchise to individuals and limits licensing its operations to companies. Starbucks retains total control over the growth and looks for logical and appropriate partners.

The mission statement of Starbucks, established in 1990, is to "establish Starbucks as the premier purveyor of the finest coffee in the world while maintaining our uncompromising principles while we grow." The principles are as follows:

- Provide a great work environment and treat each other with respect and dignity.
- Embrace diversity as an essential component in the way we do business.
- Apply the highest standards of excellence to the purchasing, roasting, and fresh delivery of coffee.
- Develop enthusiastically satisfied customers all of the time.
- Contribute positively to the communities in which we are located and help preserve the environment.
- Recognize that profitability is essential to future success.

The three basic business strategies of Starbucks are as follows:

- Utilize the recognized and respected brand "Starbucks."
- Expand market shares and develop new markets while keeping the high quality of specialty coffee and service.
- Sell not only coffee but also "coffee experiences," a place where people can relax and enjoy a conversation.

In order to support the business strategies, Starbucks develops new distribution channels and introduces new products. To extend distribution channels, Starbucks formed strategic alliances with Barnes & Noble bookstores in 1993, United Airlines in 1995, Aramark in 1996, and Albertson's in 2000. In opening Starbucks coffee shops at Barnes & Noble bookstores, both companies improved their brand image and awareness, and improved the sales. Starbucks-brewed coffee is served on United and Canadian Airlines. With these brand alliances, or cobranding, Starbucks improved brand recognition and sales. Starbucks also expanded its distribution through kiosks and carts in many types of locations. Now, kiosks and carts are at airports, universities, convention centers, and office buildings and are as important a distribution channel as freestanding coffee shops. Moreover, Starbucks has hundreds of kiosks in Albertson's grocery stores and has expanded with shops/stores within stores, such as at selected Targets.

Starbucks introduced cold and frozen specialty coffee drinks mainly for the younger generation, which is fast becoming an important market. Moreover, Starbucks started a lunch program—sandwiches and prepackaged salads priced between $3.75 and $5.95—at over 400 of their outlets to capture a new market.

Starbucks also has extended its products into retail shops, introducing Frappuccino with Pepsi in 1994 and Starbucks ice cream with Dreyer's in 1995. Starbucks coffee is sold in supermarkets as well as at retail shops.

In short, the initial success of Starbucks depended on establishing brand awareness and image. This brand recognition and perception was not established by a large traditional advertising campaign or low promotional prices, but by wide distribution and strategic brand alliances with larger partners. At present Starbucks utilizes the strong brand awareness and alliances to continue to expand.

The products of Starbucks are supported by three elements (Exhibit 12.1): quality; wide distribution through strategic alliances; and the well-recognized brand "Starbucks."

Case Discussion Questions

1. Do you believe Starbucks is still positioned as a star in the Boston Consulting Group Portfolio Box (see Chapter 10)? What are your reasons to support this or another positioning?
2. As Starbucks continues both its global expansion and brand extension strategies, what pitfalls should they look out for?

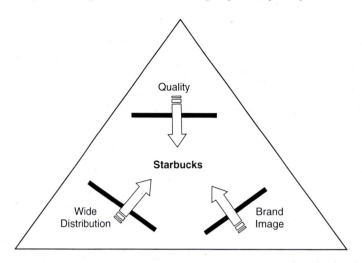

EXHIBIT 12.1. The Starbucks Product Triad

CASE 12.2. FREQUENCY PROGRAMS

It has been said that the second currency in the United States is frequency program points/miles. Frequency or loyalty reward programs permeate virtually every sector of the hospitality industry in some form or fashion. Rewards have expanded from airline miles and room nights to just about everything under the sun. Airlines, lodging chains, rental car companies, credit card companies, food service entities, themed attractions, and casinos all offer their frequent or loyal customers some type of award/reward program.

Frequency programs have grown to such an extent that their "point" liabilities now add up to hundreds of millions of dollars. Hospitality industry corporations keep the programs because they work to retain customers and in the end lower the expense of attracting new customers. (It costs five times as much on average to attract a new customer as to retain an existing one.)

For this case example, a comparison of Marriott Rewards, Hilton's HHonors, and Starwood's Preferred Guest programs are presented.[5]

Marriott Rewards

The Marriott Corporation's frequent stay program, known as Marriott Rewards, is accepted at any of its participating brands. Offering over 2,000 hotels worldwide, the program gives the guest the option of earning either points or miles for every dollar spent. Nine distinct hotel brands provide guests the opportunity for a free night or free flight. Marriott offers lodgers of all kinds the chance to earn points, whether at an extended-stay property, a moderately priced property, or a full-service luxury property. Points are awarded based on dollars spent on the full guest folio at full-service properties, and on room rate only at all other participating locations. Guests staying at most of the brands earn 10 points for every qualifying dollar spent; however, 5 points per dollar is awarded at TownPlace Suites and Residence Inn locations. Travelers have a few options when enrolling to become a member; they may call the toll-free number, sign up at any participating property, or enroll online at www. marriott.com.

Marriott has restructured their program to offer more options, greater flexibility, and better value. The new Stay Anytime Rewards program allows guests to override blackout dates during the most popular travel times—even if it's the last standard room in the hotel—for just 50 percent more points. It has also implemented a One-Call Redemption program that allows members one-to-one point-to-mile conversion rates. These benefits are available to all guests; however, an Elite membership has been set up for more frequent guests. This membership is divided into three levels, Silver, Gold, and Platinum, each offering a more prestigious set of benefits.

Silver-Level Membership

After fifteen nights per year, members can become Silver-level members with an added array of benefits. The first is an automatic credit of 20 percent bonus for those members who have chosen to earn points. Marriott will pay for the Silver-level members accommodations for the night and will send a check to compensate for the inconvenience should the reservation not be honored. Marriott has also set up a dedicated reservation line for Elite members. A priority for the requested room type will also be acknowledged upon availability. Silver-level members are also offered a priority for late checkouts. A 10 percent discount on regular Friday and Saturday night rates is also offered. Registered Silver-level members are also extended a check cashing benefit, up to $200 a day. Members also receive a 10 percent discount at Marriott-owned and -operated gift shops.

Gold-Level Membership

Once guests have stayed with Marriott for fifty nights throughout the year, they advance to the Gold-level membership where they receive all the benefits Silver members receive and more. Guests who opt to earn points are automatically credited with a 25 percent bonus. Upon check-in, Gold-level members are offered an upgrade on their room to include concierge floors, should they be available, with no superimposed charge. Select properties also offer Gold-level members access to the concierge lounge where complimentary light snacks, beverages, and continental breakfast are provided. Participating Courtyard, SpringHill Suites, and Fairfield locations also entitle Gold-level members to complimentary, unlimited local phone calls and faxes. Checks of up to $500 a day may be cashed for registered Gold-level members.

Platinum-Level Membership

The seventy-fifth night stayed at Marriott properties in a year marks eligibility for the highest level of Elite membership, the Platinum level. This level offers members the same benefits as Gold members with even more. Guests who choose to earn points will be automatically credited with a 30 percent bonus. In addition, Platinum-level members are guaranteed a room when reservations are made forty-eight hours in advance at participating properties. A welcome package will also be awaiting a Platinum-level member upon check-in.

As an added incentive to maintain guest preference, Marriott also offers additional benefits in conjunction with service and hotel partners. A Marriott Rewards Visa card is available to all guests with a 5,000 bonus point incentive for the first purchase. Three points per dollar spent at Marriott locations are earned and one point per dollar spent elsewhere using the card. The Marriott Rewards Visa card also honors guests with a complimentary Silver-level membership. Guests can earn 10 points per dollar spent when shopping at SkyMall online. A total of 500 points can be earned each time a car is rented from Hertz, Marriott's car rental partner. Other service partners Marriott works in conjunction with include American Express Membership Rewards, Click-Rewards, E*Trade, My Points, Diners Club, and AT&T Long Distance. Marriott also offers Travel Rewards with over twenty airline partners, rail travel partners, theme park partners, and cruise line partners. Up to 50,000 points can be earned when meetings or events are hosted at participating properties. Members have the opportunity to combine points with a spouse to qualify for a specific reward under the Joint Ventures program. Up to 10 percent of the required points for a reward may be purchased when sufficient points are not available.

Hilton HHonors

The Hilton HHonors frequent stay program offers members a variety of services and amenities. These exclusive privileges and benefits strive to set the guest apart from check-in to check-out. Offering over 2,000 hotels worldwide, the program gives the guest the opportunity to Double Dip, or earn both points and miles for the same stay. Eight distinct hotel brands provide guests the opportunity to earn points, whether at an extended-stay property, a moderately priced property, or a full-service luxury property. Guests earn 10 points per dollar spent on room rate and incidentals at all participating properties. Travelers have a few options to enroll to become a member; they may call the toll-free number, sign up at any participating property, or enroll online at www.hilton.com.

Members are assured that reservation requests receive special attention, especially during peak periods. In order to achieve this Hilton offers a dedicated HHonors reservation service. Hilton also offers an expedited check-in once a guest profile is established. A room will be reserved for the guest based on the preferences and credit card information that are provided on the account. Members are also given a complimentary copy of *USA Today* or the local paper each weekday morning. At participating properties HHonors members are privileged to have their spouses stay free. Late check-out is also accommodated when possible for all members should extra time be needed, along with express check-out services. Membership level is determined by stay activity—the more frequent the stays, the more generous the benefits become. Some of these benefits include bonus points, complimentary room upgrades, and health club privileges. There are four levels of membership, Blue membership, Silver VIP membership, Gold VIP membership, and Diamond VIP membership, each offering a more prestigious set of benefits.

Blue Membership

Guests can become Blue members simply by enrolling. Blue members receive 2,000 bonus points after four paid stays in a calendar quarter.

Silver VIP Membership

After a fourth qualifying stay or tenth qualifying night, guests attain Silver VIP membership status. Silver members earn 15 percent bonus on all points. Members of this group will also receive 2,000 bonus points after four paid stays as a Silver VIP in a calendar quarter. Complimentary health club privileges are also gained as members earn their Silver VIP status. Silver VIPs can also take advantage of check cashing privileges up to $200 when staying at participating Hilton hotels. Silver VIPs may also choose from an exclusive selection of rewards at special VIP-only point levels.

Gold VIP Membership

After sixteen qualifying stays or thirty-six qualifying nights in a calendar year, guests attain Gold VIP membership status. In addition to the benefits earned as a Silver VIP, Gold members earn a 25 percent bonus on all points. A 4,000-point bonus is earned after four paid stays as a Gold VIP in a calendar quarter. Gold VIP members are offered upgraded accommodations to Towers or Executive levels including a complimentary continental breakfast and amenities at participating properties. Gold VIP members also receive a welcome gift upon arrival, which includes a light snack.

Diamond VIP Membership

A twenty-eighth qualifying stay or sixtieth qualifying night in a calendar year at HHonors hotels earns a guest Diamond VIP membership level. In addition to the benefits earned as a Gold VIP, Diamond VIPs earn a 50 percent bonus on all points. Diamond VIP members enjoy a 4,000-point bonus after four paid stays as a Diamond VIP in a calendar quarter. Reservations availability is guaranteed to Diamond VIPs when reservations are made at least forty-eight hours prior to check-in, although a charge will be billed for not showing up. In addition, Diamond VIP members may redeem points nearly anytime. A RewardPlanner Service is also available to members, whether traveling for business or pleasure, that will take care of all the details according to profiles provided with membership; the charge for this service is 20,000 HHonor points.

As an added incentive to maintain guest preference, Hilton also offers additional benefits in conjunction with service and hotel partners. One of these benefits is the Travel Partner bonus points program, whereby guests traveling with one of over fifty-five airline or rail partners in conjunction with HHonors stays earn points. Hilton also cooperates with Thrifty, Avis, and National car rental partners and Norwegian and Orient cruise lines, which earn bonus points with qualifying stays. Event and Meeting Planner programs also offer bonus points for qualifying events. A 15 percent discount is offered for dinner dining experiences at participating HHonors hotel restaurants. Married members have the opportunity to combine points and stay credits to earn rewards and HHonors tier levels under the HHonors Mutual Fund program. The HHonors Reward Exchange program allows guests to turn HHonors points into airline miles and turn miles into points. Up to 20 percent of the required points for a reward may be purchased when sufficient points are not available, at $10 per 1,000 points.

Starwood Preferred Guest

Starwood's frequent guest program, Starwood Preferred Guest, is the newest of the three. It serves more than 700 hotels and resorts worldwide offering guests the option of earning points or miles. Six distinct hotel brands provide guests the opportunity to a free night or free flight. Guests earn 2 Starpoints for every eligible dollar spent, including dining in the hotels when not a registered guest. Starpoints do not expire so long as the guest stays just once a year. Starwood offers an exchange rate of 1 Starpoint to 1 airline mile/point on most major airlines. To enroll, guests may call the toll-free number, sign up at any participating property, or simply enroll online at www.starwood.com.

Since Starwood's beginning, it has offered a premier policy of no blackout dates and no capacity controls, meaning members can redeem stays anytime, anywhere. As Starwood Preferred Guest members, guests are entitled to a vast amount of benefits. Instant Awards, a spontaneous redemption program, allows immediate use of hotel services during a stay. Numerous award options allow the guests the opportunity to enjoy several different vacations and accommodations. These benefits are available to all guests; however, a more exclusive membership has been set up for the more frequent visiting guests. This membership is divided into two levels, Gold Preferred Guest and Platinum Preferred Guest, each offering a more prestigious set of benefits.

Gold Preferred Guest Benefits

After ten stays in a calendar year, members are upgraded to Gold Preferred Guests. As a Gold Preferred Guest, members will experience Starwood's benefits at a higher level. A more personalized service is offered in addition to the standard Preferred Guest benefits. As a Gold Preferred Guest, members receive a 50 percent earning bonus (a total of 3 points) for every eligible dollar spent. Gold Preferred Guests are offered a complimentary upgrade to a preferred room at check-in upon availability and can choose from leading financial and national newspapers during the week. Gold Preferred Guests are offered a 4:00 p.m. late check-out upon availability. Members are extended a check cashing benefit of up to $300 a day. Starwood also offers special member events exclusively for Gold Preferred Guests and Platinum Preferred Guests.

Platinum Preferred Guest Benefits

After twenty stays in a membership year, guests will be upgraded to a Platinum Preferred Guest status. Platinum Guests will enjoy the benefits of Gold Preferred Guest status as well as other added benefits. Platinum Guests are offered a complimentary upgrade to the best available room, including select suites, upon availability. A seventy-two-hour room guarantee is extended to Platinum Guests to secure that a room is available upon arrival. Platinum Preferred Guests also receive a welcome amenity upon arrival. Should Platinum Preferred Guests choose to fill out an online profile, they will be given the benefit of having personal preferences met with every stay.

As an added incentive to maintain guest preference, Starwood also offers additional benefits in conjunction with service and hotel partners. A Preferred Plus credit card from American Express is available to Starwood Preferred Guests along with 1,000 bonus Starpoints on the first paid stay at a participating hotel or resort. Preferred Plus holders earn 2 Starpoints for every dollar spent at participating properties. One Starpoint is earned for every dollar charged to the card. Starpoints may be redeemed in small quantities or in thousands. Starpoints may be redeemed for gift certificates at retail stores, including Gap and Saks Fifth Avenue. Vouchers are also available for Avis car rentals or AT&T prepaid phone cards.

The wide array of services and benefits offers loyal guests the opportunity to take advantage of several options during travel. Each program desires to be the best, which creates a highly competitive environment. The programs all target brand buyers, brand switchers, and especially brand loyalists. The ability to market each segment gives companies an opportunity to retain and establish frequent guests. By cooperating with "service partners" the potential market is increased and each individual program becomes better known, and this potentially results in increased membership (Exhibit 12.2).

Case Discussion Questions

1. From a marketing strategy application perspective frequency programs reward loyalty. What other marketing strategies help build repeat business?
2. Do you believe promotional concepts such as frequency programs enhance or distract from a brand's image? State your reasons for your position.

CASE 12.3. GAYLORD OPRYLAND RESORT AND CONVENTION CENTER, NASHVILLE

This chapter has focused on a number of key marketing strategies such as positioning options and perceptions. The case study that follows looks at one of the world's most successful meeting and convention destinations.[6] We will see how this facility/destination capitalized on both the "biggest" in its positioning strategy and the "most unique" in its perceptions strategy.

	Marriott Rewards			HHonors			Starwood Preferred	
	Silver Level	Gold Level	Platinum Level	Silver VIP	Gold VIP	Diamond VIP	Gold Preferred	Platinum Preferred
Redemption Options								
Ability to Earn Points	X	X	X	X	X	X	X	X
Ability to Earn Miles	X	X	X	X	X	X	X	X
Ability to Earn Both				X	X	X		
Number of Hotels		2000+			2000+		700+	
Number of Brands		9			8		6	
Points Awarded		10 per $1			10 per $1		2 per $1	
Points Earned at Dining Outlets When Not Registered							X	
Combine Points with Spouse		X			X		X	
Point Conversion		X			X		X	
Ease of Membership								
Online Enrollment		X			X		X	
1-800 Enrollment		X			X		X	
On Property Enrollment		X			X		X	
Required Nights to Become Advanced Members	15	50	75	10	36	60	10	20
Service Partners								
Airline Partners		20+			50+			
Cruiseline Partners		2			2			
Rail Partners		3			1			
Car Rental Partners		1			3			
Redemption Options								
Gift Shop Discounts		X						
Accom. Paid if Walked		X						
Room Upgrades		X	X		X	X	X	X
Room Guarantee			48 hr. adv.			48 hr. adv.		72 hr. adv.
Welcome Package			X		X	X		X
Late Check-Out		X			X		X	
Other Benefits								
Bonus Points Offered		X			X		X	
Immediate Use of Points							X	
Guest Profiles Maintained		X			X		X	
Points for Meetings/Events		Up to 50,000						
Ability to Purchase Points	10 % of required points			20% of required points				
No Blackout Policy		X						

EXHIBIT 12.2. Comparison of Frequency Programs

Gaylord Opryland Resort and Convention Center in Nashville's is the world's largest combined hotel and convention center under one roof. It has three major indoor gardens that cover more than nine acres. Opened in 1977 with 600 rooms, it has grown to 2,884 rooms and 600,000 square feet of meeting and exhibit space and boasts a variety of restaurants and lounges and thirty unique shops.

Gaylord Opryland Nashville has consistently refurbished and expends millions of dollars to maintain its number one position in the marketplace. Gaylord Opryland has a proud history of being a leader and innovator in the meetings and conventions industry. Now, it is elevating its performance to new levels so that attendees will experience a complete renewal of the Cascades Lobby, guest rooms and corridors, and many of the fine restaurants and dining venues. An $80-million transformation is in progress to reinforce Gaylord Opryland's premier position for major meetings and conventions. Upon completion, there will be over 4,000 rooms and 1 million square feet of conference and exhibit space. As part of the expansion, a computer-based audio processing and control system with state-of-the-art design has been installed. This entire system can be monitored and controlled, including local control of certain specialized sound systems via wall-mounted, custom-designed interface panels located throughout the facility. Each panel is application specific and simple for nontechnical operation.

As stated earlier, Opryland Hotel currently features over 600,000 square feet of meeting and exhibit space. Included in this vast expanse are five grand ballrooms and eighty-five breakout rooms for smaller gatherings. In fact, it's the largest convention center within a hotel in the world. Keeping with their tradition of hospitality, they also offer twenty-four-hour room service. Special services include a fully staffed business center with everything from fax machines and computers to color copiers. Rental car facilities and Opryland International Travel are all located within a complex.

Opryland also has thirty specialty shops, a variety of restaurants and lounges, three swimming pools, and a fitness center. Opryland Hotel is located in the heart of the Opryland entertainment complex, with attractions like the Grand Ole Opry, the General Jackson Showboat, and Springhouse Golf Club, home of the BellSouth Senior Classic. Other area attractions can be accessed by Opryland USA River Taxi. These include the historic Ryman Auditorium and the Wildhorse Saloon in downtown Nashville, and other Nashville river front attractions.

There are a variety of rooms to choose from at Opryland Hotel, including traditional rooms with lovely outdoor views, garden terrace rooms with private balconies that overlook acres of indoor gardens, or one of over 220 magnificent suites. In keeping with its tradition of hospitality, it offers twenty-four-hour room service.

There are a total of three indoor gardens that cover nine acres. Each of the gardens carries a theme. The Conservatory, which places an emphasis on plants, was completed in 1983. The Cascades is a water-oriented space that was completed in 1988. The most recent addition is the Delta, which opened in 1996. It's a massive subtropical garden complete with fountains, shops, restaurants, and even a river with passenger-carrying flatboats. The combination of these three indoor gardens creates an exceptional destination for convention-goers and pleasure travelers alike.

Located ten minutes or just seven miles from Nashville International Airport, Gaylord Opryland provides coach service every twenty minutes. This central U.S. location and proximity to the airport add to Opryland's attraction as a meeting destination. Meeting planners and attendees will find not only state-of-the-art group facilities capable of handling up to 6,400 people theater style or 4,560 banquet style, but also state-of-the-art full-service audiovisual support and an amphitheater. Guestrooms are also up-to-date from a technical perspective with voice mail, fax/modem hookups, and additional telephone lines. Meeting planners and attendees will find the fitness center, eighteen-hole championship golf course, three swimming pools, General Jackson Showboat, and Grand Ole Opry great additional amenities to please their attendees.

In addition to banquet capabilities to serve nearly 5,000 guests, Gaylord Opryland also offers fifteen food and beverage outlets, a multiple food facility court, contemporary and regional cuisine, steakhouse, fine-dining Italian restaurant, many lounges, and a great sports bar. Consider that all of this is under glass including more than nine acres of tropical gardens.

Other aspects of Opryland that help put this extraordinarily large facility into perspective include its own power plant capable of providing enough power for a small town. There is a substantial commissary capable of providing all the supplies for more than 10,000 meals per day plus servicing fifteen outlets and multiple banquets and group meal functions simultaneously. There is also a laundry building (not room), to handle the complex's needs. Finally, extensive state-of-the-art computer systems and programs manage everything from inventories to uniform distribution.

Technology and communications provide effective and efficient communications for successful meetings. Gaylord Opryland personnel provide extensive assistance in the areas of Internet connectivity and communications services.

Opryland, Nashville, is unique in its positioning as the world's largest meetings and convention facility under one roof. It has successfully maintained this leadership or number one positioning by consistently upgrading its facilities and technology. Further, its very well-trained staff goes the extra mile to assist meeting planners and attendees with all of their technical and nontechnical needs. There is no other single meeting and convention facility like Gaylord Opryland Resort and Convention Center. It is a great example of the concept of "unique" positioning delineated in this chapter.

Case Discussion Questions

1. What are the advantages and disadvantages of a facility the magnitude of the Opryland Resort and Convention Center?
2. What market segments would be the focal point for this facility?

NOTES

1. R. Nykiel, *The Art of Marketing Strategy* (New York: Amacor, 2001), p. 39.
2. P. Kotler, *Principles in Marketing* (Upper Saddle River, NJ: Prentice Hall, 1986), p. 57.
3. D. E. Schultz, S. I. Tannebaum, & R. F. Lauterborne, *Integrated Marketing Communications* (Lincolnwood, IL: NTC Business Books, 1993), pp. 187-202.
4. R. Nykiel, *Hospitality Management Strategies* (Upper Saddle River, NJ: Prentice Hall, 2005), pp. 154-156; www.starbucks.com.
5. Ibid., pp. 157-164.
6. www.gaylord.com.

Chapter 13

Applying Research to Brand Strategy

CHAPTER OBJECTIVES

- To delineate how branding and brand strategy is supported by marketing research and analysis.
- To identify the evolution of brands within the context of management strategy.
- To describe the key components of brand strategy.
- To demonstrate the relationship of brand strategy to managerial success and failure.

BRAND EVOLUTION

When a family decided to put its name on a building, such as Hilton, Marriott, Nordstrom's, and so on, it not only "branded" the product/service, it began to establish a positioning statement. The quality of the facility and the level of service now were described by the family name, and vice versa. This represented an early form of brand strategy. Brand strategy has been conveyed by the ownership (names), by the physical product design and packaging, and by the creations of marketing. The latter has created new brand names (W Hotels, Carnival, Enterprise, Jet Blue). Marketing also created awareness-building logos and icons (e.g., "Jack" for Jack-In-The-Box, and apple for Apple Computers). Names, logos, and icons are all part of brand strategy. In fact, anything associated with the brand's name is part of brand management. Colors, typeface, celebrity spokespersons, lighting, exterior and interior design, supplier affiliations, and so on—all need to be managed to grow and protect brands. The "look" of the brand usually represents the overall product/service image. One can close one's eyes and picture an American Airlines branded plane, a Hertz facility, or a McDonald's. One does not only picture the brand, but can describe the product, service level, and perhaps even the taste. Brand strategy is very powerful and requires research and analysis to be managed and successful.

In any ten-year time span over 100 new lodgings, hundreds of new restaurant, and dozens of new airlines, rental car brands, and so on, were launched. Some succeed, such as Southwest Airlines, and others disappear, for example, Peoples Express. Why some succeed and others fail is what brand management is all about. It is even more complex in certain segments of the industry due to how businesses are developed and grow. Regardless of the growth or development strategy there are specific areas of focus for brand management that are important to a single brand, hybrids of that brand, and even new brands launched by the same company. We have moved historically from product branding to aggressively marketing and expanding brand concepts. There are now mature as well as new brands (that have grown rapidly through franchising) that have substantial presence and awareness in the consumer's mind. Brands have reached a stage where they now have developed "equity" and are bought and sold on a fairly regular basis during contraction and expansionary periods in the economy. In addition, others absorb the original corpo-

Handbook of Marketing Research Methodologies for Hospitality and Tourism
© 2007 by The Haworth Press, Inc. All rights reserved.
doi:10.1300/5927_14

rations that have developed the brands through acquisition. The latter may result in some brands being retained and others being merged or converted to a new brand.

While brand strategy certainly is closely aligned with overall corporate strategy, the actual execution of brand strategy falls more into the realm of marketing, for branding is a key marketing weapon. Branding is the visible communicator of positioning strategy. Marketing's role is to both lead the creative process and be the "keeper" of the brand (oversee its usage). Branding is complex, involves all elements in the marketing mix, and requires often complex and careful research and analysis.

COMPONENTS OF BRAND STRATEGY

There are multiple components related to brand strategy. These include, but are not limited to, brand equity, brand loyalty, and brand awareness; perceived quality; brand associations; the name, symbol, and slogan; brand extensions; and the concept of revitalizing the brand (see Figure 13.1).

Before embarking on developing a brand or branding plan, it is essential to understand the components of brand strategy.

Brand Equity

Brand equity is the net result of all the positives and negatives linked to the brand—its name and symbols—that add value to, or subtract value from, a product or service. These assets include brand loyalty, name awareness, perceived quality, and associations.[1]

There are considerable pressures for short-term performance, in part driven by the dictum that shareholder wealth is a primary goal of business, and partly by the reality that stock prices are responsive to short-term performance measures. Short-term activities (such as price promotions) can show dramatic results, while brand-building activities (such as image advertising) may have little immediate impact. The challenge is to understand better the links between brand assets and future performance, so that brand-building activities can be justified.

Estimating the value of a brand can help show that the underlying assets do have worth. The assessment of the value of brand equity can be based on the price premium that the name supports, the impact of the name on customer preference, the replacement cost of the brand, and the stock value minus the value of other assets. The most persuasive measure, however, may be a multiplier of the earning power of the brand. The multiplier would be based upon an analysis of the earning power of the brand assets.

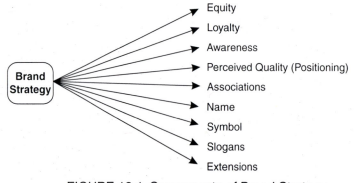

FIGURE 13.1. Components of Brand Strategy

Brand Loyalty

The core of brand equity is the loyalty of its customer base—the degree to which customers are satisfied, have switching costs, like the brand, and are committed. A loyal set of customers can have substantial value, which is often underestimated. They can also reduce marketing costs, since a customer is much less costly to keep than to gain or regain, and provide leverage over others in the distribution channel. Customers can create brand awareness and generate reassurance to new customers. Loyal customers will also give a firm time to respond to competitive advances.

Brand Awareness

Don't underestimate the power of brand awareness recognition, recall (your brand is recalled as being in a product class), and top-of-mind recall (the first recalled). People like the recognizable. Further, recognition is a basis for presence, substance, and permanence. Recall can be a necessary condition to being considered and can have a subtle influence on purchase decisions as well. It also provides the anchor to which other associations are linked.

Building awareness is much easier over a longer time period because learning works better with repetition and reinforcement. In fact, brands with the highest recall are generally older brands. Event sponsorship, publicity, symbol exposure, and the use of brand extensions all can improve awareness. However, developing recall requires a link between the brand and the product class, and just name exposure will not necessarily create that link.

Perceived Quality

Perceived quality pays off. According to recent studies using data from thousands of businesses in the PIMS (profit impact of marketing strategy) database,[2] perceived quality improves prices, market share, and ROI. In addition, it was the top-named competitive advantage in a survey of managers of business units. It provides a reason to buy, a point of differentiation, a price premium option, channel interest, and a basis for brand extensions.

The key to obtaining high perceived quality is to deliver high quality, to identify those quality dimensions that are important, to understand what signals quality to the buyer, and to communicate the quality message in a credible manner. Price becomes a quality cue, especially when a product is difficult to evaluate objectively or when status is involved. Other quality cues include the appearance of service people, public spaces, and other visible first-impression areas.

Brand Associations

"A brand association is anything mentally linked to the brand."[3] The brand position is based upon associations and how they differ from competition. An association can affect the processing and recall of information, provide a point of differentiation, provide a reason to buy, create positive attitudes and feelings, and serve as the basis of extensions.

Positioning on the basis of an association with a key tangible product attribute is effective when the attribute can drive purchase decisions, but often it can also result in a specification shouting match. The use of an intangible attribute such as overall quality, technological leadership, or health and vitality can sometimes be more enduring. The association with a customer benefit is another option. One study showed that the combination of a rational benefit and an emotional benefit was superior to a rational benefit alone.

The relative price position often is central. Is the brand to be premium, regular, or economy? Further, is it to be at the top or bottom of the selected category? Among the other association types to consider are use applications, product users, celebrities, lifestyles and personalities, product class, competitors, and country or geographic area.

Measuring Brand Associations

Insights about what a brand means to people and what motivations it taps often can be obtained by using indirect methods of eliciting associations. A customer, for example, can be asked to describe a brand user or use experience, to generate free associations with the brand, or to indicate how brands differ from each other. Another way to gain a rich profile of a brand is to ask people to consider the brand as a person (or animal, activity, magazine, etc.) and probe as to what type the brand would be.[4]

Selecting, Creating, and Maintaining Brand Associations

A successful brand association will usually follow three tenets: (1) Don't try to be something you are not. (2) Differentiate your brand from competitors. (3) Provide associations that add value and/or provide a reason to buy.

A key to creating associations is to identify and manage signals. A promotion may signal that nonprice attributes are not important unless it is structured so that it reinforces the desired image. To deliver an attribute and communicate that it exists may not be enough if the appropriate signals are not managed properly. Being consistent over time and over elements of the marketing program is crucial in maintaining associations.

Brand Name, Symbol, and Slogan

The name, symbol, and slogan are critical to brand equity, and can be enormous assets, because they serve as indicators of the brand and thus are central to brand recognition and brand associations.

A name should be selected by a systematic process involving the relation of a host of alternatives based upon desired associations and metaphors. The name should be easy to recall, suggest the product class, support a symbol or logo, suggest desired brand associations, not suggest undesirable associations, and be legally protectable. There usually are trade-offs to be made. For example, a name that suggests a product class might be strategically limiting when brand extensions are considered. A symbol can create associations and feelings. A symbol such as IBM or Sony that is based upon the name will have an edge in creating brand recognition. A symbol that includes the product class should help in brand recall where the link to the product class needs to be strong. A slogan can be tailored to a positioning strategy, and is far less limited than a name and symbol in the role it can play. A slogan can provide additional associations, or help to focus on the existing one.

Brand Extensions

One way to exploit brand equity is to extend the name to different products. An extension will have the best chance for success when the brand's associations or perceived quality can provide a point of differentiation and advantage for the extension. Extensions rarely work when the brand name has nothing to offer beyond brand awareness.

An extension should "fit" the brand. "There should be some link between the brand and the extension. The fit could be based upon a variety of linking elements, such as common use contexts, functional benefits, and links to prestige, user types, or symbols."[5] Any incongruity could damage and result in the failure of desired associations to transfer. In addition, there should not be any meaningful negative association created by the brand name. There is a risk that an extension will damage the core brand by weakening either its associations or its perceived quality. Probably the biggest risk of an extension is that the potential of a new brand name with unique associations may be lost.

IMPLEMENTING BRAND STRATEGY

Brand equity does not just happen. Its creation, maintenance, and protection need to be actively managed. Further, it involves strategic as well as tactical programs and policies. The components of a brand strategy need to be orchestrated in a plan in which all the parts work together to achieve the synergy required to market a brand. Planning requires that every detail, from the name, logo, and graphics treatment to the detailed marketing plan, be addressed. Before selecting a name, logo, and so on, it is important to start with the "positioning objective" and then develop related strategies and tactics. In the case of launching a new brand, the "perceived quality" factor becomes a driving force. When creating an entirely new brand, clear positioning within the product category and in relationship to competitive products becomes a preeminent factor. Therefore, how the brand is portrayed—the actual name and look of the new brand—take a preeminent position in the strategy. Equally important is the front-end planning. A plan needs to be in place to immediately establish a "perceived" brand equity. Positioning the new brand through its visual messages will create the perception.

Creating a brand "look," logo, icon, or package is but one creative application of software. Managing a brand's performance and meaning and its success or failure are as instantaneous as checking on the screen. Both hardware and software have greatly contributed to effective brand management.

The steps in implementing a brand strategy begin with the positioning objective and are followed by "linking" or creating the visual images that support that objective. These include name, logo, graphic treatment, and creative approach. Following these "associations" is the next step, implementing a detailed marketing plan, which includes, but is not limited to, the advertising strategy (creative and media plans); a promotional strategy (introductory promotion and retention promotion); the public relations plan (consumer and trade); the sales strategy for retention of existing business and capturing new business; the sales organizational approach; the direct mail/database marketing program; the electronic marketing strategy, and the packaging.

Brand strategy is usually a "build" or phased activity.[6] Phase 1 is the "declaration" or announcement phase; here you state your intention, positioning objective, and reveal your new "look." Phase 1 is achieved through public relations and advertising. Phase 2 is the "work in progress" stage—the kick-off plus actions from the marketing plan that state, "We are off the pad and ascending," drawing upon all the marketing weapons. Phase 3 begins the "proclamation" or statement of achievement: "We're meeting our goals—delivering as promised." This phase is achieved through public relations and advertising. Phase 4 usually employs all marketing weaponry and often is accompanied with some form of recognition, such as awards, milestones, and so on.

STRATEGIES FOR A NEW BRAND LAUNCH

The critical steps for launching a new brand need to be put in perspective and involve some key factors, as described in the following.

First is timing: The brand needs to be ready to launch. The name, logo, and graphic treatment need to be service marked or registered. The brand identifiers should have been ordered and ready to be put in place. These include look/design of the brand and any collateral materials. Once the visual associations are ready to go the brand marketing plan needs to be put into action. This begins with a "communications" plan, sometimes referred to as "memo/letter #1."

Second, memo #1 delineates the positioning so every employee in the organization can understand and explain what the new brand represents—how it is "better" than the old brand. This communiqué is usually accompanied with highlights from the overall marketing plan. It states when and where the new advertising will appear. It talks about the introductory promotions, new look, and all the other positive momentum and esprit de corps building blocks.

Third, it is absolutely essential to have the "internal launch" take place prior to the "external launch." This ensures all employees are aware of any changes.

Fourth, every business that adopts a new brand should consider a "new brand grand opening" event that reintroduces the business and people to key local contacts and the community.

Fifth, letters to existing customers should be developed and follow-up calls made to convey the new brand positioning. These letters should seek to excite and entice the customer to return or repeat purchase. An introductory incentive should be included, if possible.

Sixth, special familiarization briefings should provide information to all key intermediaries. These intermediaries include middlemen, merchant middlemen, agents, distributors, wholesalers, retailers, brokers, manufacturer agents, jobbers, and facility agents.

Seventh, a comprehensive trade media public relations plan should be rolling at the time of the launch. Interviews with key executives and spokespersons, as well as trade advertising delineating the brand positioning strategy, should be ongoing at this juncture.

Eighth, the consumer marketing plan steps also need to occur in sync with the launch. A new toll-free number, Internet address, advertisements, promotions, photos, and the like, all need to be simultaneously lined up and ready to go. These marketing activities need to be executed with a grand opening philosophy and heavy up-front expenditure level (in the first six months of the launch). In essence, spend the largest portion of the annual budget in the months following the brand launch.

Ninth, every month for the first three months recommunicate in the form of an "update" memo #1—then memo #2, memo #3, and so on—to both your internal and external constituencies. Do this again at six months and one year out.

Tenth, replace anyone who has not bought into the new brand positioning or is not communicating it with enthusiasm. This is poison to a new brand launch with both employees and customers.

In summary, it is critical to be ready before the launch with a detailed communications and marketing plan. It is essential to have the brand identifiers designed, purchased, and in place at the outset of the conversion. Finally, make sure all constituencies have been clearly and thoroughly briefed. The brand launch should have its own critical path chart, with key dates and responsibilities clearly delineated. Regular progress briefings and meetings should also occur. A sound approach is to select the launch date (after planning) then peg all the critical dates/tasks that lead up to that day. Allow for slippage with sign companies, suppliers, design issues, and such. Be sure the new brand signs are within the square-foot limitations of the existing zoning regulations before you order signs. Also, be sure you have taken and completed all legal steps such as registering your brand, slogans, and so forth.

The following can be used as a checklist for a new brand name.

Checklist for a New Brand Name

- Does the name reflect the positioning as well as product/service attributes or benefits?
- Is the name appropriate to the product/service category?
- Is it globally acceptable (translates well)?
- Is it simple and easy to remember and recognize?
- Does it convey emotion or a positive mental image?
- Is it easy to pronounce and visualize?
- Does it relate to the product/service personality?
- Does it lend itself to creative development both visually and in written copy?
- Will it work on packages/signage, and does the logo reproduce in black and white and in small and large sizes?
- Has it been protected legally (and a search completed also)?
- Will it require any special treatment when used in color, print, or broadcast media?
- How does it compare to your top three competitors?
- Have you tested it on your target market, employees, and other constituencies?

CHAPTER REVIEW

This chapter has provided a look at how brands have evolved and multiplied. Brand strategy, while part of the overall corporation's development and business expansion strategies, is largely a managerial and functional responsibility most closely linked to marketing, for it is marketing that deals with all of the visual and vocal communications aspects surrounding brands. Brand strategy is extraordinarily important, as the execution of such strategy has a direct influence on positioning, customer expectations, and pricing. Further, brand strategy is complex for it involves the management of everything associated with the brand and conveyed about the brand. The sum of all these management activities directly relates to the brand's equity, profitability, image, and actual value in the marketplace.

Building awareness, conveying perceived quality, keeping customers loyal, selecting appropriate associations, and overseeing how the brand is used are all key aspects of brand management. Selecting the proper and appropriate brand partners, extensions, and creative strategy are yet additional managerial focal points. Revitalizing maturing brands and launching new brands have become a regular and significant occurrence in business today. Selecting the best brand integration strategies for acquired or merged brands forms yet another managerial strategic task in this industry. Each of these aforementioned managerial responsibilities relies heavily on accurate and thorough marketing research.

KEY CONCEPTS/TERMS

Brand
Brand assets
Brand associations
Brand awareness
Brand equity
Brand extensions
Brand loyalty
PIMS
Product attributes
Slogan

DISCUSSION QUESTIONS

1. Which sector of the industry do you believe has developed the strongest brands? Why do you believe this is so?
2. Select a leading brand and list its assets.
3. If you were developing a "new" brand would you seek "associations"? If so, how would you research what the associations should be?
4. Name two or three brand icons and describe why you believe these contributed to the brands and how they helped.
5. Make a list of five industry brands you believe do a good job at conveying positioning. State why you believe this is so. Also, do the same for five brands that you believe are not doing a good job of conveying positioning.

CASE 13.1. CENDANT—PREMIER BRAND COLLECTOR

There is perhaps no better example of a brand collector strategy in the industry today than that of Cendant Corporation. Cendant could also be used as a case example for business development, financial, marketing, and leadership strategies. Many of the more widely known brands in the hospitality and other industries fall under the Cendant umbrella.

Cendant's brand collector strategy is based on acquiring name brands at value prices and then growing those brands through its marketing and franchising expertise. Cendant views revenue as revenue per available customer or REVPAC. Cendant offers consumers brands in multiple industries and industry sectors.

Cendant Corporation is a diversified global provider of business and consumer services primarily within the real estate and travel sectors. The company's core competencies include building franchise systems and providing outsourcing services. Cendant is among the world's leading franchisers of real estate brokerage offices, hotels, rental car agencies, and tax preparation services. Cendant is also a provider of outsourcing solutions to its business partners including mortgage origination, employee relocation, customer loyalty programs, vehicle management and fuel card services, vacation exchange services, and vacation interval sales. Other businesses include Britain's largest private car park operator and electronic reservations processing for the travel industry. With headquarters in New York City, the company operates in over 100 countries. Cendant's real estate brands include Cendant Mobility, Cendant Mortgage, Century 21, Coldwell Banker, Coldwell Banker Commercial, and ERA. Hospitality and travel-related brands include AmeriHost Inns and Suites, Avis, Budget, Days Inn, Fairfield Communities, Howard Johnson, Knights Inn, PHH Arval, Ramada, Resort Condominiums International, Super 8, Travelodge, Villager Lodge, Wingate Inn, and Wright Express. Other Cendant brands in the diversified services area include Autovantage, Benefit Consultants, Inc., Cendant Incentives, CIMS, Fisi-Madison Financial, Jackson Hewitt Tax Service, Long Term Preferred Care, National Car Parks, Privacyguard, Shoppers Advantage, Travelers Advantage, and WizCom.

Cendant owes its strategy success to CEO Henry Silverman, who clearly understands the value of brands as well as how to grow brands. Both his acquisitions and expansions through franchising and marketing have proven exceptional strategies. It is for these reasons that Cendant personifies an excellent case example of a brand collector in the hospitality industry.[7]

Case Discussion Questions

1. After acquiring a brand what strategies are implemented to increase the brand's value?
2. Cendant is one of the first corporations to view the customer as a source for multiple revenue/purchases. Do you believe the concept of REVPAC will be utilized by others in the hospitality industry? Why or why not?

CASE 13.2. SYSCO—LEADER IN THE PROCUREMENT ARENA

In virtually every sector of the hospitality industry when one thinks of purchasing, the initial response is likely to include SYSCO. The history of this supplier to the industry exemplifies multiple managerial and business strategies. SYSCO created a purchasing concept from the supplier perspective that has been unmatched to date. SYSCO strategies include acquisitions, branding co-oping, delivery systems, e-commerce, customization, and product development, to name a few. SYSCO's rich history is the best starting point for this case example.

Company Profile

In 1970 SYSCO company was established as nine entrepreneurs merged their companies in an initial public offering. One of them came to be SYSCO Food Services of Houston, LP. Through the innovative services and product, the company led its industry by 1977. In 1988 SYSCO become the first distributor with the capability to provide total, uniform services to customers across the country. Taking advantage of innovations in food technology, improved packaging, and advanced transportation techniques, the company continues to provide its customers with quality products, as preferred, delivered on time, in excellent condition, and, reflecting the quest for ever-improving efficiencies at reasonable prices.

SYSCO is the largest marketer and distributor of foodservice products in America. Operating from distribution facilities nationwide, the company provides its products and services to approximately 356,000 customers. SYSCO distribution network covers virtually the entire continental United States and includes all of its 150 largest cities as well as the Pacific Coast region of Canada.

SYSCO provides customers with over 12,000 foodservice products—fresh and frozen meats, seafood and poultry, fresh and processed produce, beverages, china, glassware and tabletop items, kitchen supplies and equipment, paper and disposable items, and chemical and janitorial supplies.

The foundation of SYSCO's success is based upon superior customer service, extensive product knowledge, consistent quality product offerings, and business-building support services. A distinctive mix of ever-evolving branded products and dedicated employees has thrust SYSCO into a new dimension from a distributor to a brand provider, supported by a depth of service unparalleled in the foodservice distribution industry. Brand width and service depth has made SYSCO the distributor of choice for the "meals prepared away from home" market.

Six strategic acquisitions completed during the year 2000 strengthened both geographical presence and product offerings. They include three custom-cutting meat operations, two broadline distributors, and a specialty produce company—through Buckhead Beef Company and Tyson Foods, Inc., to form electronic FoodService Network (EFS Network), an Internet-based, business-to-business (B2B) network. Open to suppliers, distributors, and chain restaurant operators, EFS Network is aimed at cutting costs in the foodservice supply chain by more efficiently managing the flow of information and products to the marketplace.

Commitment to Quality Control

SYSCO Corporation maintains the largest foodservice distribution technical quality assurance staff in America with over 150 representatives. SYSCO quality assurance has developed finite specifications for products marketed under brands. SYSCO quality assurance staff inspects products during production, inspects incoming and outgoing loads at redistribution centers, and audits products at each distribution center. SYSCO's high level of control of the products packed is extended to all of its high-usage products. The staff travels nationally and worldwide to conduct ongoing plant inspections and evaluations. SYSCO's commitment to quality assurance not only controls its product quality but also offers the highest-quality products in the marketplace.

Fold-Out Strategy

SYSCO's internal growth strategy involves building distribution centers in established markets that previously were being served by another SYSCO company from a distance.

When a fold-out company is formed, domiciled sales and delivery personnel become employees of the new company, a core management team is transferred from the original or other SYSCO companies, and additional employees are hired locally. Supported by a state-of-the-art facility and the SYSCO Uniform System, the new company is better able to serve its customers and SYSCO grows more rapidly in both the original and the fold-out markets.

Milestones

May 8, 1969—Incorporated in Delaware.

1970—SYSCO acquired the following companies: Frost-Pack Distributing Co. and subsidiary, Global Frozen Foods, Inc.; Houston's Food Service Co.; Louisville Grocery Co.; Plantation Foods Corp.; Texas Wholesale Grocery Corp. and subsidiary, Thomas Foods, Inc.; Justrite Foods Service, Inc. (subsidiary of Thomas Foods, Inc.); Wicker, Inc., and affiliate, Albany Frosted Foods, Inc., and affiliates, Allied Langfield, Albany, NY, and San Francisco; H&R Wholesale Co., Inc.; Sam Symons & Co.

1971—SYSCO acquired the following companies: Arrow Food Distributors, Inc.; Koon Food Sales, Inc.; Rome Foods Co.; Saunders Food Distribution, Inc.

1972—SYSCO acquired the following companies: Hallsmith Co., Inc.; the Miesel Co.; Robert Orr & Co.; Hymie Falkow Co.

1973—SYSCO acquired the following companies: Lauber, Inc.; Baraboo Food Products, Inc.; E.R. Cochran Co.; Hymie Falkow Co.

1974—SYSCO acquired the following companies: Harrisonburg Fruit and Produce Co.; Theimer Food Services; Sterling-Keeley's, Inc.; Complete Foods, Inc.; Swan Food Sales, Inc.

1975—SYSCO acquired the following companies: Tri-State General Food Supply Co.; Marietta Institutional Wholesalers; Monticello Provision Co.; Oregon Film Service, Inc.; McBreen Trucking, Inc.; Mid-Central Fish & Frozen Foods, Inc.

1978—SYSCO acquired Glen-Webb & Co.

1979—SYSCO acquired Select-Union Foods, Inc.

1982—SYSCO acquired General Management Corp. & Sub, S. E. Lankford Co.; and Frosted Foods, Inc.

1984—SYSCO acquired Pegler & Co., Bell Distributing Co.

1985—SYSCO acquired assets of PYA/Monarch of Texas, Inc.; B. A. Railton Co.; New York Tea Co.; CML Company, Inc.; DiPaolo Food Distributors.

1986—SYSCO acquired Trammell; Temple & Staff, Inc.; Deaktor Brothers Provision Co.; Bangor Wholesale Foods, Inc.

1987—SYSCO acquired General Food Service Supply, Inc.; Lawrence Foods, Inc.; Vogel's Inc.; Major-Hosking's, Inc.

1988—SYSCO acquired for cash the net assets of Staley Continental, Inc.'s foodservice distribution business known as CFS Continental; Fresh Start Foods Ltd. Partnership; sold Havi Corp. to TFP Acquisition Ltd. Partnership, sold Continental Coffee Co. of Houston to Quaker Oats, sold Gregg/RE-MI to Borden, Inc.

1989—SYSCO sold NCD Detergent, Inc., to Ecolab, Inc.

1990—SYSCO acquired Oklahoma City Food Service Distribution Business of Scrivner, Inc., and Twin City Fruit, Inc.; sold Sysco Military Distribution Division and Select-Sysco Foods.

1991—SYSCO acquired certain assets of Scrivner, Inc.

1992—SYSCO acquired certain assets of Collins Foodservice, Inc., and Benjamin Polakoff & Son, Inc.; sold Global/Sysco division.

1993—SYSCO acquired Perloff Brothers, Inc., St. Louis Assets of Clark Foodservice, Inc., Ritter Food Corp. (renamed Ritter Sysco Food Services, Inc.).

1996—SYSCO purchased Strano Sysco Foodservice Limited (formerly Strano Foodservice).

Current SYSCO Acquisition Strategy

In order to meet customer needs, six strategic acquisitions completed during the year 2000 strengthened both geographical presence and product offerings. These strategies are as follows:

1. Three custom-cutting meat operations:

- *Buckhead Beef Company (Atlanta, GA),* the #1 distributor of CERTIFIED ANGUS BEEF™ products in the world in 1999, provides customers access to the largest inventory of wet- and dry-aged USDA Prime.
- *Malcolm Meats (Toledo, OH)* distributes custom-cut meats and other protein products to customers and SYSCO broadline companies throughout Illinois, Michigan, and Ohio.
- *Newport Meat Company (Irvine, CA),* SYSCO Newport Meat Company, one of the largest purveyors of fine meats, poultry, and seafood in southern California, offers products, services, and training to SYSCO broadline companies in California, Arizona, New Mexico, and Utah. Through the custom-cutting meat operations, SYSCO now offers precision custom-cut steaks and other protein products to customers in certain areas.

These three meat-cutting operations have taken customer service to a deeper level, and each operation is a leader in its market area. They also supply other customized and portion-controlled meat and protein products, complementing SYSCO's existing broad brand capabilities. Strategically located across the United States, they offer SYSCO operating companies in certain areas the opportunity to benefit from their product range and expertise while expanding their own market reach.

2. Two broadline distributors:

- Doughtie's Food Inc. (Portsmouth, VA)
- Watson Foodservice (Lubbock, TX)

These broadline distributors enhanced customer service in the mid-Atlantic and southwestern United States. Annualized sales of these previous five companies totaled approximately $500 million in the aggregate.

3. A specialty produce company, FreshPoint, Inc., distributes specialty produce through twenty-two locations across the United States and Canada. Customers may choose from a variety of produce items, from the everyday conventional to the exotic. The company also specializes in value-added services including ripening and repacking.

This addition of FreshPoint, with approximately $750 million in annualized sales, positions SYSCO for significant future growth as broadline customers may now access a wider spectrum of unique specialty product items. Along with increased produce sales and enhanced product offerings, the FreshPoint acquisition also allows SYSCO customers to enjoy the benefits of FreshPoint's in-house ripening and repacking procedures.

SYSCO now offers a full spectrum of produce in numerous varieties, from everyday staples to the exotic. Opportunities also exist for strategic product cross-selling through both customer bases. Recently, SYSCO acquired certain operations of The Freedman Companies.

Autonomy Strategy

SYSCO is using the autonomy strategy for its acquisition process. There is no change in management when the acquisition is made. The acquired company continues its operations with its employees—only the capital structure changes. If the acquired company has a strong brand perception in the market, the acquired company can keep its original name followed by SYSCO, such as NOBEL/SYSCO. The acquired company has power to manage its own company. Only capital expansion or investing new equipment decisions needs SYSCO approval. The autonomy strategy has privileged both SYSCO and the acquired company. Exhibit 13.1 is an illustration of the autonomy strategy.

Feature	Advantage	Benefit
Efficient	Saves time in the acquisition process and cost Saves time and effort in regular operations and decision making	Generates more profit
Market	Keeping the brand perception	Keep the market segment and increase the sales
Security	No employee lay-offs	Employees feel safe in the workplace
Expertise	Employees are experts in the field	Produce better products and services

EXHIBIT 13.1. The Benefit of the Autonomy Strategy

Branding Strategies

SYSCO is determined that every product is pure, wholesome, and consistent with the high standards set by name-brand products. The largest North American foodservice supplier, SYSCO has the industry's largest, and most respected, quality assurance department. SYSCO is dedicated to creating quality products that are a part of millions of lives every day, a responsibility that is taken very seriously. Unparalleled measures are taken to ensure that each product offered is as safe as possible. The quality assurance personnels' objective is to ensure that every SYSCO product, at every level, meets or exceeds the toughest industry standards. SYSCO has made food safety top priority for over twenty-five years. The recalls on millions of pounds of ground beef, reinforce the importance of quality assurance in the foodservice industry.

The produce department of SYSCO has a quality assurance program that was developed to improve upon the performance of the daily fresh produce inspection, a unique characteristic of the foodservice industry. These programs assist in the identifying and branding of the highest quality in fresh produce in the foodservice marketplace.

The quality assurance inspection department has developed and maintains coffee specifications for each SYSCO brand product. These specifications define every aspect of the product, which includes blend, minimum quality of raw materials for each blend, decaffeinating process, grind, roast color, moisture, oxygen, and packaging and labeling.

Canned Lot Set-Aside is a unique industry program that assists in providing consistent high-quality products. The SYSCO Canned Lot Set-Aside program is a program that categorizes canned fruits, vegetables, and tomatoes.

Another monitoring program focuses on boxed beef. SYSCO is to ensure that every customer receives boxed beef products that meet all specifications set by the industry.

The commitment to delivering consistent products and exceptional value at all quality levels is unprecedented. SYSCO proudly stands behind each and every SYSCO brand product displaying the Guaranteed Quality Assured emblem and guarantees that these products conform to stringent standards for food safety, sanitation, and consistency.

Branding

SYSCO has four levels of quality for every product, which includes Imperial, Supreme, Classic, and Reliance. Imperial includes products of the best available quality that are produced in prime growing regions and packed to extremely high specifications. Supreme products are top-quality products, similar in quality to Imperial, but exclusive in that they are rare in the industry, and unique to SYSCO. The Classic products are classified as SYSCO's lead quality levels under which the finest quality products are marketed. Classic products meet and even exceed top of the line, competitive labels, and account for the largest array of products. Products with the Reliance label, an economy position, offer consistency and value in their segment of the market.

Specialty Products

Arrezzio is the family of authentic, old-world products specifically created for foodservice operations that feature Italian cuisine. Ottimo is the complete line of Italian products that provide quality at an exceptional value and is comparable with Italian distributors' brands. The Casa Solana brand south-of-the-border-style products are best suited for Mexican food. Block and Barrel is a collection of prepared products that feature a variety of deli meats and cheeses and are used mostly by delicatessen operations. Jade Mountain consists of the Asian products designed for Oriental meals. The House Recipe line consists of premium-quality tabletop products and provides exceptional value to foodservice operators.

Specialty Companies

SYSCO had the desire to create a cafeteria line, food court, or freestanding mobile cart with attractive signage to market the complete line of delicious, easy-to-prepare, heat-and-serve foods. The desire led to the creation of several different specialty companies. The Arrezzio Pizza program is an easy way to offer pizzeria-style pizza by the slice or whole. Arrezzio Italian Café offers an appetizing display of pastas and sauces, which are quite Italian. With a selection of a four-cheese Alfredo sauce to the delightful, fresh-filled pasta varieties, this specialty line is filled with flavorful Italian food. With the Casa Solana Mexican Cantina, enjoy exciting Mexican menus, featuring south-of-the-border favorites that will capture the imagination and tempt the palates of every customer. Satisfying the hunger of the health conscious, as well as those with hearty appetites, the Potato Gourmet features huge baked potatoes and a large selection of hot and cold toppings that will aid in the creation of the customer's favorite baked potato. To enjoy the taste of Asian cuisine, there is the Mein Street Wok, featuring an exciting variety of popular Asian rice bowls, including the spicy Kung Pao Beef Bowl and the Sweet and Sour Chicken Bowl, that are convenient and easy to prepare. No chopping, dicing, or slicing is necessary—just heat, assemble, and serve. A delicatessen-style program, the Block and Barrel Deli, has the most complete line of deli products available in the market. National Floor Insurance Program provides a number of dry goods to suit the front of the house, bar, back of the house, cutlery, health care, janitorial, and the outdoors. If there is any type of equipment, no matter the type of company or establishment, National Floor Insurance Program is more than able to meet their needs.

Marketing Strategy

Considering the very fast expansion SYSCO has had, one can understand why the corporation only does a short-term (usually one-year) marketing plan. There is separate marketing for different brands. However, there are some basic strategies that SYSCO utilizes to maximize its market share.

Be Present Everywhere

The total dollar purchasing volume of food and related nonfood products by every type of operation preparing food in the "away from home" market including restaurants, delis, hospitals, retirement homes, schools, colleges, hotels, cruise lines, entertainment facilities, and other locations is SYSCO'S market. This market is served by three distributor categories, as defined here, and SYSCO has its presence in every category.

- *Broadline distributors* supply a wide array of food and related items to all types of foodservice operators. These operators generally require a broad spectrum of products and their menu offerings may change frequently. SYSCO's sixty-three "traditional" operating companies are broadline distributors.
- *Customized or systems distributors,* also known as chain restaurant or quick service restaurant distributors, are supply chain restaurant operations. This customer segment generally serves a relatively fixed menu and requires a more limited product line. FreshPoint and SYGMA Network, Inc., are systems distributors. SYSCO built SYGMA fifteen years ago to accommodate this market. It is operated from the rest of the corporation and has its headquarters in Denver. Now its customers include some of the major national chains such as Wendy's and Papa Johns Pizza.
- *Specialty or niche distributors* specialize in supplying a specific product category or a specific customer segment such as ethnic foodservice restaurants. SYSCO's custom-cutting meat companies are specialty distributors.

Different Approaches to Different Markets

SYSCO divides its market into two segments:

- *Marketing associate–served customers* include independently operated foodservice locations serviced by a SYSCO marketing associate. Sales to these customers represented approximately 55.4 percent of total sales at SYSCO's sixty-three broadline, or traditional, locations. SYSCO has a team of nearly 7,000 commissioned sales professionals, or relationship managers, who provide customers with services tailored to undergird their operations and profitability. Their responsibilities include assuring that orders are timely submitted and complete, presenting new products that will enhance the customer's menu or reduce the labor required for preparation, and assisting with inventory control and menu costing and pricing.
- *Multiunit customers* include local, regional, or national foodservice operations that have multiple locations and, due to their more centralized purchasing operations, generally do not require the same degree of personalized, value-added services that marketing associates offer, but are supported by other sales personnel within the SYSCO companies. Multiunit customers contribute approximately 44.6 percent of total sales at SYSCO's sixty-three broadline, or traditional, locations.

Categorize Customers

Eighty-five percent of SYSCO's total sales come from only 25 percent of its customers. Therefore, SYSCO brackets its customers into four groups based on their order size, gross cost per stop for them, and SYSCO brand percentage in sales. It defines the top 10 percent as their Gold Customers, next 15 percent Silver, next 20 percent Bronze, and the rest "Everybody Else." They offer different special service above their standard service to different customer categories other than "Everybody Else." For example, they make special delivery arrangement for Gold Customers. By offering the special treatment, they want to motivate their customers and move them up to higher levels.

In summary, the keys to SYSCO's leadership success in the procurement arena can be attributed to the following four major management strategies.[8]

- Acquisition of key players in the industry
- Foldout strategy that economizes the system
- Concentration on SYSCO brands and specialty companies
- Responsive marketing plan

Case Discussion Questions

1. What advantages does SYSCO have over its competitors?
2. In the SYSCO case example, we stated that acquisitions were a primary management strategy. Can you identify a product/brand or service that might fit the SYSCO acquisition strategy?

NOTES

1. See D. Aaker, *Managing Brand Equity* (New York: The Free Press, 1991), pp. 15-16.

2. See R. Buzzell & T. Bradley, *The PIMS Principles: Linking Strategy to Performance* (New York: The Free Press, 1987), pp. 106-107.

3. Aaker, *Managing Brand Equity,* p. 109. Quotations from *Managing Brand Equity: Capitalizing on the Value of a Brand Name* by David A. Aaker. Copyright 1991 by David A. Aaker. Reprinted with permission of The Free Press, a Division of Simon & Schuster Adult Publishing Group. All rights reserved.

4. Ibid., p. 273.

5. See D. Aaker, *Developing Business Strategies* (New York: John Wiley & Sons, 1995), p. 264.

6. R. Nykiel, *Marketing Strategies* (New York: CORMAR Business Press, 2002), p. 110.

7. www.cendant.com.

8. R. Nykiel, *Hospitality Management Strategies* (Upper Saddle River, NJ: Prentice Hall, 2005) pp. 280-288.

Chapter 14

Applying Research to Pricing Strategy

CHAPTER OBJECTIVES

- To define pricing and its linkages to positioning, image, and perceived value.
- To delineate the breakeven analysis process and application of intuitive judgment.
- To identify the rationale for short-run and long-run pricing strategy.
- To describe the cost-plus theory and its application in selling down.
- To explain the concept of selling up and some general circumstances under which the technique may be applied.
- To summarize the use of the inflation rate plus factor.
- To explain how analyzing market segments can help maximize revenue.

PRICING BASICS

Pricing is the ultimate generator of revenues and profit. While pricing strategies are somewhat different for products than services, be it prices or rates or fares, the strategic marketing objective remains the same—maximize sales/revenue. In its simplest definition, pricing is the monetary value of a product or service. Pricing is directly reflective of your image, positioning statement, and perceived brand value. Many issues affect price. Certainly the cost of providing the product or service, competition, stage of the product life cycle, and market demand play a major role in determining a pricing strategy. In addition, the product type, seasonality, uniqueness of the product/service, trial or introductory offers, and new product/service improvements may influence pricing.[1]

Pricing is directly reflective of image, positioning, and perceived value.

Understanding Demand

With respect to demand some products/services are referred to as either "inelastic" or "elastic." A price inelastic product/service is one for which demand will remain relatively the same when the price is raised or lowered. Many top-end luxury products/services fall under this category, such as Rolex watches, Mercedes autos, and so on. Likewise, certain necessities, such as water, needed medical supplies, and so on, could be considered more inelastic than elastic. On the other hand, a price elastic product or service is one for which the demand will increase or decrease in relationship to an increase or decrease in price. An example would be increasing air-

Handbook of Marketing Research Methodologies for Hospitality and Tourism
© 2007 by The Haworth Press, Inc. All rights reserved.
doi:10.1300/5927_15

fares, new housing, and related interest rates, and so on. At the outset of determining your pricing strategies, you should view your product/service/brand category to determine its relative price elasticity.

Pricing Strategy Options

Selecting a pricing strategy may involve many options. For example, you may wish to look at pricing on a geographic basis, or with respect to timing (where in the demand cycle or purchasing cycle are you launching your product). You may desire a lower, higher, or parity pricing strategy. You may view pricing differently in an excess capacity (supply) situation. This is sometimes referred to as a "short-run" pricing situation. You set your price to cover your variable costs and to make some contribution to fixed costs, overhead, and so on. Your objective is to recover some costs while reducing your excess supply. A "long-run" pricing strategy is generally viewed as pricing that covers all costs (fixed and variable) and results in a profit. Most businesses desire the latter scenario.

BREAKEVEN ANALYSIS

To determine how to price to "break even" or generate a profit, a simple analysis is usually undertaken called a "breakeven analysis." To perform a breakeven analysis (see Figure 14.1) you must first determine your "fixed" costs. Fixed costs are costs that do not change with fluctuating sales or promotions. These include costs such as your rent, mortgage, lease, and so on. "Variable" costs also must be calculated. Variable costs are costs that vary with the volume of production or sales. Examples might be utilities, transportation costs, labor, and so on. To conduct a breakeven analysis you will also have to employ your intuitive judgment. As we have indicated, establishing the most effective price to charge for your product or service is based on many factors. The local market and competition will, in all likelihood, prove to be dominant factors in influencing a pricing decision. However, the local market conditions and your need to break even need not overly restrict your judgment or creativity in establishing a pricing strategy. Frequently, the most important factors in selecting the optimum rate or pricing strategy will come from your own intuitive judgment about what will work best for the product or service in view of the local market and competition.

Once the market has been analyzed and the competition profiled, a breakeven analysis will assist in selecting the optimum pricing strategy. A breakeven analysis is a look at the relationship between total sales and total expenses for a product/service offering. Often depicted on a simple graph, the analysis demonstrates the effects of changing the levels of total sales in terms of dollars or volumes. The vertical (*y*) axis represents revenue. The horizontal (*x*) axis represents volume in units sold, which can be expressed in whatever terminology is best for your business.

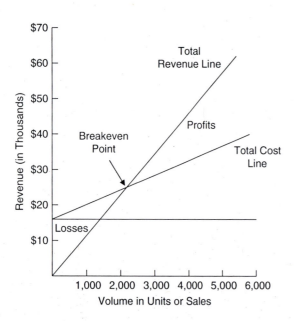

FIGURE 14.1. Sample Breakeven Chart

Total costs at the various levels of volume are plotted with a straight line that crosses the y axis at the level of fixed costs. In the simplest terms, total costs are a combination of fixed costs (costs that are incurred whether sales occur or not) and variable costs (costs that are incurred only when sales are made). Therefore, at zero sales, total costs equal fixed costs ($18,000 in Figure 14.1); at any level of sales beyond zero, total costs equal fixed costs plus the number of units sold times the variable cost per unit. Total revenue is also entered as a straight line starting at zero on both axes (since, unlike fixed costs that are incurred regardless of sales, revenue is only received as sales are made; that is, zero units sold means zero revenue). The point at which these lines cross represents the breakeven point, the point at which sales are adequate to cover total costs. Any point above the total cost line represents profits; any point below the total cost line represents losses. In the example shown in Figure 14.1, the breakeven point can be stated either in dollar volume ($24,000) or in unit volume (2,400 units).[2]

The formula for a breakeven analysis is depicted in Figure 14.2.

INFLUENCES ON PRICING STRATEGIES

As indicated at the outset of this chapter, "pricing strategies" are influenced by many factors. Let's first examine the rationale behind selecting a "low" price strategy. Following are some reasons:[3]

- To increase trial
- To preempt competition
- To expand market share
- To remain competitive
- To prevent competitive entry
- To introduce a new or improved product or service
- To increase demand and reduce inventory

Selecting a "high" price strategy may be an option for your product/service or brand. Here are some reasons to opt for a "high" price strategy:

- To substantiate a quality image/positioning (box 1 on the Marketing Strategy Grid)
- A need for fast recovery of investment
- The product/service is inelastic
- The product/service has a short life span
- The market demand is rapidly increasing
- The product/service is unique or difficult to copy or reproduce
- Profits are the focal point rather than sales
- Dollars need to be accumulated for R&D costs

There are also many reasons one might select a "parity" pricing strategy for the product/service or brand. These include the following:

- Better product/service or superior attributes compared to competition
- Better service and reputation
- Stronger guarantees/warranties
- Distribution advantage
- Newest design (look)

PX = FC + VC(X)

Where:
- P   = Price
- VC = Variable costs
- FC = Fixed costs
- X   = Volume of units produced at breakeven
      point (the number of units that must be sold)

■ Breakeven charts are useful tools, although they are not always precise. There are also two mathematical equations that can be used to calculate the breakeven points for units or sales.

■ The breakeven point in units is determined by first subtracting the variable cost per unit from the selling price per unit. The result is then divided into the total fixed costs:

$$\text{Breakeven point in units} = \frac{\text{Total fixed costs}}{\text{Selling price per unit} - \text{variable cost per unit}}$$

■ To determine the breakeven point in sales, multiply the breakeven point in units by the selling price:

Breakeven point in sales = Breakeven point in units × Selling price

■ With the tools of the basic breakeven chart and the unit and sales equations, you can use the flexible breakeven analysis to establish profit objectives and the required sales revenue to meet these objectives.

FIGURE 14.2. Breakeven Analysis Formula

PRICING TECHNIQUES

In almost all businesses, pricing can be used to maximize revenue and profit. While not every one of these techniques may apply to your business (products/services), hopefully they will stimulate your pricing strategy thought process.

Offering a "Price Range"

Most applicable for the service sector, a "price range" allows you to both "sell up" and "sell down" for a variety of factors. When demand forecasts are moving up, move up the range. When demand forecasts are weak, move down the range and take market share. Price ranges provide your customers and prospective customers the opportunity to decide if they want additional services or fewer services. Price ranges also allow for discounting off the high end of the range.

"Selling Up"

Many customers and prospects are driven by different motivations. Some factors that support "selling up" are recognizing the size of the "ego," desire, prestige, uniqueness of the product/service, value-added offers, personalization, and customization.

"Selling Down"

Many customers and prospects are "price"/"value" seekers always looking for the best deal or lower(est) price. Selling down allows you to meet price or rate resistance with a counter offer.

"Value Added"

This technique is simply including "more" for the same price. You may add 30 percent more product, provide an extra service, or include a premium or other value-added incentive to get your price.

"Pay Later"

This technique is a concept that addresses the customers' or prospects' resistance to the price based on the rationale of not having sufficient funds or not wanting to lay out the cash now for the product/service. "Pay later" pricing usually incorporates an interest or cost of cash amount factor in the stated price.

"Up Front"

This pricing technique is used to provide a perceived discount for an advance purchase. It is in essence a discount concept for paying at the time of order versus delivery or usage.

"Inflation Rate Plus Pricing"

This technique is more or less a simple rule of thumb—increase your prices at a minimum at the rate of inflation. This allows you to stay even. The "plus" factor simply means you forecast what the inflation rate is impacting your costs and add some incremental price increase (cost plus) to assure your product/service profit margins remain intact.

"Segmentation Pricing"

This is a technique that subdivides your market (be it geographically, psychographically, or by competitive pressure, distributorships, and so on) and establishes different pricing for different segments.

Pricing Checklist

There are many other creative ways to price your product/service. The strategies may vary; however, the objective is the same—sell all units/move all products/and maximize yield/revenue; the following checklist will aid you in establishing your pricing strategy:[4]

- Is the pricing strategy appropriate for the positioning/image?
- Does the product/service/brand deserve a "premium" price?
- Should the prices be adjusted based on the demand forecast?
- Should the prices be different based on the segmentation analysis?
- How will the pricing strategy be communicated to the employees, customers, and intermediaries?
- If prices are raised will competition follow?
- If prices are lowered will competition follow or undercut the prices?
- Will adding an incentive, value, or other incremental item/service allow for retention price and build volume?
- How "elastic" is the product or service?
- Is there some way to differentiate the product/service and increase the prices?
- How can the right techniques be employed to maximize revenue?
- Will upcoming promotions affect pricing strategies (own and competition's)?

CHAPTER REVIEW

This chapter pointed out the importance of pricing and the influence price has on image, positioning, and perceived value. The concepts of elasticity and inelasticity were presented along with different pricing strategies for the short run and long run. The significance of conducting a breakeven analysis in order to locate the price/volume relationship/level required to make a profit was discussed.

Influences on pricing strategies and rationale were discussed in terms of low price, high price, and parity pricing. Finally, we provided eight different pricing techniques, including the concepts of selling up, selling down, value-added pricing, pay-later pricing, up-front pricing, the inflation rate plus theory, and segmentation pricing.

KEY CONCEPTS/TERMS

Breakeven analysis
Demand
Elastic
Fixed costs
High-price strategy
Inelastic
Inflation rate plus
Low-price strategy
Parity pricing
Premium pricing
Pricing
Price range
Selling down
Selling up
Value added
Variable costs
Volume

DISCUSSION QUESTIONS

1. How does demand influence pricing for elastic products and services?
2. Why is it important to conduct a breakeven analysis before setting your price?
3. What are three reasons for using a "low price" strategy?
4. What are three reasons for using a "high price" strategy?
5. When would you use a "parity pricing" strategy?
6. Explain the minimum price increase you would recommend if the annual inflation rate were 5 percent?

CASE 14.1. SAME PRICE—THEY WIN

In some instances, the same price may be charged for an item/product or service but one provider receives more business due to a competitive advantage. This advantage may be as straightforward as having a better product or a combination of reasons. In this case example, we will look at a retailer who won with parity pricing (and sometimes even with a higher price) for many years for a number of reasons.

Let's look at Sears and specifically at the appliance and hardware areas. Sears has successfully defended its turf against the onslaught of appliance discounters, warehouse store concepts, and so on. Let's examine some of the reasons why Sears has been successful with parity pricing. First, Sears has an excellent reputation as a "service" provider after the sale. After all, you buy a Sears brand or another brand and you know who to call if a problem arises. This is not always the case with the competition. Second, Sears has a distribution/location advantage. Local chains and appliance stores may not be in the next state or market you move to—Sears is just about everywhere. Third, brand recognition and reliability are trademarks of Sears products and it stands behind its products. Its hardware is of high quality/durability and its store personnel know how to show you what the products do and how they work. The personnel are trained.

Whenever you offer more convenient and more reliable service at the same price you are likely to win. Back up that price parity with a good reputation and trained point of encounter/customer contact employees and you will have even more competitive advantages and rationale to support your parity pricing.

Case Discussion Questions

1. What role does superior service play in pricing?
2. How does locational advantage relate to pricing strategy?
3. What does reliability have to do with pricing?

CASE 14.2. PAY LATER/VALUE ADDED

Often when inventories are high and/or product models are due to be replaced, special pricing techniques are employed to "move product." One case example is that of the reduced pricing for computers at certain times during the year or during their life cycle. For example, a Compac computer and free printer (brand may vary) which regularly sell on a stand-alone basis by $999 but in certain situations (e.g., over inventory or new model about to come out) can be marketed for as low as $499, but perhaps with this condition: "The buyer is obligated to sign up with MSN for a time period equal to $400 at the time of purchase. A $100 manufacturer's rebate may be obtained from the printer company; allow up to three months for your rebate."

In this case, the "value added" is the free printer. The "pay later" aspect of this offer is your contracted monthly fees to MSN. The offer represents a strong motivation to purchase a computer product for half its price and receive a printer along with the deal. The mechanics of the rebates and allowances between Compac, the printer company, MSN, and retailer are invisible to the buyer.

Case Discussion Questions

1. Why do retailers often advertise you can pay later (e.g., next year)?
2. Why would a consumer pay "up front" for a product or service?

NOTES

1. R. Nykiel, *Marketing Your Business* (Binghamton, NY: Best Business Books, 2003), p. 147.
2. Ibid., p. 149.
3. R. Nykiel, *Marketing Strategies* (New York: CORMAR Business Press, 2002), pp. 116-117.
4. Ibid., pp. 117-118.

Chapter 15

Applying Research to Customer Service
and Quality Initiatives

CHAPTER OBJECTIVES

- To define how research plays a role in developing customer service and quality initiatives.
- To identify how strategies are deployed as major managerial strategies within the service industry.
- To present a ten-step process that identifies and supports changes in customer service and quality strategies.
- To provide a discussion of the various stages of customer development.
- To delineate the managerial strategies of continuous quality improvement and total quality management within the hospitality industry.
- To assess the likely directions and future trends for customer service and quality strategies within the hospitality industry.

UNDERSTANDING CUSTOMER EXPECTATIONS

Today, more than ever, satisfying demanding customers remains the greatest challenge and greatest opportunity in virtually every sector of the service industry. In the service industry, the consumer is not only part of the actual consumption/purchasing process but, moreover, often has preset service and quality perspectives. Today's service industry customer is increasingly time poor, more sophisticated, and more demanding. It is important to understand where the customer is coming from and what satisfaction levels the customer is expressing prior to selecting management strategies for service excellence or quality improvement.

The Role of Research

Both qualitative and quantitative research techniques are prevalent in the services sector. Questionnaires, focus groups, quantitative analysis of sales data, indices, and so forth, all have applicability and can play a supporting role to strategy selection. CSIs (customer service indices) or GSIs (guest service indices) can be used to measure performance and also be tied to managerial and employee evaluations. Bar codes and related quantitative analytical software can identify usage and preferences, price strategies, and distribution patterns. The latter can be linked to demographic, psychographic, and other socioeconomic models and data to assist in decision making, allocations, and overall product and marketing strategies. Also, most applicable in the services sector are research-based quality performance initiatives such as CQI (continuous quality improvement) and TQM (total quality management). Today, consumers have greater access to product and service information and demand that their specific needs and wants be sat-

Handbook of Marketing Research Methodologies for Hospitality and Tourism
© 2007 by The Haworth Press, Inc. All rights reserved.
doi:10.1300/5927_16

isfied. Measuring how you are satisfying the consumers and meeting their wants and needs is at the heart of consumer research and performance measurement.

Speed and Connectivity

In general, the consumer of service industry–related products and services is much like any other consumer today with respect to having less time to shop, seeking service and quality, and desiring express services at the speed of lightning. In many industries, speed has become the most valued and new competitive advantage. Speed is shortening product life cycles from years to weeks. Speed and technological progress have made transactions move from days to microseconds. Speed is expected in real-time responsiveness, twenty-four hours a day, seven days a week. Speed is what the hospitality industry consumer wants. Those who can fulfill will win; those who can't will be passed by.

Speed is one ingredient in the overall scenario for customer response and satisfaction. Another key factor linked directly to customer retention and satisfaction in the service industry is "connectivity." Connectivity means doing business in a way that is not bound by location. Connectivity means consumers can satisfy their need to access information, make a purchase, and conduct transactions anywhere, at any time, through any pertinent medium. Virtually everything in these processes can be done and accessed in some electronic form, be it on the Web, phone, screen, online, and so on. Speed and connectivity mean the service industry and its sectors must function in real time to satisfy customer needs.

Technology has enabled service industry firms to improve both the customer service experience as well as anticipate and meet the needs of consumers. Customer recognition systems, inventory search systems, frequency and other reward programs, and Web sites have all contributed to customer retention and new customer development. Data from marketing information systems feed promotional and product offerings. Certainly speed and conveniences, major needs of today's customer, have been dramatically enhanced at virtually every step of the consumption process.

The Customer Satisfaction Equation

Consumers have control of information with anytime and anyplace access. This real-time environment raises the expectations of service industry consumers, sometimes resulting in the "never satisfied customer." Increased use of the Internet to shop, make informed decisions, and purchase reinforces the role of speed and connectivity in customer satisfaction and service expectations. Consumers are savvier, with the difference between the expert seller and educated buyer becoming increasingly smaller. Consumers are better informed and more assertive buyers. Today's consumer is also more demanding as a result of having higher expectations of response times. And, perhaps most important of all, consumers have redefined customer satisfaction to include speed of service. Now customer satisfaction and, to a larger degree, the quality/value equation have been redefined. Customer satisfaction is now represented by this equation:

$$\text{Customer Expectations} \pm \text{Perceived Value Received} = \text{Customer Satisfaction}$$

Speed plays a key role in customer expectations and perceived value in the service industry. Consumers are now more demanding—they know what they want, where they want it, and when they want it. These higher levels of expectation have resulted in overall declines in traveler satisfaction levels in almost all sectors of the industry. Obviously, some of these declines are due to lack of labor, untrained personnel, and more process time related to security issues. For management, there are two overarching messages that make customer satisfaction a number one goal. First, loyalty increases with satisfaction, especially among frequent business travelers. Second, financial performance increases with loyalty. Remember, satisfied customers return and cost less than new customers.

Knowing what is really important to customers allows management to focus resources on those key areas or points of encounter. For example, if one were to look at the lodging, airline, and car rental sectors of the industry, three overall areas contribute most to customer satisfaction. First is speed and ease of reservation/check-in. Second is actual performance versus price. Here the consumer wants the flight on time, the car to be there and run well, and the room and related amenities to be ready. The third critical area of importance is the return/check-out or final transaction process. For the foodservice sector it means prompt order taking, service, and presentation of the check. Again, speed and ease (along with accuracy) are expected. Studies have shown that waiting five minutes or more to check in or be waited on greatly decreases customer satisfaction. Not surprising, membership in a frequency or VIP program increases satisfaction due in part to the program's express check-in/check-out service elements.

In summary, viewing customer satisfaction and quality service must be done with the perspective of the new consumer expectations and mindset. It is no wonder that many consider customer service to be the most valuable managerial weapon and strategy. Customer service plays a role in acquiring new customers, retaining existing loyalty, and taking market share from competitors. Good customer service is most valuable if you consider at a minimum it costs businesses five times as much to attract a new customer as it does to satisfy and retain an existing customer. It takes on new importance if you consider that a dissatisfied customer will sometimes tell more than ten other consumers/prospects about the unsatisfactory experience. So, having a customer service strategy and plan are very important in deploying this valuable marketing weapon. Some businesses fail to recognize customer service as a management weapon and underfund the function or staff it with the lowest-paid (and sometimes least-trained) employees.

POINTS OF ENCOUNTER: TEN STEPS TO SERVICE SUCCESS

Customer service strategies need to be in place at every point where the customer comes into contact with your business or any representation thereof, be it personal, vocal, electronic, and so on. Examine every potential point of encounter and you are looking at all the places/processes that your image and positioning are exposed or being tested. In this section, a ten-step process to customer service success is presented.[1]

Step One: Recognition

The points at which your employees encounter the consumer are opportunities to win (or lose) the consumer. In the age of increasing customer dissatisfaction, we must take the first step toward achieving service success: recognition. This is not the obvious recognition after the fact that service problems have caused sales to slip or that another company has taken more market share. Such problem recognition is reactive rather than proactive. For recognition to be proactive, observation and analysis of the points of encounter must occur to avoid problems before they occur. Quite simply this means we must focus on the interaction of our product or service with the consumer.

How often had you heard, "They really have a problem here. Too bad they haven't recognized and fixed it." "They" usually refers to top management, which has skipped the all important thought process known as "recognition."

A decline in sales, employee turnover, consumer complaints—these are all reactive indicators. True recognition in the proactive sense means knowing the points of encounter and assuming the customer's (also prospect's) perspective from presell to postsale.

Step Two: Identification of Problems

Recognition of points of encounter and customer problems is but one proactive step to customer service success. What is this process by which one can assure preemptive recognition and prevent loss of market share or customers? Although there are a number of approaches, placing yourself in the role of customer is one of the best. Ideally it should be done incognito and often. It will make you aware of a service problem or at least give you a fresh look at the customer's perspective. Using some periodic "acid tests" (likely to give you acid indigestion), try to be observant and analytical. Always record the problems and think about possible solutions. Here are some ways to test service:

- Call the toll-free number of one of your favorite establishments and analyze the response.
- Go incognito to outlets, service centers, units, counters, or check-in desks and make notes of your observations (you may need a big notepad). Ask other customers about their experiences at the points of encounter.
- Go to a sales office and read the literature.
- Observe the staff. Are they empathetic with customers?
- After making these observations, go through the entire purchasing process or service experience and make a list of the direct points of encounter.

Review the points-of-encounter list with the following objectives:

- Identify the critical points at which the sale, purchase, or customer's loyalty can be lost instantly if not handled properly.
- Identify the points that have to be corrected.
- Identify the points that present opportunities for making your service stand out above the competition.

Here are some additional strategies and tactics with respect to recognizing problems/opportunities and identifying solutions:

- Use shopper services to check on a business.
- Conduct your own service audit.
- Talk to and, more important, listen to customers.
- Observe and experience the offerings of the most successful competitors.
- Experience your own service as a customer.
- Personally review a random sample of complaint letters once per quarter.
- Solicit opinions of the service offering by having a focus group.
- List all points of encounter and have management focus on one of these points each quarter.
- Check current relevance of the training material and procedures for all points of encounter. Update where appropriate.
- Spend at least as much time on the points of encounter as would be spent on other aspects of your business.

Even if your business is not in the service sector per se, you can adapt these steps to check on your sales force, retailers, wholesalers, distributors, agents, and so on. This is what proactive hospitality management strategies are all about in the critical area of customer satisfaction.

Step Three: Plan of Action

Having made your observations incognito, prepared lists, identified points of encounter, and come up with several ideas, you now need a plan of action. Before implementing it on a wide scale, test it to make sure it is executed properly. Not to do so can be disastrous. Test it, modify it, and implement it.

Step Four: Reallocation of Resources

Recognition, identification, and a plan of action are sometimes not enough to make the necessary change at a point of encounter. To remain competitive and successful, a reallocation of resources sometimes may be required. These resources may be financial, personnel, or equipment.

Simple reallocations, such as putting on more phone operators to eliminate the interminable rings followed by a recorded voice telling the caller all lines or service representatives are busy, can set your company ahead of the competition. I would guess that half the callers hang up when the "next available service representative" recording comes on the line—if they haven't been disconnected or forgotten whom they'd called in the first place! If a firm never puts a customer on hold, or if the customers are always connected with a professional service representative, the chances of winning the customer are pretty good.

Step Five: Prioritization of Execution

The step least often taken and most often needed is prioritization. In a recent edition of the Sunday *New York Times,* I came across two very interesting help-wanted ads that may serve as examples. One fairly large block ad from Beth Israel Medical Center in New York City sought a "Director of Guest Relations" (new position). The other ad from a nationally recognized medical clinic read, "Wanted—Complaints Clerk." To me it was obvious that Beth Israel had (1) recognized that it was in a service business; (2) identified a point-of-encounter opportunity; (3) established a plan of action; (4) reallocated resources; and (5) prioritized the importance of its relationship with its patients. Note the difference in perspectives. Beth Israel views its patients as "guests," and the person who relates to them is at a director's level. These are the obvious signs of a healthy proactive service perspective. On the other hand, the medical clinic has the classic reactive mentality of looking for a "complaints" person and prioritizes this function with the label of "clerk." Which medical facility do you think will be perceived as better able to provide service?

Here are some additional strategies and tactics to help you reallocate and prioritize:

- In order of priority, list the points of encounter that need new or additional resources.
- In order of priority, list all "projects" (capital) dollars scheduled for allocation.
- Now prepare a new list that, in order of priority, blends the points-of-encounter items and "projects" items together.
- In prioritizing your "projects" capital needs, place first those that relate to your points of encounter.
- Review your non-point-of-encounter personnel count and payroll costs.
- Review your point-of-encounter personnel count and payroll costs.

- Allocate your resources to address the point-of-encounter personnel and the related costs to do their job right on a top priority basis. Can you imagine a firm that would spend a half-million dollars on a project and deny point-of-encounter employees an increase of 50 cents per hour as incentive pay or a $5,000 training program? Review all of your firm's expenses; this could be called "current shock."

Step Six: Training of Personnel

Ask yourself whether business is suffering from human incompetence. Today we are experiencing the end product of our formal education process in the form of employees who frequently need to be retrained. It is essential that every one of the point-of-encounter employees be trained or retrained.

Also, check on technology to see whether it is functioning properly and evaluate its ease of comprehension and use by the customer and employees. When automated systems take over, do they work and really help your customers? Or do they simply help to lose the customer/prospect and help the competition? Reflect on your own customer experiences and you will quickly perceive the importance of assessing automation.

Step Seven: Recruiting of Personnel

To recruit and hire the appropriate personnel, you have to know the right questions to ask: What are the criteria for those who will be point-of-encounter employees? Do any of these employees sell, quote prices, or directly interface with the potential customer at the critical point of encounter—the actual purchase of products/services? If so, what type of employee do you want to be responsible for bringing in revenue? Are these employees trainable, are they sufficiently intelligent to hold such positions, or are they overqualified? If you can't answer most of these questions readily, the firm either is already in trouble or will be in trouble before very long.

Well-thought-out recruiting criteria can provide very great returns and should be reviewed frequently. When was the last time a reevaluation of job descriptions and hiring criteria for point-of-encounter positions was conducted? If you believe there is no need for such reviews because the products/services offered have not changed, you are very wrong; the consumer is changing constantly. Some advocate turning the organization chart upside down, while others suggest that the pay scales be reversed. Obviously, there is no simple answer for all service industry firms. All the previous steps must be taken into account: recognition, identification, plan of action, reallocation, prioritization, training, and recruiting.

Recruiting should be attempted only after a complete review of each point-of-encounter position. Complexity of job function as well as the types of consumers encountered on a daily basis should be thoroughly analyzed. Do you have (or want) minimum-wage clerks directly interfacing with $100,000-plus executives or large-volume purchasers?

Here are some additional strategies and tactics to facilitate and sharpen your recruiting:

- Have members of top management participate in at least one point-of-encounter position training session.
- Have members of top management work at least one eight-hour day (preferably an entire week) in one of the point-of-encounter positions.
- Review your training resources (people, procedures, and related budgets) annually to determine whether they are adequate in preparing your personnel for service leadership.
- Ask customers to evaluate (via questionnaire or direct contact) how well they believe point-of-encounter employees are trained.
- Ask newly trained employees what else they believe should be taught.

- Ask the same question of your seasoned employees.
- Instruct all recruiters of point-of-encounter employees to ask themselves whether they would want to deal face-to-face with the person they are considering for the job.
- Personally participate in at least one interview session for a point-of-encounter employee.
- Consider upgrading your pay scale to attract seasoned pros away from the competition.
- Make sure your recruiters know exactly what you expect of them and then periodically check to see that they are doing exactly what you want.

Step Eight: Communications

When it comes to communicating with the customer, no one is more important than the point-of-encounter employee. It is this employee who is often the first to know when (and if) your service offering, price, policy, or procedural change is working. He or she is also a great source of information when you attempt to improve service. But, when it comes to communicating with these employees, the corporate hierarchy in general does a less than stellar job. This, in tandem with the dissatisfied consumer, works to create the environment for a disastrous customer service experience.

There are many examples of good and bad communication in the service industry. A case of good communication is CEO Bill Marriott Jr., who was renowned for his visits to virtually every hotel, restaurant, or other facility in Marriott's multibillion-dollar empire. These were not your typical "presidential" appearances, but detailed inspections as well as walk-throughs to instill motivation. Mistakes were pointed out. Employee suggestions were recorded and implemented on a broad scale if worthwhile.

Adherence to standard operating procedures is mandatory at Marriott. It is, therefore, no coincidence that Marriott's operations and services are efficient and consistent. There are other examples, but the important point is the same in all situations—good communications. The conscientious CEO goes beyond motivation and inspection. The point-of-encounter employees are made aware of top management's interest in seeing not only how the job is being done, but also who is doing the job.

By definition, communication connotes a two-way flow—up and down. Small ideas turn into big winners if communication channels are open. For some reason, it is easier to inform 1 million customers of your offer than 1,000 point-of-encounter employees. There appears to be a logical explanation. Your ad or service offer goes directly from you to the consumer, but the memo describing that offer is often handed down from the vice president of marketing through the managers, to the unit managers, to the department managers, to the shift managers, and, finally, to the point-of-encounter employees, leaving plenty of opportunity for a breakdown in communication. It happens all the time.

One thing is sure: never assume that your detailed memo of instructions, the training video, or the training manual have been read, viewed, or understood by those who must use the information. The best way to find out is to put on the consumer's hat and try to get the service offered. Don't be surprised at what you find out. Any form of change may be difficult to communicate, and the difficulty can be compounded when the change involves behavior.

Step Nine: Follow-Up to Execution

Let's go back to Bill Marriott with regard to communications. All those walk-throughs would not have amounted to much unless there had been a positive form of follow-up. A note was sent to the unit in question reaffirming the action to be taken or stating the subject to be discussed upon the next visit. Granted, the man had a phenomenal memory, but the key point is that because there is a follow-up, employees fixed what needed to be fixed.

Follow-up steps can assume a variety of forms. Some service establishments use "shopper services," which essentially are professional shoppers/customers. They are hired to work as typical consumers, logging their experiences for management. Intelligent use of these findings, of course, is crucial. The results can be negative (employee dismissals) or positive (improved training programs, plans to improve performance and eliminate problem areas).

There are many effective follow-up techniques, and what is appropriate for your particular product/service offering may require special planning. But once a plan is devised, it must be implemented. The procedure must be clearly communicated to those who will implement it, and then you must follow up to make sure it is done. Unless all these steps are taken, all the promises of your promotional ad will lead only to creating a more disappointed consumer.

Here are some strategies and tactics to improve communications and the follow-up process:

- Make a list of all point-of-encounter positions.
- Establish a personal "communications" calendar, scheduling specific frequent dates to deliver your messages to these key people.
- Consider delivering these messages either in person, by videotape, or in writing (in that order).
- Make sure all point-of-encounter employees clearly understand that their personal contact with customers represents the most critical element to conveying a good service impression.
- Listen. Listen. Listen.
- Communicate the "right" way by *showing* the employees—not merely telling them.
- Record and remember names and incidents from your own employee encounters.
- Recontact those you can with a call or a note.
- Be sincere.
- Repeat all steps regularly. (Employee turnover is the most critical factor in diluting your message and communications in general.)

Step Ten: Begin Again

For a number of reasons, this step is perhaps the most difficult. First, to some extent, having to repeat the process may imply that you have not been successful with the previous nine steps. Second, you need to go back to determine if, indeed, you did not succeed with any of the actions taken. If so, you will need to fix it or replace it. It is only appropriate that we recap here the ten steps to service success:

1. *Recognition*—knowing that there is a service opportunity and/or problem at the points of encounter
2. *Identification*—determining what they are
3. *Plan of action*—capitalizing on an opportunity or dealing with a problem
4. *Reallocation*—finding the financial and/or human resources to execute the plan
5. *Prioritization*—placing execution of the plan at the top of the list
6. *Training*—ensuring thorough preparation of those who are charged with taking action at points of encounter
7. *Recruiting*—finding the very best people for point-of-encounter positions
8. *Communications*—conveying every aspect of your plan accurately, thoroughly, and convincingly to all employees, with special focus on point-of-encounter personnel
9. *Follow-up*—rechecking all, contacting all, and ensuring all errors have been corrected
10. *Begin again!*—reviewing periodically all the processes, beginning with the steps of recognition and identification

CUSTOMER SATISFACTION STRATEGIES

Today's consumer is preconditioned and ready to challenge the product/service provider. Most surveys indicate that consumers in many product/service categories have reached a level of preconditioning that leaves them cynical toward the consumption experience.

Just as there are steps your company (and management) must take, there are steps employees must take to ensure customer satisfaction. No matter what type of service you provide, there are several keys to effective execution that will create recognition among consumers that demonstrates going beyond the points of encounter:

- *Expectations.* Recognize that you must never deliver a service that falls short of what the customers or potential customers expect for the price they are paying. Meeting or exceeding customer expectations is what ultimately determines the level of customer satisfaction. Expectation levels in the mind of the consumers are influenced by the price you charge; their prior experience with your service offering; their prior experience with your competition; and what you promise in your advertising or sales message. Meeting customer expectations is absolutely critical to repeat business.

- *Never blame the customer.* While some may argue with this categorical statement, you cannot lose by practicing it. The customer is always right, even if he or she is not! Simply stated: Let the customer win! That doesn't mean you should allow the customer to take advantage of you. This means that your employees must understand that they have the flexibility and authority to bend policy when needed to satisfy a customer.

    Most surveys show that less than 5 percent of customers will actually take the time to complain about the service received. However, these same surveys show that almost 25 percent are less than satisfied with that service. And this percentage grows dramatically when customers become increasingly cynical as a result of poor experiences with other companies offering the same type of service. When this occurs, two things can happen: (1) If you insist that your employees adhere so strictly to policy that customers are not allowed to "feel" they have won, you will lose 100 percent of those cynical customers. (2) If you have instilled in your employees the "let the customers feel they have won" philosophy, you will retain (and actually build) the loyalty of these customers.

- *Clear communication* with customers is essential to problem resolution at the point of encounter or purchase. Your employees must be able to tell customers precisely what they need and want to know or do. This is especially critical when you're involved in a promotional offer. After all, that is why the new customer has come to you in the first place. Make sure that everyone who has customer contact responsibility and supervisors are thoroughly knowledgeable about all aspects of the promotion. If necessary, provide written communiqués and training videos. Augment these with in-person training sessions, and do so in a timely manner. Never start a promotion before all employees have received complete information and thorough instructions. And always provide a central resource for clarification should questions arise.

- *Organize your procedures* to reduce the time it takes to purchase your service offering. The number one peeve of today's consumer of services is "standing in line." You must review and then revise your procedures to eliminate or at least shorten the time spent waiting in line. If the nature of your service precludes total elimination of waiting time, develop alternative plans to "fill the time." This can be in the form of a customer service representative who preprocesses the customers or socializes with them. A video entertainment or informational display will attract the customer and fill the waiting time.

- *Undo what the customers have done to themselves.* When customers discover that they are in the wrong, always avoid embarrassing them. The employee must be polite, empathetic, and tactful so that your customers "save face."

- *Never use business jargon that is unfamiliar to your customer.* You cannot assume that even those who are in the other hospitality-related businesses use the same terminology as you.
- *Trade-off time management is essential in personal contact situations.* Each point of encounter must be analyzed and a determination made as to whether the strategy should be to go for "optimum speed" or special "personal attention."
- *Employee job performance criteria* for all those in point-of-encounter positions, be they face-to-face or over the phone, should clearly focus on execution of service with efficiency and politeness. This is what it's all about, and point-of-encounter employees must know that performing their job properly is what they are being paid for!
- *Reduce time where service is expected to be fast.* Fast and efficient service leads to satisfaction, especially today. In essence, cynical consumers' negative conditioning has led them to expect long lines and slow, inefficient service. Beat that expectation! Provide faster service and you will convert the cynical consumer into one who is more than satisfied.
- *Sincere appreciation* should be expressed at virtually all points of encounter, not just at the time of purchase. This must be instilled in every point-of-encounter employee. This will ensure reinforcement of the perception that the customer is truly valued.

What follows is a recap of these customer service strategies and tactics:

Expectations must be met.
Never blame the customer.
Clear communication is essential.
Organize to reduce time.
Undo what the customer has done to himself or herself.
Never use unfamiliar business jargon.
Trade-off time management is essential.
Employee job performance criteria should focus on efficiency and politeness.
Reduce service time.
Sincere appreciation should be expressed.

Winning Characteristics

There are numerous other ways to let your customers win and to win their loyalty. Successful enterprises have "point of encounter" plans and policies in place and widely communicated. These are also the firms that demonstrate lower cost of sales (expenses), higher repeat customer levels, and customer brand loyalty.

Studying numerous successful companies and award winners at customer service reveals a number of common winning characteristics:

- Leadership
- Formalized process or plan
- Focus on understanding customer needs
- Customer and employee feedback systems
- Responding with action on feedback
- Sales and service synergy
- Customer-retention motivational and promotional programs
- Reading the marketplace and competition and responding appropriately
- Practicing innovation through research and development and through suggestion implementation
- Prominent recognition of the importance of point-of-encounter employees and giving them full support

Customer Development Stages

Customer service strategies and tactics may vary for different types of customers or be tailored based on the developmental stage of the customer (see Figure 15.1).[2] There are hundreds of customer service tactics and ideas for every customer stage and for different sizes and types of product/service businesses. The key to customer service being successful as a marketing weapon can be summarized as follows: (1) know what stage of development your customers have achieved, (2) recognize the points of encounter, (3) have a plan for customer service success, (4) empower your point-of-encounter employees with an armada of "let the customer win" tactics, (5) have a check system to see that customer service policies are being adhered to, and (6) make sure your employees' evaluations and, where possible, compensation are directly tied to your CSI.

QUALITY INITIATIVE BENCHMARKS

Even if an organization doesn't select quality leadership as its positioning, virtually all service industry firms have quality strategies. It is the nature of an industry in the services sector to focus on quality in one manner or another. It is commonplace to find organizations that have goals to consistently meet or exceed customer expectations by providing services at prices that create value for the customer and profit for the company. In the service industry, quality is a moving target and, like value, may fluctuate in definition with changing customer expectations. So where does management begin to find benchmarks for quality and specific objectives to strive to achieve? Historically, three benchmarks or paths to follow have been delineated. These include the concept of TQM, or total quality management; the concept of CQI, or continuous quality improvement; and the criteria specified by the Malcolm Baldrige National Quality Award program.

TQM and CQI have like goals in seeking to ensure quality service. Both recognize the importance of points of encounter with the customer. Quality service is measured by the customer's perception, which changes due to external and internal environmental and competitive influences. Irrespective of the change, at a point in time called the consumption point, quality service is service that meets or exceeds the customer's expectations.

High-performance companies in the service industry use components of TQM and CQI to establish guidelines and benchmarks for achieving customer satisfaction and quality service. High-performance companies provide their employees with the skills and information required to do the job of satisfying customers. The entire organization participates in delivery of quality service to reach the point of partnership (see the hierarchy of customer development in Figure 15.1). Finally, compensation, security, and the work environment are all linked to success in the high-performance company. An example of reaching the partnership level (co-owner) comes from American Express. American Express's chairman recently stated

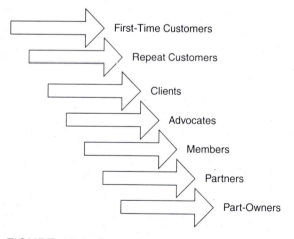

FIGURE 15.1. Customer Development Stages. *Source:* R. Nykiel, *The Art of Marketing Strategy* (New York: Amacor, 2001), p. 146.

that, by and large, over 90 percent of the company's product/ service improvements have been the direct result of customer suggestions. A high-performance company also listens and acts.

Total Quality Management

Most TQM programs have been based on Deming's fourteen points.[3] TQM is based on the overall premise that every area of the enterprise focuses on a total organization concept designed to deliver quality. Figure 15.2 recaps Deming's fourteen points.

1. Create constancy of purpose.
2. Adopt the new philosophy.
3. Cease dependence on inspection to achieve quality.
4. End the practice of awarding business on the basis of price tag.
5. Improve constantly and forever the system of production and service.
6. Remove barriers that rob employees of pride and workmanship.
7. Institute a vigorous program of education and self-improvement.
8. Put everybody in the company to work to accomplish the transformation.
9. Institute job training.
10. Institute leadership.
11. Break down barriers between departments.
12. Drive out fear.
13. Eliminate slogans.
14. Eliminate work standards (quotas).

FIGURE 15.2. Deming's Fourteen Points of TQM. *Source:* Adapted from R. Nykiel, *Hospitality Management Strategies* (Upper Saddle River, NJ: Prentice Hall, 2005), p. 215.

Continuous Quality Improvement

The concept of CQI began with Joseph Juran, who suggested that the quality of a product or service is determined by its fitness for use by external and internal customers. Juran focused on common language, process itself, and external and internal customers. It was from this philosophy that the hospitality industry concept of treating your employees as your internal customers evolved. The idea is that if management treats employees as customers, employees will treat customers better. The common denominator is that the process must produce value for the customer. "According to Juran quality equals product/ service features free from production or delivery defects. This relationship yields the defect ratio, which is frequency of defects divided by opportunity of defects. The lower the defect ratio, the higher the quality rating."[4] By striving to lower the defect ratio, CQI is reinforced. CQI leads to breakthrough performances and quality efforts become an integral part of an organization's business plan.

CQI is best delineated by the concept of continuously trying to deliver incremental improvement by enhancing or streamlining the current work process (thus, continuous quality improvement). CQI enforces the concept that striving for improvement will lead to a "breakthrough" or redesign of the work process/ delivery of service, which results in unprecedented levels of quality, speed, and savings. The CQI process focuses on the following four steps:

1. Target opportunities.
2. Analyze opportunities.
3. Develop implementation plans.
4. Evaluate the implementation plans.

A fifth unwritten step is to begin again, thus making the process continuous.

The overall CQI process is aimed at improvement in the use and mix of resources. Focal points for resource improvements include organizational concepts, physical facilities, technological systems, workplace and traffic flow design, and training systems. The ultimate goal remains customer satisfaction and retention. CQI recognizes the costs of dissatisfaction, including termination costs, recruitment and selection costs, and the cost of "bad press."

Over the years, many different techniques and tools have been developed to apply in a CQI process. Figure 15.3 lists some of the more widely applied tools and techniques for a CQI process.

Empowerment

Perhaps the one tool we hear the most about in today's hospitality industry is the concept of empowerment. Empowerment can be defined as the redistribution of power, enabling employees to perform their jobs more efficiently and effectively. "Empowerment's goal is to enhance service to the customer/guest by addressing the concern immediately. In the services sector, this process is referred to as service recovery"[5] or anticipating and handling service problems or failures. Many organizations in the casino/gaming sector and lodging sectors have successfully implemented empowerment strategies due to excellent training and specific guidelines for all involved. The concept of empowerment had its origins in the telecommunications industry when AT&T gave notoriety to the concept of "inverted pyramid" organizations (see Figure 15.4). In essence the inverted pyramid places the end-user or customer uppermost in the organizational structure. Next are direct service employees, followed by those who support them until the bottom of the pyramid is reached where management resides.

Malcolm Baldrige Award

In 1987, the National Quality Improvement Act was established and the Malcolm Baldrige National Quality Award was created. The Baldrige Award established standards of excellence for U.S. businesses with the goal to make the United States more competitive in the global marketplace. The three specific and important roles in strengthening the U.S. competitiveness were as follows:

- Help improve performance and capabilities.
- Facilitate communication/sharing of best practice information among and within organizations.
- Serve as a working tool for managing performance, planning, training, and assessment.

As conceived, the Malcolm Baldrige Award would be awarded to six firms each year—two from the manufacturing industry, two from the service industry, and two from the small business arena. To earn the award required outstanding performance in meeting the criteria of enhancing competitiveness with a focus on the delivery of ever-improving value to customers resulting in marketplace success and the improvement of overall company performance and capabilities. The Baldrige Award application categories include leadership; information and analysis; strategic planning; human resource development and

• Customer input	• Brainstorming
• Competitive analysis	• Multivoting
• Empowerment	• Priority determination charts
• Service recovery process	• Selection matrixes
	• Weighted selection matrixes

- Flow charts
- Cause-and-effect diagrams
- Fact-finding planning sheets
- Check sheets
- Bar charts, pie charts, and line graphs

FIGURE 15.3. CQI Tools and Techniques

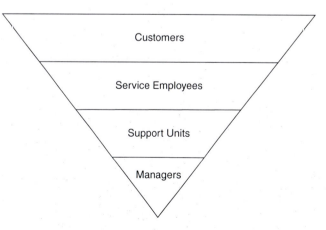

FIGURE 15.4. The Inverted Pyramid Organization

management; process management; business results; and customer focus and satisfaction. In addition to having to be the best in these categories, the Baldrige Award criteria included "core values and concepts" such as customer-driven quality, leadership, continuous improvement and learning, employee participation and development, fast response, design quality and prevention, a long-range view of the future, management by fact, partnership development, corporate responsibility and citizenship, and a results orientation.[6] All of these core values and concepts are assessed, and point values are attached to the award criteria. Figure 15.5 provides a sample of the awards criteria and point structure.

Over the years of competition many outstanding firms in the services industry have won the Malcolm Baldrige Award. In the services industry Ritz Carlton has won the prestigious award on multiple occasions. Ritz Carlton utilizes a variation of the inverted pyramid called the Ritz Carlton Interactive Team Pyramid.[7]

DIRECTIONS AND TRENDS

Technology is playing an increasingly significant role in the delivery of customer service and quality experiences in the services industry. Technology that improves value and increases the speed of the transaction is likely to have great impact on customer satisfaction. Management that seeks out such technology and that is at the forefront of implementing the technology will be leading the successful service industry firms of the future. Handheld check-in/check-out devices, scanners, security recognition systems—virtually every form of reliable automated processes—will create new benchmarks for delivery times, accuracy, and speed. Customers will demand quality service and value, including speed and connectivity, in their definition of customer satisfaction. Managerial leadership will invest, train, and implement to succeed. The process will be continuous as the customer redefines expectations due to new technologies, changing needs, and competitive moves in the marketplace. We will look closer at technology later in the text.

CHAPTER REVIEW

The service industry is service oriented by nature and as such focuses on customer satisfaction and quality service. Management strategies need to be in place throughout the organization from the points of encounter with the customer to the strategic plan. Fortunately, due to concepts such as TQM, CQI, and the Malcolm Baldrige Award, excellent guides are available by which to develop a plan for success. High-performance companies not only develop a plan, they integrate the total organization, reward systems, and measurements for success into the customer satisfaction and quality service undertakings. Management strategies require not only planning but also leadership involvement throughout the process. Management strategies seek customer input and act upon those suggestions by moving the customer through the hierarchy to partnership and ultimately to co-ownership of the process. Utilization of technology to achieve customer satisfaction, improve service recovery, and pro-

Category		Point Value
Leadership		90
Information and Analysis		75
Strategic Planning		55
HR Development and Management		140
Process Management		140
Business Results		250
Customer Focus/Satisfaction		250
Total Points		1,000

FIGURE 15.5. Sample Baldrige Award Point Structure. *Source:* Adapted from R. Nykiel, *Hospitality Management Strategies* (Upper Saddle River, NJ: Prentice Hall, 2005), p. 216.

vide the highest levels of quality service will result in sector leadership in the hospitality industry. What follows is a customer service checklist for management strategies.

Customer Service and Quality Initiative Checklist

- Is there a customer service plan/strategy in place?
- Is it adequately supported with both human and financial resources?
- Are you doing everything possible to thoroughly train and support your point-of-encounter employees?
- Do you have an empowerment policy and do all point-of-encounter personnel understand it?
- Is there a customer and (point-of-encounter) employee feedback system?
- Do all your points of encounter (human, vocal, and electronic) represent the image and positioning of your company appropriately?
- Are you performing customer perception audits either internally or with "shopper services"?
- Is customer satisfaction measurement an integral part of your employee evaluation and reward systems?.
- Are your recruiting guidelines appropriate for each of your point-of-encounter positions?
- Is customer service viewed as a marketing weapon of the highest value?
- Do you have recognition programs in place for point-of-encounter employees who provide extraordinary service?
- Is the leadership of your organization actively involved as a champion of customer service excellence?
- Is this message clearly communicated throughout the organization?
- Is the compensation of key employees appropriate and tied directly to quality service ratings?

KEY CONCEPTS/TERMS

Attitudinal research
Behavioral research
Benchmarking
Communication
Connectivity
CQI (continuous quality improvement)
Customer perceptions audit (CPA)
Customer perspective
Customer satisfaction index (CSI)
Database
Empowerment
Expectations
Focus groups
Follow-up
Job performance criteria
Level of expectation
Mystery shoppers
Platform
Point of encounter
Prioritization

Proposition
Reallocation
Recognition
Repeat factor
SOPs (standard operating procedures)
Speed
TQM (total quality management)
Trade-off time management
Walk-throughs

DISCUSSION QUESTIONS

1. How can qualitative and quantitative research techniques be utilized to support customer service and quality strategies?
2. What are the more appropriate research techniques that can help in assessing customer service and quality?
3. Why do you think so many hospitality industry companies have stated customer satisfaction is their top goal/management strategy?
4. What points of encounter do you believe are the most critical for a hospitality company in the foodservice sector? Why?
5. Why is it important to move customers through the hierarchy to the point they become "part-owner"? How would you do this in the lodging sector?
6. What do you perceive to be the critical differences between CQI and TQM?
7. Since speed has to be factored into the customer satisfaction equation, list five steps you might suggest a business take to improve in this area.
8. List three ways a firm might improve its connectivity.

CASE 15.1. SOUTHWEST AIRLINES—THE CUSTOMER'S AIRLINE

The Southwest Airlines case example[8] could be appropriately discussed under strategy selection and positioning, branding strategies, marketing strategies, communications strategies, and organizational and operating concepts. However, the more one studies Southwest Airlines the more one must admire its customer service and quality strategies. Quality strategies? Yes, if we recognize that quality is defined as a collection of attributes, which when present in a product indicates that the product has conformed to or exceeded customer expectations. Southwest Airlines would have to be recognized as meeting these criteria over the long term. A detailed review of the history, milestones, accomplishments, recognitions, and philosophies of Southwest Airlines will provide for the case of customer service and quality leadership.

Thirty years ago, Southwest Airlines put itself on the map with low fares, direct flights between three Texas cities, and attractive attendants. Today, the company still offers below-the-belt prices and has expanded its direct service to fifty-eight cities in thirty states. During the past years, Southwest has remained profitable in the face of oil crises, wars, and recessions. And while many major airlines scaled back their schedules following the September 11, 2001, terrorist attacks, Southwest continued at full operation and posts a profit (for the twenty-ninth consecutive year) in one of the most challenging operating environments that the air travel industry has ever faced. In 2001, Southwest Airlines also increased its domestic market share, made enhancements to improve its customer service, and ended the year with increased employees and aircrafts. The purpose of this case example is to point out what strategies Southwest Airlines utilized to become and remain so successful.

Milestones

Southwest Airlines began service in 1971 with flights between Houston, Dallas, and San Antonio. Today, it has become the fourth largest airline in America. It operates more than 2,700 flights a day and has more than 33,000 employees throughout the system.

The following years marked the successful steps of Southwest Airlines:

1971—Southwest Airlines takes off on its maiden voyage.

1977—Southwest stock is listed on the New York Stock Exchange as "LUV."

1987—Southwest celebrates the sixth year in a row as holder of the best customer satisfaction record of any continental U.S. carrier.

1988—Southwest is the first airline to win the much coveted Triple Crown for a month for "Best On-Time Record," "Best Baggage Handling," and "Fewest Customer Complaints."

1989—Southwest announces the billion-dollar revenue mark and becomes a "major" airline!

1992-1996—Southwest wins five consecutive annual Triple Crowns.

1994—Southwest introduces Ticketless.

Awards and Recognition

- Southwest has ranked number one in "Fewest Customer Complaints" for the last eleven consecutive years, as published in the Department of Transportation's "Air Travel Consumer Report."
- *Fortune* has consistently recognized Southwest Airlines in its annual survey of corporate reputations. Southwest came out on top as the "Most Admired Airline" in the world for 1997, 1998, 1999, and 2000. *Fortune* has listed Southwest among all industries as one of the most admired companies in the world, year after year.
- The April 2001 issue of *Fortune* placed Southwest in the "50 Most Coveted Employers" voted by MBA students.
- In April 2001, the National Airline Quality Rating (AQR) ranked Southwest Airlines number three among the top ten airlines for performance in 2000. The AQR system uses weighted averages and monthly performance data in the areas of on-time performance, baggage handling, involuntary denied boarding, and a combination of eleven customer complaint categories, all according to DOT statistics.
- Southwest Airlines has been named a charter member of the International Airline Passengers Association's Honor Roll of Airlines among the "World's Safest Airlines." It has also been recognized as one of the "World's Safest Airlines" by *Conde Nast Traveler.*
- In May 2001, *The Wall Street Journal* reported that Southwest had ranked first among airlines for the "Highest Customer Service Satisfaction."
- Since 1997, *Fortune* has ranked Southwest Airlines in the "Top Five of the Best Companies to Work for in America."
- Southwest's Rapid Rewards program was placed first in *Inside Flyer* magazine's 2001 annual Freddie Awards in the "Best Bonus Promotion" and "Best Award Redemption" categories. Southwest was also placed second in the "Program of the Year," "Best Customer Service," and "Best Web Site" categories.
- Southwest Airlines has been named in the *Forbes* Platinum 400 "America's Best Big Companies."
- In December 2001, Satmetrix Systems named Southwest Airlines the winner of the Satmetrix "Best Customer Satisfaction Award for the Transportation Industry."
- *Business Ethics* lists Southwest Airlines in its "100 Best Corporate Citizens," a list that ranks public companies based on their corporate service to various stakeholder groups.
- Southwest Airlines was listed by *Hispanic* magazine in the 2000 and 2001 Hispanic Corporate 100 for leadership in providing opportunities for Hispanics and for supporting recruitment, scholarships, and minority vendor programs.
- The Secretary of Defense presented the Employer Support of the Guard and Reserve "2001 Employer Support Freedom Award" to Southwest Airlines.
- In 2001, First Lady Laura Bush sent Southwest a personal recognition letter celebrating the company's success with the Adopt-A-Pilot program. Since its inception in 1997, the program has reached more than 25,000 students.

Key Points to Southwest's Success

Southwest has been called America's most successful airline, dramatically outperforming its competitors. It is the industry's most consistently profitable carrier, with a record the envy of its peers. Following are some of the reasons for Southwest's success.

Lower fare. Boasting the lowest costs among the major airlines, Southwest can profitably offer low fares where others can't.

Simplification. Southwest operates on a point-to-point basis instead of using a hub-and-spoke system. Its planes may land at every point along a journey, which means that the company can schedule flights for maximum utility. In addition, Southwest only uses one type of aircraft—Boeing 737—which considerably simplifies maintenance, spare parts purchase, crew training, and operations.

Efficiency. Southwest boasts some impressive statistics. Its worker-to-customer ratio is the lowest in the industry. Southwest's ground crews take twenty minutes to turn an airplane around for its next flight—half the industry average.

New technology. In January 1994, Southwest introduced a ticketless travel option, eliminating the need to print a paper ticket. Southwest also entered into an arrangement with Sabre, which was to provide ticketing and automated booking on Southwest's Web site in a cost-effective manner. In 2002, due to security requirements, Southwest introduced a new computer-generated boarding pass system.

Convenience. Southwest serves many conveniently located satellite or downtown airports, which are typically less congested than other airlines' hub airports. By so doing, Southwest provides greater convenience to passengers, has lower operating fees, and doesn't get backed up with airplane traffic on the ground that slows its quick turn-around operation style.

Focus on customers. Cheap doesn't have to mean crummy. Sure, there are no hot meals or fancy airport clubs, but Southwest's customer service is legendary. According to the "Air Travel Consumer Report" issued by the U.S. Department of Transportation in April 2002, Southwest ranked number one in on-time performance during the last fifteen years. Southwest also has the lowest passenger complaint rate—0.47. These outstanding performances provide customers a reliable and comfortable flight experience.

Employee relationship. Southwest treats its employees as well as its customers. Southwest Airlines has been listed on the top five of *Fortune*'s "100 Best Companies to Work for in America" from 1997 to 2000. Although 85 percent unionized, the airline has had only one eight-hour strike in its history while other major carriers have been beset by labor strife for the past several years.

Customer Service in Southwest Airlines

The mission statement of Southwest Airlines is "Dedication to the highest quality of Customer Service delivered with a sense of warmth, friendliness, individual pride and Company Spirit." This mission statement answers the question why a company focusing on low-price and no-frills services has been acclaimed as one of the biggest success legends in American history. As Colleen Barrett, Southwest's COO, stated so succinctly, "Southwest Airlines is not an airline with great customer service. [It is] a great customer service organization that happens to be in the airline business."

In 1971, Southwest Airlines came into being as a little three-jet upstart. Ever since then, service has been recognized as one of the core values it offers its customers. Today, Southwest has become a leader in customer service in the airline industry. Its achievements cover all aspects of service an air travel company provides. Basically, they fall into the following categories.

Safety. Safety has been a number one priority for Southwest Airlines. As a matter of fact, Southwest is the only major airline that has not had any serious accidents as of 2003.

On-time performance. According to statistics gathered and published by the U.S. Department of Transportation, Southwest has maintained one of the best cumulative on-time performance and flight schedule reliability records in the U.S. airline industry. The company enjoys a legendary turnaround time of twenty to thirty minutes, which allows it to use about thirty-five fewer aircrafts than airlines with an industry-average turnaround time. More amazingly, this is achieved with sometimes half the staff of its average competition.

When delays or cancellations do occur and overnight accommodations are needed for passengers, Southwest Airlines is among the few airline companies that address this problem in both its Customer Service Plan and Contract of Carriage agreement clearly and consistently. Southwest provides accommodations to passengers if the delay or cancellation was under the airline's control and the passenger missed the last possible flight or connection of the day to his or her destination.

Baggage handling. Southwest allows each passenger to check up to three pieces of luggage, that is, one more than most other major airlines. The company has also maintained one of the best baggage handling records in the industry.

Customer complaints. Southwest Airlines has ranked number one in fewest customer complaints for the past eight consecutive years as published in the DOT's "Air Travel Consumer Report" with a Customer Loyalty Index score of 8.63, compared with the industry score of 7.79.

Of course, nothing is perfect. Customers do complain about Southwest Airlines. The company has a set of valid and effective practices in dealing with customer complaints. A company representative answers each complaint letter personally, and each issue is addressed carefully. If the letter requires an investigation or report, a postcard will be sent to the customer acknowledging the receipt of the letter and notifying him or her as to how long the investigation should take.

The customer relations department of Southwest Airlines logs and tracks all customer complaints to make sure every issue is addressed properly and timely. The department also prepares monthly reports monitoring trends in customer complaints. Leadership of the company sometimes adjusts customer service policies according to the trends they see.

Warm, friendly, and personal services sprinkled with humor. Superb quality of service may sound incongruous with Southwest's no-frills, no-reserved-seating, and no-meals approach to air travel. Yet Southwest's employees have made the miracle by instilling a lot of warmth, friendliness, laughs, and personal attention into whatever simple service they are rendering the customer.

Southwest's customers have been constantly writing letters to the corporate office praising agents with whom they have developed friendships just from talking on the phone. In more than one case, reservations agents have met customers at their destination cities and driven them to hospitals for medical treatments. One young employee even flew his own private plane to get someone to a hospital in time for a transplant. It is not unusual for an employee to use his or her own car to drive customers four or five hours to a destination after a scheduling mix-up. Humorous touches in customer service represent yet another famous Southwest way of business that separates the company from its competition. This humorous approach to services helps ease the tension brought up by a long flight and lengthy time in a confined space. It also heightens employees' productivity so they will provide warmer and friendlier services to customers. The company encourages camaraderie between employees and customers. Southwest Airlines has built a reputation of being "the airline that loves the customer." The company adopted LUV as its stock exchange symbol to represent not only its home airport—Dallas Love Field—but also the theme of its employee-customer relationship.

Online reservations. Southwest is among the first airlines that enabled online ticket reservation. Now its Web site southwest.com is playing an essential role in furthering the low-cost and happy-customer company mission. In 2000, southwest.com generated 31 percent of the company's passenger revenues, or $1.7 billion. Booking a ticket on Southwest's Web site is an easy and straightforward process. Since March 2001, the site has also provided rental car and hotel reservations, which allowed Southwest to decide against partnering with other major airlines to form Orbitz. The concern of the company was that it wouldn't be able to control the quality of service that a Southwest customer might get from the jointly owned but separately managed travel intermediary.

Innovations in customer service. Southwest Airlines has been long acknowledged as one of the most innovative companies. It pioneered some practices that are now adopted by other airline companies. For example, Southwest was the first to implement a frequent flyer program that gives credit for the number of trips taken instead of miles flown. In 1974, it began the first profit-sharing plan in the U.S. airline industry. It is also the creator of many unique programs such as senior discounts, Fun Fares, Fun Packs, a same-day air freight delivery service, ticketless travel, and so on.

As Southwest has become a customer service star, other companies try to imitate its style. They are seldom successful. Herb Kelleher, the company's cofounder, often said, "It's the intangibles that make the difference at Southwest." Nobody can copy Southwest's success story if they don't understand what the intangibles are. The intangibles of Southwest Airlines are its happy, productive, and creative employees. It is the relentless emphasis the company puts on internal customer service that has made Southwest what it is today.

Internal Customer Service

Internal customer service refers to service directed to the internal customers, or employees, of an organization. It is the level of responsiveness, quality, communication, teamwork, and morale that help the organization succeed. As a company where employees love coming to work, Southwest has created a business strategy that focuses on its internal customers, the employees. Refer to its "inverted pyramid" structure in Exhibit 15.1. Following are areas where this strategy is borne out.

Caring about the people. Managers at Southwest encourage the "can do" and "let's try" attitudes. Employees are encouraged to generate ideas and try them. Internal competition is also encouraged. Competition at Southwest exists in a friendly and motivating way. For example, departments shower each other with ice cream, pizza, or other goodies as tokens of customer devotion. Southwest also accepts failure as a natural and forgivable occurrence. Among the rules it teaches its employees are "walk a mile in someone else's shoes," "take accountability and ownership," and "celebrate your mistakes as well as your triumphs."

As a part of the recruitment process, a "people department" sign welcomes applicants into cheerful surroundings. A popcorn machine is available to staff and applicants—Southwest's "hire for attitude, train for skill" philosophy manifests itself in every aspect of the physical surroundings and operations.

Recruitment and training. Southwest's primary focus is on its employees. The company has the lowest turnover rate in the airline industry and its employees are hardworking and dedicated. How does Southwest recruit employees? It's through the company's human resources department called the "people department." The recruiting process begins with advertisement in business publications, job fairs, and online promotions. Due to the large number of applicants, the department uses a computer program that matches applicants suitable for the jobs offered. The department chooses people based mainly on their attitudes. Even though Southwest wants its employees to be business oriented, it's not looking for a typical business-oriented person. People who are not afraid to laugh and let their personalities shine are more likely to be recruited. On some occasions résumés were sent to Southwest in cereal boxes and people appeared for interviews in gorilla costumes.

The type of interview that an applicant may go through depends on the position he or she is applying for. Basically the company uses a group interview first, which begins with the question, "Tell me how you have used humor to defuse a difficult situation." Then a paper interview is used. Once the applicant has survived the interview and becomes an employee, he or she soon realizes that Southwest puts a strong emphasis on continuous learning, training, and cross training.

Southwest's University of People trains 25,000 people a year. New employees undergo a standardized training session. In addition, every year supervisors, managers, and executives have to undergo a two-day training at the company's headquarters in Dallas, which includes the frontline leadership program for supervisors, the "Leading with Integrity" program for managers, and the "Customer-Care" training program for flight attendants, pilots, and others.

Southwest uses training as an important motivational tool. Employees are refamiliarized with the company's culture, mission statement, and corporate identity. Training prevents mistakes and employees tend to be more involved in the company and more motivated. Regular training for all ranks of employees also tends to decrease hierarchical thinking.

Communication. Good internal customer service depends on good communication. It is a policy at Southwest that every quarter, senior executives must spend one day working in field offices experiencing and seeing firsthand customer service and employment-related issues.

Southwest Airlines uses face-to-face communication, whenever possible, and always on a first-name basis. This informality helps employees build open and direct relationships and make decisions more quickly. Southwest's people communicate information through *LUV Lines,* an employee newsletter. Every issue of *LUV Lines* carries a segment called "Industry News," which keeps employees informed of what other carriers are doing. Every major event in the company, whether it's the opening of a new location or acquisition of another airline, is announced first to employees and then publicly. Southwest's financial results and performance measures are open to any employees. Southwest believes that when employees have immediate access to critical information, they can make the necessary adjustments to fix significant problems.

According to Southwest's corporate philosophy, bureaucracy exhausts the entrepreneurial spirit,

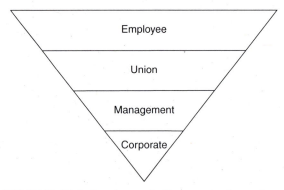

EXHIBIT 15.1. Southwest's Corporate Organization

slows the organization down, and constrains its competitive position. Southwest's leanness gives control, ownership, and responsibility to those who are closest to the action. Due to its leanness and informality, Southwest has an atmosphere that fosters active and personal involvement on the part of its managers. The company tries to avoid formal communication channels. Such channels foster communication that is distant and cold. Southwest trusts its employees and gives them the latitude, discretion, and authority they need to do their jobs. Southwest's corporate philosophy of employees first has helped to create a successful and enjoyable communication environment.

Building employee relationships. Good employee relationships characterize Southwest's organizational culture. Southwest's employees think of the company as a family, feeling personally involved, responsible, and motivated. Southwest is described as a decentralized company with simultaneous loose/tight properties and strong leadership.

A large sign at the main lobby of the home office displays a message by Herb Kelleher: "The people of Southwest Airlines are the creators of what we have become—and what we will be." In Southwest's corporate headquarters photographs of employees, their families, and even their pets cover the hallway.

There are two tools applied by Southwest Airlines to build employee relationships. One is creating a good work environment and the other is job security.

Southwest believes that treating employees like family will foster the kind of intimacy that builds strong relationships and makes work fun. The company encourages employees to take their jobs and the competition seriously. On the other hand, it creates an environment where play, humor, creativity, and laughter flourish.

Southwest Airlines is recognized for providing the greatest job security for employees in the airline industry. Although the company does not have a formal no-layoff policy, it has never laid off any employees, in spite of the cyclical nature of the industry. The turnover rate is also low. Instead of pursuing short-term profits, Southwest focuses on the match of employees' and the company's longer-term interests. In order to avoid layoffs, the company hires very sparingly. In 2001, Southwest reviewed 194,821 résumés and hired 6,406 new employees. The strict recruiting procedures and the commitment to job security have helped the company keep the labor force smaller and more productive than those of their competitors.

The other factor to keep employees at the job is allowing them to feel liberated when they come to work. To foster problem solving and cooperation, Southwest has a "Walk a Mile" program, in which any employee can do somebody else's job for a day. This program helps employees better understand one another's jobs. About 75 percent of 20,000 employees have participated in this program. In 2000, Southwest Airlines was included in *Fortune*'s list of the "100 Best Companies to Work for in America," which particularly praised the company's culture, high rate of internal promotions, and job security.

Establishing a unique culture. Southwest Airlines has a strong reputation as an employee-centered company with a nonhierarchical culture. The company spends a lot of energy in maintaining this culture. Starting from hiring, it focuses on looking for those who have a good sense of humor and who are interested in performing as a team and take pride in team results instead of personal accomplishments.

The other key to the company's culture is communication. Managers spend a lot of time with employees and communicate with them in a variety of ways. The philosophy of the management is to make employees feel fulfilled and happy, and to treat employees as individuals and be interested in their personal lives. Distinguished from other airlines, Southwest has a culture that values efficiency, hard work, innovation, and simplicity. Southwest established a culture committee in the early 1990s. The committee's mission is to regularly visit all sectors of the company promoting the original history and spirit of the airline.

Creating excellent benefits for employees. To support the belief that people take better care of things they own, and that this special care is ultimately passed on to the customer, Southwest created a profit-sharing program and a broad-based stock option plan that allows employees to participate in the financial benefits of an ownership culture. Ownership extends beyond just the profit sharing and is manifested in the priority the company places on employee initiative and responsibility. Southwest is built on the principle that employees are expected to take on an entrepreneurial role in being proactive owners who are cognizant of corporate values and confident enough with their empowerment to participate in decision making and the continuous improvement process. This entrepreneurial spirit provides employees with freedom and responsibility to take effective action and the financial participation through ownership that allows them to benefit from the company's overall performance.

Southwest is the only airline to offer stock ownership without asking for wage concessions. The company provides a profit-sharing plan, which is at the core of its benefits program. Almost all of the employees are rewarded with a percentage of the company's profits divided up and allocated by relative salary. Employees are free to choose to increase the amount. Twenty-five percent of an employee's profit sharing goes to the purchase of Southwest's stock. Employees own more than 13 percent of the company's stock through this plan. The shares held by employees are spread broadly among most of the company's workers.

The unique ownership culture has really empowered employees to take on responsibility for maintaining the high-performance standards with few complications. Southwest has the most productive workforce in the industry with 2,400 customers served per employee annually, double its competitors' average. Southwest also has the lowest turnover rate among airlines, with less than 4.5 percent of employees leaving per year.

Southwest's internal culture is what sets it apart from other companies in the industry. Every employee is given the general guidelines of his or her responsibilities and role in the company, then expected and encouraged to go outside those guidelines fearlessly. This is an airline that takes the boredom out of flying and makes it fun again. Southwest takes every chance it gets to be funny and out of the ordinary. It seems the employees of Southwest love the benefits of watching their actions create personal financial rewards through stock ownership.

Conclusion

Over thirty years ago, when Rollin King and Herb Kelleher decided to put together a different kind of airline, the philosophy it was based on was as follows: "If you get your passengers to their destinations when they want to get there, on time, at the lowest possible fares, and make darn sure they have a good time doing it, people will fly your airline."

They have lived up to their commitment. All the strategies that have made Southwest Airlines a huge success were smartly built around this original philosophy. Southwest has been famous for positioning at a low fare, great convenience, and no-frills service market. Speed, efficiency, and customer service are the three pillars on which the company has built its value. Southwest has achieved its stellar customer service records through a company culture that puts employees first, cares about people, and makes work fun for everybody. When internal customers are satisfied, so are the external customers. Southwest Airlines is exemplifying this business notion each and every day—not for one year but every year. This is why Southwest Airlines was selected for the case example on customer service and quality.

Case Discussion Questions

1. Meeting or exceeding a customer's expectations results in customer satisfaction. Name three steps you would take to identify a customer's expectations.
2. Building employee relationships and establishing a company-employee "culture" are important in the services industry. What are some of the things you would expect management to do to help develop good employee relationships and a winning culture?

CASE 15.2. HERTZ CORPORATION—CONTINUOUSLY IMPROVING PRODUCT AND CUSTOMER SERVICE DELIVERY

In this chapter the concept of CQI (continuous quality improvement) was discussed. For a hospitality industry company, this means continually improving in the delivery of your product or service offering to the consumer. In this case study, we look at how technology has played a role in continually improving the service delivery process and customer experience for Hertz.[9]

Hertz is the world's largest car rental company and one of the largest construction and industrial equipment rental businesses in the United States. In total, Hertz operates from approximately 7,000 locations in the United States and in more than 140 countries around the world. Their aim is to provide consistent and seamless service and a high level of quality on a global basis generating a perceived value that distinguishes Hertz from its competitors. This case study provides a synopsis of the company's history and looks at some of the many customer service innovations implemented by Hertz. These innovations required management's commitment of substantial resources and even changing the way Hertz conducted its business.[10]

The pioneer of auto renting was Walter L. Jacobs who in September of 1918, at the age of twenty-two, opened a car rental operation in Chicago. Starting with a dozen Model T Fords, which he repaired and repainted himself, Jacobs expanded his operation to the point where, within five years, the business generated annual revenues of about $1 million. In 1923, Jacobs sold his car rental concern to John Hertz, president of Yellow Cab and Yellow Truck and Coach Manufacturing Company. Jacobs continued as Hertz's top operating and administrative executive. In 1932, Hertz opened the first airport car rental location at Chicago's Midway Airport. In 1938, the first Hertz location was opened in Canada. In 1950, the first Hertz European location was opened in France.

In 1953, the Hertz properties were bought from GMC by the Omnibus Corporation, which divested itself of its bus interest and concentrated solely on car and truck renting and leasing. A year later, a new name was taken—the Hertz Corporation—and it was listed for the first time on the New York Stock Exchange. Jacobs became Hertz's first president and served in that post until his retirement in 1960. On April 25, 1997, Hertz became a publicly traded company, listed on the New York Stock Exchange, under the symbol "HRZ." And on March 9, 2001, Ford reacquired Hertz's outstanding stock, making the company once again a wholly owned subsidiary of Ford. Hertz is headquartered in Park Ridge, New Jersey, since 1988. Prior to that, the corporation was based in New York and, before that, in Chicago. Car rentals, the largest and best known of Hertz's activities, are conducted from approximately 1,900 U.S., corporate, and licensee locations outside the United States. Hertz offers a wide variety of current-model cars on a short-term rental basis—daily, weekly, or monthly—at airports, in downtown and suburban business centers, and in residential areas and resort locales. Today, Hertz's Worldwide Reservations System handles approximately 40 million phone calls and delivers in total approximately 30 million reservations annually.

Hertz has scored many "firsts" in the industry. Hertz was the first to move car rental locations out of back-street garages and to offer a coast-to-coast network of customer convenient, attractive car rental locations. The company was the first to make available cars in many sizes, makes, and models, allowing customers to choose vehicles to meet various needs. Another Hertz first in the car rental industry has made it easier for customers to find their destination once they leave the Hertz lot. Introduced in 1984, Computerized Driving Directions (CDD) provides customers with detailed directions to local destinations, including estimated time and distance. Today in the United States, customer-friendly, self-service CDD terminals and kiosks are available at most major Hertz airport and downtown locations and printed directions in six languages are provided. CDD directions are also available in Canada, across Europe, and in Australia at major airport and downtown locations. CDD in Europe provides directions in nine languages.

Hertz was a pioneer in fast check-in and check-out with such customer-oriented services as the Hertz Number One Club, which preregisters your rental and lets you go right to the car of your choice. Also, Hertz embraced the handheld computer/printer for quick check-ins at most all locations—a great service to the time-pressured business customer.

While most all of the innovative customer-oriented services were made available to most customers, Hertz also developed an extraordinary popular service for a select list of VIPs called "The Platinum Service." In this case, the senior management of Hertz came up with a most interesting strategy. Hertz management targeted only a few thousand corporate CEOs and senior executives for the "by invitation only" Platinum Service. Platinum Service members are individuals who have the power to make or influence key decisions potentially beneficial to Hertz—decisions such as which rental car company to use on a preferred basis for a corporation's travelers and which rental car company should provide leased vehicles to the corporation. These few thousand Platinum Service members receive extraordinary customer service, which includes a private toll-free phone number, reservationists who know the customer by name as well as his or her car preference history, automatic upgrades to luxury class autos (when available) at no charge, and personalized service at many airports subject to security restrictions ("meet and greet" personnel bring the car to you or pick it up where you leave it). Many more services and amenities are offered to the Platinum Service members.[11]

In the late 1990s Hertz introduced a concept called Hertz Local Editions, offering hundreds of convenient locations. This network of local rental locations offers fast customer pickup and return service. All the customers need to do is call and Hertz will come and get them at their home or office. This pickup/return service is available with one-hour advance notice and is usually provided within fifteen minutes.

Many things contribute to great customer service. For the hospitality industry customer, especially frequent travelers, much of what Hertz does on a global basis adds up to great customer service. Exhibit 15.2 summarizes Hertz's ongoing quality service driven by its management and service delivery innovations.

EXHIBIT 15.2. Hertz's Customer Service

Case Discussion Questions

1. Convenience has become an essential component of successful customer service in today's marketplace. Select a hospitality business and identify three ways you could make the purchasing process and customer service experience more convenient for the customer.
2. In the Hertz case example, technology and innovation were combined to offer seamless service. Select another sector of the hospitality industry and identify where you believe technology will have a great impact and improve customer service/satisfaction in the future.

CASE 15.3. GLENEAGLES COUNTRY CLUB—CUSTOMER SATISFACTION THROUGH CREATIVE MARKETING

This chapter focused on points of encounter and their relationship to customer satisfaction. One of the most challenging areas within the hospitality industry in terms of customer satisfaction and marketing is dealing with club members and marketing clubs. The case example that follows presents a club which excels at both satisfying its customers as well as using creative strategies in its marketing.

Gleneagles Country Club in Plano, Texas, is one of ClubCorp's holdings, which owns or operates nearly 200 golf courses, country clubs, private business and sports clubs, and resorts internationally.[12] Founded in 1957, Dallas-based ClubCorp has $1.6 billion in assets. Among the company's nationally recognized club properties are Pinehurst in the Village of Pinehurst, North Carolina (the world's largest golf resort, home of the 2005 U.S. Open); Firestone Country Club in Akron, Ohio (site of the 2003 World Golf Championships—NEC Invitational); Indian Wells Country Club in Indian Wells, California (site of the Bob Hope Chrysler Classic); The Homestead in Hot Springs, Virginia (America's first resort founded in 1766); and Mission Hills Country Club in Rancho Mirage, California (home of the Kraft Nabisco Championship). The more than fifty business clubs and business and sports clubs include the Boston College Club; City Club on Bunker Hill in Los Angeles; Citrus Club in Orlando, Florida; Columbia Club in Seattle; Metropolitan Club in Chicago; Tower Club in Dallas; and the City Club of Washington, DC. The company's 19,000 employees serve the more than 215,000 members and households and 200,000 guests who visit ClubCorp properties each year.

Gleneagles was established in 1985. The Clubhouse has a very "clubby" feel with the mahogany walls, ten-foot doors, and huge chandeliers. The membership enjoys socializing together. Parties and events have become traditions. As you walk through the front doors you are immediately welcomed by the tenured Gleneagles staff.

Gleneagles Country Club is comprised of members who are looking for an environment that is professional as well as personal. The club has members who need only a place to dine and enjoy the camaraderie of the other members and those who want to have it all—golf, tennis, and fitness.

Gleneagles has two impeccably kept championship golf courses, eighteen well-lit tennis courts, and pools to enjoy in the summer. The beautifully appointed clubhouse has been ranked top in the area for many years.

Gleneagles also offers a state-of-the-art fitness center with a full line of Cybex resistance equipment, a Cycle Reebok studio, a group exercise and cardiovascular area, a massage and nutrition center, and a child care center. The fitness center is also the home of the Wimbledon Grill as well as the site for the Gleneagles All Star Junior Tennis Program.

Gleneagles is perhaps best known for its golf course, thirty-six holes of championship golf, designed by the team of Von Hagge and Devlin. Bentgrass greens and water views on the majority of the fairways are course signatures.

Gleneagles cultivates its members' children for the future. The club introduces them to the game of golf and what a privilege it is to belong to a club. Year-round instruction and summer clinics give these girls and boys the opportunity to learn the game. Several juniors have competed on a national level and few have moved on to the PGA Tour.

Gleneagles also provides a private event specialist for members. The event specialist plans the events and works with the executive chef on the menu planning and event details. The facility is available for a full range of events.

The city of Plano, Texas, has an unusually young population and so does Gleneagles. The majority of the membership consists of families wanting family programs. Many of these younger families live in the large substantial homes surrounding the golf course. A very affluent group of residents are not only Gleneagles neighbors but also the members. Like most clubs, the membership is demanding and, in the Gleneagles case, very active. Gleneagles staff must relate to the entire family, from the children to the parents, every day of the week.

Gleneagles believes in the concepts outlined in this chapter. Points of encounter, from the moment the valet parks one's car, to the doorman's welcome and the greeting upon passing through the doors by a well-trained greeter, make members feel this is "their" club. Further, flexibility is something the entire staff is taught. Staff is empowered to prepare items to the members' request, even if they are not on the very extensive menu. Staff accommodates the membership in every way possible—taking care of errands, retaining forgotten items, and so on.

Satisfying a range of customers that comprises children and adults is no easy task. Gleneagles offers a very creative and comprehensive calendar of events that meets everyone's needs.

In addition to special events related to golf and tennis, the club offers an extensive list of other daily activities each month to keep members and their families involved. Examples include a wine club, happy hours, "two for one" days, themed dinner nights such as "southern home-style night," "prime rib night," "Italian night," "Caribbean night," and so on. There are ladies nights and events, and children's entertainment, menus, and events. Each holiday is a special event and the club is themed for the day. For example, on Easter, the Easter Bunny is there for the children along with a magnificent children's buffet (kids have the option of their own seating area) and of course the traditional Easter egg hunt. There are a plethora of summer camps including a golf camp, tennis camp, and swimming camp. From happy hour to happy children's events there is always something to please the membership irrespective of age.

All of these activities are well marketed with everything from newsletters, to the monthly calendar mailing, to special invitations. Members are encouraged to make their suggestions and are often rewarded with small prizes of appreciation. Many of the themed nights, parties, and activities are the direct result of club members' suggestions.

Gleneagles goes the extra mile for its club members. This point can be best exemplified with this actual holiday experience. Like most clubs, the Christmas holidays often create demand beyond the capacity for a club. Frequently, all December dates and event space are fully reserved and utilized. Such was the case when this one newer club member tried to hold a holiday event for his company executives at the club. Most clubs would say they were sorry the dates weren't available and offer to book it for another time. The events staff member at Gleneagles sensed the new member's disappointment and apparent frustration. She offered an alternative idea to the member. Having visited the member's magnificent home, she felt there was more than adequate space in the home for the event. Naturally, the spouse who was planning the event did not want to be cooking and serving. The Gleneagles staff member offered to provide everything from the setup, to bartenders, to the food, to the chef and servers, to the cleanup crew, and, yes, even arrange for valet parking and holiday plants.

The new member couple were amazed that the club would go this extra mile for them and agreed to the idea. The event was an immense success and the new member and spouse received numerous comments from their guests on how warm and nice it was to have this year's executive gathering at a home versus a club. Exceptional service and going the distance for its membership is one reason for Gleneagles' success and satisfied membership.

Gleneagles demonstrates an in-depth understanding of its target market (families) and how to meet their needs. The club understands marketing and creating activities that drive club members to participate and use the club. Gleneagles understands the community it resides in and how to go the extra mile for its members. Moreover, the well-trained staff at Gleneagles knows how to serve its membership. From the multiple points-of-encounter greetings to the "exceptions to the rules," Gleneagles aims for member satisfaction.

Case Discussion Questions

1. Many clubs have rules and limitations. When do you believe rules should be broken and flexibility be utilized?
2. Having a full activity schedule/calendar is only an informational or planning tool. What steps do you believe a club should take to market the calendar of events?

NOTES

1. Nykiel, R. (1988). *Points of Encounter* (New York: Amacor), p. 14.

2. Nykiel, R. (2001). *The Art of Marketing Strategy* (New York: Amacor), p. 146.

3. Deming, W. (1982). *Out of Crisis* (Cambridge, MA: Massachusetts Institute of Technology, Center for Advanced Engineering Study), pp. 23-24.

4. Woods, R. & King, J. (1996). *Quality Leadership and Management* (East Lansing, MI: Educational Institute—AH&MA), p. 39.

5. Ibid., p. 104.

6. Material adapted from the Malcolm Baldrige National Quality Award 1995 Award Criteria (Gaithersburg, MD, National Institute of Standards and Technology).

7. Ritz Carlton Human Resources Department.

8. Information derived from http://www.southwest.com, http://www.iflyswa.com/about_swa/press/factsheet.html (updated June 19, 2001), and http://www.iflyswa. com/about_ swa/financials/investor_relations_ index.html.

9. Information derived from www.hertz.com/myprofile.htm and www.thehertzcorporation.com.

10. Nykiel, R. (1990). *You Can't Lose If the Customer Wins* (Stamford, CT: Longmeadow Press), p. 121.

11. Ibid.

12. Information derived from www.clubcorp.com.

PART IV:
PLANNING AND COMMUNICATIONS

In Part I, we delineated approaches and techniques related to qualitative, quantitative, and integrative research methodologies. In Part II, we focused on market analysis and research approaches and techniques related to locational analysis, site selection, and feasibility and market area studies. And, in Part III, we discussed research applications related to overall marketing strategy, positioning, brands, pricing, and customer satisfaction. All of these research approaches, techniques, analyses, and studies can be most effective only if they are organized to support a plan and are properly communicated. These latter two items, planning and communications, are the focal points of Part IV. This part begins with Chapter 16, which presents a guideline to preparing a research-based business review. This chapter points out the significance of accurate market information and the key components of the business review process. In Chapter 17, the strategic marketing planning process is presented along with the concept of zero-base budgeting, a strategic marketing plan guideline, and a sample plan. Finally, in Chapter 18, methods for effective presentation of research findings and plans along with some communications techniques are suggested.

Chapter 16

Preparing a Research-Based Business Review

CHAPTER OBJECTIVES

- To define the concept of a business review.
- To provide guidelines for preparing a business review.
- To present a ten-step multifaceted business review process.
- To delineate how to utilize primary data and secondary data in the development of a business review.
- To suggest sources for data that support conducting and assessing a business review process.

A business review is where key qualitative and quantitative research findings are related to the current and future marketing and strategic plans of an organization. The business review provides an information decision-making base for the subsequent strategic marketing plan and the rationale for all strategic marketing decisions. Most important, it provides a consumer and customer orientation to the organization's marketing communications.

This chapter provides a business review process that incorporates key research findings to support plan rationale and marketing decisions. Following a structured review process as suggested in this section will help create a more effective database from which to make decisions. It is very important to look not only inward at the organization, but externally at the competition and the respective industry, and ahead at future trends that may impact the plan. The industry category is the overall business in which you compete. For example, American Airlines is in the travel industry.

It should be pointed out that throughout the business review process consumers and customers are a consistent focal point. In order to analyze company trends, it is essential to investigate through various research methodologies the behavior of customers or of the product/service offered. Also, in order to compare internal company trends to the industry the product/service is associated with, it is also necessary to look at the purchase behavior of consumers.

THE SIGNIFICANCE OF MARKET INFORMATION

Today, consumers have more product choices than ever before. They also have more information about the choices. The combination of more competition (from small niche marketers to large dominant category killers) and a bombardment of communication from the many competitive alternatives means marketers have to work much harder to affect target market behavior in today's environment. Thus it is more important now than at any time in the history of marketing to really understand your target market and to let this understanding drive not only your marketing decisions, but the entire decision-making framework of the company.

Handbook of Marketing Research Methodologies for Hospitality and Tourism
© 2007 by The Haworth Press, Inc. All rights reserved.
doi:10.1300/5927_17

Today it is more important than at any time in the history of marketing to understand the target market.

Many business successes have come about not because of great business management, but because the organization had tremendous consumer insight—insight developed through a deep understanding of the target market, the business environment, and the competition. Examples are numerous of companies that translated the insights and applied the research findings to successfully compete and even dominate their respective industry sector—companies such as Southwest Airlines, Wal-Mart, Dell, and Disney, to name a few. Newer market entrants have also demonstrated a thorough knowledge of their target market needs—companies such as Jet Blue, Lexus automobiles, Amazon.com, and Enterprise Rental Cars.

A substantial portion of the target market innovation in today's marketing environment is coming from retailers, service firms, package goods companies, and business-to-business firms who are interacting with their target markets with a new level of urgency. Technological innovations in the retail industry, such as "smart cash registers," increased use of research, and marketing databases, have provided marketers with a wealth of customer information. The more successful business-to-business firms are spending less time selling what they have and more time defining their customers' needs, and package goods companies faced with parity of product and a sales promotion environment are exploring new ways to build brand equity and value-added incentives with the products. Marketers who are on the front lines, engaging in dialogue with the consumer on a daily basis, are the ones who are often closest to the consumer and target market demands. This "closeness" is bringing about a change in the way many marketing-oriented companies are doing business.

Marketing intelligence information systems are now capable of defining sets of unique needs or consumption behavior, allowing marketers to quickly and realistically adjust their offerings to affect the segment's behavior.

As a result of instantaneous access to product and service information through the Internet, consumers are truly more educated and more demanding. This knowledge combined with the consumers' desire for fast service and stress-free purchasing has moved marketing just about completely away from the Four Ps—product, price, place, and promotion—to and beyond the Four Cs—consumer wants and needs, consumer cost, convenience, and communications. In fact, some marketeers believe we have now moved to a new set of Five Ps—preparation (research and analysis), positioning, perception, proclamation, and power thrusts.[1]

Creating a perception in line with consumer needs and current behavior and getting that message through the clutter is what successful marketing is all about today.

Marketing remains a broad-based discipline, dynamic and reliant upon research and analysis. Marketers must make strategic decisions such as which customers should be targeted, what is the message to interest them, and what is the price to move them to purchase. Moreover, marketers must decide what are the best channels of communication and distribution. These strategic marketing decisions require a systematic review based on factual data.

KEY COMPONENTS OF THE BUSINESS REVIEW

Many organizations look at their business review as an annual exercise. This may have been fine in the past, but in today's marketplace the business review process needs to be ongoing in many areas. If you don't think so, look at what happened to one of the fastest-moving rising stars—Krispy Kreme Donuts. Riding a straight line upward in stock price, unit growth, and profits, Krispy Kreme was expanding rapidly when an external trend known as the high-protein (low-carbohydrate) diet swept the country in 2004. The immediate impact of this desire to be thin was a flattening of revenue and the first quarter ever of loss for Krispy Kreme. When something like this external trend occurs, you can't wait for the annual assessment to come up—you need to adjust right away or have to hope the trends go away. So before we begin to describe the key components of the business review process, it is important to remember that change is constant, not annual. Identify a method to keep monitoring, assessing, and reporting significant changes on a daily, weekly, or monthly basis. Given this ongoing monitoring, we can now look more in depth at the business review process.

There are five key components in the business review process. Some researchers break the process into fewer pieces and others into many more. The number of key components may well vary by the nature and complexity of the business itself. For the purposes of this text, we will utilize five components as depicted in Figure 16.1.[2]

Parameters. The scope of the business review process is identified. In this first key step a definition of the current core competencies, marketing capabilities, and strengths and weaknesses of the organization are usually topics for assessment. Parameters with respect to how in depth and what is the breadth of the assessment will also need to be specified. By predefining the parameters/scope a prioritization step is automatically being undertaken. Areas within the parameters are what our mission encompasses and areas not within the parameters of the review are currently not of interest.

Product/service review. Here the focal point for review and assessment is the actual product/service category and the organization's status within the category. The relationship to consumers, consumer preferences, competition, and potential threats or opportunities is assessed. Multiple perspectives are important during this key component of the business review. The most important perspective is that of the customer, then consumers, and last management itself. During this assessment process, it is likely there will be a "gap" between the customer's perspective and management's perspective. Thus, it is essential to conduct a GAP analysis to see why, how, and where consumer's perspective is differing from management's. This exercise is extremely important in the services sector due to the nature of most service-related businesses.

Market review. Much like the product review, which assesses the first layer of consumer and customer behavior, the market review seeks to do the same by looking at the total product/service category, total market, consumer demand, and major customer segments. In this component of review, sales trends are analyzed both for the product/service category and for the company/brand(s). Pricing strategy is reviewed along with distribution channels and competition. The

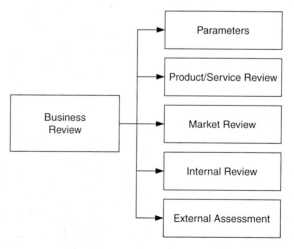

FIGURE 16.1. Key Components of the Business Review

market review usually looks at historical (recent history) demand, the current scenario, and projects a future demand line premised on identified assumptions. Also, in this section pertinent statistical comparisons may be presented such as market share, pricing trends, unit sales or dollar sales per employee, outlet or channel, and so forth.

Internal review. This component of the business review focuses on the operations and delivery of the product/service offering(s). Customer service indices (CSIs) are reviewed, quality ratings assessed, effect ratios compared, and various productivity measures analyzed. This component of the review process is also where policies and procedures, organizational structure logistics, and other internal areas are reviewed.

External assessment. In this component of the business review process, the probes focus on external areas that are likely to impact the business or strategy. For example, the external assessment might focus on government regulations, new technologies, major consumer attitudinal or behavioral changes, consumption trends, and so on.

Through researching and assessing these five key component areas a list is compiled of up-to-date information on strengths and weaknesses, opportunities and threats, core competencies, and marketing capabilities. Further, this process should cause a reexamination of the corporate organizational philosophy, goals, objectives, strategies, and even tactics. The process may also result in changes in pricing and distribution.

Special attention should be paid to assessments and trends that can have a major effect (positive or negative) on the target market.

The target market may be affected in a positive or negative manner by numerous factors. Some of these to look for during the review process are summarized in Figure 16.2.

MORE IDEAS AND APPLICATIONS

There are many detailed tasks to be undertaken during a business review. Some helpful ideas include developing a list of key questions that need to be answered for each of the five components of the business review process. Market researchers can also utilize data charts to help structure their search for relevant information. The data chart allows for quick reference if organized with key headings and columns. Developing the data charts before conducting the research makes it possible to focus on what you need to look for, not on what you have found.

It is a good idea to develop comparative reference points so that data findings are placed into some perspective. For example, your organization's sales growth (trend line) alone is one reference/dimension. However, when the chart includes the product/service category growth line and the sales trend lines for your top three competitors, it provides enough perspective/dimension to allow for actionable item discussions. Whenever possible, it is a good practice to use a meaningful (to the business) trend line from a historical perspective, for example, five years or three years, and the like. This allows for further identification of events that may have impacted the business and also may create a sense of urgency with respect to actions. In essence, it takes data from being static to being dynamic.

Comparisons can be a valuable tool in a market review. It is impor-

Positives	Negatives
✓ Favorable demographic changes	✓ Customer tenure
✓ Product/service enhancements	✓ Changing demographics
✓ Lifestyle changes	✓ Lifestyle trends
✓ Technological improvements	✓ Channels of distribution
✓ Cost efficiencies	✓ Newer/better product/service
✓ External environmental trends	✓ Technology/product/service

FIGURE 16.2. Select Major Target Market Effectors

tant to compare how the various measurements stack up within the company, that is, declining volumes per salesperson, and so forth. This also allows the business to compare the company to both key competitors and to the industry/category. Over time (years/months) "benchmarks" can be established that allow the comparative quantitative assessments. The importance of these benchmarks is that they become the key signals for action(s).

Organizing and communicating the business review is no easy process. Approaches include issuing monthly reports/assessments, "flash" reports or bulletins, summary statements, and a detailed written business review document. In all cases make it objective, use the third-party approach, and prioritize from the urgent to the interesting as a general rule of thumb. Conciseness, bullet points, charts, diagrams, and so on, all help to get the critical data across and understood.

The researcher's role in marketing and management is to get the significant findings concisely communicated and their implications understood by all who need to know.

CHAPTER REVIEW

This chapter discussed the importance of an ongoing business review process. It also indicated that the business review is where key qualitative and quantitative research findings are related to the current business and future strategic marketing plan. The business review process may vary in components based on the complexity of an organization, products or services, and markets served. The five key components to a business review process would include setting parameters, conducting a product/service review, as well as undertaking a comprehensive market review, internal review, and external assessment. The findings from conducting a business review will likely include the positive and the negative "effectors" with respect to the target market. Finally, the importance of concise and timely communications and the need for effective presentation of the data/findings was stressed.

KEY CONCEPTS/TERMS

Behavior
Benchmarks
Business review
Comparisons
Customer service index (CSI)
Defect ratio
Dynamic
Effectors
Five Ps
Four Cs
Four Ps
GAP analysis
Parameters
Target market
Trend line

DISCUSSION QUESTIONS

1. Why is it important to have an ongoing business review process?
2. What types of key research findings might be included within the business review process?
3. Why is it a good practice to present trends/data such as sales/revenues over a multiple-year time frame?
4. Why is it important to view industry/category and competitive trends/data over the same multiple-year time frame?
5. What is a "gap analysis" and why do you think management usually rates itself higher (better) than customers?
6. How would you describe the researcher's role in the marketing and management decision process?

CASE 16.1. HOLIDAY INNS, INC.—RECOGNIZING CHANGE

A key component to a successful strategic plan is to recognize macro trends and driving forces that will have an impact on your business strategy. As indicated in this chapter, if one does not recognize macro trends or driving forces with direct implications, the business strategy may be falsely premised and ultimately fail. In the case example that follows, we will view the opposite—how one company paid attention to both internal and external driving forces and made very successful strategic managerial decisions.

In the mid-1970s, Holiday Inns, Inc., was experiencing both internal and external driving forces that were pressuring its older senior management on multiple fronts. These driving forces included aging product; new product that did not fit/match up with the word "inn" (high-rise hotels) with resultant pressure from franchisees with the new product; court mandates to dispose of some manufacturing businesses that supplied products for the Holiday Inn system; competition in many markets; market saturation (too many Holiday Inns in a given market); and shifting interstate highway patterns, new airports, new suburbs, and decaying inner-city locations.

From a "positioning" perspective, due to its sheer size, market share, and franchising and royalty fee inflow, Holiday Inns was a very profitable cash cow (see Exhibit 16.1, the Boston Consulting Group Portfolio Box).

One major problem was the fact that many of the inns were becoming obsolete due to age and/or location deterioration. Facing the multitude of problems and threats, senior management decided upon some major strategic steps and initiatives. These included reviewing all existing businesses, such as the bus company, steamship line, various manufacturing businesses, and their lodging holdings, and listening to franchisee pressure, and bringing in select new management, including a new vice chairman of the board, new president of the then Inn Development Division, new executive vice president from Inn Development, new marketing officer, and new Senior Vice President for Planning and Development (responsible for strategic planning). Within a few months the new team completed the first formal competitive and environmental analysis and a comprehensive SWOT analysis, which focused on demand generators in each market (see Exhibit 16.2).

These analyses revealed that nearly 35 percent of the existing product would need replacement or be obsolete (due to the product itself and/or market location) within 120 months (see Exhibit 16.3).

The analysis further revealed the need to immediately conduct some in-depth property-by-property financial analysis to determine how big this aging problem was, where it was (franchise system and/or parent company owned inns), and when the impact on the "cash cow" would arrive. In addition, a financial analysis model was created looking at everything from book values to dispositions. Given the fundamental questions about the health of the "cash cow," the senior management proposed to the board that a comprehensive strategic planning effort be undertaken and funded immediately. The board agreed and suggested that an internal strategic planning team be assembled of those considered the "key players and most qualified." Further, they suggested that this "team" move off-site away

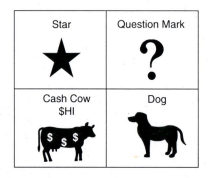

Star	Question Mark
★	?
Cash Cow $HI	Dog

EXHIBIT 16.1. Boston Consulting Group Portfolio Box

- ➤ Air Deplanements
- ➤ Convention Activity
- ➤ Corporate Activity (national and regional headquarters)
- ➤ Government Activity (federal white-collar employment)
- ➤ Feeder Market Significance
- ➤ Destination Market
- ➤ Population/Migration Trend
- ➤ Performance
- ➤ Fair Market Share
- ➤ Other Indicators

Development Point Index	_____Points		Total _____Rank
INDICATOR	Points	Bonus	Points Earned
Airport Activity			
Convention Activity			
Corporate Activity			
Government Activity			
Feeder Market Significance			
Destination Market			
Population/Migration Trend			
Performance Factor			
Fair Market Share			
Other			
Total			

EXHIBIT 16.2. Summary of Demand Generators

_____ **SMSA**

Development Timing	SMSA Recommended Product	Motel/Inn	Motor Hotel	Hotel
Immediate to 24 Months				
24 to 60 Months				
60 to 120 Months				
Always				
LOCATION TYPE:	CODE			
Airport	A			
Suburban	S			
City	C			
Highway	H			
Resort/Destination	D			

Comments:

EXHIBIT 16.3. Summary of Development Recommendation

from their current duties and be devoted full-time to the effort. Also, the strategic planning team was to engage a reputable consulting firm to help provide objectivity and contribute to the process. A new position for a Vice President of Strategic Planning was created, the team assembled, and the process set under way with the assistance of Temple, Barker and Sloane, a Boston area based consulting firm. The approach to the strategic planning effort was unique for its time and can be delineated as follows.

First, the team studied all the recently completed competitive and environmental data, the analysis of the condition of the 1,200 plus inns in the system and their respective markets, and the financial analysis. A comprehensive matrix was developed that profiled the inns with respect to an "immediate to ten year time frame" and also delineated the specific market with respect to growth, competition, obsolescence, and opportunity. This matrix was completed for all inns and the composite results analyzed for part one of the process—the condition and future of the Holiday Inn system/brand.

Second, based on the previous findings, various financial scenarios were developed to look at options ranging from a selling/disposition strategy for existing parent company product to new inn/concept development and room additions in growth markets.

Third, the strategic planning team and external consultant studied the company from a future profit and cash flow perspective; studied the industry to ascertain its business cycle; and studied all other industries to ascertain potential opportunities for entry, acquisitions, or development. A comprehensive business/industry cycle model was developed that compared the Holiday Inns' profit cycle to other industry sectors' and leaders' profit patterns. This was done to look for potential acquisitions that would support a desired consistent earnings flow and higher return on invested capital. All other existing businesses were reviewed with respect to their profit contributions and potential/market growth.

Fourth, a time/sequence strategy implementation model was developed. This model was premised on maintaining profit objectives, cash flow, and raising various levels of incremental cash from the sales of identified assets, including parent company owned inns and manufacturing and transportation businesses.

Fifth, new product concepts, brand segmentation, and incremental revenue generation all related to the lodging industry were explored.

Finally, a strategic plan was developed to communicate recommended business strategy charges, including strategies to overcome anticipated resistance by select board members and shareholders who might be opposed to any change or any of the changes to be recommended. This strategic communications plan would prove to be very valuable over the months ahead.

What were the direct and indirect results of this substantial undertaking? Before looking at significant events and their related timeline, here is a list of ten of the strategies/changes recommended as a result of the process:

1. Consider disposition of all manufacturing and transportation related to businesses.
2. Consider investment (either start-up or acquisitions) in businesses that have profit/cash flow patterns that will support consistency in earnings at that time. (These were identified as the gaming industry or discount retail/drugstores.)
3. Sell off parent company inns that have no or low book values and/or fall within the "obsolete" market/product category within the next sixty months. Utilize proceeds for new concept development and/or acquisitions.
4. Make ownership investment in Las Vegas casino on the strip.
5. Segment product by tiering—hotels, inns, and so on.
6. Develop new brands.
7. Utilize the demographic and market analysis models to fit new product type to market segment demand/needs for future development.
8. In view of the aging of the Holiday Inn product and changes in the marketplace over the next 120 months, consider disposing of the Holiday Inn brand at maximum pricing.
9. Accelerate new businesses (i.e., gaming) and new lodging concepts to replace Holiday Inn brand over the next sixty months and capitalize on companies' reservations/technical strengths, marketing, franchising, and development expertise for new businesses/brands.
10. Offer existing franchise base new concepts/products to also accelerate growth and build a new franchise system around each new brand.

Needless to say, these findings and recommendations were an extraordinary shock to many of those senior executives and board members. This was also compounded by the fact that the vice chairman of the board, the corporate CEO and president, and executive vice president were of strong religious beliefs that gaming was a sinful enterprise. In addition, the board's external directors had many among their ranks who sympathized with that antigaming position. The strategic planning team had anticipated this reaction and commissioned a survey of all shareholders (and lenders) to ascertain their perspective on this issue. The models showed that the numbers were overwhelming in support of the strategy recommendations. In fact, one mega hotel/casino (defined as over 1,000 rooms with a large gaming area) would produce as much or more profit than the entire corporation was then generating in year two of its operation. In addition, unlike some of the other manufacturing and transportation business, the payback on the gaming investment was substantially shorter (i.e., two to eight years) versus ongoing losses for many years for some of the other businesses. Needless to say, over 80 percent of the shareholders surveyed supported entry into the gaming business.

All the recommendations were presented to the board, along with a specific opportunity in Las Vegas. The meeting ended after some heated discussions without approval. After considerable internal maneuvering and shareholder/franchisee pressure, a few months later the board was reconfigured. The vice chairman retired, the president and CEO and executive vice president resigned, and the new senior management team (reduced in number) was reconfigured and the board of directors was put in place. Most of the strategic plan recommendations were approved for implementation. While the specific Las Vegas deal was lost to other investors, the timeline/history that follows exemplifies a strategic planning process that really resulted in change.

Milestones

1952—First Holiday Inn is built by Kemmons Wilson and Wallace Johnson in Memphis, Tennessee.

1954-1974—Company becomes vertically integrated with products group distributing supplies, equipment, and so on, to lodging, housing, health care, and foodservice markets.

1955—Sells franchises; Bill Walton hired to lead franchise expansion.

1957—Becomes public company to raise money to continue rapid expansion.

1968—Diversifies to maintain growth; acquires TCO Industries, holder of Continental Trailways Bus and Delta Steamship Lines.

Early 1970s—Growth slows.

1971 to 1979—Trailways profits decline.

1978—Expands overseas. Strategic decision is made to enter gaming.

1979—Kemmons Wilson resigns as chairman of board; Roy Winegardner appointed chairman; Lem Clymer resigns as president and director; Mike Rose is appointed president and CEO. Acquires Perkin's Cake and Steak and 40 percent of the River Boat Casino. Sells Continental Trailways. Enters into gaming industry.

1980—Purchases Harrah's (Harrah's Tahoe and Reno).

1981—Holds 99 percent ownership of Harrah's Marina, Atlantic City (purchases remaining 1 percent in 1983).

1982—Enters joint project with Donald Trump, Harrah's Boardwalk (Atlantic City). Purchases remaining 60 percent of the River Boat Casino. Forms two new chains—Hampton Inns and Embassy Suites. Sells Delta Steamship Lines.

1983—Opens first Holiday Inn Crowne Plaza Hotel. Winegardner retires as chairman of board; Rose appointed chairman.

1984—Acquires Granada Royale and converts property to Embassy Suites. Opens first Embassy Suite and Hampton Inn.

1985—Changes name from Holiday Inns, Inc., to Holiday Corporation to project multiple nature of corporation. Enters joint venture with Communications Satellite Corporation to turn Holiday's HI-Net communications satellite network into the world's largest privately owned satellite communication system (in-room entertainment and teleconferencing). Transfers Perkin's Restaurant chain to Tennessee Restaurant Co. in exchange for an initial 79 percent of the new company's stock, without voting control. Acquires 50 percent interest in Residence Inns.

1986—Sells 50 percent interest in Trump's Boardwalk. Announces major restructuring.

1987—Sells interest in Residence Inns for $51.4 million (Residence Inns goes indirectly to Marriott). Lake Tahoe Casino opens. Implements $2.6 billion recapitalization plan to enhance shareholder value. Closes announced sale of 14 domestic and 140 international Holiday Inn hotels to Bass PLC (Holiday Inns and Crowne Plaza).

1988—Harrah's Del Rio Casino/Hotel in Laughlin, Nevada, opens. Reenters extended-stay market through Homewood Suites.

1989—Announces second restructuring: sells Holiday Inn brand to Bass PLC for $1.98 billion and creates new company.

As the milestones indicate, almost all of the ten recommendations were fully implemented by the new management of the company over the next 120 months. The evolution/revolution initiated by Roy Winegardner and Mike Rose would ultimately culminate in the sale of Promus's lodging holdings to Hilton and result in Harrah's as the remaining entity encompassing the gaming/casino holdings.

What Holiday Inn management did so well was not only to recognize the internal and external forces of change, but also to identify the opportunities these same forces presented. In today's hospitality environment the pace of change and the impact of driving forces have accelerated. This has had a direct impact on shortening the strategic planning process to virtually an ongoing process.[3]

Case Discussion Questions

1. Can you identify three or four macro trends or driving forces that are likely to impact the hospitality industry in the next five years?
2. Select one of the macro trends or driving forces and present your thoughts on how you would respond. What actions would you undertake? What changes would you implement?

NOTES

1. R. Nykiel, *The Art of Marketing Strategy* (New York: Amacor, 2001), pp. 35-36.
2. R. Hiebing & S. Cooper, *The Successful Marketing Plan: A Disciplined and Comprehensive Approach* (2nd ed.) (Lincolnwood, IL: NTC Business Books, 1996), pp. 9-10.
3. http://www.USATODAY and Hospitality Industry Hall of Honor and Archives located at the Conrad N. Hilton College, University of Houston, Houston, TX.

Chapter 17

The Strategic Marketing Planning Process

CHAPTER OBJECTIVES

- To define the strategic marketing planning process.
- To present the different types of marketing information required to complete a strategic marketing plan.
- To delineate step-by-step the structure and contents of a strategic marketing plan.
- To demonstrate the relationship between research findings and plan strategies.

You cannot develop an effective marketing plan without knowing your consumers and which marketing tools to use to sell to consumers. The purpose of this chapter is to provide an outline for a marketing plan that ties together the research and application phases of marketing.

The issues and strategies addressed in this chapter can be applied, with some modification, to most sectors of the industry.

FINANCIAL CONSIDERATIONS

With few exceptions, there are rarely sufficient financial resources to support all of the programs and tools that a marketer desires. Many marketers approach their marketing plans in a traditional fashion—they sit down with last year's plan and apply additional dollars or cut out certain programs as a result of budgetary constraints. Those who do approach a marketing plan in this way ignore the basic premise of marketing—researching and knowing the consumer. They may feel comfortable "ballparking" marketing budget allocations because they have become familiar with their markets over time.

You cannot develop an effective marketing plan without knowing your customers and which marketing tools to use.

To develop a truly effective marketing plan and to make the best use of financial resources, you need to know your consumers' needs today. You also need to know to which direction their needs are moving. You must learn the consumers' habits, preferences, and perceptions of your products or services as well as how consumers perceive your competition. You must know your problem areas, whether they are markets, cities, specific products, or people. Finally, you must identify your strengths and related opportunities. Don't commit one marketing dollar until you have exhaustive knowledge of all these areas. For planning purposes, begin with the zero-base budgeting concept.

Handbook of Marketing Research Methodologies for Hospitality and Tourism
© 2007 by The Haworth Press, Inc. All rights reserved.
doi:10.1300/5927_18

Zero-Base Budgeting

Zero-base budgeting is a broad concept that can help you prioritize where you want to spend your limited resources. With zero-base budgeting, no expenditure is justified just because it was made last year. Every expense is reanalyzed and justified annually to determine whether it will yield better results than spending the same amount in another way.[1]

One note of caution: frequently there are vital expenses that must be maintained at certain minimum levels. For example, a sales force or reservation system must retain certain expenses that relate to those functions and one should use extreme caution in applying zero-base budgeting. Some marketers subdivide the marketing budget into a "vital core" of expenses and "all other" categories and apply the concept only to the "all other" category. Some consider this a violation of the principle of zero-base budgeting, while to others it is simply common sense. You are the best qualified to determine which approach is most applicable.

RESEARCH AND REQUIRED INFORMATION

The first step in developing a complete marketing plan is to research and gather required information. After defining the parameters, required research and information can be divided into four major areas:

1. Market segmentation, needs identification, and measurement of customer perceptions
2. Facts about your competition
3. External facts
4. Internal facts

Market Segmentation, Needs Identification, and Measurement of Customer Perceptions

You may already know a great deal about your market and its segments, based on internal customer-origin analysis, your customer database, or external marketing information you purchased. To update your knowledge and make the most of your marketing expenditures, use the following nine-step process (see also Figure 17.1):

1. Identify the markets that yield the greatest number of customers (this is likely where your facilities/units are located).
2. Using the major geographic markets identified in step 1 for research sampling, determine the proper segmentation of the total market.
3. During the segmentation process, roughly determine the demographic characteristics of each segment, including the segment's approximate size and trend. With respect to "trend," you should be looking for which direction each segment is heading—Is the segment increasing or decreasing as a percentage of your business? Is the segment itself growing or declining? (Research techniques are available to more accurately and specifically determine the demographics, but the costs of extensive research may outweigh its value. An approximate demographic definition should be adequate.) Then select appropriate media to promote your product or service to these segments.
4. Evaluate the target market and submarkets in each of the demographic segments you want to reach. A national probability sample will give you a fairly accurate assessment of these trends. When you add the results of this sampling technique in your in-house demographic

data, you can project meaningful trends for your targeted segments. These will probably be sufficient for your initial efforts in strategic marketing planning.

5. Decide which segments you want to pursue and which you do not want to pursue. In making these decisions, consider such facts as these:

   - Suitability of your existing products/services to meet the needs of these segments
   - Each segment's trend—whether it is growing or shrinking
   - The profitability of the segment

   For the most part, such decisions will not change your marketing approach. However, for certain segments peripheral to your current business mix, these decisions will be very important, and you will need more information. Defer the marketing decision on whether to pursue the peripheral segments until you get a better idea of the suitability of your product/service to the defined needs of these segments.

6. Identify in detail the specific needs of each of the segments you hope to reach. Determine what factors, products, or services are most and least important to customers in each segment. Trained interviewers can glean this information from focus groups. (Step 9 helps further measure customer perceptions through focus groups.) As previously discussed, a focus group is a small representative sample of your customer base or potential customer base. The group is subjected to a structured interview or series of questions; responses are then analyzed to glean marketing information.

7. Analyze how well your existing products and services meet the needs of each segment. Does your offering fall short in providing the products or services required by each segment? Can your existing products and services be adapted to meet the needs of each segment? Remember to be objective when analyzing your own products and services. Customer perceptions of your products and services often differ from yours. At this point, you may eliminate additional segments from your potential market if your products/services don't meet the needs of the segments.

8. Identify all major companies that serve your total market. To do this, you will have to analyze the companies based in your market, the type of offices they have (i.e., corporate headquarters, regional offices, district offices, and so on), and their major suppliers/visitors and where they come from (their origin points).

9. Conduct focus group interviews with customers from each market segment to measure their perceptions of both your products/services and those of all competitors serving in the industry sector. This should be done in several steps:

   - Determine which products or services are preferred by customers in the segment. What characteristics do customers in that segment prefer? How do segment customers perceive your product? Which attributes relate best to customers in the segment and why?
   - Determine customer perceptions of other (nonpreferred) products and services. What characteristics are seen as positive and negative?
   - Determine how each product/service is perceived to meet the most important need of your segment (as identified in step 6).

   Make sure your products and/or services are considered equally with those of other competitors. You want an objective measurement of how customers in different market segments view each of their options.

   The perceptions customers have of each competitor are the result of the quality and/or operations and of advertising and promotion schemes. Likewise, the solutions to making any changes in your image will lie equally in operations and marketing.[2]

Information obtained through research may not be entirely new to you. However, information on how you compare to your competition will probably be more objective than you have ob-

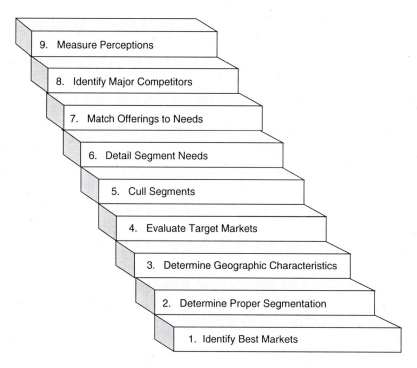

FIGURE 17.1. Summary of the Nine-Step Process for Market Segmentation, Needs Identification, and Measurement of Customer Perceptions

tained before and, therefore, should be more useful to you. For example: Where do you have real advantage over your competition? What are your weak spots? What are your competitors' weak spots? Into which new segments can you expand your market? Which segments (if any) absolutely don't want your products or services?

With the nine-step process, you have identified the following information:

- Your market's segments, as classified by needs plus rough demographics
- The size of each market segment and its growth trends—which segments are growing and which are shrinking
- The specific needs of each segment and the relative importance of these needs
- An objective measurement of how well your firm and product or service is perceived to fulfill these needs in relation to your competition
- An identification of which competitors/companies best relate to each segment and why

With this information you will be able to more accurately position your products or services in the marketplace.

Facts About the Competition

You may tend to dismiss the effects of competition on your business. However, when you ignore the competition, you may overlook several variables that affect marketing planning. Focusing solely on your present strengths is also shortsighted in situations involving increased competition, especially in a given market segment.

Although you regard all the things you do as important, consumers may not always agree with you. They often have different priorities than you. Furthermore, consumers in different segments have different priorities. Price, service level, and an overall good experience are extremely important. It is important to know how you stack up against your competitors in these areas.

To evaluate your competition, you need the following information: market share data, competitive marketing strategies and practices, and any performance statistics on data available.

Market Share Data

Market share data provide a long-range overview of how you are faring in relation to your major competitors. Often, accurate figures on the size of the total market are unavailable; however, you can get a fairly useful measurement by comparing your own figures against the total of all your major competitors or against a smaller select group of competitors. This can be accomplished on a local, regional, and national level by subscribing to and participating in various industry services, by reviewing market reports issued by industry accounting firms, and by reviewing tax records.

Competitive Marketing Strategies and Practices

Be aware of your competitors' current marketing programs when formulating your own marketing strategies. The most effective way to get information about your competitors' marketing programs is to clip all of their advertising from magazines and newspapers for a period of several months. A clipping service can do this or your advertising agency may be able to help.

It is also useful to get a fix on other media and methods for competitors' marketing activities, including the following:

- Radio and TV
- Outdoor/billboard advertising
- Direct mail
- Direct solicitation
- Trade solicitation
- Publicity
- Sales promotion

This information will be more difficult to obtain, but there may be ways to learn more about these areas. Most advertising agencies subscribe to syndicated services that supply such data. You may also obtain market information on your own from advertising sales representatives and other individuals who work for the various media outlets (magazines, radio stations, etc.).

The information you gather about competitors' marketing programs doesn't have to be precise or detailed. Try to get enough information to answer the following questions:

- What segments are your competitors pursuing?
- What are their strategies in terms of image building?
- What media or marketing methods are they using?
- How successful do their marketing programs seem to be?

After gathering this information over a period of time, you will be able to detect shifts in competitive marketing strategies.

External Facts

External data on market industry trends and sales patterns will be useful when you are ready to develop your own marketing strategies.

Trends in the Overall Market

Look for a broad overview of major segment trends, such as signs of growth or decline in different market segments and/or any other information you can obtain regarding growth trends of the other market segments. This information will be very general, but it will help you determine a marketing strategy.

Internal Facts

Marketing Expenditures

Look at your marketing costs objectively. Marketing cost should be defined as "that amount necessary to procure the sale." Using this definition, include as part of your marketing costs all of the following expenses and reductions to income:

- Salesperson salaries and administrative expenses
- Advertising expenditures
- Public relations expenditures
- Travel relations expenditures
- Coupon discounts
- Distribution systems expenses
- Credit card fees you pay to credit card companies
- Others

This definition may not conform to a uniform system of accounts, but it will give you a clearer picture of your actual marketing costs. When you combine an overview of expenditures with a trend analysis, you should be able to more objectively determine the proper allocation of funds needed to carry out the marketing strategies you develop.

Trends in Your Mix of Business

Measure trends in your sales in the following areas:

- By price
- By segment
- By location
- New versus repeat business

This information will tell you what is really happening when sales go up or down. You need to know how effective your efforts are in building business in a particular segment. When you have a decrease in sales, you need to know in what segment the problem lies so that you may take immediate, focused corrective action.

In short, trends in sales are your monitoring system—the indicator of what is happening and how effective you are in your marketing planning and execution.

ANALYSIS OF RESEARCH AND INFORMATION

The following questions identify specific areas to target in the strategic marketing program. Information needed to answer the questions will come from the market segmentation, needs identification, and customer perceptions research discussed earlier.

Customer Needs, Preferences, and Perceptions

1. Which market segments relate best to your products or services?
2. In which areas of need are your products or services perceived to be strong by current market segments? In which areas are they weak?
3. In which areas of need do your strengths (as perceived by the segment) correspond to the first priority needs of the segment?
4. In each weak area (as perceived by the market segment), are there operational factors that contribute to the perceived weakness, or is it purely an image or awareness problem? Is it a marketing problem?
5. In each market segment with which you presently best identify, who are your major competitors and what are their major strengths and weaknesses (as perceived by the segment)?
6. Are your main markets presently within the segments that best identify with your product or service or are there any areas of need in which your competition is perceived as doing a superior job?
7. Which market segments relate least to your product or service? Is this a result of your past marketing programs being focused in other directions, or does it stem from an inaccurate or inadequate awareness of the product or service itself?
8. In each market segment where you see an opportunity to broaden your market, who are your major competitors and what are their major strengths and weaknesses (as perceived by the segment)?

Competitive Trends

1. How has your business fared against competitive businesses in recent years?
2. What are the primary marketing directions of your major competitors?
3. What are the major competitive threats facing your business now and in the near future?

Immediate Problems

What are the immediate problems that must be corrected this year? The following list suggests examples of problems that must be addressed immediately:

1. Sales problems at specific units or locations
2. Declining business volumes in particular market segments
3. Quality and service problems
4. Pricing problems
5. New competitors that are expected to have an adverse effect on a particular market
6. Existing marketing strategies that are unsuccessful

Long-Range Major Problems

What are the major marketing problems you face that must be solved to achieve greater success over the next five years? For example:

1. Change of image required
2. Industry-wide declining business volumes in particular market segments
3. Increasing success of a particular competitor as a result of design, quality and service, marketing, in overall results, or in combinations of these items
4. Changes in preferences and needs of a particular market segment
5. Pricing
6. Adverse trends or yields in marketing expenditures

Opportunities and Alternatives

1. What are the major weaknesses of your competitors that you would exploit more fully?
2. What unsatisfied needs have been identified in your present market segments? Is it possible to provide a service or product that will satisfy these needs?
3. What market segments peripheral to your current marketing thrust offer opportunities for you to broaden your market?

THE STRATEGIC MARKETING PLAN

The following list provides an overview of the total marketing plan:

- Analysis of research and information
- Objectives
- Marketing program
- Marketing appropriations (the marketing budget)
- Sales goals
- Action programs
- Communication of assigned responsibilities
- Monitoring of action program

Now that you have examined the first part of the total marketing plan structure (your business review), asked the right questions, and obtained factual answers, you can start the actual strategic marketing plan.

In the strategic marketing plan, you analyze what you have learned about your business and translate it into action programs. By combining all of your research into one document, you force yourself to see

- how (and whether) everything you are doing actually fits together;
- whether it is logical and sound;
- whether, in total, it is possible to accomplish with the manpower and money available.

You also clearly establish guidelines for handling day-to-day matters in a manner consistent with your longer-range objectives.

Objectives

What are the overall objectives of your marketing program? These objectives should be determined on the basis of your research and information analysis. Objectives should correspond to the following areas:

- Identification of customer preferences and the desire to change customers' perceptions of your product or service
- Changes in marketing direction desired after comparing your present markets with shifts in the total market
- Defensive and offensive marketing moves dictated by competitive successes and new competitive directions
- Immediate problem solving
- Long-range problem solving
- Taking advantage of opportunities to grow and expand

In order to make the marketing program as effective as possible, restrict the number of marketing objectives to the major items of the highest priority.

The whole purpose of marketing planning is to separate the wheat from the chaff and to focus on those areas that will yield the greatest results. Attempting to focus on everything will result in more work, greater expenditures, minimal results, and frustration for all. By separating priority from nonpriority objectives, you can achieve positive results; hence, it is desirable to limit the number of objectives you establish.

Marketing Program

This section suggests an approach to developing your total marketing program for the next several years, with emphasis on the first year. This section, like the whole marketing plan, should be updated each year.

Overall Strategy

First, state the proposition. That is, define, in general terms, what you are trying to provide and sell to your markets. The proposition should be the promise that can be made to have the strongest appeal to the customers' self-interests. It should be based on the information gathered during the research steps of this marketing planning process. It must be truthful, possible to achieve, and unique. It must clearly distinguish you over the competition.

You may need a different proposition for each market segment. If so, make sure there are no inconsistencies among the propositions.

Next, clarify the platform. Your marketing platform is the list of benefits to the customer and advantages over the competition that your property provides. Spell out, item by item, all the claims you plan to make to your customers. This is not another general statement; it includes the details that support the proposition. Your promotion and advertising will be based on the platform.

Media Strategy

Use your established objectives to identify precise target markets to which to aim the media. Establish specific advertising, public relations, and direct mail programs, and clearly determine the intent of the program, media selection, dates, and dollars for each.

Each of the advertising, public relations, and direct mail programs should be compared with previous media programs. Program changes should be made on the basis of how the new program will achieve the desired objectives and results better than did the old program. Also, compare your media programs to those of your competitors and address any obvious deficiencies.

Selling Strategy

Specific strategies should be developed for sales and promotion to each market segment. Development of selling strategies must be accomplished at two levels:

- Identify activities that will be carried out by your national sales departments' marketing staffs. Also, identify overall sales strategies to be implemented by segment and product/service offering.

- Develop specific sales targets and strategies for each location, unit, etc. Again, identify a few major strategies rather than attempting all the possible ways of building sales.

Compare these sales strategies with competitors' sales programs and correct any obvious deficiencies. Strategies should also be compared with previous strategies to determine whether there are sufficient differences to achieve your desired changes.

You must also identify new staffing requirements and the difference in cost from the preceding programs.

Changes in Operations

Identify the changes in operations or procedures required to achieve the desired marketing objectives and establish timing costs.

Marketing Appropriations

Amount

Determine how much funding is needed to achieve the agreed-upon marketing objectives and supporting programs. What is the difference between the amount needed and available funds? Ultimately, a final amount should be determined. If incremental funding is used, keep in mind that there should be an expected offset in incremental revenue.

Allocation

Determine the allocation of available funds among the various functions of marketing: advertising, publicity, sales force, travel agents' commissions, discount coupons, preopening campaigns, and research. Use zero-base budgeting, wherein all expenditures must be fully analyzed and their justifications verified each year. This approach may help in reallocating resources from year to year into areas where they will do the most good.

Since there rarely will be sufficient funds available to execute all the programs needed, available funds should be apportioned according to costs and benefits.

Justification

The justification for the marketing budget is the research and analysis you conduct. If you have approached the marketing planning process in an analytical and pragmatic way, then you will have a strong argument for your budget. If management does not allocate sufficient funds to achieve the necessary results, or if these funds are not efficiently spent, then you must accept something less than the desired objectives.

Sales Goals

Sales goals can be both macro and micro in nature, but they should always be quantified. You may be looking at a sales increase measured in dollars, or you may want to increase your sales percentage as measured against the entire product or service line average. The following is a list of questions that can help you identify sales goals:

1. What is the total sales goal for all products and services? This may be expressed as revenue or in terms of a percentage increase.
2. What is the revenue per available outlet, unit, or whatever is your best measure?

3. What is the average sales goal for all units?
4. What are the average price rate increases for all properties?
5. What are the goals for sales in each major business segment? Determine the percent for each segment.
6. How much additional sales will be generated this year (over last year) for the increase in marketing expenditures over those of last year? Estimate the increase in dollars.

Action Programs

List, in chronological order, all the specific strategies that were allocated available marketing funds. Identify specific target dates, budget-approved expenditures, and responsibility. Figure 17.2 shows one way of organizing this information.

Monitoring of Action Program

To properly monitor progress on the action program, institute an adequate follow-up process. The following section of this chapter presents a simple worksheet to help you allocate the marketing budget by expenditure and by market segment (see Sample Strategic Marketing Budget Plan Summation). The worksheet can be modified and applied at the individual unit level.

The first attempt at completing a strategic marketing planning process of this nature is always the most difficult. Updating and scheduling periodic research will provide you with an ongoing flow of relevant and applicable information. You must be careful to make sound judgments at stages before the research is completed. However, depending on management's judgment, knowledge, and expertise, some of the data may have immediate application and be beneficial to your marketing program.

A SAMPLE STRATEGIC MARKETING PLAN

Up to this point the focus has been on multiple research methodologies, assessing focal points, and providing the rationale for actual strategy selection. Parameters for competitive and environmental research were provided. Key concepts such as positioning, brand strategy, and target markets were also defined.

Now the focus shifts to the structure and content of the "strategic marketing plan" from an organizational perspective. Where applicable, definitions and samples of each section or component of a strategic marketing plan are provided. These examples will be "generic" (you can fill in your business or change the content to suit your individual case). Let us begin with the first section or topical area in a strategic marketing plan, the "preface."

Item	Target Date	Approved Expenditures	Responsibility
Media Plan			
Selling Plan			

FIGURE 17.2. Marketing Program Organization Chart

The Preface

The first step in the marketing plan is the preface, which is an introductory statement that briefly delineates what the document is all about or what to expect. Let's look now at a sample preface.

Sample Preface

This strategic marketing plan contains many recommendations from a mission statement to specific tactics that provide both generators of revenue and product/positioning improvements. Its focus is strategic, covering the next one to three years with respect to the overall market, as well as tactical, in that it addresses more immediate action steps to increase returns in the current and subsequent fiscal years. The strategic and tactical elements should be viewed as interlinked, and, to a large extent, they are by-products of each other.

Overall, the strategies and tactics, while seeking to generate revenue, are based on the premise of improving market share by selling more to existing customers and creating new demand. The environmental and competitive assessment highlights the strengths, weaknesses, opportunities, and threats. The mission statement suggests an overall vision that, once agreed upon, should be the focal point upon which future actions are based.

Finally, this strategic marketing plan is realistic in its application of resources, focus, and recommended action steps. It suggests specific ways to achieve the goals and objectives either from an operation and manpower methodology or a resource allocation perspective. It strongly urges coordination, cooperation, and communication to support the achievement of the mission.

Executive Summary

Following the preface, the written plan should move on to the executive summary. This is the key to presenting, communicating, and convincing ownership, investors, shareholders, and stakeholders to pay attention and to read on. The executive summary should articulate the organization's mission statement, goals and objectives, strategies and tactics, as well as address issues and highlight the planning document's recommendations. Let's examine a typical executive summary.

Sample Executive Summary

An environmental and competitive assessment of the strengths, weaknesses, opportunities, and threats reveals a crossroads in terms of the market. The overall ingredients for success are based in the assets of the brands, yet the accumulation of weaknesses and threats can disrupt the status quo. A major downturn in sales and the incremental deterioration of the distribution infrastructure are potential and real threats.

In summary, we are at that 50 to 60 percent threshold, where we can secure our position, "change and rejuvenate" the distribution system, or we can struggle to maintain the current status quo. The recommendations contained in this marketing plan focus on the former option.

At this point in time, and for the duration of the plan's three-year period, the following mission statement is appropriate: "To become the industry leader known for product innovation, extraordinary customer service, and the best value in the marketplace."

Strategic marketing, infrastructure improvements, and new product development need to be targeted with action plans to offset pending market and related economic declines. A reasonable goal to strive for is a 7 to 10 percent annual growth, measured in revenues, during the planning period.

Five objectives have been identified to address this goal:

1. Enhance the overall product/offering, both quantitatively and perceptually.
2. Develop the infrastructure (including a new distribution system) to be customer friendly and to increase repeat purchases.
3. Broaden the customer base while providing for new revenues.
4. Maximize resources for strategic marketing.
5. Improve communications to all audiences, including current customers, suppliers, distributors, investors, and employees.

In order to achieve these objectives, three primary driving forces need to be addressed in the focal points of the strategy:

1. Enhance the perceptions of our existing brands.
2. Identify and select new pricing strategies and cooperative selling opportunities.
3. Accelerate the number of new products developed and shorten the development cycle.

To address these driving forces, this plan suggests the full use of all marketing weaponry—promotions, advertising, cooperatives, sales, events, and public relations—to work in synergy with the overall goal of revenue generation. Related strategies and tactics for each category of weaponry are suggested within the plan.

Further, the objectives are supported with over forty specific recommendations; some require immediate attention, and others are to be implemented during the planning period. Also presented are the budget-planning approaches. Highlights from these recommendations include the following:

- Selecting a vision or theme for the future (two are suggested for selection)
- Optional packaging concepts to immediately improve the first impression for all brands
- Potential development concepts to provide additional attractive new brands, while broadening the customer base
- Infrastructure improvements to increase the movement of products to the market
- Utilization of a full-service advertising agency and public relations agency
- A promotions and events calendar
- A public relations and communications strategy
- A specific cooperative opportunity

This marketing plan strongly urges development of a new image through the selection and communication of a vision or theme. Two such themes and appropriate supporting slogans are presented for discussion.

Six primary issues emerge for decision making: (1) the need for a full-time marketing function or an advertising and public relations agency; (2) the selection of a new vision or theme; (3) the need for new product development; (4) an immediate plan for infrastructure and product-to-market delivery improvements; (5) changing visual perceptions and improving communications; and (6) consideration of a 7 percent versus a 5 percent budget increase.

Acting on the recommendations, reallocating budget expenditures, and the resolution of the previous issues should result in a measurable increase in revenues of 7 to 10 percent on an annual basis.

Competitive and Environmental Assessment

A section usually located in the beginning of the planning document is the competitive and environmental assessment. This step provides a realistic assessment of the business's strengths and weaknesses and its surrounding opportunities and threats (commonly referred to as the SWOT analysis) and then takes a close look at its competition. A strength is an asset or a resource of your business that can be used to improve its competitive position, such as strong brand equity, a new product, or a strong distribution system. A weakness is just the opposite—a deteriorating resource or lack of capability that may cause your business to have a less competitive position, which can adversely affect market share. For instance, an antiquated distribution system and lack of a major market are categorized as weaknesses. Opportunities are developed from a business's or brand's strengths, or set of positive circumstances, and can include superior products, high awareness levels, or the opportunity for unique products within your category. Threats are viewed as problems that focus on your weaknesses and which can create a potentially negative situation. Depressed wholesaler activity and a new competitor with substantial financial resources are examples of threats.

Your business/brand marketing plan strategies should be based on a realistic assessment of your operating environment and competitive position. This assessment should include a factual SWOT (strengths, weaknesses, opportunities, and threats) analysis that is both objective and subjective in nature. The perspective should also include looking around at your competition, looking within at the business itself, and looking ahead to the next one to three years.

Sample Competitive and Environmental Assessment

Strengths:

- Excellent brand equity/reputation
- Market share leadership
- Breadth of product line
- Retailer relationships
- Superior sales force

Weaknesses:

- Major brands losing share
- Competitors increasing with each new product
- "Generics" undercutting margins
- Distribution system too slow/cumbersome

Opportunities:

- Capitalize on retailer relationships to launch new product
- Give sales force more product lines to sell
- Develop state-of-the-art distribution system or acquire competitor with one
- Retake market share through short-term aggressive lowest price strategy

Threats:

- Projected major economic downturn
- External distribution system deteriorating
- New costly proposed government regulations
- Acquisition of major competitor by cash-rich corporation
- New products with superior qualities

Summary and Assessment: Our brands/reputation provide us a base of strength and opportunity to take greater market share by pricing and new product introductions. Replacing the distribution system is critical to remain competitive.

The Mission Statement

The core of the actual marketing planning document begins with the mission statement, which is a concise narrative statement summarizing your organization's objectives and ultimate goals. It provides a clear direction for everyone working in your organization, serves as a basis for communication, asserts a philosophy for doing business, and provides a basis for evaluating your organization. In essence, a mission statement outlines why you are in business.

A mission statement represents the end result of your objectives as well as the achievement of your ultimate goals, while defining what your organization is all about. Once agreed upon, it becomes the benchmark against which all strategies and human and financial resource allocations are measured. Furthermore, a mission statement is a communications vehicle, whose purpose is to be clear, concise, and directional while focusing on the planning period as well as the future. A mission statement is ultimately the end product of the leadership of your organization.[3] Let's now view a sample mission statement.

Sample Mission Statement

"To become the industry leader known for product innovation, extraordinary customer service, and the best 'value' in the marketplace."

Goals and Objectives

The next step, which immediately follows the mission statement, is the section titled goals and objectives. Goals are both qualitative and quantitative, which means that they are comprised of both data-based estimates and educated guesses, although realistic estimates are preferred. Objectives outline "what" needs to be accomplished during the time frame of the plan. They must be specific, measurable in a quantifiable manner, related to a specific time period, and focused on affecting the behavior of your market. Although the overall goal is the fulfillment of your mission statement, a very specific and quantifiable goal could be exemplified as in the following sample.

Sample Goal and Objectives

Goal: To seek to offset pending economic declines (as a minimum target) with the achievement of actual growth through new product introduction producing an annualized rate of (up to) 10 percent incremental revenue growth during the plan's duration.

Reaching this goal would be based upon the achievement of the following primary objectives:

1. Enhance the overall product offering both quantitatively and perceptually.
2. Broaden the customer base by providing new products.
3. Redevelop a new distribution infrastructure to be user friendly and maximize marketing resources to facilitate repeat business.
4. Increase market share by 5 percent.
5. Improve communications to all audiences, including current customers, suppliers, distributors, investors, and employees.

Each of these primary objectives is supported with a set of strategies and tactics for their implementation in the strategy section of this plan.

Driving Forces

It is important to recognize that three major driving forces are of such magnitude that they need to be discussed individually from the strategic issues. These driving forces, although interrelated to a large degree, should be viewed both individually and collectively as they support your business's objectives and strategies.[4] Let's look now at a sample presentation of these forces.

Sample Driving Forces

Driving force #1—Perception. We are clearly positioning as the current "value" leader in terms of quality product at a fair price. Our brands and sales force are perceived as the finest in the industry. Our overall perception by customers and competitors is one of leadership. We need to reinforce this perception or lose this advantage.

Driving force #2—Pricing. Our pricing strategies have made us the most attractive company to deal with and provided us with great sales advantages. Supported by our lower cost structure and quality product we have been able to take the number one market share position in most product/brand categories. We will need to capitalize on this and be even more aggressive to thwart new competition and maintain share in the opening economic downturn.

Driving force #3—New product development. Our competitors and customers know us as the new product innovator. Our ability to develop and launch new products ahead of the competition is threatened only by the many new specialty product upstarts and our deteriorating distribution system. We can protect this driving force by rapid implementation of the new/proposed distribution system and accelerated schedule of new product launches.

Strategies and Tactics

The next step of the strategic marketing plan focuses on "how" the goals and objectives as previously outlined will now be achieved. This section is called the strategies and tactics section of the planning process. Strategies simply detail "how" the plan's objectives will be achieved. Tactics are the "detailed items" related to the strategies.

Note in the following "sample" strategies and tactics the use of different marketing weapons, that is, brand strategies, packaging, public relations, database and electronic marketing, promotions, pricing, sales, co-ops, etc. Also, note how one objective is supported by multiple marketing weaponry working in concert with each other.

Sample Strategies and Tactics

Reference: Objective #1—enhance overall product offering quantitatively and perceptually.

Supporting strategies:

- Launch all brand extensions in the next eighteen months.
- Introduce one new product per quarter.
- Implement the new package and signage designs over the next six months.

Tactics:

- Begin brand extensions on West Coast first.
- Introduce first new product in New York for media proximity and coverage.
- Unveil new signage designs at new unit opening in Chicago during franchise convention.

Reference: Objective #2—develop a new distribution infrastructure to be user friendly and facilitate repeat purchases.

Supporting strategies:

- Design the new system to allow online customers access for order tracking.
- Increase the discount percentages for multiple-term contracts.
- Launch a new frequent purchaser incentive rewards program.

Tactics:

- Provide major (category 1) customers with complementary software at time of system implementation (co-op with vendor).
- Run sales contest when discounts are announced.
- Unveil at franchise/distributor show.

Reference: Objective #3—broaden the customer base while providing for new revenues.

Supporting strategies:

- Expand the database list program and electronic marketing efforts.
- Launch new advertising campaign at twice the GRPs (gross rating points).
- Implement a new more aggressive promotions calendar.
- Expand the sales coverage into Canada and Mexico.

Tactics:

- Mail new prospects special introductory offers.
- Purchase incremental prime-time network television.
- Increase the number of promotions and include minimum of three trial offers during the cycle.
- Lease offices by December 1 and have fully staffed by March 1.

Program Plans

In some cases, an objective and related strategy may be of such magnitude or so extraordinary in nature that a separate detailed "program plan" or "action plan" is delineated within the actual body of the strategic marketing plan, incorporated in the appendix, or provided as a separate document (even though summarized in the strategic marketing plan). In our "generic" examples the new distribution system might be meritorious of this type of treatment.

Certainly it is appropriate to include items such as the media plan, the promotions calendar, new packaging, new pricing strategies, etc. These may also be included within the "program plans" section or in tabled appendixes.

Recommendations

Now that the strategic marketing plan detail has been outlined, it is time to provide specific recommendations for both short- and long-term perspectives. Typically, these recommendations are related to the objectives previously detailed in the goals and objectives section of the plan. This interrelationship between the recommendations and objectives should permeate daily decisions and actions in a manner consistent with the long-term success of the overall strategy. Once the necessary decisions are made, specific action takes place. Let's now look at some sample recommendations.

Sample Recommendations

- To enhance the overall product offering we recommend the acquisition of a new line of products (brand X and/or company Y). This will also help us quickly broaden our customer base (supports objectives #1 and #3).
- Immediate reallocation of an additional $5.0 million to expedite the implementation of the new distribution system (supports objective #2).
- Retain our outside design expertise to refresh all packing, brands, and corporate logo (supports objectives #1 and #5).
- Establish a new "communications" function to oversee all communications functions and coordinate all efforts including the newly proposed "customer friendly" order/distribution system communications (supports objectives #1, #2, #4, and #5).

The Vision

In many strategic marketing plans, a section outlining the company's vision is often included. The "vision" is a statement that vividly describes the desired outcome of the overall strategic plan. Often the section including the company's vision will present alternative scenarios for its future while providing both direction and purpose for its interim strategies and activities. Let's review a sample "vision" statement.

Sample Vision Statements

- "To be viewed as the industry leader by customers, investors, employees, and shareholders as a result of our innovative products, service-oriented employees, and strong financial performance."
- "To achieve preeminence as the industry leader through award-winning customer service, flawless product quality and delivery, and dedicated personnel worldwide."

Slogans

In many business or corporate strategic marketing plans, a company's mission, vision, goals, and objectives become reflected in slogans. Slogans help build identity and can convey a company's position in the marketplace, which is demonstrated by examples such as "Quality IS Job Number One" or "Innovation Through Investigation." Slogans can also be created and associated with marketing campaigns. Ultimately, a slogan becomes an image with which almost everyone—current and potential customers—can identify. Let's now take a look at some sample slogans.

Sample Slogans

- "Leadership Through Innovation"
- "The Quality/Value Leader"
- "Beyond Expectations"
- "Customer Driven Product Excellence"
- "The Company of Tomorrow"

Issues

In the process of undertaking any strategic marketing plan, several issues will surface. It is recommended that these issues be collected during the planning process and set aside for appropriate discussion at the end of the actual plan. Although some issues may resolve themselves during the planning process, others may divert the process or cause delays. Addressing the issues at the end of the plan enables the company to put the issues into perspective in relation to the plan in its entirety. Let's look at some sample issues.

Sample Issues

- Currently, 25 percent of brands (units, etc.) are in the decline phase of their life cycle and 35 percent are projected to be in thirty-six months. Do we sell or rejuvenate?
- Our top three leading brands/products are not doing well against the biggest newly emerging market.
- Competitors' new products are taking major market share.
- We are "underpenetrated" (not enough stores/outlets) in three major markets and "overpenetrated" (too many stores/outlets) in three other markets.
- We lack presence in Mexican and Canadian markets.
- Our antiquated technology system in distribution is hurting sales and customer relations.

Measurements and Results

In order to ensure success, all of the activities within a strategic marketing plan need to be measurable. This can be achieved in two ways—either the expected results are specific and quantifiable or they are related to key dates, milestones, or timetables. Likewise, qualitative accomplishments can be measured within time parameters or other established criteria, including polls, image assessments, or opinion surveys. Specifying these expectations is critical in determining which goals are being achieved and, as a result, whether strategies need to be modified. Let's review some sample key measurements and results.

Sample Key Measurements and Results

- Increase product/brand offerings by 20 percent during the planning period.
- Reverse the downtrend in the CSI (customer service index) and bring it back up to the 90 percent level by December 1.
- Have the new distribution system up and running (within budget) by June 1.
- Open the Mexico City, Toronto, and Vancouver sales centers by March 1.
- Consummate two cooperative product-marketing agreements—one by March 1 and the second by April 1.

- Review brand awareness levels after the new advertising campaign has run six weeks to ascertain whether the 15 percent increase has been achieved against the target markets segment.

Budget

A key component of any plan is the budget plan, as it may often seem that there are never enough marketing dollars available for the execution of the plan. Although strategic marketing plans may offer a means for measuring various targets, such as increasing the revenue from 7 to 10 percent, the achievement of these goals is contingent upon budget allocations and meeting revenue goals to fund future objectives. Thus, it is first necessary to determine the plan's priorities and the costs associated with their execution. Then comes the balancing act—weighing what needs to be accomplished with what is affordable.

In a strategic context, numerous scenarios or options may be selected, and each can be interlinked with existing and new marketing strategies. For example, "If we exceed our revenue growth goal of 10 percent in year one, we will move to option #2, increase the budget, and accelerate the new product development."

The budget plan should be prepared by using a summation format and any desired (significant) calendars (promotions/events) and any "special" program plans. The following is a sample overview of a marketing budget plan summation, including sample promotions and events calendars. All examples are theoretical/generic for exhibit purposes.

Sample Strategic Marketing Plan Budget Overview

This $31.0 million budget* is designed to achieve a 10 percent annualized growth in revenues during the planning period. The budget is premised upon the on-time introductions of all new products and the projected slow downturn in economic conditions. Key objectives and strategies supported include the following:

- Achieving annualized revenue growth of 10 percent
- Adding 1.2 million purchases from new customers
- Increasing unaided brand awareness by 10 points
- The successful launch of six new products and achievement of each of their year-one targeted revenue and sales objectives
- Launch of a new frequent buyer's promotion in conjunction with the launch of the new distribution system
- Development and implementation of an entirely new Internet site with linkages to the new customer-oriented distribution system

The budget plan has taken into consideration the changes in pricing strategy, new packaging, and product introduction. It is in line with industry sector and competitive spending ratios. We do, however, recommend consideration be given to option #2 presented in the appendix, which we believe would accelerate revenue growth by an incremental 10 percent annually, with an incremental spending level of $2.0 million or 4 to 6 percent.

---

*This represents an 8.5 percent increase over the previous year; however, it incorporates the six new product launches and new packaging costs.

Sample Strategic Marketing Budget Plan Summation

OPTION #1*—YEAR 1

Weapon/Tool	$(M)	% of Total	% Change
Advertising			
Media	$10.0	32.3	10
Production	1.5	4.8	(2)
Promotions	7.5	24.2	5
Merchandising	1.0	3.3	—
Sales	5.0	16.0	8
Events	1.0	3.3	1
Direct Mail	1.5	4.8	5
Electronic	1.5	4.8	12
Packaging	.5	1.6	6
Research	.5	1.6	(12)
Miscellaneous	1.0	3.3	(15)
TOTAL	$31.0	100	8.5

A "promotions" calendar (see Figure 17.3) and "events" calendar (see Figure 17.4) follow.

The Appendix

The final section of a strategic marketing plan is the appendix. Although appendixes are often included within the original document, it is suggested here that relevant statistical data and research findings be presented in an accompanying volume. This will ensure that the marketing plan remains an action document and is not weighted down with excessive numbers and data. A sample of items that form an appendix follow.

Sample Appendix Table of Contents

   I. Optional Budget Plans at Incremental and/or Reduced Levels
  II. Marketing Budget Review Chart—Historical Trends
 III. Research Findings Which Support or Negate Strategies
 IV. Distribution of Marketing Dollars by Weaponry (Detailed)
  V. Detailed Promotional Calendar
 VI. Detailed Current Customer Trends
VII. Information on Potential Co-Op Partners
VII. Other Data: New Logos, Package Designs, etc.

---

*Incremental marketing expenditure options are contained in the appendix.

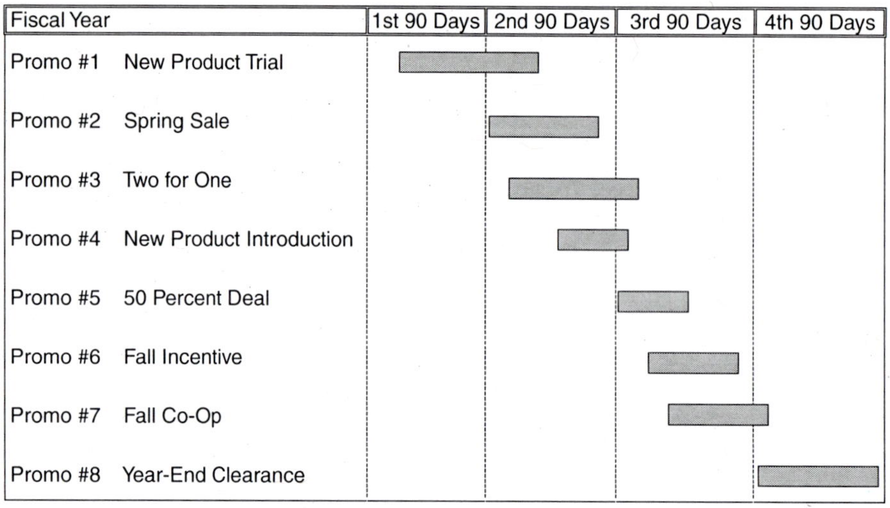
Fiscal Year
1st 90 Days
2nd 90 Days
3rd 90 Days
4th 90 Days
Promo #1 New Product Trial
Promo #2 Spring Sale
Promo #3 Two for One
Promo #4 New Product Introduction
Promo #5 50 Percent Deal
Promo #6 Fall Incentive
Promo #7 Fall Co-Op
Promo #8 Year-End Clearance

FIGURE 17.3. Sample Promotions Calendar

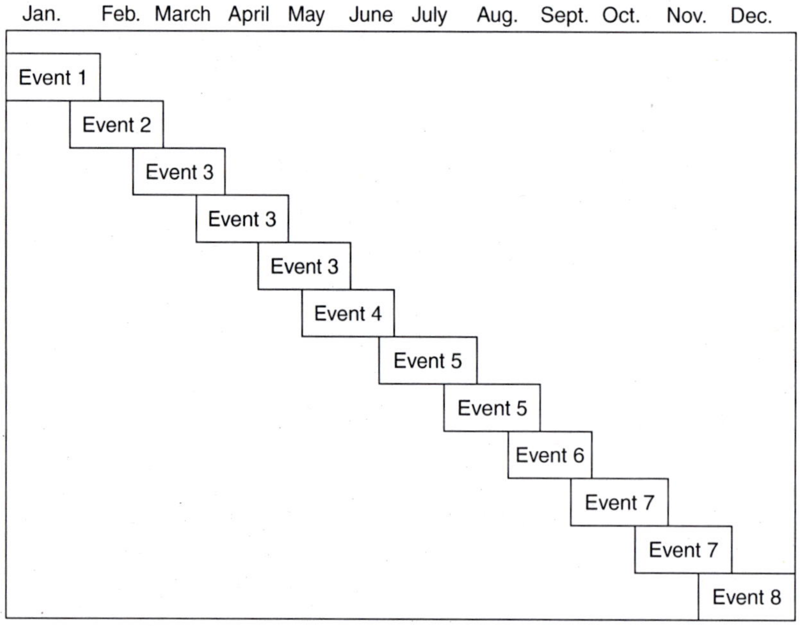
Jan. Feb. March April May June July Aug. Sept. Oct. Nov. Dec.
Event 1
Event 2
Event 3
Event 3
Event 3
Event 4
Event 5
Event 5
Event 6
Event 7
Event 7
Event 8

1. Super Bowl related
2. Winter related
3. Spring related
4. New product related
5. Summer related
6. Fall kick-off related
7. Holidays related
8. Year-end related

FIGURE 17.4. Events Calendar

CHAPTER REVIEW

This chapter related the steps and results of the business review process to the development of a strategic marketing plan. The importance of market segmentation, needs identification, and measurements of customer perceptions were discussed. Further, the significance of assessing and analyzing key competitors and external and internal facts as an important step in the preparation of a strategic marketing plan was pointed out. Key questions to be answered as part of the initial research information-gathering criteria were suggested. Finally, a sample strategic marketing plan (in generic format) was presented. As part of the process we covered the concept of zero-base budgeting, which infers that marketing strategy priorities be identified and funds allocated each time the strategic marketing plan is prepared versus budgeting based on the previous years' expenditures.

KEY CONCEPTS/TERMS

Action program
Competition
Consumer needs
Customer perceptions
Driving forces
Focus group
Growth rate
Market segment
Marketing planning
Milestones
Mission statement
Objectives
Strategy
Zero-base budgeting

DISCUSSION QUESTIONS

1. Why is it important to know as much as possible about your competitors?
2. What are the three ways market segment information might affect your strategies?
3. Why is a mission statement important and why should it be widely communicated to all constituencies?
4. Select a company and discuss what you believe are key driving forces.
5. Why is linking objectives and strategies important in a strategic marketing plan?
6. Why is it important to isolate issues for discussion at the end of the plan?
7. How many areas can you identify where a business review might impact strategic selection?

CASE 17.1. CONTINENTAL AIRLINES

This chapter pointed out that for a strategic plan to be successful it must be championed by the company leadership as well as extensively communicated to all constituencies. There is perhaps no better example of both of the aforementioned factors than that of Continental Airlines' "Go Forward Plan" (see Exhibit 17.1). Briefly looking at the airline's history will help place the extraordinary success of this strategic plan into perspective.

From its humble beginnings in the 1930s as Varney Speed Lines to the multibillion-dollar corporation of today, Continental Airlines has had an interesting and somewhat volatile history.

Throughout its history, Continental has had its share of ups and downs. It has merged or consolidated with several airlines to become the third largest airline in the United States. The company has had to reorganize during Chapter 11 bankruptcies. It has gone from being one of the worst airlines to one of the best, and it has won numerous awards for being the best in the industry. Continental has also supported war efforts by modifying military aircraft and transporting deploying U.S. service personnel.

In the past decade, Continental Airlines has changed its CEO and its corporate culture. It has gone from a company where employees were embarrassed to be associated with the brand, to a company that is considered one of the top 100 companies to work for.

This case example will focus on Continental Airlines' history, Gordon Bethune's Go Forward Plan, and how that strategic plan changed the airline.

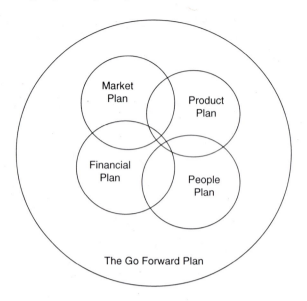

EXHIBIT 17.1. Continental Airlines—Components of the Go Forward Plan

Historical Highlights

Walter T. Varney and his partner Louis Mueller founded Varney Speed Lines, the precursor to Continental Airlines, over sixty years ago. On July 15, 1934, Varney Speed Lines flew their first flight, a 530-mile route from Pueblo, Colorado, to El Paso, Texas, with stops in Las Vegas, Nevada, and Santa Fe and Albuquerque, New Mexico. That same year, Varney ceded control to Mueller. Two years later, Mueller sold 40 percent of the new company to Robert F. Six, who led the company for more than forty years. On July 1, 1937, Robert F. Six changed the company's name to Continental Airlines and moved its headquarters from El Paso to Denver.

During World War II, many U.S. companies found themselves focusing on government contracts and assisting in the war effort. At this time, Continental Airlines built the Denver Modification Center where it modified B-17 Flying Fortresses and B-29 Super Fortresses for the U.S. war effort.

On December 10, 1953, Continental signed a merger agreement with Pioneer Airlines that added sixteen new cities in Texas and New Mexico to its growing route map. And in 1959, Continental's first true jet flight (a Boeing 707-120) took place.

Continental moved its headquarters to Los Angeles in 1963. During the Vietnam War, Continental transported U.S. troops to the Orient. And Continental's Pacific experience during the war led to the formation of Air Micronesia. Its first flight covered more than 4,000 miles from Saipan to Honolulu. In 1969, the first Continental Mainland-Hawaii service began.

Continental's route map underwent significant growth in the 1970s. In August 1976, the Civil Aviation Bureau awarded Air Micronesia with routes between Saipan and Japan. For Continental, the most significant expansion was President Carter's approval of a new route from Los Angeles to New Zealand and Australia in 1977.

In 1982, the airline merged with Texas International led by Frank Lorenzo (retaining the Continental name), offering service to four continents (North and South America, Asia, and Australia) with a fleet of 112 aircraft.

The 1978 airline industry deregulation turned the 1980s into a decade of turbulence for Continental. In 1983, Continental filed to reorganize under Chapter 11 of the Federal Bankruptcy Code. Rebuilding the company began immediately and by the end of 1984, Continental recorded a $50 million profit. In 1986, Continental emerged from Chapter 11, and then became the third largest U.S. airline with the consolidation of Frontier, People Express, and New York Air.

In 1987, the One Pass Frequent Flyer Program was created. And in 1988, Continental Airlines formed their first global alliance with Scandinavian Airline Systems (SAS).

The 1990s remained unstable as Frank Lorenzo's disassociation from Continental began when he sold most of his direct and indirect investments in the airline during the summer of 1990. In late 1990, rising fuel costs due to the Iraqi invasion of Kuwait led to Continental's second bankruptcy filing.

In February 1991, Continental unveiled its new blue and gray identity. It introduced a new logo and color scheme that symbolized the airline's real and growing potential to link the countries of the globe together. In 1992, Continental launched the award-winning Business First service on transoceanic flights. In November 1992, Air Partners/Air Canada invested $450 million in Continental, leading to Continental's second bankruptcy emergence in April 1993.

In early 1995, Continental's CEO Gordon Bethune unveiled his four-point strategic Go Forward Plan designed to improve Continental's operational performance and working environment for employees and achieve sustained profitability. During this year, Continental Airlines was recognized twice as being number one out of the ten largest U.S. airlines for its domestic on-time performance.

In July 1995, Continental announced the largest quarterly profit in its history. At the end of this year, *Business Week Magazine* named Continental the Best NYSE stock for the year. Continental's Class B Common Stock had risen from a low of $6.50 per share in early January to a high of $47.50 in December. Continental closed out 1995 with the largest annual profit in its sixty-one-year history ($224 million).

In addition, during the fourth quarter of 1995, the airline ranked first in on-time performance and baggage handling and second in least complaints. In 1997, Continental became the first airline ever to receive back-to-back J. D. Power Awards for Best Airline on flights of 500 miles or more. The same year, the airline had a record annual profit of $640 million, and it announced a plan to consolidate Houston Headquarters into downtown Houston—Continental Center.

In late 1998, Continental Airlines and Northwest Airlines formally announced their alliance to enhance competition and improve consumer travel options. The alliance created a fourth major U.S. airline network competitive with "The Big Three" U.S.-based airlines.

In 1999, Continental launched daily nonstop service from Houston to Tokyo, Japan. This was the first nonstop flight from Houston to Asia. The same year, Gordon Bethune was named as one of the fifty best CEOs in America by *Worth* magazine. Continental Airlines and America West Airlines became the first two U.S. airlines to implement interline e-ticketing. And it started implementing its Customer First program and fine-tuned customer service policies, established new functions, and provided training to thousands of staff.

In 2000, Continental Airlines was ranked as the nation's number one airline in customer satisfaction for both short-distance and long-distance flights in an independent study conducted by *Frequent Flyer* magazine in conjunction with J. D. Power and Associates. Continental won Best Short Haul Executive/Business Class and Best Frequent Flyer Program. In September 2000, Continental Airlines ranked as the number one innovative user of information technology among all airlines, according to the released *InformationWeek* 500 list.

On January 22, 2001, Continental Airlines celebrated its independence. In April, Continental Airlines' One Pass Frequent Flyer Program garnered four top Freddie Awards, including "Program of the Year" and "Best Elite-Level Program," during *Inside Flyer*'s thirteenth Annual Freddie Awards ceremony. The One Pass program also received the "Best Award" in recognition of reduced miles from the United States to Latin America, as well as "Best Web Site" for 2000.

The Go Forward Plan

In 1994, Continental was the worst airline among the ten largest players in the airline industry, according to the U.S. Department of Transportation's statistics. From 1994 to 2001, Gordon Bethune, the CEO of the company, not only turned around the company but also established a culture by implementing the Go Forward Plan. This plan touched four key strategic elements of the business: market, finance, product, and people.

Market Strategy

Bethune and his team set up a goal for the Go Forward Plan: to make Continental *fly to win* by

- determining the target market;
- fitting the product to market by effective pricing and positioning strategy;
- making the product accessible to the customers.

First, Continental eliminated 18 percent of the routes that did not generate a profit to the company and concentrated on its market strength. Then, it cut back flights between small cities and the low-cost airline—Continental Lite. Meanwhile, the company increased flights out of the hubs including Houston, Cleveland, and Newark. Based on market research, such promising routes as those between Raleigh-Durham and New York were created.

In order to market the product efficiently, Continental contracted the major travel agents because they brought nearly 80 percent of the business to the company, and it also reestablished commissions to a fair price to rebuild the relationship with those agents. The award-winning frequent flyer program was restored to retain customers' loyalty, and e-ticket terminals were built in major airports around the country to make the product more accessible.

Financial Strategy

Before Bethune took over the company, Continental's financial system could neither provide reliable information for its daily cost and daily revenue nor make a forecast on cash and revenue. This system was then replaced with an updated financial system. The new system was not only able to estimate cost based on the industry average and to forecast the number of flights landing each day according to the schedule, but also to measure the weight of each plane and the landing fees. The valuable information provided by the system created substantial profit for the company. For instance, Continental found out that an extraordinary amount of money was made on the European flights. After further analyzing those flights, Continental raised the price of the tickets to European destinations. This helped the company create an additional $10 million per year.

The following financial strategies were implemented:

- Renegotiating some leases
- Postponing some payments
- Refinancing some of the large debt
- Adjusting the price structure

When the renegotiation with the creditors, including General Electric and Air Canada, and the renegotiation of leases and debt structure took place in 1995, Continental saved $25 million on long-term debt. When some unproductive flights, such as A300s, were removed from the fleet, Continental enhanced its return on the investment.

Product Strategy

In the 1980s, Continental was a heterogeneous mixture of several airlines: Continental, Frontier, People Express, and New York Air. Gordon Bethune and his management team recognized the damage of the mixed product to Continental's overall brand image and managed to eliminate some of the product. The management also enhanced the fleet by reducing the average age of the fleet. Thus, primary maintenance was significantly reduced. Meanwhile, Continental customized its product to meet the consumers' needs by

- cutting the flights and the cities the company flies to;
- flying where people want to go;
- providing desirable customer services.

According to a survey conducted by the U.S. Department of Transportation, the quality of the airline's product is measured by on-time arrival percentage, lost-baggage claims, complaints received, and the number of passengers denied upon boarding. The 1997 J. D. Power and Associates Airline Customer Satisfaction Study also indicated that on-time performance counted for 22 percent of a customer's overall satisfaction. It was wise for Bethune to create an incentive program that rewarded every employee with a $65 bonus each month on a condition that the company was among the top five on-time carriers nationwide. Since his program was so successful, the company's on-time performance bounced from last place to first place within only six months.

People Plan

Although the people plan is listed last in the Go Forward Plan, the first step taken by Bethune resulting in Continental's turnaround was related to his people plan. He demonstrated his open-door management style by opening the executive suite's door to every Continental employee, and he broke the barriers of communication from the top. Then, Bethune implemented the people plan step-by-step and re-created the Continental corporate culture. The steps employed follow:

- Casual dress on Friday
- "On-time" started with the managers' meeting

- Nonsmoking in Continental Airlines buildings and flights
- Burned the employee manual to enhance employees' creativity and capability
- Repainted every single plane
- Rewarded cooperation

Thus, synergy was created when the market-planning people and the operating people worked together to improve the schedule. A positive environment was facilitated when valuable people were brought into the company. The open book policy allowed employees to see the true financial status of the company. Trust was built when Continental restored wage levels once the financial situation of the company was improved. A coherent relationship was established when Continental started treating travel agencies as its business partners. Customized service was provided when the frequent flyer program was restored. In essence, Bethune turned the company around by creating a win-win-win situation among the customer, business partner, and Continental itself.

In the Wake of 9/11

The horrific events of September 11, 2001, affected millions of people worldwide. Here is a brief overview of important issues and an assessment of the factors affecting the company's strategic decisions.

Financial Implications

Continental Airlines reported a 2001 fourth quarter loss of $149 million dollars. The company's net loss for the full year was $95 million, despite a $174 million dollar grant donated to Continental by the government for industry stabilization purposes. Revenue for the fourth quarter of 2001 dropped 28.4 percent from the same period in 2000. Revenues were cut about in half from the previous year to $1.74 billion from $2.43 billion.

The company has produced a wide variety of stock price levels (currently around $30 USD per share). The high for 2001 was $52.32 USD in July. After the September 11 attacks, Continental stock dropped to a low of $12.35 USD per share. With over 10 million shares traded in one day in September, and almost that amount in the days that followed, the company was reeling with the reaction of the nation—one can almost see the panic that followed.

Maintaining Standards

Throughout 2001, Continental led the major airlines in on-time performance and reliability. After the attacks, it maintained meal service, in-flight entertainment, blankets, pillows, and magazines. It decided to drop employees and flights rather than reduce quality. Air Transport World named Continental "Airline of the Year" for 2001.

As for future operations, Continental decided to defer the delivery of twenty-eight Boeing jets that were supposed to be delivered in 2002. Instead, it took only twenty of the forty-eight aircraft it had ordered for this year. Between 2003 and 2008 is the delivery date for the next twenty-eight. During that time it is scheduled to take thirty-nine more jets that were ordered previously.

Employee Perspective

For the third consecutive year, the company was named one of the "100 Best Companies to Work For." It was the only passenger airline among those companies named in the February 4 issue of *Forbes Magazine*. This award is based on an evaluation of work environment, company culture, compensation and benefits, and other measures of job satisfaction. The company paired down flights after the attacks and reduced its workforce by 21 percent.

Continental reduced management compensation and did not pay employee profit-sharing amounts. Gordon Bethune, who made about $5.5 million dollars in 2000, and President Larry Kellner, who made around $3.7 million in 2000, decided not to take compensation after September 26, 2001, in order to help decrease the amount of employees laid off.

Creating Strategy

Continental Airlines has infused its marketing messages with core values detailed in the four points of the Go Forward Plan, created by Gordon Bethune, for the previous seven years. This plan initiated a philosophy wherein four key strategic points are emphasized and subsequently manifested in its marketing presentations by way of clever and catchy phrases designed to both inform and entertain the customer. The key points are *Fly to Win, Fund the Future, Make Reliability a Reality,* and *Working Together.* Within these points, the core values of dependable on-time performance, safety and reliability, and award-winning service excellence have been emphasized as an advertising standard. These slogans encompass divergent yet essential business acumens ensuring the company's sustained presence and determination to enjoy further business success.

Continental does not advertise nationwide on network television or cable at all, as it considers this to be an inefficient use of its marketing dollars. It pinpoints those markets that constitute only the greatest revenue-generating potentials (those being Continental's route hub cities of New York, Cleveland, and Houston), advertising in only as much as that particular market may return in sales. Continental does, however, advertise to a lesser degree in Miami, Washington, DC, Boston, San Francisco, and Los Angeles. Continental's marketing strategies employ sports event sponsorship, magazine and newspaper print, billboards, network and cable television (in its target markets), radio and Internet mediums, whose most-valued target market is the high-yield male and female business traveler aged twenty-five to fifty-five. This group, who travels within three days of booking, in total, generates more cumulative revenue than does the leisure traveler despite the fact that it represents only 25 percent of all passengers accommodated. The optimum mix is a preferred 50 percent–50 percent, to which Continental has, and is now still, committed to achieve. With this objective, Continental directs virtually all media toward this business market, avoiding depiction of beautiful vacation scenes in any form whatsoever, and devoting as much as 70 percent of its spending allowance in the New York metropolitan area alone.

Despite the downturn in air travel post September 11, 2001, Continental remains steadfast in its committed delivery of uncompromised service. Cost-cutting changes in other carriers come in the form of reduced flights and airport lounge amenities, closed ticket offices, removal of ticket kiosks, omitted in-flight food, blankets, pillows, and complimentary reading material. Continental is unwilling to degrade its product in order to save money, realizing that the product itself is the selling point to which the customer responds and consciously chooses. And, Continental continues to target the high-yield business traveler with incentive programs designed to stimulate sales activities by offering complimentary bonus programs through customer participation. MeetingWorks, BUSINESSbonus, RewardOne, and Miles of Thanks programs have been created to accrue points redeemable for upgrades, travel certificates, discounted fares, discount freight handling, and President's Club memberships. Media messages displayed most recently address the business traveler specifically with copy focusing on Continental's added international destinations, new airplanes, and BusinessFirst service. Of course, all these efforts are intended to restore a financially viable, growing company. Time will ultimately tell with measurable results whether this steadfast strategy continues to work.[5]

Case Discussion Questions

1. World events decimated the travel industry in the 2001-2003 time frame. Some airlines filed for bankruptcy; others folded completely. Assume your airline went bankrupt and they continued to operate and eventually emerged from bankruptcy. What would be the key objectives of your strategic plan during and following bankruptcy?
2. In the Continental case what do you believe were the strongest management strategies within the Go Forward Plan?

NOTES

1. R. Nykiel, *Marketing in the Hospitality Industry* (4th ed.) (East Lansing, MI: Educational Institute of the American Hotel and Motel Association, 2004), pp. 263-264.

2. Ibid., p. 284.

3. R. Nykiel & E. Jascolt, *Marketing Your City USA* (Binghamton, NY: The Haworth Press, 1998), p. 23.

4. B. Tregoe & J. Zimmerman, *Top Management Strategy* (New York: Simon and Schuster, Inc., 1980), pp. 40-41.

5. R. Nykiel, *Hospitality Management Strategies* (Upper Saddle River, NJ: Prentice Hall, 2005), pp. 368-376.

Chapter 18

Effective Presentation and Communication of Research Findings

CHAPTER OBJECTIVES

- To discuss the relationship between research findings and presentation techniques and tools.
- To provide a process for communicating research findings to various audiences.
- To present an ongoing approach to research and analysis and the communications of significant data.
- To delineate oral and written presentation approaches which effectively communicate research findings and related recommendations.

RESEARCH FINDINGS AND PRESENTATION TECHNIQUES

Presentations, be they oral, written, or electronic are the usual format in which research findings and studies are communicated. Just as with people, no matter how brilliant the individual researcher or research, if poorly presented or communicated, the less likely it is to get a decision or the job. Research for research's sake is useless just as theoretical research that cannot be effectively communicated to an applied environment is usually useless to the corporate sector. Research that clearly communicates findings, analyses, and recommendations is valuable and most likely actionable. The bottom line is that how we communicate research findings is as important as the research itself in many instances. Communication of research findings in an appropriate and professional manner is more likely to result in enhancing the value and credibility of the research. And, likewise, poorly presented research is most likely to create a negative impression and detract from the findings and recommendations.[1]

Every research presentation should be scripted taking into account the audience, complexity of the research, and desired outcome or action (reaction) sought by the researcher. First, an assessment of the primary audience needs to be made. Normally, the higher up the corporate organizational hierarchy, the briefer and more to the point (conclusions and recommendations) the better. A guarantee of failure with this audience is to spend too much (if any) time on the technicalities of the process (methodology). This audience is interested in what you did and how to use it for action. Obviously, if your research is being presented back to researchers (i.e., the corporate market research department contracts with a market research service to conduct a project) to some degree the opposite may hold true—focus on the methodology, accuracy, and validity of the research. Also, the specific nature (type) of the research conducted may well dictate the best method or format for presentation. The point is there is no single magical presentation approach for research projects. The presentation must be tailored to the audience, the scope of the project, and the methodologies utilized. For example, video clips from a customer focus group will have an instant impact and reaction compared to reading from a transcript. The more visual (versus verbal or written) the presentation, the more likely there is of retention of the results. If you wish to stimulate discussion of the research you will not succeed with a bland statement or reference to a finding. Likewise, if you make a startling statement or quote an overwhelming statistic, such as "Over 90 percent of our customers indicated . . . ," you are likely to stimulate others to express their interpretations or perspectives. Competitive comparisons also work well to stimulate responses from the audience. Role-playing and audience involvement, if properly managed, can also help to convey key findings.

APPEALING TO THE SENSES

Throughout this text we have emphasized the importance of the visual, be it a graph, table, figure, map, or analytical tool. The old adage "a picture conveys a thousand words" is absolutely true when it comes to research presentations. Figure 18.1 presents a delineation of effective presentation techniques.

Likewise we know that the more interactive and participative the presentation, the more likely the faith in the process and ownership of the results.

Visuals

Data and findings can often be presented in more than one fashion or more than one technique. For example, differences can be presented in a graph, bar chart, table, and so forth. Opinions and preferences can be presented visually (videotaped), with audio (recorded), or in written format. Selecting the best or most appropriate presentation format for the data/information/findings at hand should be thought out in advance of any formal or informal discussion of research. This, along with developing a script and flow for the presentation, is more likely to bring the research success.

Figure 18.2 presents a simple research finding in a number of different ways. Which do you think is the more effective?

Use Color

We live in a world of color and it works well to support the conveyance of findings and data. For example, if using a scale, the upper end (100 percent range) might be in green tones while the lower end might be in shades of red. Green signifies money, profits, growth, and success, whereas red immediately flags failure, risk, and loss. Remember to use contrast when using color. Yellows will not copy or reproduce well on a white background; black and red will contrast the greatest with a white background. Likewise, reds and oranges are warm colors and blues and yellows are cool colors. Another use of color is in written presentations. Executive summaries or recommendations may be on other than white paper, such as gray or blue, to flag their importance, while the body of the research report is on white. Finally, visuals should be simple—so simple that one glance conveys the point or findings.

Other Techniques

For research that is ongoing, using a flash report or bulletin to convey a key finding or trend is very effective. A more formal but equally effective tech-

Sense/Technique	% Retention of Data/Findings
• Visual • Verbal • Written	• 94 • Less than 90 • Less than 70

FIGURE 18.1. Presentation Techniques and Response Recollections

nique for ongoing research is a monthly report or update. It can take the form of a competitive and environment report that is bulleted and in brief sentence format to highlight key occurrences and trends during the selected time frame. A word of caution here—executives scan, so make it easy to scan by using bold-face or italic type, and so on. Also, be sure it fits in a briefcase or it may never be read, as most executives read their correspondence while commuting, traveling, or at home. Depending on the current technical sophistication of the audience, other electronic formats, such as a DVD, may be very effective to convey results.

Research Reports

We have already stated the importance of scanning and use of color to make key sections of a research report stand out. There are

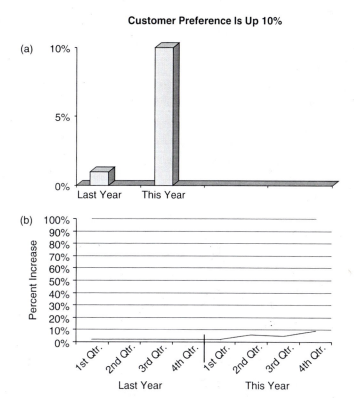

FIGURE 18.2. Sample Presentations of a Research Finding

numerous other ways to enhance the written research report. These include using a multiple part approach. Here there are two or three major components to the written presentations. One is the executive summary. It may be a "stand alone" section or located in the front of the actual report. The second is the actual written report, which should be factual and concise (to the point). The third part should be (if needed) an appendix, which contains whatever is necessary to satisfy the audience or reader. Include methodology descriptions if necessary, other pertinent statistical data, additional competitive information, trend data, questionnaires, surveys, or other research tools used in the project research.[2] The use of bullets, dashes, fonts, print weights, italics, boxes, shading, and so forth are all good if consistent and not overdone. These should enhance the appearance, expedite the scan, and highlight the important items. One more item to be included is visuals, be they PowerPoint or charts. Be sure to have on hand copies of these visuals or an electronic site at which they can be located and downloaded.

Researcher's Role

The role of the researcher is to conduct valid and accurate research and provide meaningful analysis. In development research and planning, pointing out or categorizing markets that are underrepresented (growth opportunities) or oversaturated (potential dispositions) is fine from a research or analytical perspective. All researchers need to remember that their role is to provide the rationale for managerial decisions, not to predetermine or make strategic decisions. Even contracted research consultants usually make recommendations—not decisions. Going beyond one's role can dramatically shorten a career or contract. Researchers should be prepared to respond objectively, based on research and not their opinion, to questions that may be of a strategic nature.

The researcher should point out issues which have resulted from the findings as well as make recommendations based on the research. Most researchers utilize a disclaimer at the outset of their report that states the data/findings being presented are based on the information collected and sources identified. Further, there is usually a statement which separates/protects the researcher from decisions or other steps taken by the client based on the data, since the data are primarily generated from secondary sources. Many times the research will uncover the need to address other areas with additional research. These needs should be pointed out in a straightforward objective manner, not with a sales pitch for more research. If the data and analysis do not provide the answer, don't try to provide one or speculate, but instead simply state, "That could not be ascertained by the scope of the research."

It should be pointed out that market and development research is a very good position for career advancement. The research position within a corporation allows the individual to potentially learn more about the company, competition, environment, and industry than most in the company. Further, it provides an excellent channel for legitimate exposure to management and the opportunity to identify a mentor within the organization. In larger corporations, the function itself is of substantial significance for a career in research. Likewise, working for a good market research firm provides a great learning opportunity through exposure to multiple clients. Many senior executives have moved up from the position of a researcher.

SCRIPTING THE PRESENTATION

Just as a good researcher develops a plan of attack for a research project, a plan or script should be developed for presenting and communicating the results of the research (see Figure 18.3).

Part I—Setting the Stage

Based on the audience and the presentation techniques, set up the room (if possible) to communicate effectively and not so the audience is fragmented. This may mean moving chairs from the back of the room or completely changing the room.

Part II—Implementing the Script

Implementation begins once you are satisfied with the staging and are ready to execute the presentation plan or script. The script should include and flow along the following:

- Supply introductions (if needed).
- State the objective of the research.
- Briefly (very briefly) state the approach utilized.
- Present the key findings (results) including recommendations.
- Point out where detailed backup data can be found (e.g., appendix).
- If issues were identified, simply present these in a list or bullet format.
- Solicit questions and discussion.

Part III—Follow-Up

This should be based on detailed notes taken during the presentation (by a colleague or recorder). Assess what was discussed; note any key questions that require further research and/or points requiring follow-up. Transmit a follow-up report as soon as feasible to your key client contact. Remember to say thank you at three key points—when you begin, when you end, and in

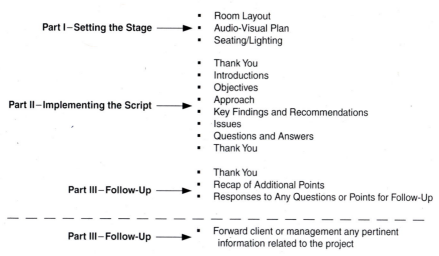

FIGURE 18.3. Recap of Presentation/Communication Process

your follow-up report. Even if the assignment ends, it is a good practice to forward to the client any additional relevant data that cross your desk. The same is true for internal research.

CHAPTER REVIEW

This chapter has pointed out that for research to be of maximum value it needs to be clearly and concisely communicated. The research presentation process and communication of results is a major responsibility of the researcher. It was suggested that the presentation process be scripted and that key findings be presented visually by use of graphs, pictorials, videos, charts, and so forth. An organization process for presentation of written development plans including samples of data presentation formats was delineated. The parameters of the researcher's role were defined, along with some commentary boundaries. A three-part process was described for presenting research results and included setting the stage, scripting, and trend follow-up.

KEY CONCEPTS/TERMS

Assessment
Attention span
Audio-visual
Bar charts
Competitive/environmental reports
Disclaimer
Discussion
Executive summary
Flash reports
Flow
Graphics
Issues
Key findings
Key result areas
Management perspective
Opinions

Outside expertise
Recommendations
Results measurements
Script
Timing

DISCUSSION QUESTIONS

1. Why is it important to script the presentation of research findings?
2. What is the three-part process for presenting research findings?
3. Why is it important to utilize visuals in presenting research findings?
4. How would you organize a long-term development plan research presentation?
5. What goes in an appendix to a research plan?
6. How would you define the role of the external or contracted researcher and that of the internal company researcher?

CASE 18.1. VERY EFFECTIVE PRESENTATIONS AND COMMUNICATIONS—LOSE-WIN-WIN

Effective presentations and superior communications require thorough preparation. The preparation needs to take into consideration the complexity of the issue, magnitude of the decision, and perspective of the audience. Given these three premises, this is a case example that demonstrates how the rationale and thorough presentation eventually overcame the irrational reaction.

A senior executive of a major corporation was given the assignment to thoroughly prepare a presentation to the board of directors that would substantially change the entire company. The time frame was the mid- to late 1970s. The company was the largest in its industry but its core product was aging and many of its other holdings were being sold off as part of a long-term strategic plan. The company would be classified as a "cash cow" in the Boston Consulting Group Portfolio Box. The founders and senior management were getting on in years and a younger team of senior managers had recently been recruited into select positions. The board of directors had grown and also aged. There was recent discontentment among its franchisees and also some major shareholders. It was becoming apparent that it was a time for change.

The senior executive given the assignment was provided all the financial and human resources needed to complete the project. The assignment was multifold. First, the company had been approached to acquire what was considered the best location in the major gaming market in North America. Further, the related developer proposed what would have been the first "mega" hotel and casino in the market. The assignment was to develop a bulletproof presentation, which should cover everything that could reasonably be anticipated.

The "team" was assembled and the project assignment undertaken. A detailed site selection and project feasibility study were undertaken. A complete assessment of every individual and entity was completed. Even a shareholders' survey was completed to obtain their feelings on the concept, project, and entry into the gaming business. All financial and market analyses were completed. A profile of every current board member was also completed to anticipate questions as well as to help prepare rationale to support the project. In summary, it was thought no stone was unturned and the special board meeting was scheduled a month before the option on the land would expire.

Preparation for the actual board presentation included a scripted format, video, flip charts, premeeting detailed booklets, a slide presentation, and the independent survey of the shareholders. The senior executive selected to head the research/assignment team was selected to present the findings supported by a senior external consultant. The research findings presented were basically bulletproof. Here are just a few of the key points for purposes of understanding how overwhelmingly positive this project would be for the corporation.

First, the project would generate more cash and profits for the company than all other current businesses owned and operated by the company combined. Second, despite the magnitude of the project investment, the payback period would be two to three years or twenty-seven months. Third, 84 percent of all shareholders surveyed looked favorably upon the company entering the gaming business. Fourth, because of the company's other real estate holdings, it could quickly become the leader in the gaming business through the addition of casinos and/or acquisition of another gaming company. Fifth, the long-term prospects for the gaming industry were very strong. And sixth, the profit cycle for gaming was most compatible with the profit cycle for other businesses owned by the corporation, thus ensuring a consistent performance. There were a number of other reasons to support the positive decision.

What transpired in the boardroom is perhaps one of the most fascinating examples of rationale versus irrational. The senior executive/presenter concluded the presentation and opened up the meeting for discussion. The first to speak was the executive vice president of the corporation, who placed a box of twenty-year-old *Reader's Digest*s on the table. He picked one up and pointed out a story of "sin and prostitution" in the gaming market. He really got into his presentation by actually throwing the *Reader's Digest* at the presenter. One of the vice chairmans of the board (quite elderly) asked an inappropriate question about medications or prescriptions. The president of the company then spoke and said he and at least six other board members would resign on the basis of their religious beliefs if the full board approved the entry into the gaming business or the project. The chairman briefly spoke and encouraged all to be rational but didn't want to take a position on the matter at the present time. Just then, the other vice chairman stood up and took his lit cigar and placed it lit side down into the cherry wood board table. As he ground the cigar into the wood, he stated, "As the largest shareholder present, I am adjourning this session of the board." With that he and about half of the twenty-five board members present abruptly left. So did the senior executive/presenter.

You might think this is a real loss for research, presentation thoroughness, and so on. You surely might think this if you knew the land and the "deal" were to be lost due to time running out on the land option. However, here is the rest of the story.

At 11:00 p.m. that night the senior executive/presenter received a phone call from his boss and the vice chairman of the board who had abruptly terminated the board of directors meeting earlier that Friday. The essence of the call was that the senior executive/presenter was to distribute and collect (wait for signature) a letter to all of the officers (senior VPs, division presidents, EVPs, etc.) of the company over the weekend. Excluded from the distribution were the president, corporate executive vice president, vice chairman of the board, and the current chairman. All signed letters were to be hand delivered to the vice chairman's (cigar smoker) office by 8:00 a.m. Monday. The letter would be preceded by a personal call from the vice chairman and the division president. The call would convey the fact that the group headed by the vice chairman (cigar smoker) now held more voting shares of the company stock than those opposed to gaming. The letter would ask for the support of the senior management team (officers). The letter also included an attachment, which in essence was a letter of resignation; should the above referenced vice chairman's group of shareholders (block) find it necessary these resignation letters would be used as additional support for the upcoming changes planned by the large block of shareholders under the leadership of the vice chairman.

The behind-the-door process went on for a few weeks and shortly after the land option was lost, a new board meeting was announced. The essence of the new board meeting and related events were as follows. The vice chairman (cigar smoker) would now be the chairman and CEO of the corporation. The executive VP and division president would become the president and COO. A new board of directors had been formed and would be substantially smaller than the old board. The chairman and other vice chairman of the board "retired"; the *Reader's Digest*–throwing EVP was no longer with the company, and the president (at the time of the first board meeting) resigned. Six other board members closely affiliated with the now retired chairman were not included on the new board. Let's just say the specific deal was lost but a "win" in terms of strategy had just occurred.

At the first official meeting of the new board of directors, the vote to seek entry into the gaming business was unanimously approved. Within the next few months, the company began acquiring small casinos next to its real estate/properties. Within the next thirty-six months, the company had disposed of the businesses identified in the strategic plan research and had acquired one of the largest and most successful gaming companies in the United States. Let's just call that another win.

Case Discussion Questions

1. Why is it important to try to identify all possible objections (rational or irrational) that might occur with research recommendations?
2. Do you believe it is beneficial or detrimental to provide research presentation findings and reports prior to the actual presentation meeting?

NOTES

1. R. Nykiel, *Marketing Your Business* (Binghamton, NY: Best Business Books, 2002), pp. 234-235.
2. Ibid., pp. 229-231.

APPENDIXES

Appendix I

Marketing Intelligence Information Sources

The sources listed here can provide a variety of secondary research information. You should obviously search the Internet and also contact the U.S. Government Web site. There are numerous government publications issued by virtually every branch of the government on a regular basis. The Department of Commerce has numerous field offices, as does the Small Business Administration. Also, check the Government Printing Office Publications Center in Washington, DC. You can order publications directly from this source. Specific marketing and consumer related information is also abundant from the U.S. Census, Bureau of the Census. Also, media representatives and trade and consumer publications (e.g., *American Demographics*) are excellent sources of data. There are a number of non-government-related sources that provide a variety of marketing information services.

SOURCE	PROVIDES
A. C. Neilsen Company 299 Park Avenue New York, NY 10171 212-707-7500	Demographics, retail sales, and media information for each DMA (designated market area) in the United States (e.g., television audience data, retail purchases, etc.)
The Arbitron Company 142 West 57th Street New York, NY 10019 212-887-1300	Local market demographic/product usage profiles and media usage reports with target audience profiles, etc.
The Circulation Book P.O. Box 994 22619 Pacific Coast Highway Malibu, CA 90265	Circulation and penetration for all daily newspapers, Sunday papers, newspaper supplements, and magazines by metro area and TV viewers.
Claritas, Inc. 1525 Wilson Blvd., Suite 1000 Arlington, VA 22209-2411 1-800-234-5973	PRIZM, a market segmentation system which divides the United States into numerous lifestyle clusters and social groups.
ClusterPlus 2000 Strategic Mapping, Inc. Corporate Headquarters 3135 Kifer Rd. Santa Clara, CA 95051-0827 1-800-472-6277	Demographic, media habits, and purchasing data on over fifty classifications of American consumers in geographic targets down to the block level.
Dun's Marketing Services Offices nationwide 1-800-526-0651	Direct mail lists and 516 (standard industrial classifications) category and geographical information on business.

Handbook of Marketing Research Methodologies for Hospitality and Tourism
© 2007 by The Haworth Press, Inc. All rights reserved.
doi:10.1300/5927_20

SOURCE	PROVIDES
Equifax National Decision Systems 1979 Lakeside Parkway Tucker, GA 30084-5847 770-496-7171	Micro Vision, a service which classifies consumers into over fifty segments down to the zip + 4 level.
Fairchild Fact Files Fairchild Books 7 West 34th Street New York, NY 10001 212-630-3880	Files on market trends, buying habits, advertising expenditures, sales and demographic profiles by product category.
Gale Research Company 835 Penobscot Building Detroit, MI 48226-4094 1-800-877-4523	The encyclopedia of associations (U.S. and international), consultant directories, and the Trade Show and Professional Exhibits Directory. Also, management information guides and a variety of topical reports.
Leading National Advertisers (LNA) 11 West 42nd Street, 11th Floor New York, NY 10036 212-789-1400	Competitive spending information by medium, summary of national advertising expenditures by brand and industry category, etc.
Radio TV Reports, Inc. 317 Madison Avenue New York, NY 10017 212-309-1400	Source for copies of all competitive radio and television ads.
Rome Report 11 West 42nd Street, 11th Floor New York, NY 10036 212-789-1400	Business-to-business and trade advertising expenditures.
SRI International 333 Ravenswood Avenue Menlo Park, CA 94025-3493 415-859-3032	Source of the VALS (values and lifestyles) program, which segments U.S. consumers into a number of distinct lifestyle groups for predicting consumer behavior.
Simmons Market Research Bureau, Inc. (SMRB) 420 Lexington Avenue New York, NY 10170 212-916-8900	Products/services including MRI and SMRB which provide information on demographics, size, and media habits of the user/purchaser groups for various products/brands, etc.
Standard Rate and Data Service (SRDS) 1700 West Higgins Road Des Plaines, IL 60018 708-375-5000	Newspaper rates and data service for population, expenditures for individual states, counties, etc., with household information. Also, numerous "source books" for mailing lists, media rate information, etc.
Viking and Penguin Books Viking Penguin, Inc. 375 Hudson Street New York, NY 10014 212-366-2000	Information U.S.A., a reference guide for direct access to government experts, commerce data sources, census data sources, etc.
Yesawich, Pepperdine & Brown 1900 Summit Tower Blvd., Suite 600 Orlando, FL 32810 407-875-1111	MONITOR, an annual research tool that provides insight into social, behavioral, and travel related trends among American consumers.

Appendix II

Marketing-Related Associations

The marketing discipline is fortunate to have a number of outstanding professional associations that form yet another source for information sharing/intelligence. The following is a brief listing of some of these associations.

ASSOCIATION	FOCUS
Advertising Research Foundation (ARF) 641 Lexington Avenue New York, NY 10022 Telephone: (212) 0751-5656 Fax: (212) 319-5265	Conducts/provides impartial and objective research on advertising effectiveness. Membership includes agencies, research firms, advertisers, media companies, and educational institutions.
American Association of Advertising Agencies (Four A's) 666 Third Avenue New York, NY 10017 Telephone: (212) 682-2500 Fax: (212) 953-5665	Provides counsel to ad agencies on operations and management and provides for professional development.
American Hotel & Motel Association (AH&MA) 1201 New York Avenue, NW, Suite 600 Washington, DC 20005-3931 Telephone: (202) 289-3157 Fax: (202) 289-3110 www.ah&ma.org	Provides a resource for statistical information and special studies for the lodging industry. Addresses governmental/legislative issues with potential impact on marketing.
American Marketing Association (AMA) 250 South Wacker Drive Chicago, IL 60606 Telephone: (312) 648-0536 Fax: (312) 993-7542	Assists in the professional development of the individual professional through a variety of educational programs and publications focused on marketing.
Association of Coupon Processors (ACP) 500 North Michigan Avenue, Suite 1400 Chicago, IL 60614 Telephone: (312) 661-1700 Fax: (312) 661-0769	Concentrates on improving the coupon industry from numerous perspectives, e.g., regulation, practices, etc.
Association of Incentive Marketing (AIM) 1600 Route 22 Union, NJ 07083 Telephone: (908) 687-3090 Fax: (908) 687-0977	Promotes the education, quality, and ethical standards for those involved in incentive marketing.

Handbook of Marketing Research Methodologies for Hospitality and Tourism
© 2007 by The Haworth Press, Inc. All rights reserved.
doi:10.1300/5927_21

ASSOCIATION	FOCUS
Association of In-Store Marketing (AISM) 66 North Van Brunt Englewood, NJ 07631 Telephone: (201) 894-8899 Fax: (201) 894-0529	Promotes the awareness and use of in-store media/marketing programs. Offers guidelines/standards and a speakers bureau.
Association of National Advertisers (ANA) 155 East 44th Street New York, NY 10017 Telephone: (212) 697-5950 Fax: (212) 661-8057	Serves interests of corporations that advertise regionally and nationally (represents 80 percent + of all ad expenditures in the United States).
Association of Retail Marketing Services (ARM) 3 Caro Court Red Bank, NJ 07001 Telephone: (908) 842-5070 Fax: (908) 219-1938	Represents suppliers of incentive services to retailers; provides educational research and information programs.
Council of Sales Promotion Agencies (CSPA) 750 Summer Street Stamford, CT 06901 Telephone: (203) 325-3911 Fax: (203) 969-1499	An association for full-service promotion agencies that provides educational and informative information to its membership.
Direct Marketing Association (DMA) 11 West 42nd Street New York, NY 10036-8096 Telephone: (212) 768-7277 Fax: (212) 768-4546	Provides conferences, meetings, and publications on direct mail and represents its membership in government-related issues.
Food Marketing Institute (FMI) 800 Connecticut Avenue, NW Washington, DC 20006-2701 Telephone: (202) 452-8444 Fax: (202) 429-4519	Provides research, education, and industry relations for its membership of food retailers and wholesalers.
Grocery Manufacturers of America (GMA) 1010 Wisconsin Avenue, NW, Suite 900 Washington, DC 20007 Telephone: (202) 337-9400 Fax: (202) 337-4508	Made up of manufacturers and processors of food and nonfood products sold to retail grocery stores; provides public policy, trade relations, scientific, and educational advocacy programs.
Hotel Sales & Marketing Association International (HSMAI) 1300 L. Street, NW, Suite 1020 Washington, DC 20005 Telephone: (202) 789-0089 Fax: (202) 789-1725 www.hsmai.org	Provides educational seminars, certificate programs, publications, and local/national networking opportunities for those involved in selling meetings, group business, etc., to the hotel industry.
Licensing Industry Merchandisers Association (LIMA) 350 Fifth Avenue, Suite 6210 New York, NY 10118-0110 Telephone: (212) 244-1944 Fax: (212) 563-6552	Concentrates on those involved in the marketing of licensed properties and provides information, publications, seminars, and speakers.
National Association of Demonstration Companies (NADC) P.O. Box 1189 Bloomfield, NJ 07003-1189 Telephone: (800) 338-NADC Fax: (201) 338-1410	A group of hundreds of organizations in the direct marketing area; supports the use, acceptance, and reputation of in-store demonstrations.

ASSOCIATION	FOCUS
National Association for Information Services (NAIS) 1250 Connecticut Avenue, NW, Suite 600 Washington, DC 20036-2603 Telephone: (202) 833-2545 Fax: (202) 833-1234	Interest is in the interactive tele-media area as an advocate of the industry. Members include cable television, long-distance carriers, regional telephone companies, and publishing companies.
National Restaurant Association (NRA) 1200 Seventeenth Street, NW Washington, DC 20036-3097 Telephone: (202) 331-5996 Fax: (202) 331-2429	Provides readership on national issues related to the restaurant industry as well as major trade shows and associated educational programs through the foundation.
The Point-of-Purchase Advertising Institute (POPAI) 66 North Van Brunt Englewood, NJ 07631 Telephone: (201) 894-8899 Fax: (201) 894-0529	Serves all constituencies involved in/with POP (point-of-purchase) products and services. Acts to promote, protect, and advance issues for the industry.
Promotion Marketing Association of America (PMAA) 257 Park Avenue South New York, NY 10010 Telephone: (212) 420-1100 Fax: (212) 982-PMAA	As the largest organization in the promotions field, PMAA provides educational programs, information, and publications to its membership, with a focus on entertainment marketing, in-store marketing, product sampling, and small business.
Specialty Advertising Association International (SAAI) 3125 Skyway Circle North Irving, TX 75038-3526 Telephone: (214) 252-0404 Fax: (214) 258-0949	Provides leadership and information to those interested in the promotional products industry.
Travel Industry Association of America (TIA) 1100 New York Avenue, NW, Suite 450 Washington, DC 20005-3934 Telephone: (202) 408-8422 Fax: (202) 408-1255 www.tia.org	As the largest association serving the broadest spectrum of the industry, TIA provides extensive marketing information, publications, and seminars (including the Marketing Outlook Forum) and represents the industry on travel-related matters nationally and internationally.

Appendix III

Top Fifty U.S. Research Firms and Web Sites

U.S. Rank 2003	Organization	Headquarters	Web site	U.S. Research Revenues* ($ in millions)
1	VNU, Inc.	New York	vnu.com	1,609.0
2	IMS Health, Inc.	Fairfield, CT	imshealth.com	537.9
3	Information Resources, Inc.	Chicago	infores.com	388.0
4	Westat, Inc.	Rockville, MD	westat.com	381.6
5	TNSUSA	London	tns-global.com	366.3
	TNS	London	tns-i.com	199.7
	TNS NFO	Greenwich, CT	nfow.com	166.6
6	The Kantar Group	Fairfield, CT	kantargroup.com	339.8
7	Arbitron, Inc.	New York	arbitron.com	265.7
8	NOP World US	New York	nopworld.com	205.6
9	Ipsos	New York	ipsos-na.com	176.1
10	Synovate	Chicago	synovate.com	161.1
11	Maritz Research	St. Louis, MO	maritzresearch.com	122.9
12	J.D. Power and Associates	Westlake Village, CA	jdpower.com	119.1
13	Harris Interactive, Inc.	Rochester, NY	harrisinteractive.com	111.0
14	The NPD Group, Inc.	Port Washington, NY	npd.com	96.8
15	Opinion Research Corp.	Princeton, NJ	opinionresearch.com	84.7
16	GfK USA	Nuremberg, Germany	gfk.com	58.5
	GfK Custom Research, Inc.	Minneapolis	customresearch.com	32.3
	V2 GfK	Blue Bell, PA	vanderveer.com	26.2
17	Lieberman Research Worldwide	Los Angeles	lrwonline.com	57.7

Handbook of Marketing Research Methodologies for Hospitality and Tourism
© 2007 by The Haworth Press, Inc. All rights reserved.
doi:10.1300/5927_22

U.S. Rank 2003	Organization	Headquarters	Web site	U.S. Research Revenues* ($ in millions)
18	Abt Associates, Inc.	Cambridge, MA	abtassociates.com	51.7
19	C&R Research, Inc.	Chicago	crresearch.com	48.1
20	Wirthlin Worldwide	McLean, VA	wirthlin.com	40.1
21	Market Strategies, Inc.	Livonia, MI	marketstrategies.com	34.3
22	Burke, Inc.	Cincinnati	burke.com	31.5
23	ICR/International Communications Research	Media, PA	icrsurvey.com	29.7
24	MORPACE International, Inc.	Farmington Hills, MI	morpace.com	27.0
25	Knowledge Networks, Inc.	Menlo Park, CA	knowledgenetworks.com	26.0
26	Arbor, Inc.	Media, PA	arborinc.com	25.5
27	Walker Information	Indianapolis	walkerinfo.com	25.2
28	National Research Corp.	Lincoln, NE	nationalresearch.com	24.4
29	Lieberman Research Group	Great Neck, NY	liebermanresearch.com	24.1
30	comScore Networks, Inc.	Reston, VA	comscore.com	23.5
31	Marketing and Planning Systems, Inc.	Waltham, MA	mapsnet.com	23.0
32	Marketing Research Services, Inc.	Cincinnati	mrsi.com	22.2
33	Peryam & Kroll Research Corp.	Chicago	pk-research.com	21.1
34	OTX Research	Los Angeles	otxresearch.com	19.1
35	Flake-Wilkerson Market Insights LLC	Little Rock, AR	fw-mi.com	17.8
36	Directions Research, Inc.	Cincinnati	directionsrsch.com	17.6
37	Data Development Corp.	New York	datadc.com	17.5
38	RDA Group, Inc.	Bloomfield Hills, MI	rdagroup.com	17.0
39	The PreTesting Company, Inc.	Tenafly, NJ	pretesting.com	16.3
40	Catalina Marketing Research Solutions	Crestview Hill, KY	cmresearchsolutions.com	15.5
41	Schulman, Ronca & Bucuvalas, Inc.	New York	srbi.com	15.3
42	The Marketing Workshop, Inc.	Norcross, GA	mwshop.com	14.7

U.S. Rank 2003	Organization	Headquarters	Web site	U.S. Research Revenues* ($ in millions)
43	Simmons Market Research Bureau, Inc.	Deerfield Beach, FL	smrb.com	13.9
44	Savitz Research Cos.	Dallas	savitzresearch.com	13.5
45	Cheskin	Redwood Shores, CA	cheskin.com	11.9
46	Market Probe, Inc.	Milwaukee	marketprobe.com	11.7
47	Marketing Analysts, Inc.	Charleston, SC	marketinganalysts.com	11.4
48	Ronin Corp.	Princeton, NJ	ronin.com	10.8
49	MarketVision Research, Inc.	Cincinnati	mv-research.com	10.6
50	Data Recognition Corp.	Maple Grove, MN	datarecognitioncorp.com	10.1
			TOTAL	5,803.9
	All others (147 CASRO** companies) not included in the Top 50 Total			584.5
				6,388.4

*Estimated by Top 50. U.S. and worldwide revenues may include nonresearch activities for some companies that are significantly higher.

**Council of American Survey Research Organizations.

Appendix IV

Top Twenty-Five Global Research Organizations and Web Sites

Rank 2003	Organization	Head-quarters	Parent Country	Web Site	No. of Countries with Sub-sidiaries/ Branch Offices	U.S. Research Revenues ($ in millions)
1	VNU N.V.	Haarlem	Netherlands	vnu.com	81	3,048.3
2	Taylor Nelson Sofres plc	London	U.K.	tns.global.com	70	1,565.1
	Taylor Nelson Sofres	London	U.K.	tns.global.com	54	1,050.5
	NFO World Group, Inc.	Greenwich, CT	U.K.	tns-global.com	40	514.6
3	IMS Health, Inc.	Fairfield, CT	U.S.	imshealth.com	75	1,381.8
4	The Kantar Group	Fairfield, CT	U.K.	kantargroup.com	61	1,002.1
5	GfK Group	Nuremberg	Germany	gfk.com	48	673.6
6	Ipsos Group S.A.	Paris	France	ipsos.com	36	644.6
7	Information Resources, Inc.	Chicago	U.S.	infores.com	18	554.3
8	Westat, Inc.	Rockville, MD	U.S.	westat.com	1	381.6
9	Synovate	London	U.K.	synovate.com	46	357.7
10	NOP World	London	U.K.	nopworld.com	6	335.6
11	Arbitron, Inc.	New York	U.S.	arbitron.com	3	273.6
12	Maritz Research	St. Louis	U.S.	maritzresearch.com	4	188.8
13	Video Research Ltd.	Tokyo	Japan	videor.co.jp	4	166.7
14	J.D. Power and Associates	Westlake Village, CA	U.S.	jdpower.com	6	144.8

Handbook of Marketing Research Methodologies for Hospitality and Tourism
© 2007 by The Haworth Press, Inc. All rights reserved.
doi:10.1300/5927_23

Rank 2003	Organization	Head-quarters	Parent Country	Web Site	No. of Countries with Sub-sidiaries/ Branch Offices	U.S. Research Revenues ($ in millions)
15	Harris Interactive, Inc.	Rochester, NY	U.S.	harrisinteractive.com	4	137.0
16	Opinion Research Corp.	Princeton, NJ	U.S.	opinionresearch.com	6	131.2
17	INTAGE, Inc.	Tokyo	Japan	intage.co.jp	2	122.3
18	The NPD Group, Inc.	Port Washington, NY	U.S.	npd.com	11	117.6
19	AGB Group	Milan	Italy	agb.com	19	81.6
20	Market & Opinion Research Int'l	London	U.K.	mori.com	2	64.4
21	Lieberman Research Worldwide	Los Angeles	U.S.	irwonline.com	1	63.2
22	Dentsu Research, Inc.	Tokyo	Japan	dentsuresearch.co.jp	1	57.0
23	Abt Associates, Inc.	Cambridge, MA	U.S.	abtassociates.com	3	54.0
24	Nikkei Research, Inc.	Tokyo	Japan	nikkeiresearch.com	4	52.1
25	Wirthlin Worldwide	McLean, VA	U.S.	wirthlin.com	4	52.0
				TOTAL		11,651.0

Source: Marketing News, August 15, 2004, p. H4.

Glossary

accuracy (of measurement): Closeness of the agreement between the result of a measurement and a true value or reflection of the "real world."

action program: A list of actions that must be taken to fulfill the marketing plan. It includes target dates, approved expenditures (as differentiated from unapproved estimated costs), and the person(s) responsible for implementing each action.

action research: Research that results in a problem-solving strategy.

advertising medium: The vehicle (e.g., newspaper or direct mail) used to carry the advertising message from the sender to the intended receiver.

agent: One authorized to transact business for another (principal) within the scope of a defined authority.

aided awareness: Awareness generated by asking individuals which brands, products, and so on, they are familiar with after reading or reviewing a list.

algorithm: A logical or computational procedure that, if correctly applied, ensures the solution of a problem.

alternative hypothesis: Takes in all possible cases that are not treated by the stated hypothesis.

analytical tools: Anything that turns raw data into usable information.

ANOVA: Analysis of variance.

attribute: A quality, character, characteristic, or property.

automation: The computerization of manual functions.

average: Numbers used to represent or characterize a group of numbers. The most common type is the arithmetic mean.

barter: The furnishing of products by an advertiser as full or partial payment for broadcasting time or free mentions on television or radio. Time so purchased is called barter time, and its purchase is usually arranged by a broker.

bell-shaped curve: The normal distribution.

benchmarking: A control source against which you compare the area you are studying.

benefit and need segmentation: Divides a market into groups of consumers on the basis of the benefits they seek, the needs they expect to satisfy, and, in some instances, the factors they hope to avoid.

Handbook of Marketing Research Methodologies for Hospitality and Tourism
© 2007 by The Haworth Press, Inc. All rights reserved.
doi:10.1300/5927_24

binomial distribution: A discrete probability distribution in which there are two alternatives (e.g., heads/tails, success/failure).

brainstorming: A conference technique of solving specific problems, amassing information, stimulating creative thinking, developing new ideas, and so on, by unrestrained and spontaneous participation in discussion.

brand: The name or symbol used to identify and differentiate a product or service from competing products or services.

brand development index: A measure of the concentration of a brand's consumption; typically, the units or dollars of a product consumed per thousand population in a year's time.

brand image: The pattern of feelings, associations, and ideas held by the public at large regarding a specific brand. Also brand personality.

brand loyalty: A measure of how loyal customers are over a period of time.

breakeven analysis: An analysis of the level of sales at which a project would make zero profit.

breakeven calculation: A technique to determine the absolute or percent sales increase needed to pay for the cost of a promotion.

buying habits: The frequency and method of purchase.

CAPI: Computer-assisted personal interviewing.

case study research: Employing multiple sources of information to study a single, limited situation through one particular contemporary period of time.

category development index: Determines product category's strength on a market-by-market basis.

CATI: Computer-assisted telephone interviewing.

central limit theorem: The means of samples from a normally distributed population are themselves normally distributed, regardless of the sample size used to calculate the mean. This is a robust theorem! As sample size increases then the means of samples drawn from a population of any distribution will approach a normal distribution.

channel of distribution: The sequence of marketing agencies (such as wholesalers and retailers) through which a product passes on its way from the producer to the final user.

characteristic: Property that helps distinguish between items of a given population.

chronological work plan: A listing of action steps to be taken in date order, with identification of responsibility.

city pairs: Origin and destination points of a flight segment.

cluster analysis: The identification of groups of respondents who give similar responses to two or more variables.

coefficient of determination: This is the square of the correlation coefficient (r^2). This is thought to be an easier value to interpret than r. It is the proportion of variance in one variable (y) that can be explained by variance in the other (x). Again, it varies from 0 to 1 and is always less than the absolute magnitude of r.

coefficient of variance (CV): CV = 100 × standard deviation/mean. CV is unitless. It may be used to check for repeatability (reproducability) of within-subjects data.

committee: A body of persons delegated to consider, investigate, take action on, or report on some matter.

competition: Any business concern, product, or concept that competes for customers in your market.

competitive research: Marketing research that compares your product or service to the products or services of competitors and tries to discover how consumers perceive and experience your product/service offering in relation to the competitors' products/services.

concentration: The percent within a given demographic target market segment that purchases the product; for example, of all persons eighteen to twenty-four years old, 80 percent are purchasers of the product.

concept development: Opportunity identification, opportunity analysis, idea generation and enrichment, idea selection, and concept definition.

confidence interval: The degree of accuracy desired by the researcher and stipulated as a level of confidence in the form of a percentage.

confidence limits: The upper and lower values between which the true mean will lie with particular probability (e.g., 95 percent or 99 percent).

consumer's perspective: The consumer's attitude toward a product or service that centers on the needs that it satisfies.

core competencies: The capability at which a company does better than other firms that provides them with a distinctive competitive advantage and contributes to acquiring and retaining customers.

correlation: Relating one variable to another by calculating the extent to which one increases as the other is increased.

correlation coefficient: Linear correlation is measured by the "correlation coefficient" or r, which varies from −1 (complete negative correlation) to +1 (complete positive correlation). The further the value from 0 and toward −/+1, the better the correlation. The following are conventional terms given to different levels of r: very weak correlation = 0.00-0.19; weak correlation = 0.20-0.39; modest correlation = 0.40-0.69; strong correlation = 0.70-0.89; very strong correlation = 0.90-1.00.

cost-plus theory: The recognition of the need to price or sell a product or service in periods of low demand by discounting the price beyond fixed and variable cost levels to stimulate sales.

CQI (continuous quality improvement): The ongoing efforts within a company to meet the needs and exceed the expectations of customers by changing the way work is performed so that products and services are delivered better, faster, and at less cost than in the past.

CSI (customer service index): Customer buying profiles and churn analysis are examples of decision support activities that can affect the success of customer relationships.

customer needs: What a customer really looks for or wants in a product or service.

customer perceptions: The ways in which the customer, in his or her own mind, look at a product. They include the customer's image of the product. Customer perceptions often differ from management's beliefs and perceptions.

customer satisfaction: Meeting the identified needs of each guest with a level of service and product quality that matches or exceeds the expectations created by your property's marketing message and related pricing.

database: A program or system for storing information that can be used to search, sort, and produce outputs. In marketing, databases are most often associated with customer or prospect records.

database marketing: A sales and marketing methodology that sells and promotes by selective direct mail with the objective of increasing sales and profits.

demand: The customer side of a commercial relationship (demand and supply).

demographic profile: Demographic data describing characteristics of consumers related to specific products or services.

demographics: Description of the vital statistics or objective and quantifiable characteristics of an audience or population.

demographic segmentation: The division of a market by like characteristics such as sex, age, income, home ownership, martial status, occupation, and education.

descriptive statistics: Statistics used to describe sample data in some way (e.g., means, standard deviations) or to describe relationships in the form of odds ratio, relative risk, etc.

discriminant analysis: Comparable to factor analysis; aims to relate variables together into similar groups called discriminant factors. The difference between factor and discriminant analysis is the basis of the grouping.

distribution: An account of all the values of a variable is called its distribution.

driving force(s): The method of delivering the product to the customer—channels of distribution. Also, how and where the product is sold (geographic).

elasticity: Measures the extent volume shifts in response to a shift in the variable under consideration.

environmental impact study: A report that describes environment impacts for both the short and long term of a specific project.

environmental research: Marketing research that focuses on external forces (economic, social, political, technological, etc.).

ethnographic research: The study of ethnic groups by geographic area.

evaluation: To determine the significance, worth, or condition of something, usually by careful appraisal and study.

expense plus approach: Estimate of sales levels to cover expenses and make a projected profit.

exposure: The number of consumers actually hearing or seeing your advertising.

factor analysis: Simplifying data by identifying relationships between variables in the data set.

feasibility study: The methods and techniques used to examine technical and cost data to determine the economic potential and the practicality of project applications.

feeder markets: Geographic locations that "feed" an area its business; for example, 8.5 percent of all San Francisco's hotel rooms were booked from Los Angeles.

fixed costs: Costs that do not change with fluctuating sales or promotion.

focus group: A marketing research technique that combines personal-opinion solicitation in the form of group discussion with a structured set of questions.

franchise: In marketing, a contract right or license granted by a franchisor for compensation, usually to multiple franchisees, to do business under a certain name legally controlled by the franchisor and usually involving specific territorial, field-of-use, and product-quality traits. A contractual relationship establishing a means of marketing goods or services giving certain elements of control to the supplier (franchisor) in return for the right of the franchisee to use the supplier trade name or trademark, usually in a specific marketing area.

frequency: How often a particular score or event occurs.

full-service agency: An advertising agency that has a full range of services for research and development.

GAP analysis: The difference between projected outcomes and desired outcomes. In product development, the GAP is frequently measured as the difference between expected and desired revenues or profits from currently planned new products if the corporation is to meet its objectives (the difference in total funding needed for a proposal and the amount of funding already made available).

geodemographic segmentation: The division of a market along geographic and demographic dimensions; for example, linking the number of people with similar characteristics (age, income, etc.) with specific geographic locations.

grid concept: A tool that views both the present, future markets, and competitive conditions that allows the user to gain a perspective on products and services through the evaluation process.

gross rating point (GRP): A unit of measurement of audience size for television, radio, or outdoor advertising, equal to 1 percent of the total potential audience universe; used to measure the exposure of one or more programs or commercials without regard to multiple exposure of the same advertising to individuals. Also, the product of media reach times exposure frequency.

heavy user: A frequent purchaser or repetitive user of a product or service.

horizontal integration: Acquiring other operators at the same producer or processing level in the supply chain.

hypothesis: Most commonly takes the form of an exact specification as to what the population parameter value is.

incentive: Cash, merchandise, or travel offered to consumers, salespeople, or dealers as a tangible reward for a purchase or sales performance. A premium.

independent variable: Determines at least partly the value of the dependent variable.

index preference scale: Plus or minus 10 from 100 (90–100–110).

inference: A form of logic in which you make a generalization about an entire class based on what you have observed about a small set of members of that class.

inferential statistics: Statistics that test sample data for significance and include calculation of the "*p*" value, confidence intervals, etc.

inflation plus factor: A method for increasing prices that is based on the premise that increases should be at the inflation rate plus a percent target.

in-house: A term used to describe a company that implements one or more services within the company as opposed to contracting with outside suppliers.

inside micro approach: Your own sales history review/projected three-year trend (with judgment).

integrative research: The combination of two different research techniques to obtain multiple data about a single situation.

interactive: A two-way information system whereby the information receiver can communicate directly with the information supplier.

intercepts: Consumer interviews conducted on the street, in malls, and so forth.

intermediary: An individual or firm that facilitates transactions between consumers and suppliers. There are two types: commercial (those earning commissions) and captive (those who facilitate transactions as part of their regular jobs and do not earn commissions).

internal data: Operational data on such items as sales, credit, and lists generated within the firm.

intrabrand competition: Competition between or among the distributors, wholesalers, or retailers of the product of a particular manufacturer of that product.

investigative consumer report: When a company gathers information about a person's credit history (according to the Fair Credit Reporting Act).

laddering: A probing technique, used in one-on-ones and focus groups, designed to delve into the real reasons for participants' attitudes and behaviors toward a topic.

level of expectation: The quantity or quality of your product or service, as expected by your customers. A basic premise of advertising is that you never promise more than your product or service can actually fulfill.

Likert scales: Common scales used to measure attitudes or perceptions.

list rental: An arrangement in which a list owner furnishes names and/or addresses on a list to a mailer, together with the privilege of using the list (unless specified) one time only. A list can be selected from a mass-compiled list on geographic, demographic, or psychographic bases, or it can be rented from a firm whose clientele closely resembles that desired (subject to the practice of many mailers and the Direct Marketing Association to permit consumers to remove their names from unwanted lists). The list owner is paid a royalty by the mailer, usually a specific fee per name. The list owner will establish a specific date on which the user has the obligation to mail to a specific list.

long-term objectives: Objectives to be accomplished in one to three years.

mailing list: A collection of names and addresses maintained on a computer to generate mailings.

mapping: Utilizing multidimensional models based on quantitative and qualitative research to position products/brands/attributes against competitors in the marketplace.

market area: A geographical section of the United States that becomes a cohesive area for marketing. It tends to have the same distribution patterns, the same supply sources, and, frequently, political boundaries.

market assessment: An evaluation of a market to establish its viability for business entry or other actions.

market development index: The number of units or dollar value of all brands of a product or service category that have been sold per thousand population within an area in a stated period, usually a year. Also category development index. Loosely, a product's, service's, or category's degree or rate of usage in markets and market segments to which it is available.

market planning: An arranged structured process to determine the target market, its needs and wants, and how to fulfill these.

market potential: Sales volume for a product or service that is available to or desired by a supplier; influenced by category development and often expressed in terms of share of market.

market research: Marketing research that seeks to quantify and segment market demand.

market segment: A portion of the total market wherein all of those particular customers have something in common. There are many ways of segmenting a market; the most widely used is by demographics, such as sex, age, income, education, etc.

market share: Your product's or service's piece of the total market for that product or service, usually expressed as a percentage or on a point scale.

marketing: The process of determining the target market, the market's needs and wants, and fulfilling these better than the competition.

marketing concept: A management philosophy which holds that the best means to satisfy corporate objectives is to focus all corporate efforts to find ways to permit customers to satisfy their desires.

marketing plan: (1) A strategy for marketing a product or service. (2) A comprehensive document containing background, rationale, and supportive detail regarding a marketer's objectives and strategies. Also plan.

Marketing Strategy Grid: A presentation/analytical marketing tool designed to help you select strategies to improve your market share and gain on the competition.

mean: The most widely used measure of location. The sum of all observations divided by the number of observations. Sample means are symbolized by $\overline{X}$, while population means are generally symbolized as μ.

measurement: Set of operations having the object of determining a value of a quantity.

media: As used in promotion, all the different means by which advertising reaches its audience.

media mix: The different media (magazines, radio, TV, etc.) to be used.

median: The "middle value" if the data are listed in rank order. If there are two central values, then the median is simply the average of these. The median is a useful statistic when we are dealing with highly skewed data.

medium use: Types, ad sizes, day part, length of commercials, etc.

megatrend: A massive qualitative or quantitative trend that has a substantial impact on an enterprise or society.

merge/purge: A computer process whereby lists may be "merged" together to facilitate zip code sequencing and testing segments and "purged" of duplicate names, pander names, and undesirable names that are to be saved for later mailing.

metropolitan statistical areas: A geographic segmentation technique that divides a market into areas within a large county or within a number of small counties; the core of such an area is usually a major city.

mission statement: A concise narrative statement summarizing your objectives and ultimate goals.

mode: The most commonly observed value (or set of values) in a data set. For continuous variates we cite the modal class (or classes). The mode is a useful characteristic when we wish to quote the most "fashionable" observation.

moderator: A person who conducts focus groups or panels.

morpho box: A matrix tool that breaks a product down by needs met and technology components, allowing for targeted analysis and idea creation.

most commonly used level of confidence: By far, the most commonly used level of confidence in marketing research is the 95 percent level, corresponding to a 1.96 standard error.

motivation research: Research that attempts to relate behavior to underlying desires, emotions, and intentions, in contrast to research that enumerates behavior or describes a situation; it relies heavily on the use of techniques adapted from psychology and other social sciences.

multivariate: A procedure that represents a type of inferential analysis dealing with several variables at the same time.

mystery customer/shopper: A researcher playing the role of a customer to evaluate services and customer interface points.

nixie: A piece of mail that is undeliverable.

normal distribution: An important continuous distribution, characterized entirely by its mean and standard deviation. Sometimes referred to as the Gaussian distribution, it is the classical bell-shaped curve with the mean, median, and mode all lying on the line of symmetry. It is widely used in statistics, not least because the central limit theorem dictates that repeated sample means drawn from a normally distributed population will themselves tend to be normally distributed.

objectives: What needs to be accomplished during the planning period, expressed quantitatively and/or qualitatively.

observational research: Research from viewing a situation and recording it for additional analysis.

outside macro approach: The trend in total market or category sales for the next three years.

overpenetrated: Too many stores/outlets in a trading area.

parameters: Values that are computed from a complete census and are considered to be precise and valid measures of the population, as contrasted with values that are computed from information provided by a sample, or the sample's statistics.

parametric and nonparametric data: Data from a population that follow a normal distribution. Data from a population that do not follow a normal distribution (or nominal or ordinal data) are called nonparametric data. Statistical tests that use the parameters (mean and standard deviation) of such a normal population to calculate the test statistic and "*p*" value are called parametric tests. Those that do not use the parameters of the population but use ranks of the variables to calculate the test statistic and "*p*" value are called nonparametric tests.

patent: Exclusive right (monopoly) to manufacture, sell, or otherwise use an invention for a limited period.

penetration: The total number of outlets/units a market will support.

perception: A mental image.

phenomenology: The study of a whole phenomenon in a concentrated way.

phenomenon: A thing that appears, or is perceived or observed, or an occurrence which causes question.

Poisson distribution: A discrete probability distribution that models the outcome of rare and random events.

position: In marketing strategy, the consumer perception of a product's or service's benefit or benefits, in comparison to its competition, which its manufacturer attempts to create and encourage via advertising, packaging, and/or promotion. Also positioning, as in product positioning, and near product position. Also, the placement of an advertisement in a publication in terms of page number, side, etc., or of a commercial in a program.

positioning: The relationship of your product or service offering in relationship to all others.

preface: Introductory statement that briefly delineates what the document is all about or what to expect in the document.

price elastic product: One for which the demand will increase or decrease in relationship to an increase or decrease in price.

price inelastic product: One for which the demand will remain relatively stable when the price is raised or lowered.

price points: Specific levels of pricing at which sales may be stimulated to increase or the points at which price increases begin to impact sales negatively.

price segmentation: Identifies groups of consumers within a market whose purchase of products or services is within the limits of certain dollar amounts.

prima facie: At first sight; a fact that is presumed to be true unless disproved by contrary evidence.

prioritization: To list or rate (as projects or goals) in order of priority.

product life cycle: The stages that a product goes through from starting out as a new product perhaps being adopted only by innovators, to increased adoption and acceptance by more customers, to maturity and sales decline. The four stages that a new product goes through are introduction, growth, maturity, and decline.

product or service research: Marketing research that usually focuses on your product's or service's strengths and weaknesses in relation to the products/services of competitors.

product/service attributes: Items of importance derived from the consumers' perceptions.

proposition: The strongest factual statement you can make on behalf of your product or service.

prospect research: Marketing research aimed at providing a profile of present and future customers.

prototype: A physical model of the new product concept; depending upon the purpose, prototypes may be nonworking, functionally working, or both functionally and aesthetically complete.

psychographic segmentation: A method of subdividing a market based on like needs and psychological motivations of consumer groups.

psychographics: Characterization of differences between people in terms of lifestyles, social class, and personalities, especially important in determining a target market and to pursue a marketing plan.

qualitative data: Data such as sex, color, post code, genotype, etc., which cannot be ordered by way of severity or extent, as opposed to quantitative data. Also called nominal data.

quality: The collection of attributes that, when present in a product, means a product has conformed to or exceeded customer expectations.

quantitative data: Data that give an idea of the amount of the variable. There are three kinds: (1) Continuous: numerical data that are continuous in distribution; i.e., they can take any value including fractions/decimals. (2) Discrete: data that although numerical do not include decimals/fractions. (3) Ordinal: data that consist of ranks or ordered categories.

questionnaire: A data collection vehicle similar to a survey but usually briefer and less complex in content.

random error: Result of a measurement minus the mean that would result from an infinite number of measurements of the same measure and carried out under repeatability conditions. (1) Random error is equal to error of measurement minus systematic error. (2) In practice, random error may be estimated from twenty or more repeated measurements of a measure and under specified conditions.

range: The difference between the highest and lowest values. Perhaps the simplest measure of dispersion in data, but, by definition, it is strongly influenced by extreme untypical values.

ratio analysis: A way of expressing relationships between a firm's accounting numbers and their trends over time that analysts use to establish values and evaluate risks.

raw data: Data to which nothing has been done to extract any numbers or information.

region: A geographic subdivision within a country, often defined by natural borders such as mountains, major rivers, etc.

regression analysis: Determines whether two sets of data fit a straight line graph with the standard mathematical formula $y = ax + c$.

repeat factor: The measurement of brand loyalty as indicated by the percentage of customers who are repeat purchasers.

response rate: The percentage of the total audience mailed to that replies.

retention: The ability to retain customers for future business.

revenue maximization: Achieving the highest potential revenue through management of market mix, pricing strategies, and yield management.

REVPAC (revenue per available customer): Integral component to measuring long-term customer value.

REVPAR (revenue per available room): Used in evaluating the performance of the lodging industry.

risk: The standard deviation of the return on total investment or the degree of uncertainty of return on an asset.

ROAM (return on assets managed): A concept utilized by companies who are managing others' assets under a contract.

ROI (return on investment): "Payback time"—the amount of time it takes to get your money back after investing it in a project.

ROIC (return on invested capital): A measure of financial performance and a financial performance forecasting tool.

sample: A smaller portion of an overall population that reflects the composition of that population.

sampling: Delivery of a product to the consumer with the intent of encouraging trial of the product. The size of the sample will vary depending on consumer behavior and costs.

saturation: The supplying of a market with as much of a product as it will absorb.

scanning: To examine, especially systematically with a sensing device.

seasonality index: A measurement that expresses the variation of sales of goods or services, for a brand or category, from an even distribution throughout the year as influenced by seasonal factors; for example, suntan lotions have an extremely high summer seasonality index.

segment profitability: The profitability of a particular type of consumer or market segment, determined by analyzing the revenues generated through the sale of products and services to that type of consumer or segment.

segmentation: The process of dividing the broad consuming market into manageable segments with common characteristics.

share: (1) The percentage of total retail purchases, in terms of dollars or units, for a given category of product that is enjoyed by any product or brand in that category. Also share of market, share of retail sales. (2) A rating survey of the percentage of the television or radio audience in a coverage area that is tuned to the program being rated.

share point: One percent of the total market or audience.

short-term objectives: Objectives to be accomplished in the immediate time frame, or through the current year.

significance level (*p* value): This is the level of probability below which a result is taken to be statistically significant. This is equal to the type I error (alpha). Common measures are <0.05 = significant; <0.01 = highly significant; <0.001 = very highly significant.

standard deviation: The square root of the variance. This important measure of dispersion is essentially an attempt to undo the effect of squaring when the variance is calculated.

standard error: A measure of the variability in the sampling distribution based on what is theoretically believed to occur were we to take a multitude of independent samples from the same population.

standard error of mean (SEM): The standard deviation (SD) of the sample means in a population (*N*). SEM = SD of the population/root of *N*.

standard metropolitan statistical area: A federally designated urban area consisting of counties that meet certain standards for population, urban character, and economic and social integration.

standardization: To bring into conformity with a standard.

standards: Something set up and established by authority as a rule for the measure of quantity, weight, extent, value, or quality.

statistical inference: A set of procedures in which the sample size and sample statistics are used to make estimates of population parameters.

statistics: Values that are computed from information provided by a sample are referred to as the sample's statistics, whereas values that are computed from a complete census, which are considered to be precise and valid measures of the population, are referred to as parameters.

strategic marketing plan: A broad structure that guides the process of determining your target market, detailing the market's needs and wants, and then fulfilling these needs and wants better than your competitors.

strategy: How you plan to achieve the objectives you have set. For example: To increase our business by 10 percent within the next twelve months, we will (1) increase outdoor advertising and (2) shift some of our advertising to promotions.

survey: A structured research document designed to elicit consumer opinion, uncover facts, and gain insights on potential trends.

SWOT analysis: Strengths, weaknesses, opportunities, and threats; used to align your internal strengths with external opportunities and conversely try to identify important threats and ensure that these external threats are not focused on your weaknesses in such a way that you will fail commercially.

tactics: Specific items or steps to support your strategies.

target market: The most likely purchasers of your product.

***t* distribution:** t = sample mean − population mean/SEM = $m - \mu$/SEM. This distribution is similar to the Gaussian distribution, but wider. As the sample size increases, its similarity to the Gaussian distribution increases. It has a mean of 0.

test market: A limited geographical area in which a test of an alternate marketing plan variable or new product is conducted.

tort: An injury or wrong committed, either with or without force, to the person or property of another.

TQM (total quality management): A business improvement philosophy that comprehensively and continuously involves all of an organization's functions in improvement activities.

trade media: A group of publications and/or broadcast media that follows a specific industry.

trade-out: An exchange of your product or service for advertising coverage. Also barter.

trading area: The geographic territory where your customer lives.

traffic counts: The recording of the vehicles and pedestrians passing a given point; used by TAB (Traffic Audit Bureau for Media Measurement, Inc.) to authenticate the potential exposure of outdoor advertising structures.

trend research: Identification of quantitative and qualitative preferences and attitudinal and behavioral directions in which the market or segments thereof are moving.

triangulation: A term used in land surveying to fix the exact position of topographical features. The principle of triangulation is to take bearings upon an unknown point from two known ones.

unaided awareness: Considered more accurate, it involves consumers recalling specific brands, products, etc., without any assistance.

underpenetrated: Too few stores/outlets to take advantage of the market's potential.

universal product code (UPC): A special code number and striped visual code on the package used by optical scanners at checkout counters to automatically record the brand and its price.

validity: Analogous to accuracy, reflecting a research technique's ability to give a true picture of the study object.

variable: A characteristic or property that describes a person, an object, or a situation, comprising a set of different values or categories.

variable costs: Costs that vary with the volume of production or sales.

variance: The most important measure of dispersion. It is the average squared deviation of values from their mean. Estimating the variance in a population as judged from a sample is by far the most common practice.

vertical integration: Occurs in a supply chain anywhere from raw materials to end customers; an organization would be described as vertically integrating, or vertically integrated, when it acquires or owns operations at different and usually sequential levels of the supply chain.

vision: A statement that vividly describes the desired outcome of the strategic marketing plan.

volume: A measure of units sold expressed within a given time frame, such as daily, hourly, monthly, etc.

zero-base budgeting: A budgeting concept that is premised on starting from zero and building up based on the resources required to achieve the plan objectives.

zip codes: Postal designations by which key demographic and purchasing information can be sorted/mailed.

Bibliography

Aaker, D. A. (1991). *Managing brand equity.* New York: The Free Press.

Aaker, D. A. (1996). *Building strong brands.* New York: The Free Press.

Argyris, C. R. (1985). *Action science.* San Francisco: Jossey-Bass.

Arnold, D. (1992). *The handbook of brand management.* Reading, MA: Addison-Wesley.

Babbie, E. R. (1979). *The practice of social research* (2nd ed.). Belmont, CA: Wadsworth Publishing.

Bagozzi, R., Rosa, J., Celly, K., & Coronel, F. (1998). *Marketing management.* Upper Saddle River, NJ: Prentice Hall.

Berrigan, J., & Finkbeiner, C. (1992). *Segmentation marketing: New methods for capturing business markets.* New York: HarperBusiness.

Berry, L. L., & Parasuraman, A. (1991). *Marketing services: Computing through quality.* New York: The Free Press.

Block, T. B., & Robinson, W. A. (1994). *Sales promotion handbook* (8th ed.). Chicago: Dartnell.

Bogart, L. (1967). *Strategy in advertising.* New York: Harcourt, Brace and World.

Boltin, B., Callahan, T. E., & Keeling, J. M. (1996). *Hotel development.* Washington, DC: Urban Land Institute.

Bulmer, M. (1986). *Social science and social policy.* London: Allen & Unwin.

Churchill, G. A. (1991). *Marketing research: Methodological foundations* (5th ed.). Hillsdale, IL: Dryden Press.

Clancy, K. J., & Shulman, R. S. (1991). *The marketing revolution: A radical manifesto for dominating the marketplace.* New York: HarperBusiness.

Cravens, D. W. (1987). *Strategic marketing* (2nd ed.). Homewood, IL: Richard D. Irwin.

Cravens, D. W., & Piercy, N. F. (2003). *Strategic marketing* (7th ed.). New York: McGraw-Hill.

Denzin, N. K. (1970). *The research act in sociology.* Chicago: Aldine.

Drucker, P. (1974). *Management—Tasks, responsibilities, practices.* New York: Heineman.

Eden, C., & Huxham, C. (1996). Action research for management research. *British Journal of Management, 7,* 75-80.

Feig, B. (1993). *The new products workshop: Hands-on tools for developing winners.* New York: McGraw-Hill.

Glaser, B. G., & Strauss, A. L. (1967). *The discovery of grounded theory: Strategies for qualitative research.* New York: Aldine.

Gottschalk, J. A. (1993). *Crisis response.* Detroit, MI: The Visible Ink Press.

Hackman, J. R., & Oldham, G. R. (1980). *Work design.* Reading, MA: Addison-Wesley.

Hammersley, M. (1990). *The dilemma of qualitative method: Herbert Blumer and the Chicago tradition.* New York and London: Routledge.

Hamper, R. J., & Baugh, S. L. (1998). *Strategic market planning.* Lincolnwood, IL: NTC Business Books.

Harris, N. (1989). *Service operations management.* London: Cassell.

Hatton, A. (2000). *Marketing planning.* London, UK: Pearson Education Limited.

Hayden, C. (1986). *The handbook of strategic expertise.* New York: Free Press.

Hiebing, R. G., & Cooper, S. W. (1996). *The successful marketing plan* (2nd ed.). Lincolnwood, IL: NTC Business Books.

Holloway, R., & Hancock, R. (Eds.) (1969). *The environment of marketing behavior* (2nd ed.). Lincolnwood, IL: NTC Business Books.

Johns, N. (1994). Managing quality. In P. L. Jones & P. Merricks (Eds.), *The management of foodservice operations* (pp. 245-261). London: Cassell.

Johns, N., & Lee-Ross, D. (1998). *Research methods in service industry management.* London: Cassell.

Kast, F. E., & Rosenzweig, J. E. (1985). *Organization and management: A systems and contingency approach.* New York: McGraw-Hill.

Kerin, R., & Peterson, R. (1998). *Strategic marketing problems* (8th ed.). Upper Saddle River, NJ: Prentice Hall.

Kerlinger, F. H. (1986). *Foundations of behavior research* (3rd ed.). New York: Holt, Reinhart & Winston.

Handbook of Marketing Research Methodologies for Hospitality and Tourism
© 2007 by The Haworth Press, Inc. All rights reserved.
doi:10.1300/5927_25

Kinnear, T. C. (1991). *Marketing masters.* New York: American Marketing Association.

Kotler, P. (1972). *Marketing management.* Englewood Cliffs, NJ: Prentice Hall.

Kotler, P. (1999). *Kotler on marketing.* Englewood Cliffs, NJ: Prentice Hall.

Lazerfeld, P. (1955). *Survey design and analysis.* New York: The Free Press.

Lele, M. M. (1992). *Creating strategic leverage.* New York: Wiley.

Levitt, T. (1986). *The marketing imagination.* New York: The Free Press.

Lovelock, C., & Wright, L. (2001). *Services marketing* (4th ed.). Upper Saddle River, NJ: Prentice Hall.

Lovelock, C., & Wright, L. (2002). *Principles of service marketing and management* (2nd ed.). Upper Saddle River, NJ: Prentice Hall.

Magrath, A. J. (1992). *The 6 imperatives of marketing: Lessons from the world's best companies.* New York: AMACOM.

Magrath, A.J. (1995). *Marketing strategies for growth in uncertain times.* Lincolnwood, IL: NTC Business Books.

Manning, G. L., & Reece, B. L. (1998). *Selling today.* Upper Saddle River, NJ: Prentice Hall.

Marriott International Corp. (2000). Marriott Annual Report 1999. Bethesda, MD: Author.

Mayo, E. (1933). *The human problems of an industrial civilization.* New York: Macmillan.

McKay, E. S. (1993). *The marketing mystique* (Rev. ed.). New York: AMACOM.

McNeill, D., & Freiberger, P. (1993). *Fuzzy logic: The discovery of a revolutionary computer technology and how it is changing our world.* New York: Simon & Schuster.

Michalko, M. (1991). *Tinkertoys: A handbook of business creativity for the '90's.* Berkeley, CA: Ten Speed Press.

Miller, S. (1986). *Experimental design and statistics* (2nd ed.). London and New York: Metheun.

Myers, J. H. (1996). *Segmentation and positioning for strategic marketing decisions.* New York: American Marketing Association.

Myers, J. H., & Tauber, E. (1997). *Market structure analysis.* Chicago: American Marketing Association.

Nykiel, R. A. (1992). *Keeping customers in good times and bad.* Stamford, CT: Longmeadow Press.

Nykiel, R. A. (1994). *You can't lose if the customer wins.* New York: Berkeley.

Nykiel, R. A. (1997). *Marketing in the hospitality industry* (3rd ed.). East Lansing, MI: Educational Institute—AH&MA.

Nykiel, R. A. (1998). *Marketing your city USA.* Binghamton, NY: The Haworth Press, Inc.

Nykiel, R. A. (1998). *Points of encounter.* Kingston, NY: Amacor.

Nykiel, R. A. (2005). *Hospitality management strategies.* New York: Pearson/Prentice Hall.

Ott, L. (1984). *An introduction to statistical methods and data analysis.* Boston: PWS Publishers.

Parmerlee, D. (1992). *Developing successful marketing strategies.* Lincolnwood, IL: NTC Business Books.

Patching, D. (1990). *Practical soft systems analysis.* London: Pitman.

Posch, R. J., Jr. (1988). *Marketing and the law.* Englewood Cliffs, NJ: Prentice Hall.

Rapp, S., & Collins, T. (1988). *MaxiMarketing: The new direction in advertising, promotion and marketing strategy.* New York: New American Library.

Ray, M., & Myers, R. (1986). *Creativity in business.* Garden City, NJ: Doubleday.

Reich, A. Z. (1997). *Marketing management for the hospitality industry.* New York: John Wiley & Sons.

Reis, A., & Trout, J. (1981). *Positioning: The battle for your mind.* New York: McGraw-Hill.

Reis, A., & Trout, J. (1986). *Marketing warfare.* New York: McGraw-Hill.

Reis, A., & Trout, J. (1986). *Positioning: The battle for your mind.* New York: McGraw-Hill.

Reis, A., & Trout, J. (1993). *The 22 immutable laws of marketing: Violate them at your own risk!* New York: HarperBusiness.

Richey, T. (1994). *The marketer's visual tool kit.* New York: AMACOM.

Ryan, C. (1995). *Researching tourist satisfaction: Issues, concepts, problems.* London: Routledge.

Schwartz, P. (1991). *The art of the long view: Planning for the future in an uncertain world.* New York: Doubleday Currency.

Sherlock, P. (1991). *Rethinking business-to-business marketing.* New York: The Free Press.

Silverman, D. (1993). *Interpreting qualitative data.* London: Sage.

Slattery, M. (1986). *Official statistics.* London: Tavistock.

Staruss, A., & Corbin, J. (1990). *Basics of qualitative research: Grounded theory procedures and techniques.* London: Sage.

Summer, J. R. (1985). *Improve your marketing techniques: A guide for hotel managers and caterers.* London: Northwood Books.

Teare, R., Atkinson, C., & Westwood C. (Eds.) (1944). *Achieving quality performance.* London: Cassell.

Tregoe, B. B., & Zimmerman, J. W. (1980). *Management strategy.* New York: Simon & Schuster.

U.S. Government Printing Office (1995). *Directory of national trade associations of businessmen.* Washington, DC: Author.

Vavra, T. G. (1992). *Aftermarketing: How to keep customers for life through relationship marketing.* Homewood, IL: Business One Irwin.

Von Bertalanffi, L. (1968). *General systems theory.* New York: Braziller.

Walker, O. C., Boyd, H. W., Mullins, J., & Larreche, J. (1999). *Marketing strategy* (4th ed.). New York: McGraw-Hill.

Whyte, W. F. (1945). *Human relations in the restaurant industry.* New York: McGraw-Hill.

Wilson, A. (1992). *New directions in marketing: Business-to-business strategies for the 1990's.* Lincolnwood, IL: NTC Business Books.

Yin, R. K. (1989). *Case study research: Design and methods.* London: Sage.

Index

Page numbers followed by the letter "f" indicate figures; those followed by the letter "t" indicate tables.

Handbook of Marketing Research Methodologies for Hospitality and Tourism
© 2007 by The Haworth Press, Inc. All rights reserved.
doi:10.1300/5927_26

THE HAWORTH HOSPITALITY
& TOURISM PRESS™
Hospitality, Travel, and Tourism
K. S. Chon, PhD, Editor in Chief

THAILAND TOURISM by Arthur Asa Berger. (2007).

CULTURAL TOURISM: GLOBAL AND LOCAL PERSPECTIVES edited by Greg Richards. (2007). "An excellent collection of material that builds upon the editor's previous studies in the field as well as the work of ATLAS. Not only does the book reflect extremely well on the high quality of work that comes out of the ATLAS network on cultural tourism, but the work further reinforces Greg Richards' profile as a leader in the cultural tourism field." *C. Michael Hall, BA (Hons), MA, PhD, Professor, Department of Tourism, University of Otago*

GAY TOURISM: CULTURE AND CONTEXT by Gordon Waitt and Kevin Markwell. (2006). "This book provides an international overview of gay destinations and spaces. It addresses issues of how the tourism industry, in its search for the 'pink dollar,' yet again seeks to commodify and normalize experiences within commercial settings, and thus creates stereotypes that are not wholly satisfying for gay men. The authors are not afraid to court controversy by addressing gay issues in Islamic societies. In short, there is much in this book for tourism researchers unfamiliar with the social context of gay tourism. Such readers will emerge both better informed and with further questions to prompt their own thinking." *Chris Ryan, PhD, Professor of Tourism, University of Waikato Management School, New Zealand*

CASES IN SUSTAINABLE TOURISM: AN EXPERIENTIAL APPROACH TO MAKING DECISIONS edited by Irene M. Herremans. (2006). "As a tourism instructor and researcher, I recommend this textbook for both undergraduate and graduate students who wish to pursue their careers in parks, recreation, or tourism. The text is appropriate both for junior and senior tourism management classes and graduate classes. It is an excellent primer for understanding the fundamental concepts, issues, and real-world examples of sustainable tourism." *Hwan-Suk Chris Choi, PhD, Assistant Professor, School of Hospitality and Tourism Management, University of Guelph*

COMMUNITY DESTINATION MANAGEMENT IN DEVELOPING ECONOMIES edited by Walter Jamieson. (2006). "This book is a welcome and valuable addition to the destination management literature, focusing as it does on developing economies in the Asian context. It provides an unusually comprehensive and informative overview of critical issues in the field, effectively combining well-crafted discussions of key conceptual and methodological issues with carefully selected and well-presented case studies drawn from a number of contrasting Asian destinations." *Peter Hills, PhD, Professor and Director, The Centre of Urban Planning and Environmental Management, The University of Hong Kong*

MANAGING SUSTAINABLE TOURISM: A LEGACY FOR THE FUTURE by David L. Edgell Sr. (2006). "This comprehensive book on sustainable tourism should be required reading for everyone interested in tourism. The author is masterful in defining strategies and using case studies to explain best practices in generating long-term economic return on your tourism investment." *Kurtis M. Ruf, Partner, Ruf Strategic Solutions; Author,* Contemporary Database Marketing

CASINO INDUSTRY IN ASIA PACIFIC: DEVELOPMENT, OPERATION, AND IMPACT edited by Cathy H.C. Hsu. (2006). "This book is a must-read for anyone interested in the opportunities and challenges that the proliferation of casino gaming will bring to Asia in the early twenty-first century. The economic and social consequences of casino gaming in Asia may ultimately prove to be far more significant than those encountered in the West, and this book opens the door as to what those consequences might be." *William R. Eadington, PhD, Professor of Economics and Director, Institute for the Study of Gambling and Commercial Gaming, University of Nevada, Reno*

THE GROWTH STRATEGIES OF HOTEL CHAINS: BEST BUSINESS PRACTICES BY LEADING COMPANIES by Onofre Martorell Cunill. (2006). "Informative, well-written, and up-to-date. This is one title that I shall certainly be adding to my 'must-read' list for students this year." *Tom Baum, PhD, Professor of International Tourism and Hospitality Management, The Scottish Hotel School, The University of Strathclyde, Glasgow*

HANDBOOK FOR DISTANCE LEARNING IN TOURISM by Gary Williams. (2005). "This is an important book for a variety of audiences. As a resource for educational designers (and their managers) in particular, it is invaluable. The book is easy to read, and is full of practical information that can be logically applied in the design and development of flexible learning resources." *Louise Berg, MA, DipED, Lecturer in Education, Charles Sturt University, Australia*

VIETNAM TOURISM by Arthur Asa Berger. (2005). "Fresh and innovative…. Drawing upon Professor Berger's background and experience in cultural studies, this book offers an imaginative and personal portrayal of Vietnam as a tourism destination…. A very welcome addition to the field of destination studies." *Professor Brian King, PhD, Head, School of Hospitality, Tourism & Marketing, Victoria University, Australia*

TOURISM AND HOTEL DEVELOPMENT IN CHINA: FROM POLITICAL TO ECONOMIC SUCCESS by Hanqin Qiu Zhang, Ray Pine, and Terry Lam. (2005). "This is one of the most comprehensive books on China tourism and hotel development. It is one of the best textbooks for educators, students, practitioners, and investors who are interested in China tourism and hotel industry. Readers will experience vast, diversified, and past and current issues that affect every educator, student, practitioner, and investor in China tourism and hotel globally in an instant." *Hailin Qu, PhD, Full Professor and William E. Davis Distinguished Chair, School of Hotel & Restaurant Administration, Oklahoma State University*

THE TOURISM AND LEISURE INDUSTRY: SHAPING THE FUTURE edited by Klaus Weiermair and Christine Mathies. (2004). "If you need or want to know about the impact of globalization, the impact of technology, societal forces of change, the experience economy, adaptive technologies, environmental changes, or the new trend of slow tourism, you need this book. *The Tourism and Leisure Industry* contains a great mix of research and practical information." *Charles R. Goeldner, PhD, Professor Emeritus of Marketing and Tourism, Leeds School of Business, University of Colorado*

OCEAN TRAVEL AND CRUISING: A CULTURAL ANALYSIS by Arthur Asa Berger. (2004). "Dr. Berger presents an interdisciplinary discussion of the cruise industry for the thinking person. This is an enjoyable social psychology travel guide with a little business management thrown in. A great book for the curious to read a week before embarking on a first cruise or for the frequent cruiser to gain a broader insight into exactly what a cruise experience represents." *Carl*

Braunlich, DBA, Associate Professor, Department of Hospitality and Tourism Management, Purdue University, West Lafayette, Indiana

STANDING THE HEAT: ENSURING CURRICULUM QUALITY IN CULINARY ARTS AND GASTRONOMY by Joseph A. Hegarty. (2003). "This text provides the genesis of a well-researched, thoughtful, rigorous, and sound theoretical framework for the enlargement and expansion of higher education programs in culinary arts and gastronomy." *John M. Antun, PhD, Founding Director, National Restaurant Institute, School of Hotel, Restaurant, and Tourism Management, University of South Carolina*

SEX AND TOURISM: JOURNEYS OF ROMANCE, LOVE, AND LUST edited by Thomas G. Bauer and Bob McKercher. (2003). "Anyone interested in or concerned about the impact of tourism on society and particularly in the developing world, should read this book. It explores a subject that has long remained ignored, almost a taboo area for many governments, institutions, and organizations. It demonstrates that the stereotyping of 'sex tourism' is too simple and travel and sex have many manifestations. The book follows its theme in an innovative and original way." *Carson L. Jenkins, PhD, Professor of International Tourism, University of Strathclyde, Glasgow, Scotland*

CONVENTION TOURISM: INTERNATIONAL RESEARCH AND INDUSTRY PERSPECTIVES edited by Karin Weber and Kye-Sung Chon. (2002). "This comprehensive book is truly global in its perspective. The text points out areas of needed research—a great starting point for graduate students, university faculty, and industry professionals alike. While the focus is mainly academic, there is a lot of meat for this burgeoning industry to chew on as well." *Patti J. Shock, CPCE, Professor and Department Chair, Tourism and Convention Administration, Harrah College of Hotel Administration, University of Nevada–Las Vegas*

CULTURAL TOURISM: THE PARTNERSHIP BETWEEN TOURISM AND CULTURAL HERITAGE MANAGEMENT by Bob McKercher and Hilary du Cros. (2002). "The book brings together concepts, perspectives, and practicalities that must be understood by both cultural heritage and tourism managers, and as such is a must-read for both." *Hisashi B. Sugaya, AICP, Former Chair, International Council of Monuments and Sites, International Scientific Committee on Cultural Tourism; Former Executive Director, Pacific Asia Travel Association Foundation, San Francisco, CA*

TOURISM IN THE ANTARCTIC: OPPORTUNITIES, CONSTRAINTS, AND FUTURE PROSPECTS by Thomas G. Bauer. (2001). "Thomas Bauer presents a wealth of detailed information on the challenges and opportunities facing tourism operators in this last great tourism frontier." *David Mercer, PhD, Associate Professor, School of Geography & Environmental Science, Monash University, Melbourne, Australia*

SERVICE QUALITY MANAGEMENT IN HOSPITALITY, TOURISM, AND LEISURE edited by Jay Kandampully, Connie Mok, and Beverley Sparks. (2001). "A must-read. . . . a treasure. . . . pulls together the work of scholars across the globe, giving you access to new ideas, international research, and industry examples from around the world." *John Bowen, Professor and Director of Graduate Studies, William F. Harrah College of Hotel Administration, University of Nevada, Las Vegas*

TOURISM IN SOUTHEAST ASIA: A NEW DIRECTION edited by K. S. (Kaye) Chon. (2000). "Presents a wide array of very topical discussions on the specific challenges facing the tourism industry in Southeast Asia. A great resource for both scholars and practitioners." *Dr.*

Hubert B. Van Hoof, Assistant Dean/Associate Professor, School of Hotel and Restaurant Management, Northern Arizona University

THE PRACTICE OF GRADUATE RESEARCH IN HOSPITALITY AND TOURISM edited by K. S. Chon. (1999). "An excellent reference source for students pursuing graduate degrees in hospitality and tourism." *Connie Mok, PhD, CHE, Associate Professor, Conrad N. Hilton College of Hotel and Restaurant Management, University of Houston, Texas*

THE INTERNATIONAL HOSPITALITY MANAGEMENT BUSINESS: MANAGEMENT AND OPERATIONS by Larry Yu. (1999). "The abundant real-world examples and cases provided in the text enable readers to understand the most up-to-date developments in international hospitality business." *Zheng Gu, PhD, Associate Professor, College of Hotel Administration, University of Nevada, Las Vegas*

CONSUMER BEHAVIOR IN TRAVEL AND TOURISM by Abraham Pizam and Yoel Mansfeld. (1999). "A must for anyone who wants to take advantage of new global opportunities in this growing industry." *Bonnie J. Knutson, PhD, School of Hospitality Business, Michigan State University*

LEGALIZED CASINO GAMING IN THE UNITED STATES: THE ECONOMIC AND SOCIAL IMPACT edited by Cathy H. C. Hsu. (1999). "Brings a fresh new look at one of the areas in tourism that has not yet received careful and serious consideration in the past." *Muzaffer Uysal, PhD, Professor of Tourism Research, Virginia Polytechnic Institute and State University, Blacksburg*

HOSPITALITY MANAGEMENT EDUCATION edited by Clayton W. Barrows and Robert H. Bosselman. (1999). "Takes the mystery out of how hospitality management education programs function and serves as an excellent resource for individuals interested in pursuing the field." *Joe Perdue, CCM, CHE, Director, Executive Masters Program, College of Hotel Administration, University of Nevada, Las Vegas*

MARKETING YOUR CITY, U.S.A.: A GUIDE TO DEVELOPING A STRATEGIC TOURISM MARKETING PLAN by Ronald A. Nykiel and Elizabeth Jascolt. (1998). "An excellent guide for anyone involved in the planning and marketing of cities and regions. . . . A terrific job of synthesizing an otherwise complex procedure." *James C. Maken, PhD, Associate Professor, Babcock Graduate School of Management, Wake Forest University, Winston-Salem, North Carolina*